KRIEGSMARINE U-BOATS

1939–45

THE SPELLMOUNT SUBMARINE IDENTIFICATION GUIDE

KRIEGSMARINE U-BOATS 1939–45

CHRIS BISHOP

SPELLMOUNT

British Library Cataloguing in Publication Data:
A catalogue record for this book is available
from the British Library

ISBN-13: 978-1-86227-352-8
ISBN-10: 1-86227-352-9

First published in the UK in 2006 by
SPELLMOUNT LTD
The Mill
Brimscombe Port
Stroud
Gloucestershire GL5 3QG

Tel: 01453 883300
Fax: 01453 883233
e-mail: enquiries@spellmount.com
Website: www.spellmount.com

Editorial and design by
Amber Books Ltd
Bradley's Close
74-77 White Lion Street
London N1 9PF
www.amberbooks.co.uk

Project Editor: Michael Spilling
Design: Hawes Design
Illustrations: Julian Baker and Patrick Mulrey
– Art-Tech/Midsummer Books

Printed in Dubai

Picture Credits

Art-Tech/Aerospace: 28, 29, 31, 32, 44, 82, 111, 119
Art-Tech/MARS: 12, 34
Popperfoto: 14, 42, 46
Süddeutscher Verlag: 6, 40, 172
TRH Pictures: 9, 10, 13, 20, 56, 58, 68, 69, 70, 76, 84, 93, 104, 111, 131, 132, 139, 140, 149, 156, 160, 162

Contents

Introduction

Ranging far out into the Atlantic and preying on seaborne British trade, the *Kriegsmarine*'s U-boat fleet was the greatest threat to Britain's survival during World War II. In 1939, half the food eaten in the United Kingdom came from overseas. Two-thirds of the raw materials required by Britain's war industries were imported, too. If German U-boats could stop this flow of goods by sinking Allied merchant ships, Hitler might win the war. The *Kriegsmarine*'s submarine supremo, Admiral Karl Dönitz, understood well his priorities. Dönitz calculated that a fleet of around 250 or 300 submarines would be necessary to stifle British supply lines. But the High Command's obsession with battleships delayed the submarine building programme, and was, in the view of Dönitz, irrelevant. He believed that only submarines offered a realistic prospect of blockading Britain.

◀ **Hitler's grey wolves**

A Type IX boat sets out on patrol in its element – on the surface. In the first year of the war, before the introduction of radar, U-boats attacking on the surface at night wreaked havoc on Allied Atlantic convoys.

KARL DÖNITZ HAD LEARNED his craft in U-boats during World War I. The Imperial German Navy was the first to make extensive use of submarines in attacking an enemy's supply lines, and in spite of the primitive nature of the boats of the period, achieved considerable success.

U-boats wreaked havoc on British shipping in the Mediterranean, and the unrestricted submarine warfare of 1917 and 1918 came within a whisker of bringing Britain to its knees. It was a major reason why after the war Germany was denied a submarine force under the terms of the treaty of Versailles. In spite of the ban, Germany set up clandestine U-boat design offices in Holland in 1922 and in Berlin in 1927. In 1932, months before Hitler's rise to power, the Weimar government approved a naval building plan which included 16 U-boats.

Rearmament

The rise of the Nazis accelerated the navy's plans. In 1935 Hermann Göring announced Germany's intent to rearm, repudiating the Treaty of Versailles. Hitler managed to push through an Anglo-German naval agreement that allowed German warship construction up to a ceiling of 45 per cent of the Royal Navy. Curiously, since the British had painful experience of what submarines could do, the agreement also allowed Germany to match the Royal Navy's submarine force, ton for ton.

Dönitz was given command of Germany's first post-war submarine flotilla in 1935 and set about training a new U-boat fleet that could succeed where his generation had, by a narrow margin, failed. Once in charge of the German submarine force, he was able to define the types of boat best suited to near and distant operations as well as the number required to beat a fully-organized convoy system.

U-Boat construction

At the outbreak of war Germany had three main types of U-boat in construction. One requirement identified was that of a coastal submarine, and the Type II quickly went into production. Type II U-boats proved to be handy and manoeuvrable, and could crash-dive in 25 seconds. Their low profile and lively handling earned them the nickname of 'canoes'. But their small size and weapons load were handicaps in the open-ocean combat, and construction ceased in 1941.

The majority of U-boats that fought the battle of the Atlantic were Type VIIs. Like the Type II, the Type VII was based on a boat originally designed for Finland and built in 1930. Type VIIs were built in huge numbers, with more than 800 being completed by the end of the war. Although intended for ocean operations, size was limited to allow the maximum number of boats to be built within treaty limits. This had the added advantage of making them agile and quick to dive.

As with most submarines of the period, the Type VII was powered by diesel engines on the surface and used battery-driven electric motors underwater. Under diesel drive a Type VII could make more than seventeen knots – enough to run rings around a slow-moving convoy. Underwater it could not do much more than five knots, and that for only a few hours.

The Type VII carried between 11 and 14 torpedoes. Early boats also had a deck gun, but as the war progressed, this was often replaced with heavy anti-aircraft armament.

The Type IX class was designed for ocean warfare. Loosely based on the far smaller Type II, it differed

▼ Type XXI

With a crew of 57 and considerably more powerful than its predecessors, the late-war Type XXI was designed for long range operations. Unlike the Type VIIs, Type XXIs could stay submerged for much longer and were as fast under water as they were on the surface. But the Type XXI was not introduced until late in 1944, by which time the war at sea had already swung decisively against Germany.

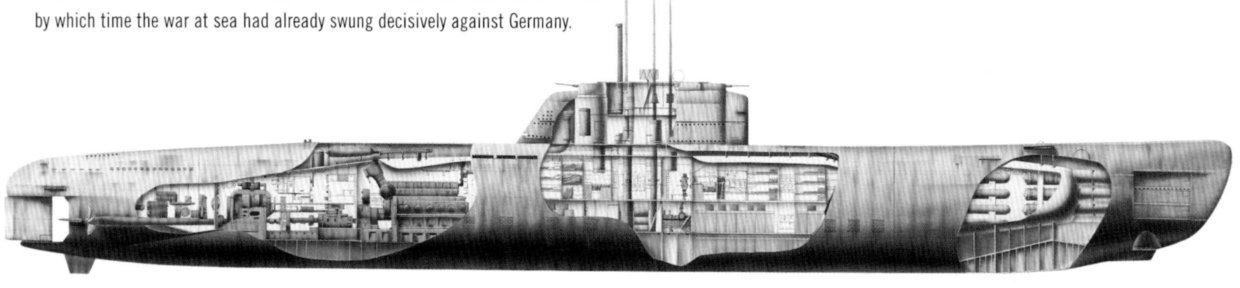

fundamentally in having a double hull. This increased useable internal volume by enabling fuel and ballast tanks to be sited externally. In turn, the extra hull improved survivability by cushioning the inner (pressure) hull from explosive shock and gave the boats greatly improved handling on the surface.

Early Type IXs had enough range to operate in the southern hemisphere, mounting long patrols into the South Atlantic. Later versions with increased range could reach the Indian Ocean and even the Pacific without refuelling.

Outbreak of war

As late as the summer of 1939, Hitler was telling the German Navy that there was little danger of war. The *Kriegsmarine*'s building schedule was based on the assumption that there would be no conflict until the mid-1940s, by which time they hoped to match the Royal Navy.

However, when Britain and France declared war in September 1939 Dönitz had only 46 operational submarines, of which more than half were the coastal 'ducks' – Type IIs – primarily used for training.

For the first eight months of the war U-boat activity against Britain's vital supply lines was limited and directed almost entirely against the few ships that sailed independently rather than in convoy. Indeed, during the Norwegian campaign (April 1940), all U-boats were withdrawn from the Atlantic for operations in the North Sea.

New tactics

But that was about to change. Between the wars, Dönitz had developed theoretical group attack tactics. Once in control of the *U-bootwaffe*, he tested the concept of the 'wolf pack' – co-ordinated strikes by groups of submarines far out into the ocean.

At the outbreak of war, some 3000 ocean-going merchant ships flew the British flag and another 1000 coasters plied the waters around the UK: a combined total of 17.5 million tons of shipping. The ships were organised into convoys, typically protected by four to six escorts armed with depth-charges.

Although the heavy cruiser *Hipper*, the battlecruisers *Scharnhorst* and *Gneisenau* and the 'pocket battleships' *Scheer* and *Graf Spee* snapped up a number of ships on raiding cruises, it was soon apparent that Germany's small surface fleet could not inflict serious damage on British convoys.

▲ **Torpedo loading**

A U-boat crew bring a torpedo on board. Initial problems with reliability were soon overcome and as German torpedoes improved, so the *U-bootwaffe* quickly became a deadly fighting force.

However, the prospect of a heavy German warship or two getting in amongst a convoy kept British naval staff awake at night. But although there were some close shaves, Hitler's big ships failed to land a significant blow against the convoy routes. The pride of the *Kriegsmarine* had failed, and it was up to the U-boats to carry the war to the enemy.

KEY TO SPECIFICATIONS

All measurements are given in metric followed by imperial in parenthesis. For both 'Max Speed' and 'Displacement', 's/d' shows measures for when the U-boat was either surfaced or dived.

Combat Flotillas

Once a U-boat and its crew had completed their training, they were assigned to a combat, or 'Front', *flottille* (flotilla). The six prewar combat flotillas bore the brunt of operations for the first two years of the war. Originally based at Kiel and Wilhelmshaven, the Front flotillas were transferred to bases in Norway and France after those countries were conquered in the campaigns of 1940. The new bases enabled the boats to reach their main patrol areas more quickly, without having to make the perilous voyage around the British Isles. By the end of the war, 16 Front flotillas had been established and had seen combat in war zones as far afield as the Caribbean, the Indian Ocean and the East Indies. However, the bulk of operational U-boats and their crews fought and died in the key battlegrounds of the Atlantic.

◀ A meal above deck

A U-boat crew enjoy a rare meal in the open air. On operational patrol, crews would spend many weeks within the cramped confines of their submarine.

1 Unterseebootsflottille

Plans for German rearmament, circumventing the provisions of the Treaty of Versailles, had been under way since the days of the Weimar Republic in the 1920s. That rearmament came into the open in 1935, two years after Hitler came to power.

NAZI GERMANY'S FIRST U-BOAT UNIT, *U-Flottille* Weddigen, was officially founded on 27 September 1935 under the command of Fregkpt. Karl Dönitz, later to become commander of the U-boat arm, commander-in-chief of the Navy, and last *Führer* of the Reich after Hitler's suicide in 1945. The flotilla was named after Kptlt. Otto Weddigen, who as commander of U-9 sank the armoured cruisers HMS *Aboukir*, HMS *Cressy* and HMS *Hogue* in September 1914.

In 1939 the flotilla, based at Kiel, was renamed 1. *Unterseebootsflottille* (1st Flotilla). Its first boats had been dispatched into the North Sea before the

1ST FLOTILLA BASE LOCATIONS

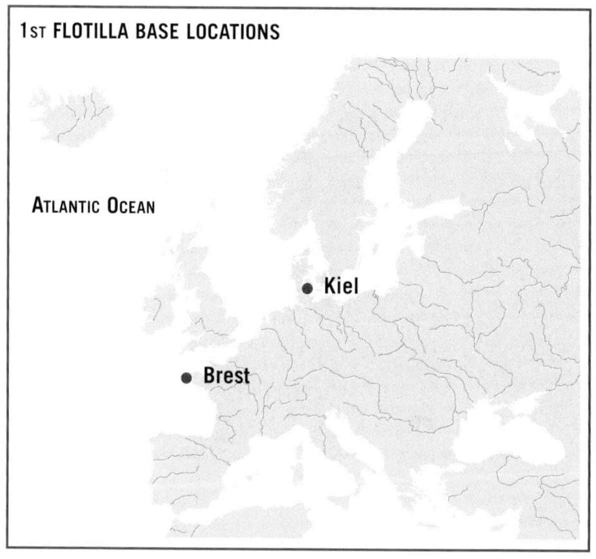

▼ Under attack

1st Flotilla boats served throughout the war, seeing early triumph change to defeat. Here, U-625 is about to be sunk by a Canadian Sunderland in 1944.

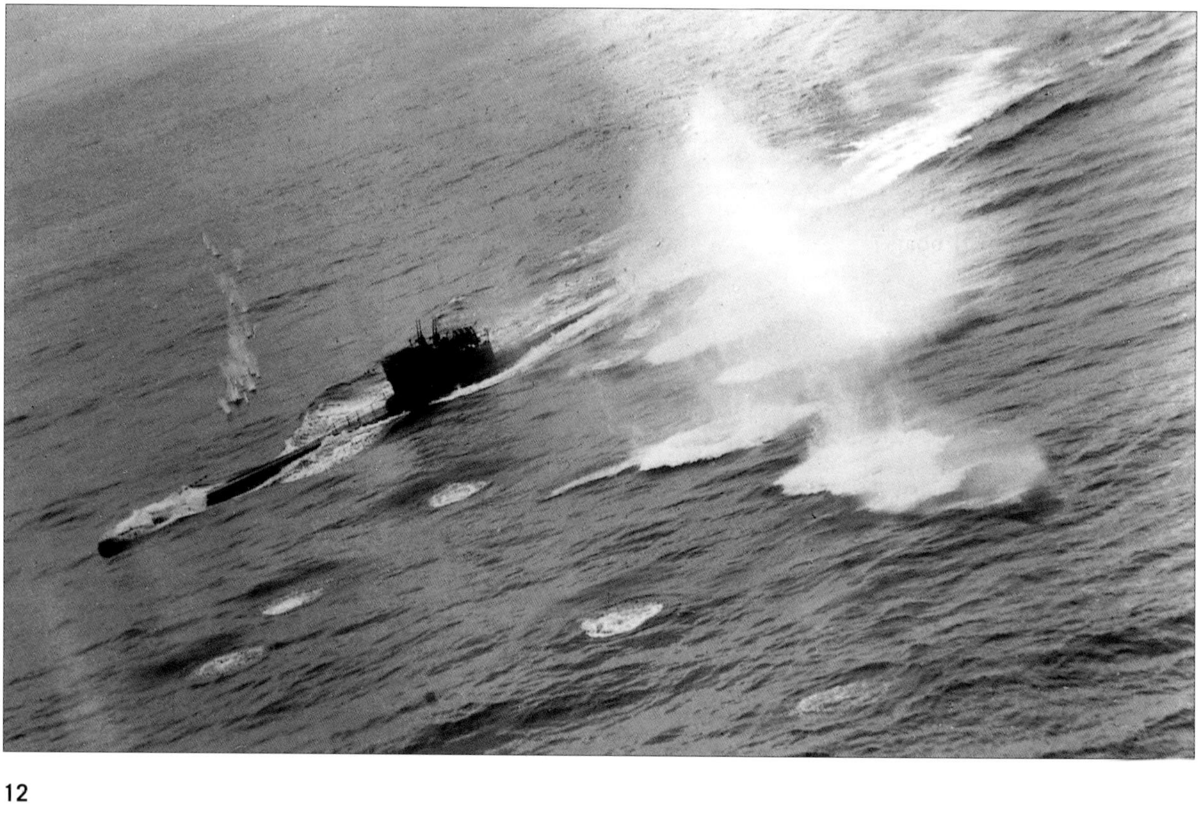

▲ **U-563**

The crew of U-563 pose beneath the conning tower of their Type VIIC in the summer of 1942. The U-boat was sunk with all hands on 31 May 1943, southwest of Brest, by depth charges from British and Australian Handley Page Halifax and Sunderland aircraft.

Commanders

Kpt. z. S. Karl Dönitz *(Sep 1935 – Dec 1935)*
Kpt. z. S. Loycke *(Jan 1936 – Sep 1937)*
Kptlt. Hans-Günther Looff *(Oct 1937 – Sep 1939)*
Korvkpt. Hans Eckermann *(Sep 1939 – Oct 1940)*
Korvkpt. Hans Cohausz *(Nov 1940 – Feb 1942)*
Kptlt. Heinz Buchholz *(Feb 1942 – Jul 1942)*
Korvkpt. Werner Winter *(Jul 1942 – Sep 1944)*

1st FLOTILLA INSIGNIA

Many U-boats had insignia (*Bootswappen*) painted on their conning towers. The first examples were individual, but later boats often carried a flotilla insignia as well. This is the 1st Flotilla's emblem.

1ST FLOTILLA

Type	Boats on strength
Type IIB	14
Type IIC	8
Type IID	13
Type VIIB (after 1941)	3
Type VIIC (after 1941)	81
Type VIIC/41 (after 1941)	2
Type XB (after 1941)	2

outbreak of war, and achieved some successes against Britain's coastal convoys. However, it was clear that the small Type II boats were only marginally effective in a long-distance war, and they began to be replaced by the larger Type VII boats.

Atlantic bases

The *Wehrmacht*'s victory in the Battle of France in 1940 allowed the *Kriegsmarine* to base its U-boats on the French Atlantic coast, doing away with the need for the long and risky passage around the British Isles. In January 1941 construction of massive concrete pens began in the French ports, and from June 1941 the 1st Flotilla was based at Brest in Brittany.

The flotilla was the basic command unit of the *Kriegsmarine* for organizational purposes, but boats were often moved from flotilla to flotilla. Control of boats on operations was held by the various *Führer der Unterseeboote*, or FdU, or even by the commander-in-chief himself. Once they left port on patrol, the 1st Flotilla's boats were directed by FdU *West* from a base at Paris, which was later moved to Angers. Many of the *Kriegsmarine*'s top aces served at one time or another with the 1st Flotilla, including Otto Kretschmer, Erich Topp, Adalbert Schnee, Reinhard Suhren and Wolfgang Lüth.

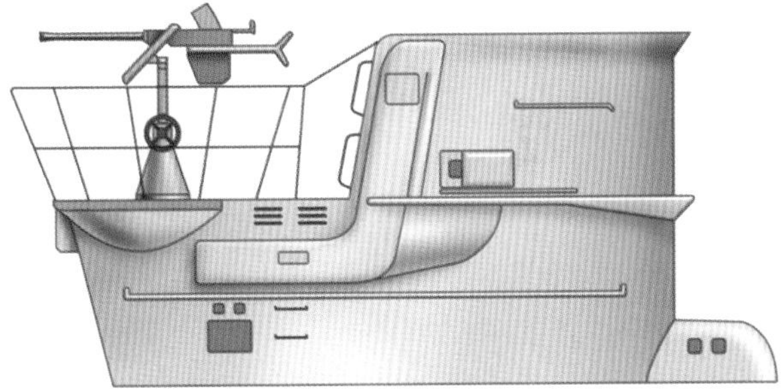

▲ **Type VIIB conning tower**

Early Type VII boats had simple conning towers, with little or no provision for anti-aircraft armament. By 1940, however, boats were being fitted with a widened bridge to allow the carriage of a single C/30 2cm (0.8in) cannon. The gun was known to have reliability problems, so the conversion was considered to be an interim measure until an improved twin mounting was available. Early war towers were also fitted with wave deflectors halfway up and around the bridge.

Star commanders

1935–45

The 1st Flotilla served throughout the most active phases of World War II, and numbered among its commanders many U-boat aces.

Grossadmiral Karl Dönitz

In September 1935 Karl Dönitz took command of the *U-Flottille* Weddigen with the Type II boats U-7, U-8 and U-9. On 1 January 1936 he became the *Führer der Unterseeboote* (FdU), a position that was renamed *Befehlshaber der Unterseeboote* (BdU) after the outbreak of war. He had been a successful U-boat captain in World War I and remained in the trade between the wars, developing the wolfpack tactics that concentrated U-boats on a convoy to attack it in strength.

Korvettenkapitän Adalbert Schnee

Schnee was born on 31 December 1913 in Berlin. He joined the *Kriegsmarine* as part of Crew 34. In May 1937 he joined the U-boat arm, serving under *Oberleutnant* Otto Kretschmer aboard U-23. His first command was U-6, followed by U-60, U-121, U-201 and U-2511, the first Type XXI boat to make an operational patrol in the last days of the war. He made 12 patrols, sinking 21 ships totalling 90,847 GRT and two auxiliary warships of 5700 GRT as well as damaging three ships with a total tonnage of 28,820 GRT. He was awarded the Oak Leaves to the Knight's Cross after his seventh patrol in U-201, during which he sank over 41,000 GRT of shipping.

Kapitänleutnant Rolf Mützelburg

Born on 23 June 1913 at Kiel, Mützelburg joined the *Reichsmarine* as part of Crew 32. After two years on minesweepers, he joined the U-boat arm in October 1939. He received his first combat experience on Schepke's U-100. He commanded U-10 in 1940 before taking command of U-203. In seven patrols, his boat sank 19 ships for a total of 81,987 GRT and damaged three more totalling 17,052 GRT. Awarded the Knight's Cross in November 1941, he received the Oak Leaves in July 1942. Mützelburg died accidentally while swimming on his last patrol on 11 September 1942. Diving from the conning tower, he struck the deck with his head and shoulder when the boat lurched suddenly in the swell. He was buried at sea on 12 September 1942.

STAR COMMANDERS

Commander	Patrols	Ships Sunk
Grossadmiral Karl Dönitz	None	None
Korvettenkapitän Adalbert Schnee	12	21
Kapitänleutnant Rolf Mützelburg	7	19
Kptlt. Friedrich Guggenberger	10	14

▲ **Admiral Dönitz**

Admiral Karl Dönitz (right) shown with propaganda minister Albert Speer, following the surrender of Nazi Germany, May 1945.

Kapitänleutnant Friedrich Guggenberger

Born in Munich in 1915, Guggenberger joined the *Reichsmarine* as part of Crew 32. His first U-boat was U-28, commanded by Günther Kuhnke. During the autumn of 1940 Guggenberger took over U-28, and later he commanded U-81, U-847 and U-513. He made 10 patrols, sinking 14 ships of 41,025 GRT plus one auxiliary warship of 1150 GRT. His greatest triumph was the sinking of the 22,963-tonne (22,600-ton) British carrier HMS *Ark Royal* in the Mediterranean in November 1941. Guggenberger died on 13 May 1988 at Erlenbach am Main.

Early U-boat organization

1935–39

To the outside world, the *Kriegsmarine*'s U-boat arm seemed to spring into existence in an astonishingly short time in 1935, but in fact it was the product of years of secret planning.

UNDER THE TERMS of the Treaty of Versailles, the German *Reichsmarine* had specifically been barred from designing or building submarines, but the clandestine work of the 1920s and 1930s meant that Germany was already well into the process of U-boat development when Hitler came to power. When Hermann Göring announced that the Third Reich was casting aside the shackles of Versailles, most of the preliminary work on the first boats for the German Navy had already been done.

The first U-boat officers and crewmen had been trained at the *U-Abwehrschule* at Kiel, established on 1 October 1933. Nominally intended to teach anti-submarine tactics, it was actually used to provide theoretical instruction for future U-boat officers and crews. U-boat building did not get under way until 1935, but all of the preparatory work was done in the preceding two years.

U-boats in service

The first Type IIA boats were completed in 1935, with U-1 to U-6 being reserved as training boats while U-7, U-8 and U-9 were assigned to the *U-Flottille* Weddigen, under the command of Karl Dönitz. The U-boat school, initially at Kiel, was moved to Neustadt north of Lübeck. A second flotilla, the *Flottille* Salzwedel, was established on the North Sea at Wilhelmshaven in September 1936, followed by *Flottille* Lohs, *Flottille* Emsmann and *Flottille* Wegener at Kiel and *Flottille* Hundius at Wilhelmshaven.

U-boat headquarters was established aboard the depot ship *Hai* at Kiel, where Dönitz, now promoted to *Kapitän zur See* and *Kommodore*, set up his staff. Although numbers of U-boats in service were still relatively small, Dönitz's aim was to create a large administration network that would be able to control the large number of submarines which he hoped and believed would be entering service in the near future.

CREW 36 EMBLEM

Germany hosted the Olympic Games in 1936, and many officers who joined the *Kriegsmarine* in Crew 36 adopted the Olympic rings for their commands, including the 1st Flotilla boats U-20, U-23 and U-59.

Specifications

Crew: 44
Powerplant: Diesel/electric
Max Speed: 29.6/14.8km/hr (16/8kt) s/d
Surface Range: 7964km (4300nm)
Displacement: 636/757 tonnes (626/745 tons) s/d
Dimensions (length/beam/draught): 64.5 x 5.8 x 4.4m (211.6 x 19 x 14.4ft)
Commissioned: Jul 1936 – April 1937
Armament: 11 torpedoes (4 bow/1 stern tubes); 1 x 8.8cm (3.5in) and 1 x 2cm (0.8in) guns

▲ **U-27 – U-36**

Type VIIA

The first Type VII boats were commissioned in 1936, in time to serve alongside British and French vessels on neutrality patrol during the Spanish Civil War. A total of 10 were built before construction was switched to the improved Type VIIB.

U-9

Type IIB

Built by Germania-Werft at Kiel, U-9 was laid down on 8 April 1935 and was launched on 30 July of the same year. The boat was commissioned into 1st Flotilla on 21 August.

U-9 was one of the boats sent out on patrol before the outbreak of war. After that she had a successful combat career in the first year of the war, during which she sank eight ships totalling more than 24,000 GRT, as well as the French submarine *Doris*.

The war in the North Sea was very much what the small Type II boats had been designed for, the short distances involved meaning that their low endurance was no real handicap. However, all that was about to change. Although successful, the Type II boats were too small for the Atlantic campaign, and U-9 was transferred to 24 Flotilla at Danzig, where she was used as a torpedo instruction boat. She was then moved to 21 Flotilla at Pillau, where she was used as a school boat to train new recruits.

U-9 Commanders

Korvkpt. Hans-Günther Looff *(Aug 1935)*
Oblt. Werner von Schmidt *(Sep 1935 – Oct 1937)*
Kptlt. Ludwig Mathes *(Oct 1937 – Sep 1939)*
Oblt. Max-Martin Schulte *(Sep 1939 – Dec 1939)*
Oblt. Wolfgang Lüth *(Dec 1939 – Jun 1940)*
Wolfgang Kaufmann *(Jun 1940 – Oct 1940)*
Kptlt. Joachim Deecke *(Oct 1940 – Jun 1941)*
Kptlt. Hans-Joachim Schmidt-Weichert *(Jul 1941 – Apr 1942; Oct 1942 – Sep 1943)*
Oblt. Heinrich Klapdor *(Sep 1943 – Aug 1944)*
Oblt. Martin Landt-Hayen *(Apr 1944)*
Kptlt. Klaus Petersen *(Apr 1944 – Jun 1944)*

After two years spent as a training boat, U-9 was dismantled and shipped overland to the Black Sea, where she mounted a further 12 patrols. U-9 was sunk on 20 August 1944 while in harbour at Konstanza on the Black Sea by bombs during a raid by Soviet aircraft.

Specifications

Crew: 25
Powerplant: Diesel/electric
Max Speed: 33/15.4km/hr (17.8/8.3kt) s/d
Surface Range: 3334km (1800nm)
Displacement: 283/334 tonnes (279/329 tons) s/d
Dimensions (length/beam/draught): 42.7 x 4.1 x 3.8m (140.1 x 13.5 x 12.5ft)
Commissioned: 21 Aug 1935
Armament: 6 torpedoes (3 bow tubes); 1 x 2cm (0.8in) gun

IRON CROSS EMBLEM

U-9 was the first boat to carry an individual insignia, a metal Iron Cross being mounted on the conning tower of the boat during the pre-war period. This was to commemorate the famous U-9 of World War I.

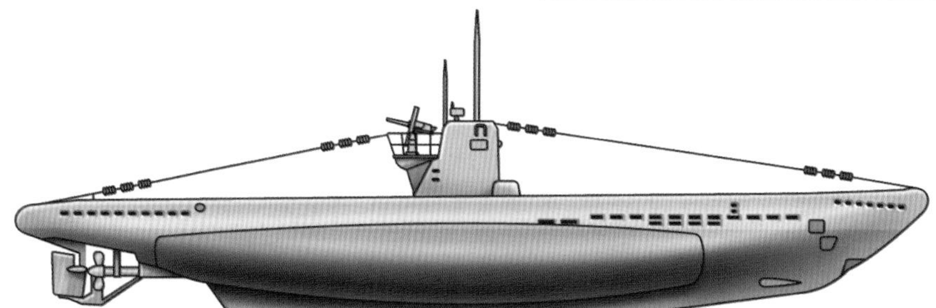

▲ **U-9**

Type IIB

Known as 'canoes' to their crews, the Type II coastal boats carried too few torpedoes to be really effective in combat, and most became training vessels.

U-9 TIMETABLE

Patrol Dates	Operational Area	Ships Sunk
25 Aug 1939 – 15 Sep 1939	Reconnaissance of English coast	0
16 Jan 1940 – 22 Jan 1940	North Sea	2
5 Feb 1940 – 17 Feb 1940	North Sea	2
14 Mar 1940 – 20 Mar 1940	North Sea submarine hunting	0
4 Apr 1940 – 24 Apr 1940	Norwegian invasion	0
5 May 1940 – 30 May 1940	Low Countries	4

U-201

TYPE VIIC

Laid down on 20 January 1940, U-201 was a Type VIIC boat, a member of the largest class of submarines ever built and the mainstay of the *U-Bootwaffe* throughout the war.

A HIGHLY SUCCESSFUL BOAT, commanded by U-boat ace Adalbert Schnee for much of its existence, U-201 carried out nine patrols in the Atlantic between April 1941 and February 1943. In that time the boat accounted for more than 100,000 GRT of Allied merchant shipping as well as sinking a fighter/catapult ship and an anti-submarine warfare (ASW) trawler.

U-201 Commanders

Kptlt. Adalbert Schnee *(Jan 1941 – Aug 1942)*

Kptlt. Günther Rosenberg *(Aug 1942 – Feb 1943)*

U-201 took part in Operation *Paukenschlag*, the U-boat offensive on the east coast of the United States. Schnee was succeeded by Günther Rosenberg in 1942, and it was under his command that U-201 was sunk with all hands on 17 February 1943 in the North Atlantic by depth charges from the British destroyer HMS *Viscount*. The boat was previously thought to have been sunk east of Newfoundland by the destroyer HMS *Fame*. This attack actually sank U-69.

U-201 TIMETABLE

Patrol Dates	Operational Area	Ships Sunk
22 Apr 1941 – 18 May 1941	Transit from Kiel to Brest	2
18 May 1941 – 19 Jul 1941	Central N Atlantic	0
14 Aug 1941 – 25 Aug 1941	W of Ireland/W of Portugal	3
14 Sep 1941 – 30 Sep 1941	W/SW of Ireland	5
29 Oct 1941 – 9 Dec 1941	W of Ireland	0
24 Mar 1942 – 21 May 1942	US East Coast	3
27 June 1942 – 8 Aug 1942	Central Atlantic SE of the Azores	6
6 Sep 1942 – 26 Oct 1942	Central Atlantic/Caribbean	3
27 Dec 1942 – 29 Dec 1942	Returned after developing fault	0
3 Jan 1943 – 17 Feb 1943	N Atlantic	0

U-441

TYPE VIIC FLAK CONVERSION

U-boats in transit across the Bay of Biscay were becoming increasingly vulnerable to aggressive Allied aircraft attacks, and it was decided to give the U-boats the chance to fight back.

IN APRIL–MAY 1943, U-441 was rebuilt as U-Flak 1, the first of three U-Flak boats. Designed to lure aircraft into battle, she was equipped with an enlarged bridge on which were mounted two Flakvierling 2cm (0.8in) quad mounts and a 3.7cm (1.5in) Flak gun, along with extra MG 42 machine guns. The crew was increased from around 46 to 67.

On her first patrol, U-441 shot down a Sunderland but was still vulnerable. With the boats unable to fight off Allied air attacks, Admiral Dönitz decided that the U-Flak experiment had failed. In late 1943, U-Flak 1 was converted back to a more conventional configuration.

U-441 Commanders

Kptlt. Klaus Hartmann *(Feb 1942 – May 1943)*

Kptlt. Götz von Hartmann *(May 1943 – Aug 1943)*

Kptlt. Klaus Hartmann *(Aug 1943 – Jun 1944)*

U-441 was sunk with all hands on 8 June 1944 in the English Channel by depth charges from a Liberator of No. 224 Sqn RAF.

Specifications

Crew: 67

Powerplant: Diesel/electric

Max Speed: 31.5/14.1km/hr (17/7.6kt) s/d

Surface Range: 12,040km (6500nm)

Displacement: 773/879 tonnes (761/865 tons) s/d

Dimensions (length/beam/draught): 67.1 x 6.2 x 4.8m (220.1 x 20.34 x 15.75ft)

Commissioned: 21 Feb 1942

Armament: 14 torpedoes; 1 x 3.7cm (1.5in) and 2 x quad 2cm (0.8in) guns

▲ **U-441**

Type VIIC Flak conversion

In spite of her impressive anti-aircraft armament, U-441 was severely damaged on each of the patrols she mounted as a Flak boat, and she was converted back to normal Type VIIC configuration.

U-441 TIMETABLE

Patrol Dates	Operational Area	Ships Sunk
17 Sep 1942 – 27 Sep 1942	Transit from Kiel to Trondheim	0
1 Oct 1942 – 7 Nov 1942	Transit to Brest, patrol N of Ireland	0
7 Dec 1942 – 11 Dec 1942	Returned after developing fault	0
13 Dec 1942 – 22 Jan 1943	Central Atlantic	1
27 Feb 1943 – 11 Apr 1943	Central N Atlantic	0
22 May 1943 – 25 May 1943	Bay of Biscay	1
8 July 1943 – 13 Jul 1943	Bay of Biscay	0
17 Oct 1943 – 8 Nov 1943	NW coast of Spain	0
18 Jan 1944 – 14 Mar 1944	W and NW of the British Isles	0
1 May 1944 – 3 May 1944	Returned after developing fault	0
20 May 1944 – 28 May 1944	Western English Channel	0
6 June 1944 – 8 June 1944	Normandy Invasion Front	0

U-556

Type VIIC

On 27 May 1941, U-556 was ordered to collect the War Diary of the battleship *Bismarck*, then being chased down by the Royal Navy.

U-556 TIMETABLE

Patrol Dates	Operational Area	Ships Sunk
1 May 1941 – 30 May 1941	Transit from Kiel to Lorient	5
19 June 1941 – 27 June 1941	N Atlantic	0

U-556 HAD ALREADY had a successful patrol when she was ordered to close with the *Bismarck*. Force H (aircraft carrier *Ark Royal* and battlecruiser *Renown*) came within the boat's sights, but U-556 was at the end of a patrol and had no more torpedoes. The boat had not reached the battleship by the time the *Bismarck* was pounded into ruin and sank. The U-boat herself did not last much longer. She was sunk on 27 June on her next patrol, southwest of Iceland, by depth charges from the corvettes HMS *Nasturtium*, HMS *Celandine* and HMS *Gladiolus*. Five of her crew were killed and 41 survived.

U-556 Commander

Kptlt. Herbert Wohlfarth *(Feb 1941 – Jun 1941)*

Specifications

Crew: 44
Powerplant: Diesel/electric
Max Speed: 31.5/14.1km/hr (17/7.6kt) s/d
Surface Range: 12,040km (6500nm)
Displacement: 773/879 tonnes (761/865 tons) s/d
Dimensions (length/beam/draught): 67.1 x 6.2 x 4.8m (220.1 x 20.34 x 15.75ft)
Commissioned: 6 Feb 1941
Armament: 14 torpedoes (4 bow/1 stern tubes); 1 x 3.7cm (1.5in) and 2 x twin 2cm (0.8in) guns

▲ **U-556**

Type VIIC

U-556 was one of a number of boats ordered to attack Convoy HX 113 in June 1941. Located by the convoy escorts on 27 June, U-556 was depth-charged and forced to the surface, where she was destroyed.

Convoy HG 76

December 1941

HG 76 was an important convoy comprising 32 ships sailing from Gibraltar in December 1941. Powerfully escorted, it was targeted by equally strong U-boat forces.

U-BOATS INVOLVED IN THE BATTLE included Wolfpack *Seeraüber*, comprising U-67 (Type IXC), U-107 (Type IXB), U-108 (Type IXB), U-131 (Type IXC), U-434 (Type VIIC). The group was reinforced by U-125 (Type IXC), U-71, U-567, U-574 and U-751 (all Type VIIC). They faced the Royal Navy's 36th Escort Group under Commander F. J. Walker, including two sloops, *Deptford* and *Stork*,

Specifications

Crew: 48–55
Powerplant: Diesel/electric
Max Speed: 33.7/13.5km/hr (18.2/7.3kt) s/d
Surface Range: 16,110km (8700nm)
Displacement: 1068/1197 tonnes (1051/1178 tons) s/d
Dimensions (length/beam/draught): 76.5 x 6.8 x 4.7m (251 x 22.31 x 15.42ft)
Commissioned: Jul 1936 – Apr 1937
Armament: 22 torpedoes (4 bow/2 stern tubes); 1 x 8.8cm (3.5in), 1 x 3.7cm (1.5in) and 1 x 2cm (0.8in) guns

▲ **U-107**

Type IXB

Although a part of 2. *Flottille*, U-107 took part in the attack on convoy HG 76. While unsuccessful in this operation, U-107 did sink 37 ships over the course of 14 patrols, making her one of the most successful U-boats of the war.

and seven corvettes, *Rhododendron*, *Marigold*, *Convolvulus*, *Penstemon*, *Gardenia*, *Samphire* and *Vetch*. The group was supported by the prototype escort carrier *Audacity* and the escort destroyers *Blankney*, *Exmoor* and *Stanley*.

The battle around the convoy was to be one of the most important of the war. At this time, U-boats seemed to be sinking merchantmen at will, but the strength of the escort of HG 76, as well as the presence of the escort carrier, promised to be more of a challenge. The loss of four boats in this battle came as a severe shock to the U-boat arm. The strong escort allied to the aggressive tactics developed by Commander Walker had defeated a wolfpack for the first time, but until these could be applied to every convoy, losses would continue to mount. The battle around HG 76 was a portent of things to come.

▲ **Depth charges**

Depth charges were the convoy escort's primary weapon in the struggle against the U-boat – at least when the boat was submerged.

CONVOY HG 76 BATTLE TIMETABLE

Date	Event
16 Dec	Contact is established. U-67, U-108 and U-131 are driven off by the escorts
17 Dec	U-131 is repeatedly attacked and damaged by aircraft from the *Audacity*. Unable to dive, the crew scuttle the boat
17/18 Dec	U-434 keeps contact during the night, but in the morning is detected by the escort and sunk. Two Fw 200 Condors are shot down by Martlets (Grumman Wildcats) from the *Audacity*. U-107 and U-67 are driven off by the convoy escort
19 Dec	U-574 sinks HMS *Stanley*. Lit up by 'snowflake' illuminating rounds, the boat is forced to dive. Damaged by depth charges from the *Stork*, U-574 is forced to the surface, where it is rammed and sunk. While the escort is occupied, U-108 sinks one ship
20/21 Dec	U-107 maintains contact, but the wolfpack is unable to penetrate the escort
21 Dec	Reinforced by U-71, U-567 and U-751 the wolfpack presses home its attack. U-567, under ace commander Endrass, sinks one ship, but is herself sunk by the *Deptford*. U-751 finds the *Audacity*, and sinks the escort carrier
22 Dec	The convoy escort is reinforced by two destroyers. U-71 and U-125 are driven off
23 Dec	U-751 loses contact

Wolfpack groups *Star*, *Specht* & *Fink*

April 1943

The spring of 1943 saw the Battle of the Atlantic coming to a climax. U-boats were in service in large numbers, but Allied escort forces were also getting stronger.

THE *STAR* WOLFPACK was formed in April 1943, incorporating the *Meise* Group, which had been operating southeast of Greenland, together with a number of new boats. The group was instructed to form a patrol line south of Iceland, with the aim of intercepting a westbound convoy. Convoy ONS 5 passed the northern end of the patrol line, but bad weather meant that only five boats made contact, and only one ship was sunk. On 1 May, the *Star* boats were directed to an eastbound convoy, SC 128, which had been sighted and lost by another wolfpack, the 18-strong *Specht* Group. Now numbering 30 boats, the combined wolfpacks were renamed Group *Fink*.

After searching for SC 128, the *Fink* boats again encountered ONS 5, which had been delayed by a storm. ONS 5 was a slow outward-bound convoy of 42 ships that had sailed for North America on 22 April. It was given the crack B7 Escort Group led by Commander Peter Gretton, which was reinforced later by the 1st and 3rd Support Groups.

Early in May, Ultra intelligence and high-frequency direction-finding intercepts warned the British of an imminent attack by the powerful wolfpack. On the night of 3 May the boats attacked the escort, with the operation being directed by Admiral Dönitz himself from his headquarters. Scenting a major success, the admiral urged his U-boat commanders to press home their attacks. However, the escorts proved so effective at keeping the U-boats at bay by night that they switched to submerged attacks by day.

On 5 May the convoy lost 12 ships. However, this was the last occasion when the U-boats would make such a killing, and it came at a very high cost. The convoy escort attacked more than 15 boats in the fog that had descended, and six were destroyed, with another seven sustaining serious damage.

Following these severe losses, over the next few weeks the U-boats were unable to successfully attack any other convoy.

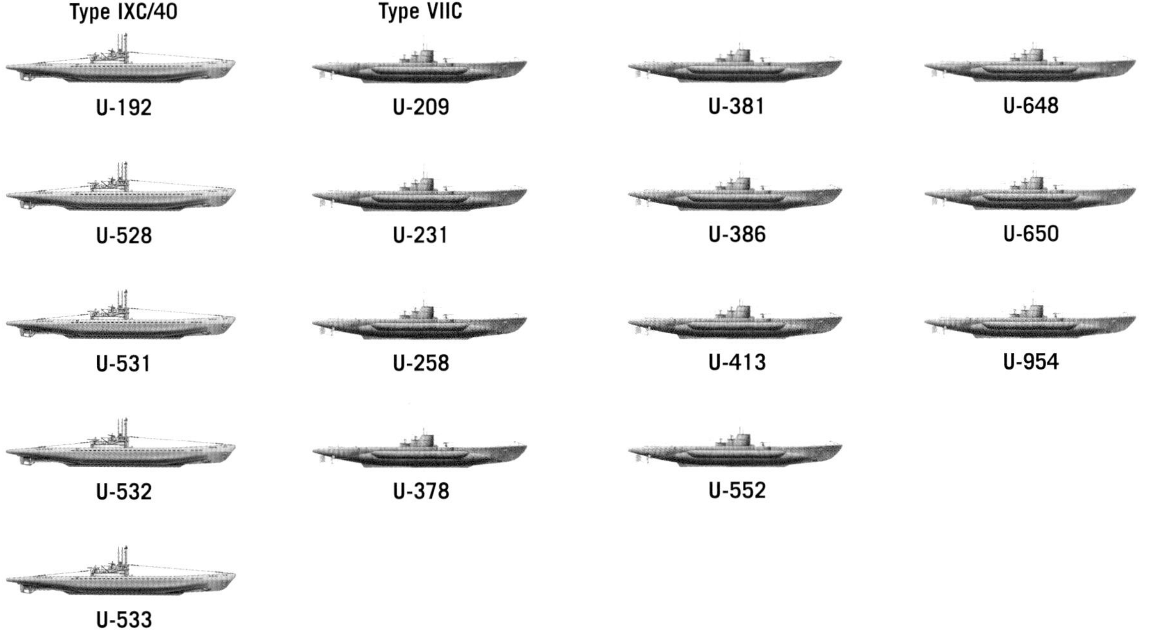

BOATS THAT SERVED WITH 1ST FLOTILLA (111 BOATS)

U-Boat	Type	Commissioned	Flotilla(s)	Patrols	Fate
U-8	IIB	5-Aug-35	13 Apr 1940 – 30 Jun 1940 from U-Bootschulflottille	1 patrol	to 24. Flottille
U-9	IIB	21-Aug-35	1 Sep 1935 – 30 Jun 1940	19 patrols. 7 ships sunk: total 16,669 GRT; 1 warship sunk: total 561 t/552 tons; 1 warship damaged: total 419 t/412 tons	to 24. Flottille
U-10	IIB	9-Sep-35	27 Sep 1935 – 3 Oct 1937 from U-Bootschulflottille	5 patrols. 2 ships sunk: total 6356 GRT	to 3. Flottille
U-11	IIB	21-Sep-35	1 Jul 1940 – 30 Nov 1940 (school boat) from U-Bootschulflottille	None	to 21. Flottille
U-13	IIB	30-Nov-35	1 Sep 1935 – 31 May 1940	9 patrols. 9 ships sunk: total 28,056 GRT	Sunk 31 May 1940, southeast of Lowestoft, by depth charges from the sloop HMS *Weston*. 26 survivors (no casualties)
U-15	IIB	7-Mar-36	1 Mar 1936 – 30 Jan 1940	5 patrols. 3 ships sunk: total 4532 GRT	Sunk with all hands 30 Jan 1940 in the North Sea; accidentally rammed by the German torpedo boat *Iltis*. 25 dead

BOATS THAT SERVED WITH 1ST FLOTILLA (111 BOATS)

U-Boat	Type	Commissioned	Flotilla(s)	Patrols	Fate
U-17	IIB	3-Dec-35	1 Dec 1935 – 31 Oct 1939	4 patrols. 3 ships sunk: total 1825 GRT	to U-Ausbildungsflottille
U-18	IIB	4-Jan-36	4 Jan 1936 – 1 Aug 1939	14 patrols. 3 ships sunk: total 1985 GRT; 1 ship damaged: total 7745 GRT; 1 warship damaged: total 57t/56 tons	to 3. Flottille
U-19	IIB	16-Jan-36	1 Jan 1936 – 30 Apr 1940	20 patrols. 14 ships sunk: total 35,430 GRT; 1 warship sunk: total 448t/441 tons	to 1. U-Ausbildungsflottille
U-20	IIB	1-Feb-36	1 Jan 1940 – 30 Apr 1940 from 3. Flottille	17 patrols. 14 ships sunk: total 37,669 GRT; 1 ship damaged beyond repair: total 844 GRT; 1 ship damaged: total 1846 GRT	to 1. U-Ausbildungsflottille
U-21	IIB	3-Aug-36	1 Aug 1936 – 30 Jun 1940	7 patrols. 5 ships sunk: total 10,706 GRT; 1 aux warship sunk: total 605 GRT; 1 cruiser damaged: total 11,685t/11,500 tons	to 21. Flottille
U-22	IIB	20-Aug-36	1 Jan 1940 – 27 Mar 1940 from 3. Flottille	7 patrols. 6 ships sunk: total 7344 GRT; 2 auxiliary warships sunk: total 3633 GRT; 1 warship sunk: total 1499t/1475 tons	Missing with all hands 27 March 1940 in the North Sea/Skagerrak, possibly lost to a mine. 27 dead
U-23	IIB	24-Sep-36	1 Sep 1936 – 30 Jun 1940	16 patrols. 7 ships sunk: total 11,094 GRT; 2 warships sunk: total 1433t/1410 tons; 3 ships damaged beyond repair: total 18,199 GRT; 1 ship damaged: total 1005 GRT; 1 warship damaged: total 57t/56 tons	to 21. Flottille
U-24	IIB	10-Oct-36	18 Oct 1939 – 30 Apr 1940 from 3. Flottille	20 patrols. 1 ship sunk: total 961 GRT; 5 warships sunk: total 580t/571 tons; 1 ship a total loss: total 7886 GRT; 1 ship damaged: total 7661 GRT	to 1. U-Ausbildungsflottille
U-56	IIC	26-Nov-38	1 Jan 1940 – 31 Oct 1940 from 5. Flottille	12 patrols. 3 ships sunk: total 8860 GRT; 1 auxiliary warship sunk: total 16,923 GRT; 1 ship damaged: total 3829 GRT	to 24. Flottille
U-57	IIC	29-Dec-38	1 Jan 1940 – 3 Sep 1940 from 5. Flottille	11 patrols. 11 ships sunk: total 48,053 GRT; 1 auxiliary warship sunk: total 8240 GRT; 1 ship damaged beyond repair: total 10,191 GRT; 2 ships damaged: total 10,403 GRT	to 22. Flottille
U-58	IIC	4-Feb-39	1 Jan 1940 – 31 Dec 1940 from 5. Flottille	12 patrols. 6 ships sunk: total 16,148 GRT; 1 auxiliary warship sunk: total 8401 GRT	to 22. Flottille
U-59	IIC	4-Mar-39	1 Jan 1940 – 31 Dec 1940 from 5. Flottille	13 patrols. 16 ships sunk: total 29,514 GRT; 2 auxiliary warships sunk: total 864 GRT; 1 ship damaged beyond repair: total 4943 GRT; 1 ship damaged: total 8009 GRT	to 22. Flottille
U-60	IIC	22-Jul-39	1 Jan 1940 – 18 Nov 1940 from 5. Flottille	9 patrols. 3 ships sunk: total 7561 GRT; 1 ship damaged: total 15,434 GRT	to 21. Flottille
U-61	IIC	12-Aug-39	1 Jan 1940 – 14 Nov 1940 from 5. Flottille	10 patrols. 5 ships sunk: total 19,668 GRT; 1 ship damaged: total 4434 GRT	to 21. Flottille
U-62	IIC	21-Dec-39	1 Jan 1940 – 30 Sep 1940 from 5. Flottille	5 patrols. 1 ship sunk: total 4581 GRT; 1 warship sunk: total 1372t/1350 tons	to 21. Flottille
U-63	IIC	18-Jan-40	18 Jan 1940 – 25 Feb 1940	1 patrol. 1 ship sunk: total 3840 GRT	Sunk 25 Feb 1940 in the North Sea south of the Shetlands by depth charges and torpedoes from the destroyers HMS *Escort*, HMS *Inglefield*, HMS *Imogen* and the submarine HMS *Narwhal*. 1 dead and 24 survivors
U-79	VIIC	13-Mar-41	13 Mar 1941 – 30 Sep 1941	6 patrols. 2 ships sunk: total 2983 GRT; 1 warship damaged b/r: total 635t/625 tons;1 ship damaged: total 10,356 GRT	to 23. Flottille
U-80	VIIC	8-Apr-41	8 Apr 1941 – 30 Apr 1941 (training)	None	to 26. Flottille
U-81	VIIC	26-Apr-41	26 Apr 1941 – 30 Nov 1941	17 patrols. 23 ships sunk: total 39,711 GRT; 1 auxiliary warship sunk: total 1150 GRT; 1 aircraft carrier (HMS *Ark Royal*) sunk: total 22,960t/22,600 tons; 1 ship damaged beyond repair: total 5917 GRT; 2 ships damaged: total 14,143 GRT	to 29. Flottille
U-83	VIIB	8-Feb-41	8 Feb 1941 – 31 Dec 1941	12 patrols. 5 ships sunk: total 8425 GRT; 1 auxiliary warship sunk: total 91 GRT; 1 ship damaged: total 2590 GRT; 1 auxiliary warship damaged: total 6746 GRT	to 23. Flottille
U-84	VIIB	29-Apr-41	29 Apr 1941 – 7 Aug 1943	8 patrols. 6 ships sunk: total 29,905 GRT; 1 ship damaged: total 7176 GRT	May have been sunk with all hands returning from the Caribbean on 7 Aug 1943 by a Mk 24 homing torpedo from a US Navy Liberator of VB-105. 46 dead. For many years the boat was erroneously thought to have been sunk southwest of the Azores on 24 Aug 1943 by torpedoes from an Avenger of the escort carrier USS *Core*.
U-86	VIIB	8-Jul-41	1 Sep 1941 – 14 Dec 1943	7 patrols. 3 ships sunk: total 9614 GRT; 1 ship damaged: total 8627 GRT	Listed as missing with all hands 14 Dec 1943 in the North Atlantic after failing to answer radio calls. 50 dead. Previously believed to have been sunk 29 Nov 1943 east of the Azores by depth charges from aircraft of the escort carrier USS *Bogue*. That attack was actually against U-764, which escaped undamaged
U-116	XB		1 Feb 1942 – 6 Oct 1942 from 2 Flottille	4 patrols. 1 ship sunk by mines: total 4284 GRT; 1 ship damaged by mines: total 7093 GRT	Declared missing with all hands in Oct 1942 in the North Atlantic, details and position not known. The last radio message was sent on 6 Oct 1942. 56 dead
U-117	XB	25-Oct-41	1 Feb 1942 – 14 Oct 1942 from 2 Flottille	5 patrols. 2 ships damaged by mines: total 14,269 GRT	to 11. Flottille
U-137	IID	15-Jun-40	15 Jun 1940 – 19 Dec 1940	4 patrols. 6 ships sunk: total 24,136 GRT; 1 ship damaged: total 4917 GRT; 1 auxiliary warship damaged: total 10,552 GRT	to 22. Flottille
U-138	IID	27-Jun-40	27 Jun 1940 – 31 Dec 1940	5 patrols. 6 ships sunk: total 48,564 GRT; 1 ship damaged: total 6993 GRT	to 22. Flottille
U-139	IID	24-Jul-40	24 Jul 1940 – 3 Oct 1940 (training)	2 patrols	to 21. Flottille
U-140	IID	7-Aug-40	7 Aug 1940 – 31 Dec 1940	3 patrols. 3 ships sunk: total 12,410 GRT; 1 warship sunk: total 209t/206 tons	to 22. Flottille
U-141	IID	21-Aug-40	21 Aug 1940 – 23 Oct 1940 (training)	4 patrols. 4 ships sunk: total 6801 GRT; 1 ship damaged: total 5133 GRT	to 3. Flottille
U-142	IID	4-Sep-40	4 Sep 1940 – 16 Oct 1940 (training)	4 patrols	to 24. Flottille
U-143	IID	18-Sep-40	18 Sep 1940 – 2 Nov 1940 (training)	4 patrols. 1 ship sunk: total 1409 GRT	to 24. Flottille

BOATS THAT SERVED WITH 1ST FLOTILLA (111 BOATS)

U-Boat	Type	Commissioned	Flotilla(s)	Patrols	Fate
U-144	IID	2-Oct-40	2 Oct 1940 – 19 Dec 1940 (training)	3 patrols. 1 warship sunk: total 209t/206 tons	to 22. Flottille
U-145	IID	16-Oct-40	16 Oct 1940 – 18 Dec 1940 (training)	3 patrols	to 22. Flottille
U-146	IID	30-Oct-40	30 Oct 1940 – 31 Dec 1940 (training)	2 patrols. 1 ship sunk: total 3496 GRT	to 22. Flottille
U-147	IID	11-Dec-40	Dec 1940 (training)	3 patrols. 3 ships sunk: total 8636 GRT	to 22. Flottille
U-149	IID	13-Nov-40	13 Nov 1940 – 31 Dec 1940 (training)	1 patrol. 1 warship sunk: total 209t/206 tons	to 22. Flottille
U-150	IID	27-Nov-40	27 Nov 1940 – 31 Dec 1940 (training)	None	to 22. Flottille
U-201	VIIC	25-Jan-41	25 Jan 1941 – 17 Feb 1943	9 patrols. 22 ships sunk: total 103,355 GRT; 2 aux warships sunk: total 5700 GRT; 2 ships damaged: total 13,386 GRT	Sunk with all hands 17 Feb 1943 in North Atlantic by depth charges from the British destroyer HMS *Viscount*. 49 dead. Previously thought to have been sunk east of Newfoundland by depth charges from the destroyer HMS *Fame*. This attack actually sank U-69
U-202	VIIC	22-Mar-41	22 Mar 1941 – 2 Jun 1943	9 patrols. 9 ships sunk: total 34,615 GRT; 5 ships damaged: total 42,618 GRT. One special operations mission, landing 4 saboteurs on Long Island, New York, on 12 Jun 1942	Sunk 2 Jun 1943 southeast of Cape Farewell, Greenland, by depth charges and gunfire from the sloop HMS *Starling*. 18 dead and 30 survivors
U-203	VIIC	18-Feb-41	18 Feb 1941 – 25 Apr 1943	11 patrols. 21 ships sunk: total 94,296 GRT; 3 ships damaged: total 17,052 GRT	Sunk 25 April 1943 south of Cape Farewell, Greenland, by depth charges from Swordfish aircraft of No. 811 Sqn off the escort carrier HMS *Biter* and by the destroyer HMS *Pathfinder*. 10 dead and 38 survivors
U-204	VIIC	8-Mar-41	8 Mar 1941 – 19 Oct 1941	3 patrols. 4 ships sunk: total 17,360 GRT; 1 warship sunk: total 1077t/1060 tons	Sunk with all hands 19 Oct 1941 near Tangier by depth charges from the corvette HMS *Mallow* and the sloop HMS *Rochester*. 46 dead
U-208	VIIC	5-Jul-41	1 Sep 1941 – 7 Dec 1941 from 5. Flottille (training)	2 patrols. 1 ship sunk: total 3872 GRT	Sunk with all hands 7 Dec 1941 in the Atlantic west of Gibraltar by depth charges from the destroyers HMS *Harvester* and HMS *Hesperus*. 45 dead. Previously thought to have been destroyed by the corvette HMS *Bluebell*, but this attack was probably against U-67 and caused only minor damage
U-209	VIIC	11-Oct-41	1 Mar 1943 – 7 May 1943 from 11. Flottille	7 patrols. 4 ships sunk: total 1356 GRT	Missing with all hands on 7 May 1943 in the North Atlantic in approximate position 52N, 38W. Possibly lost in a diving accident after being damaged on 4 May by a Canadian Catalina. 46 dead. Originally thought to have been sunk by the frigate HMS *Jed* and the sloop HMS *Sennen* on 19 May 1943; in fact U-954 was sunk.
U-213	VIID	30-Aug-41	1 Jan 1942 – 30 Apr 1942 from 5. Flottille (training)	3 patrols	to 9. Flottille
U-225	VIIC	11-Jul-42	1 Jan 1943 – 15 Feb 1943 from 5. Flottille (training)	2 patrols. 1 ship sunk: total 5273 GRT; 4 ships damaged: total 24,672 GRT	Sunk with all hands 15 Feb 1943 in the North Atlantic by depth charges from a Liberator aircraft of No. 120 Sqn RAF. 46 dead. Sinking previously credited to US Coast Guard cutter *John C. Spencer* on 21 Feb 1943 in the North Atlantic – actually against U-604, which escaped damage.
U-238	VIIC	20-Feb-43	1 Aug 1943 – 9 Feb 1944 from 5. Flottille (training)	3 patrols. 4 ships sunk: total 23,048 GRT; 1 ship damaged: total 7176 GRT	Sunk with all hands 9 Feb 1944 southwest of Ireland by depth charges from the sloops HMS *Kite*, HMS *Magpie* and HMS *Starling*. 50 dead
U-243	VIIC	2-Oct-43	1 Jun 1944 – 8 Jul 1944	1 patrol	Sunk 8 Jul 1944 in the Bay of Biscay west of Nantes by depth charges from a Sunderland of No. 10 Sqn RAAF. 11 dead and 38 survivors
U-247	VIIC	23-Oct-43	1 Jun 1944 – 1 Sep 1944 from 5. Flottille (training)	2 patrols. 1 ship sunk: total 207 GRT	Sunk with all hands 1 Sep 1944 near Land's End by depth charges from the Canadian frigates HMCS *St. John* and HMCS *Swansea*. 52 dead
U-263	VIIC	6-May-42	1 Nov 1942 – 20 Jan 1944	2 patrols. 2 ships sunk: total 12,376 GRT	Sunk with all hands 20 Jan 1944 in the Bay of Biscay near La Rochelle during deep dive trials. 51 dead
U-268	VIIC	29-Jul-42	1 Feb 1943 – 19 Feb 1943 from 8. Flottille (training)	1 patrol. 1 ship sunk: total 14,547 GRT	Sunk with all hands 19 Feb 1943 in the Bay of Biscay west of Nantes by depth charges from a Vickers Wellington of No. 172 Sqn RAF. 45 dead
U-271	VIIC	23-Sep-42	1 Jun 1943 – 28 Jan 1944 from 8. Flottille	3 patrols. No ships sunk or damaged. Served as a Flak boat September–November 1943	Sunk with all hands 28 Jan 1944 west of Limerick by depth charges from a US Navy PB4Y Liberator of VB-103. 51 dead
U-276	VIIC	9-Dec-42	1 Mar 1944 – 1 Jul 1944 from 8. Flottille	3 patrols	to 31. Flottille
U-292	VIIC/41	25-Aug-43	1 May 1944 – 27 May 1944 from 8. Flottille	1 patrol	Sunk with all hands 27 May 1944 west of Trondheim by depth charges from a Liberator of No. 59 Sqn RAF. 51 dead.
U-301	VIIC	21-Jan-43	1 Oct 1942 – 31 Dec 1942 from 5. Flottille	3 patrols	to 29. Flottille
U-304	VIIC	5-Aug-42	1 Apr 1943 – 28 May 1943 from 8. Flottille	1 patrol	Sunk with all hands 28 May 1943 southeast of Cape Farewell, Greenland, by depth charges from a Liberator of No. 120 Sqn RAF. 46 dead.
U-305	VIIC	17-Sep-42	1 Mar 1943 – 17 Jan 1944 from 8. Flottille	4 patrols. 2 ships sunk: total 13,045 GRT; 2 warships sunk: total 2601t/2560 tons	Lost with all hands in the North Atlantic 16 Jan 1944, possibly to one of its own torpedoes. 51 dead. Previously credited to the destroyer HMS *Wanderer* and the frigate HMS *Glenarm* on 17 Jan 1944. That attack probably sank U-377.

BOATS THAT SERVED WITH 1ST FLOTILLA (111 BOATS)

U-Boat	Type	Commissioned	Flotilla(s)	Patrols	Fate
U-306	VIIC	21-Oct-42	1 Mar 1943 – 31 Oct 1943 from 8. Flottille	5 patrols. 1 ship sunk: total 10,218 GRT; 2 ships damaged: total 11,195 GRT	Sunk with all hands 31 Oct 1943 in the Atlantic northeast of the Azores by depth charges from the destroyer HMS *Whitehall* and the corvette HMS *Geranium*. 51 dead
U-311	VIIC	23-Mar-43	1 Dec 1943 – 22 Apr 1944 from 8. Flottille	2 patrols. 1 ship sunk: total 10,342 GRT	Sunk with all hands on 22 Apr 1944 southwest of Iceland by depth charges from the frigates HMCS *Matane* and HMCS *Swansea*. 51 dead
U-331	VIIC	31-Mar-41	31 Mar 1941 – 14 Oct 1941	10 patrols. 1 auxiliary warship sunk: total 9135 GRT; 1 battleship sunk (HMS *Barham*): total 31,599t/31,100 tons; 1 warship damaged: total 378t/372 tons	to 23. Flottille
U-336	VIIC	14-Feb-42	1 Dec 1942 – 5 Oct 1943 from 5. Flottille	5 patrols. 1 ship sunk: total 4919 GRT	Sunk with all hands 5 Oct 1943 southwest of Iceland by rockets from a Hudson of No. 269 Sqn RAF. 50 dead. Previously credited to a US Navy Ventura of VB-128 on 4 Oct 1943, which actually sank U-279
U-353	VIIC	31-Mar-42	1 Oct 1942 – 16 Oct 1942 from 5. Flottille	1 patrol	Sunk 16 Oct 1942 in the North Atlantic by depth charges from the destroyer HMS *Fame*. 6 dead and 39 survivors
U-354	VIIC	22-Apr-42	1 Oct 1942 – 14 Oct 1942 from 5. Flottille	20 patrols. 1 ship sunk: total 7179 GRT; 1 warship sunk: total 1320t/1300 tons; 1 warship damaged beyond repair: total 11,603t/11,420 tons; 1 ship damaged: total 3771 GRT	to 11. Flottille
U-371	VIIC	15-Mar-41	15 Mar 1941 – 31 Oct 1941	19 patrols. 8 ships sunk: total 51,401 GRT; 1 aux warship sunk: total 545 GRT; 2 warships sunk: total 2323t/2286 tons; 2 ships damaged beyond repair: total 13,341 GRT; 4 ships damaged: total 28,072 GRT; 2 warships damaged: total 2540t/2500 tons	to 23. Flottille
U-372	VIIC	19-Apr-41	19 Apr 1941 – 13 Dec 1941	8 patrols. 3 ships sunk: total 11,751 GRT; 1 auxiliary warship sunk: total 14,650 GRT	to 29. Flottille
U-374	VIIC	21-Jun-41	1 Sep 1941 – 13 Dec 1941 from 5. Flottille	3 patrols. 1 ship sunk: total 3349 GRT; 2 auxiliary warships sunk: total 992 GRT	to 29. Flottille
U-379	VIIC	29-Nov-41	1 Jul 1942 – 8 Aug 1942 from 8. Flottille	1 patrol. 2 ships sunk: total 8904 GRT	Sunk 8 Aug 1942 in the North Atlantic southeast of Cape Farewell, Greenland, by ramming and depth charges from the corvette HMS *Dianthus*. 40 dead and 5 survivors
U-392	VIIC	29-May-43	1 Dec 1943 – 16 Mar 1944 from 5. Flottille	2 patrols	Sunk with all hands 16 Mar 1944 in the Straits of Gibraltar by depth charges from the frigate HMS *Affleck*, the destroyer HMS *Vanoc* and from 3 US Navy PBY Catalinas of VP-63. 52 dead
U-394	VIIC	7-Aug-43	1 Apr 1944 – 31 May 1944 from 5. Flottille	2 patrols	to 11. Flottille
U-396	VIIC	16-Oct-43	1 Jun 1944 – 30 Sep 1944 from 5. Flottille	5 patrols	to 11. Flottille
U-401	VIIC	10-Apr-41	10 Apr 1941 – 3 Aug 1941	1 patrol	Sunk with all hands 3 Aug 1941 southwest of Ireland by depth charges from the destroyer HMS *Wanderer*, the Norwegian destroyer *St. Albans* and the corvette HMS *Hydrangea*. 45 dead
U-405	VIIC	17-Sep-41	1 Mar 1942 – 30 Jun 1942 from 8. Flottille	11 patrols. 2 ships sunk: total 11,841 GRT	to 11. Flottille
U-413	VIIC	3-Jun-42	1 Nov 1942 – 20 Aug 1944 from 8. Flottille	8 patrols. 5 ships sunk: total 36,885 GRT; 1 warship sunk: total 1118t/1100 tons	Sunk on 20 Aug 1944 in the Channel south of Brighton by depth charges from the escort destroyer HMS *Wensleydale* and the destroyers HMS *Forester* and HMS *Vidette*. 45 dead and 1 survivor
U-415	VIIC	5-Aug-42	1 Mar 1943 – 14 Jul 1944 from 8. Flottille	7 patrols. 1 ship sunk: total 4917 GRT; 1 warship sunk: total 1362t/1340 tons; 1 ship damaged: total 5486 GRT	Sunk by a mine on 14 Jul 1944 west of the torpedo-net barrier at Brest. 2 crewmen killed
U-418	VIIC	21-Oct-42	1 May 1943 – 1 Jun 1943 from 8. Flottille	1 patrol	Sunk with all hands 1 Jun 1943 northwest of Cape Ortegal by rockets from a Bristol Beaufighter of No. 236 Sqn RAF. 48 dead
U-422	VIIC	10-Feb-43	1 Aug 1943 – 4 Oct 1943 from 8. Flottille	1 patrol	Sunk with all hands on 4 Oct 1943 north of the Azores by Avenger and Wildcat aircraft from the escort carrier USS *Card*. 49 dead. U-422 was being resupplied by 'milk cow' U-460, which was also sunk. A third boat, U-264, escaped with serious damage
U-424	VIIC	7-Apr-43	1 Oct 1943 – 11 Feb 1944 from 8. Flottille	2 patrols	Sunk with all hands 11 Feb 1944 southwest of Ireland by depth charges from the sloops HMS *Wild Goose* and HMS *Woodpecker*. 50 dead
U-426	VIIC	12-May-43	1 Nov 1943 – 8 Jan 1944 from 1. Flottille	2 patrols. 1 ship sunk: total 6625 GRT	Sunk with all hands 8 Jan 1944 west of Nantes by depth charges from an Australian Sunderland of No. 10 Sqn RAAF. 51 dead
U-435	VIIC	30-Aug-41	1 Jan 1942 – 30 Jun 1942 from 5. Flottille	8 patrols. 9 ships sunk: total 53,712 GRT; 1 auxiliary warship sunk: total 2456 GRT; 3 warships sunk: total 869t/855 tons	to 11. Flottille. Sunk with all hands 9 Jul 1943 west of Figueira, Portugal, by 4 depth charges from a Wellington of No. 179 Sqn RAF. 48 dead
U-439	VIIC	20-Dec-41	1 Nov 1942 – 4 May 1943 from 5. Flottille	4 patrols	Sunk on 4 May 1943 west of Cape Ortegal, Spain, in a collision with U-659. 40 dead and 9 survivors
U-440	VIIC	24-Jan-42	1 Sep 1942 – 31 May 1943 from 5. Flottille	5 patrols	Sunk with all hands 31 May 1943 northwest of Cape Ortegal, Spain, by depth charges from a Short Sunderland of No. 201 Sqn RAF. 46 dead
U-441	VIIC	21-Feb-42	1 Oct 1942 – 8 Jun 1944 (as U-Flak 1 from 1 May 1943 – 1 Nov 1943) from 5. Flottille	11 patrols. 1 ship sunk: total 7051 GRT	Converted as the first Flak boat with anti-aircraft armament in April/May 1943. Shot down a Sunderland on its first patrol, but was badly damaged by Beaufighters on its second. Returned to a normal configuration in Oct 1943. Sunk with all hands on 8 Jun 1944 in the English Channel by depth charges from a Liberator of No. 224 Sqn RAF. 51 dead

BOATS THAT SERVED WITH 1ST FLOTILLA (111 BOATS)

U-Boat	Type	Commissioned	Flotilla(s)	Patrols	Fate
U-456	VIIC	18-Sep-41	1 Dec 1942 – 12 May 1943 from 11. Flottille	11 patrols. 6 ships sunk: total 31,528 GRT; 1 auxiliary warship sunk: total 251 GRT; 1 warship (HMS *Edinburgh*) damaged: total 11,685t/11,500 tons	Almost certainly sunk with all hands in a diving accident on 12 May 1943 while avoiding the destroyer HMS *Opportune* in the North Atlantic. The boat was crash-diving after being badly damaged by a Fido homing torpedo from a Liberator of No. 86 Sqn RAF. 49 dead. Sinking was previously credited to the corvette HMCS *Drumheller*, the frigate HMS *Lagan* and a Canadian Sunderland of No. 423 Sqn
U-471	VIIC	5-May-43	1 Nov 1943 – 30 Apr 1944 from 5. Flottille	3 patrols	to 29. Flottille
U-556	VIIC	6-Feb-41	6 Feb 1941 – 27 Jun 1941	2 patrols. 6 ships sunk: total 29,552 GRT; 1 ship damaged: total 4986 GRT	Sunk 27 Jun 1941 southwest of Iceland by depth charges from the corvettes HMS *Nasturtium*, HMS *Celandine* and HMS *Gladiolus*. 5 dead and 41 survivors
U-557	VIIC	13-Feb-41	13 Feb 1941 – 4 Dec 1941	4 patrols. 6 ships sunk: total 31,729 GRT	to 29. Flottille
U-558	VIIC	20-Feb-41	20 Feb 1941 – 20 Jul 1943	10 patrols. 17 ships sunk: total 93,186 GRT; 1 auxiliary warship sunk: total 913 GRT; 1 warship sunk: total 940t/925 tons; 1 ship damaged beyond repair: total 6672 GRT; 2 ships damaged: total 15,070 GRT	Sunk 20 Jul 1943 in the Bay of Biscay northwest of Cape Ortegal by depth charges from a British Halifax and a US B-24 Liberator of No. 58 Sqn RAF and the 19th A/S Sqn. 45 dead and 5 survivors
U-559	VIIC	27-Feb-41	27 Feb 1941 – 31 Oct 1941	10 patrols. 4 ships sunk: total 11,811 GRT; 1 warship sunk: total 1077t/1060 tons	to 23. Flottille
U-561	VIIC	13-Mar-41	13 Mar 1941 – 31 Jan 1942	15 patrols. 5 ships sunk: total 17,146 GRT; 1 ship damaged beyond repair: total 5062 GRT; 1 ship damaged: total 4043 GRT	to 23. Flottille
U-562	VIIC	20-Mar-41	20 Mar 1941 – 31 Dec 1941	9 patrols. 6 ships sunk: total 37,287 GRT; 1 ship damaged: total 3359 GRT	to 29. Flottille
U-563	VIIC	27-Mar-41	27 Mar 1941 – 31 May 1943	6 patrols. 3 ships sunk: total 14,689 GRT; 1 warship sunk: total 1900t/1870 tons; 2 ships damaged: total 16,266 GRT	Sunk with all hands 31 May 1943 southwest of Brest by depth charges from British and Australian Handley Page Halifax and Sunderland aircraft. 49 dead
U-564	VIIC	3-Apr-41	3 Apr 1941 – 14 Jun 1943	9 patrols. 18 ships sunk: total 95,544 GRT; 1 warship sunk: total 914t/900 tons; 4 ships damaged: total 28,907 GRT	Sunk 14 Jun 1943 northwest of Cape Ortegal by depth charges from an Armstrong Whitworth Whitley of No. 10 OTU RAF. 28 dead and 18 survivors
U-565	VIIC	10-Apr-41	10 Apr 1941 – 31 Dec 1941	21 patrols. 3 ships sunk: total 11,347 GRT; 3 warships (including cruiser HMS *Naiad* and HM Submarine *Simoom*) sunk: total 7829t/7705 tons; 3 ships damaged: total 33,862 GRT	to 29. Flottille
U-566	VIIC	17-Apr-41	17 Apr 1941 – 24 Oct 1943	11 patrols. 6 ships sunk: total 38,092 GRT; 1 warship sunk: total 2301t/2265 tons	Scuttled 24 Oct 1943 in the North Atlantic west of Leixoes after being seriously damaged by depth charges from a Vickers Wellington of No. 179 Sqn RAF. 49 survivors and no casualties
U-574	VIIC	12-Jun-41	12 Jun 1941 – 19 Dec 1941	1 patrol. 1 warship sunk: total 1209t/1190 tons	Sunk 19 Dec 1941 in the North Atlantic east of the Azores by ramming and depth charges from the sloop HMS *Stork*. 28 dead and 16 survivors
U-582	VIIC	7-Aug-41	1 Jan 1942 – 5 Oct 1942 from 5. Flottille	4 patrols. 6 ships sunk: total 38,826 GRT	Sunk with all hands 5 Oct 1942 southwest of Iceland by depth charges from a US Navy Catalina of VP-73. 46 dead. Previously credited to a Hudson on the same day, which sank U-619
U-584	VIIC	21-Aug-41	1 Dec 1941 – 31 Oct 1943 from 5. Flottille	10 patrols. 3 ships sunk: total 18,478 GRT; 1 warship sunk: total 209t/206 tons. Landed 4 saboteurs south of Jacksonville, Florida, on 18 Jun 1942	Sunk with all hands 31 Oct 1943 in the North Atlantic by a Fido homing torpedo from Avenger aircraft of the escort carrier USS *Card*. 53 dead (including one man lost overboard on 10 Oct)
U-597	VIIC	20-Nov-41	1 Jul 1942 – 12 Oct 1942 from 8. Flottille	4 patrols. 2 ships sunk: total 9295 GRT; 1 ship damaged: total 6197 GRT	Sunk with all hands 12 Oct 1942 southwest of Iceland by depth charges from a Liberator of No. 120 Sqn RAF. 49 dead
U-599	VIIC	4-Dec-41	1 Sep 1942 – 24 Oct 1942 from 8. Flottille	1 patrol	Sunk with all hands 24 Oct 1942 northeast of the Azores by depth charges from a Liberator of No. 224 Sqn RAF. 44 dead
U-603	VIIC	2-Jan-42	1 Dec 1942 – 1 Mar 1944 from 5. Flottille	5 patrols. 4 ships sunk: total 22,406 GRT	Sunk with all hands 1 Mar 1944 in the North Atlantic by depth charges from the destroyer escort USS *Bronstein*. 51 dead
U-625	VIIC	4-Jun-42	1 Nov 1943 – 10 Mar 1944 from 13. Flottille	9 patrols. 3 ships sunk: total 18,751 GRT; 2 auxiliary warships sunk: total 939 GRT	Sunk with all hands 10 Mar 1944 west of Ireland by depth charges from a Sunderland of No. 422 Sqn RCAF. 53 dead
U-628	VIIC	25-Jun-42	1 Dec 1942 – 3 Jul 1943 from 5. Flottille	4 patrols. 4 ships sunk: total 21,765 GRT; 3 ships damaged: total 20,450 GRT	Sunk with all hands 3 Jul 1943 northwest of Cape Ortegal, Spain, by depth charges from a B-24 Liberator of No. 224 Sqn RAF. 49 dead
U-629	VIIC	2-Jul-42	1 Nov 1943 – 7 Jun 1944 from 11. Flottille	11 patrols	Sunk with all hands 7 Jun 1944 west of Brest by depth charges from a B-24 Liberator of No. 53 Sqn RAF. 51 dead. Previously credited to a 224 Sqn Liberator on 8 June, but that probably sank U-441.
U-632	VIIC	23-Jul-42	1 Jan 1943 – 6 Apr 1943 from 5. Flottille	2 patrols. 2 ships sunk: total 15,255 GRT	Sunk with all hands 6 Apr 1943 southwest of Iceland by depth charges from a B-24 Liberator of No. 86 Sqn RAF. 48 dead
U-637	VIIC	27-Aug-42	1 Jun 1944 – 5 Jul 1944 from 5. Flottille	3 patrols. 1 warship sunk: total 57t/56 tons	to 8. Flottille
U-643	VIIC	8-Oct-42	1 Jul 1943 – 8 Oct 1943 from 5. Flottille	1 patrol	Sunk 8 Oct 1943 in the North Atlantic by depth charges from Liberators of Nos. 86 and 120 Sqns. 30 dead and 18 survivors
U-651	VIIC	12-Feb-41	12 Feb 1941 – 29 Jun 1941	1 patrol. 2 ships sunk: total 11,639 GRT	Sunk 29 Jun 1941 south of Iceland by depth charges from destroyers HMS *Malcolm* and HMS *Scimitar*, corvettes HMS *Arabis* and HMS *Violet* and minesweeper HMS *Speedwell*. All 45 crew survived

BOATS THAT SERVED WITH 1ST FLOTILLA (111 BOATS)					
U-Boat	**Type**	**Commissioned**	**Flotilla(s)**	**Patrols**	**Fate**
U-653	VIIC	25-May-41	25 May 1941 – 15 Mar 1944	8 patrols. 3 ships sunk: total 14,983 GRT; 1 warship sunk: total 853t/840 tons; 1 ship damaged: total 9382 GRT	Sunk with all hands 15 Mar 1944 in the North Atlantic by depth charges from a Swordfish of escort carrier HMS *Vindex*, and from sloops HMS *Starling* and HMS *Wild Goose*. 51 dead
U-654	VIIC	5-Jul-41	1 Nov 1941 – 22 Aug 1942 from 5. Flottille	4 patrols. 3 ships sunk: total 17,755 GRT; 1 warship sunk: total 914t/900 tons	Sunk with all hands 22 Aug 1942 in the Caribbean north of Colon by depth charges from a Douglas B-18 of US Army 45 BS. 44 dead
U-656	VIIC	17-Sep-41	1 Jan 1942 – 1 Mar 1942 from 5. Flottille	2 patrols	Sunk with all hands 1 Mar 1942 in the North Atlantic south of Cape Race by depth charges from a US Navy PBO-1 Hudson of patrol squadron VP-82. 45 dead. This was the first U-boat sunk by the US Navy
U-665	VIIC	22-Jul-42	1 Feb 1943 – 22 Mar 1943 from 5. Flottille	1 patrol. 1 ship sunk: total 7134 GRT	Sunk with all hands 22 Mar 1943 west of Ireland by depth charges from a Whitley of No. 10 Operational Training Unit RAF. 46 dead. Previously credited to a No. 172 Sqn Wellington in Biscay, which actually attacked U-448, causing no damage
U-669	VIIC	16-Dec-42	1 Jun 1943 – 7 Sep 1943 from 5. Flottille	2 patrols	Missing with all hands in the Bay of Biscay on or after 8 Sep 1943. 52 dead. Previously credited to a Canadian aircraft northwest of Cape Ortegal on 7 Sep, but that attack was actually against U-584 and caused no damage
U-722	VIIC	15-Dec-43	1 Aug 1944 – 30 Sep 1944 from 31. Flottille	3 patrols. 1 ship sunk: total 2190 GRT	to 11. Flottille
U-731	VIIC	3-Oct-42	1 May 1943 – 15 May 1944 from 8. Flottille	4 patrols	Sunk with all hands 15 May 1944 near Tangier by depth charges from HMS *Kilmarnock*, trawler HMS *Blackfly* and 2 US Navy PBY Catalinas from VP-63. 54 dead
U-732	VIIC	24-Oct-42	1 May 1943 – 31 Oct 1943 from 8. Flottille	3 patrols	Sunk 31 Oct 1943 near Tangier by depth charges from trawler HMS *Imperialist* and destroyer HMS *Douglas*. 31 dead and 18 survivors
U-736	VIIC	16-Jan-43	1 Apr 1944 – 6 Aug 1944 from 8. Flottille	2 patrols	Sunk 6 Aug 1944 west of St Nazaire by depth charges from frigate HMS *Loch Killin*. 28 dead and 19 survivors
U-740	VIIC	27-Mar-43	1 Apr 1944 – 6 Jun 1944 from 8. Flottille	2 patrols	Missing with all hands in the Channel after 6 Jun 1944. The boat may have been sunk on 7 Jun by a Liberator of No. 53 Sqn or on 8 Jun by a Liberator of No. 224 Sqn. 51 dead
U-741	VIIC	10-Apr-43	1 Nov 1943 – 15 Aug 1944 from 8. Flottille	5 patrols. 1 warship damaged: total 1651t/1625 tons	Sunk 15 Aug 1944 northwest of Le Havre by depth charges from corvette HMS *Orchis*. 48 dead and 1 survivor
U-743	VIIC	15-May-43	1 Jul 1944 – 21 Aug 1944 from 8. Flottille	1 patrol	Missing with all hands in the Atlantic or Arctic after 21 Aug 1944. 50 dead. Previously credited to corvette HMS *Porchester Castle* and frigate HMS *Helmsdale* on 9 Sep 1944, but the boat destroyed in that attack was U-484. A wreck discovered off the coast of Northern Ireland may be U-743, in which case she was probably lost to unknown causes in mid-September.
U-754	VIIC	28-Aug-41	1 Dec 1941 – 31 Jul 1942 from 5. Flottille	3 patrols. 13 ships sunk: total 55,659 GRT; 1 ship damaged: total 490 GRT	Sunk with all hands 31 Jul 1942 north of Boston by a Lockheed Hudson of No. 113 Sqn RCAF. 43 dead
U-767	VIIC	11-Sep-43	1 May 1944 – 18 Jun 1944 from 8. Flottille	1 patrol. 1 warship sunk: total 1392t/1370 tons	Sunk 18 Jun 1944 southwest of Guernsey by depth charges from the destroyers HMS *Fame*, HMS *Inconstant* and HMS *Havelock*. 49 dead and 1 survivor
U-773	VIIC	20-Jan-44	1 Aug 1944 – 30 Sep 1944 from 31. Flottille	3 patrols	to 11. Flottille
U-821	VIIC	11-Oct-43	1 Mar 1944 – 10 Jun 1944 from 4. Flottille	2 patrols	Sunk on 10 Jun 1944 in the Bay of Biscay by attacks from 4 Mosquitoes of No. 248 Sqn and by depth charges from a Liberator of No. 206 Sqn RAF. 50 dead – 1 survivor
U-925	VIIC	30-Dec-43	1 Aug 1944 – 24 Aug? 1944 from 4. Flottille	1 patrol	Missing with all hands in the North Atlantic or Arctic on or after 24 August 1944. 51 dead
U-956	VIIC	6-Jan-43	1 Jul 1943 – 31 Dec 1943 from 5. Flottille	13 patrols. 1 warship sunk: total 1209t/1190 tons; 1 ship damaged beyond repair: total 7176 GRT	to 11. Flottille
U-963	VIIC	17-Feb-43	1 Aug 1943 – 31 Oct 1944 from 5. Flottille	10 patrols	to 11. Flottille
U-987	VIIC	8-Jul-43	1 Mar 1944 – 31 May 1944 from 5. Flottille	1 patrol	to 11. Flottille
U-1007	VIIC/41	18-Jan-44	1 Jun 1944 – 31 Jul 1944 from 31. Flottille	1 patrol	to 24. Flottille
U-1199	VIIC	23-Dec-43	1 Aug 1944 – 9 Nov 1944 from 8. Flottille	2 patrols. 1 ship damaged beyond repair: total 7176 GRT	to 11. Flottille
UB	British S class	30-Nov-40	30 Nov 1940 – May 1941	None; used for trials	Launched at Admiralty Dockyard Chatham on 27 Sep 1938. Commissioned into Royal Navy as HMS *Seal* 28 Jan 1939. Captured after being damaged while minelaying 29 Apr 1940. Transferred to 3. Flottille in May 1941
UD-1	British H class	21-Nov-40	Nov 1940 – Apr 1941	Trials boat	Originally commissioned as the US-built British submarine H 6 at Quebec in Canada on 10 Jun 1915. Interned after running aground at Schiermonnikoog in the Netherlands on 16 Jan 1916. Purchased by the Dutch Government and commissoned as O 8. Taken over by the German Navy on 14 May 1940 at Den Helder, Netherlands. Transferred to 3. Flottille
UD-4	Dutch O 21 class	28-Jan-41	Jan 1941 – Apr 1941	School boat	Laid down in 1938 as the Dutch submarine O 26. Captured while being built at the Rotterdam yard on 14 May 1940. Launched 23 May 1940 and commissioned on 28 Jan 1941. Transferred to 3. Flottille

2 Unterseebootsflottille

Founded a year after the 1st Flotilla, the 2nd U-Boat Flotilla was established on Germany's North Sea coast at Kiel in September 1936 but moved to Wilhelmshaven within weeks. It was known as the U-Flottille Saltzwedel, and its first commander was *Fregattenkapitän* Werner Scheer.

THE FLOTILLA WAS NAMED after World War I U-boat ace *Oberleutnant zur See* Reinhold Saltzwedel, who commanded UB-10, UC-10, UC-11, UC-21, UC-71 and UB-81 in the Great War. In the course of 22 patrols, he sank 111 ships for a total of 172,262 tonnes (170,526 tons). He was killed on 2 December 1917, when UB-81 was sunk by a mine in the English Channel. On 1 February 1935 Hitler unveiled the existence of a new U-boat force and on 16 March repudiated the terms of the Versailles Treaty. It was also at this time that the *Kriegsmarine* (Combat Navy) and *Unterseebootwaffe* (U-boat arm) were officially formed. Unknown to other nations at that time, Germany had already begun construction on 12 new U-boats as early as 1934 – by January 1935, the parts were awaiting assembly in Kiel and building began to be undertaken openly.

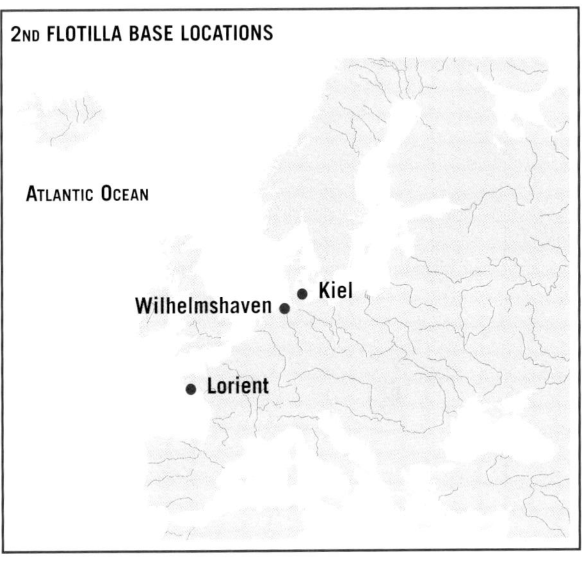

U-boat expansion

The Anglo-German Naval Agreement of 1935 allowed the *Kriegsmarine* to legally construct up to 35 per cent of the tonnage of the Royal Navy. Submarine tonnage allowed was up to 45 per cent and could be raised to 100 per cent with due notification. As part of that expansion, the Saltzwedel Flotilla was created.

The Saltzwedel Flotilla was intended for longer-range operations than the Weddigen Flotilla, and in addition to the two large Type IA boats, it contained the first examples of the new medium Type VII boats. U-33 and U-34 were sent to the Mediterranean to support Nationalist Spain. U-34 encountered the Republican submarine C-3 and sank it – the first

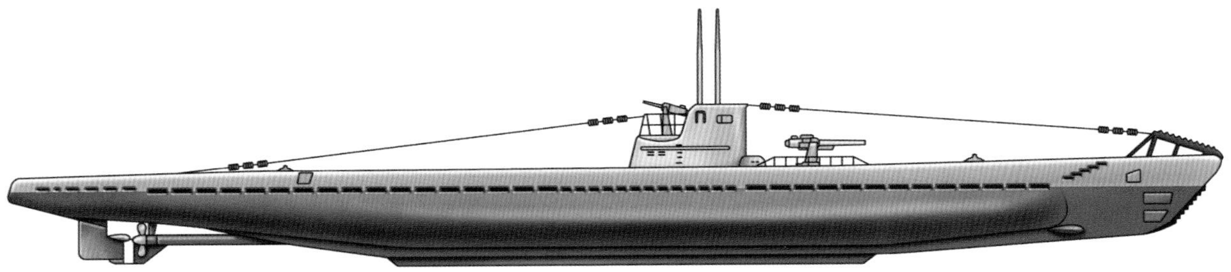

Specifications

Crew: 43

Powerplant: Diesel/electric

Max Speed: 33/15.4km/hr (17.8/8.3kt) s/d

Surface Range: 12,410km (6700nm)

Displacement: 876/999t (862/983 tons) s/d

Dimensions (length/beam/draught): 72.4 x 6.2 x 4.3m (237.5 x 20.34 x 14.11ft)

Commissioned: 6 April 1936

Armament: 14 torpedoes (4 bow/2 stern tubes); 1 x 10.5cm (4.1in) and 1 x 2cm (0.8in) guns

▲ **U-25**

Type IA

The Type I was the precursor to the Type IX long-range boat, and its design began under the Weimar Republic. It was difficult to handle; the two completed examples had difficulty maintaining periscope depth and rolled heavily in any kind of sea.

success for the *Kriegsmarine's* fledgling U-boat arm.

Three years later, Fritz-Julius Lemp's sinking of the Montreal-bound liner *Athenia* in another Saltzwedel boat marked the beginning of Germany's U-boat war against England. Leading the attack on the Americas, India, Africa and the oil-rich Caribbean merchant traffic, ace commanders like Werner Hartenstein and Reinhard Hardegen wreaked havoc among Allied trade shipping in distant waters. However, while the 2nd U-boat Flotilla mounted some of the most shattering submarine offensives of World War II, it was the intact capture of two of its boats, complete with their Enigma code machines, that would contribute greatly to the Allied defeat of Germany's U-boat arm.

▲ **Kiel harbour**

This 1939 photograph shows in the foreground the 2nd Flotilla boats U-27, U-33 and U-34 (all Type VIIAs) as well as two Type IIAs (background, left). Kiel was one of the chief bases and production areas for U-boats throughout the war.

2ND FLOTILLA

Type	Boats on strength
Type IA	2
Type VIIA	10
Type VIIC	2
Type IX	5
Type IXB	14
Type IXC	27
Type IXC/40	28
Type XB	2
UA (originally built for Turkey)	1
Dutch Type O 21	1

Commanders

Fregkpt. Werner Scheer *(Sep 1936 – Jul 1937)*
Korvkpt. Hans Ibbeken *(Oct 1937 – Sep 1939)*
Korvkpt. Werner Hartmann *(Jan 1940 – May 1940)*
Korvkpt. Heinz Fischer *(May 1940 – Jul 1941)*
Korvkpt. Victor Schütze *(Aug 1941 – Jan 1943)*
Fregkpt. Ernst Kals *(Jan 1943 – Oct 1944)*

2ND FLOTILLA INSIGNIA

The 2nd Flotilla insignia consisted of a U-boat transfixed by a shaft of lightning, otherwise known as the *Siegesrune*. This symbol was a runic depiction of the letter 'S', standing for *Sieg*, or victory.

Star commanders
1939–44

In the first years of the war, the 2nd Flotilla included the *U-Bootwaffe*'s long-range boats in its operational strength, and some of its Type IX commanders were particularly successful.

Korvettenkapitän Reinhard Hardegen

Born on 8 March 1913 in Bremen, Hardegen joined the Navy as part of Crew 33 soon after the Nazi seizure of power. In 1935 he began training as a naval aviator, but after being seriously injured in a crash he transferred to the U-boat arm in 1939. His first boat was the Type IXB U-124, in which he served under Kptlt. Wilhelm Schulz.

On 11 December 1940, Hardegen took command of the small Type IID boat U-147, which on its single patrol with Hardegen in command sank a Norwegian freighter of nearly 5000 GRT. On 16 May 1941, he succeeded Kptlt. Karl-Heinz Möhle in the successful Type IXB boat U-123. Even though he had been declared unfit for U-boat duty thanks to the injuries suffered in his pre-war plane crash, Hardegen sank five ships totalling more than 21,000 GRT on his first patrol off West Africa. U-123 was one of five boats sent by Dönitz on Operation *Paukenschlag*, or *Drumbeat*, the opening act of the U-boat offensive on the east coast of the United States. In this second 'Happy Time', U-123 sank nine ships for a total of 53,173 GRT. During his second *Drumbeat* patrol in March 1942, Hardegen sank a further 10 ships for a total of 57,170 tons. He was awarded the Oak Leaves to his Knight's Cross while still at sea.

Hardegen left U-123 at the end of July and spent the remainder of the war as an instructor. After the war he spent a year as a POW, returning to Bremen in 1946. Subsequently he became a successful businessman and a member of parliament.

EDELWEISS EMBLEM

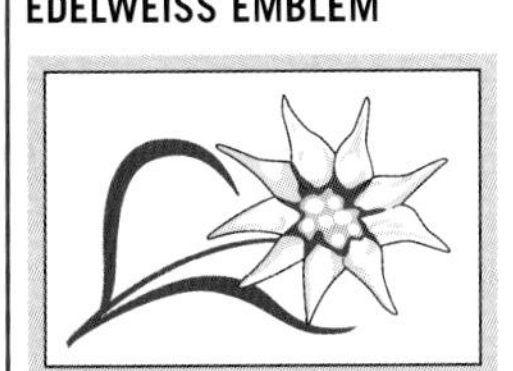

The crew of U-124 had served aboard U-64, lost off Norway in April 1940. German mountain troops rescued them and in gratitude they adopted the *Gebirgsjäger* emblem, the edelweiss.

Kapitänleutnant Fritz-Julius Lemp

Born on 19 February 1913 in Tsingtao, China, Lemp joined the *Reichsmarine* as part of Crew 31. His first command was U-28, on which he served briefly before taking command of U-30.

Lemp was operating west of the British Isles on the first day of the war when he sank a large vessel thought to be an armed merchant cruiser. In fact, it was the liner *Athenia*, and 112 of its passengers died in the incident. From a controversial start, Lemp went on to considerable success, sinking 17 ships and damaging one.

Promoted to command the Type IXB U-110, on 9 May 1941 Lemp was forced to the surface by the destroyers *Bulldog* and *Broadway* on his second patrol. His boat was captured by the British, a priceless intelligence coup, and Lemp was mysteriously killed, or possibly committed suicide.

▼ U-32

This grainy photograph shows U-32 moving through friendly waters, probably off northern Germany. U-32 is famous for having sunk the largest vessel of any U-boat, the 43,030-tonne (42,350-ton) liner *Empress of Britain*, in October 1940.

STAR COMMANDERS		
Commander	**Patrols**	**Ships Sunk**
Korvettenkapitän Reinhard Hardegen	5	21
Kapitänleutnant Fritz-Julius Lemp	10	19
Kapitän zur See Wolfgang Lüth	15	46

Kapitän zur See Wolfgang Lüth

Born on 15 October 1913 in Riga, Latvia, Wolfgang Lüth joined the Navy as part of Crew 33. He transferred to U-boats in February 1937 and served aboard U-27 on neutrality patrol during the Spanish Civil War. His first combat command was the Type IIB boat U-9, in which he made six patrols. Transferring to the Type IID U-138, he sank four ships on his first patrol. He transferred to the large Type IX U-43, and in five patrols sank 12 ships totalling 69,169 tonnes (68,077 tons). In May 1942 Lüth commissioned the new long-range Type IXD2 boat U-181. On his first patrol off South Africa and in the Indian Ocean, Lüth's boat sank 12 ships for a total of more than 55,000 GRT, for which he was awarded Oak Leaves to the Knight's Cross. His next patrol, at 205 days the second longest of the war, saw U-181 sink a further 10 ships of more than 45,000 GRT. In January 1944, after more than five years of uninterrupted duty on U-boats, *Korvettenkapitän* Wolfgang Lüth became the commanding officer of the 22nd Flotilla, the unit responsible for training future U-boat commanders. Lüth then became the youngest commander of the *Marineschule*, the German Naval Academy, at Flensburg-Mürwik. He died on 13 May 1945 at the *Marineschule*, shot in error by one of his own sentries.

Specifications

Crew: 48–50
Powerplant: Diesel/electric
Max Speed: 33.7/13.5km/hr (18.2/7.3kt) s/d
Surface Range: 16,110km (8700nm)
Displacement: 1068/1197t (1051/1178 tons) s/d
Dimensions (length/beam/draught): 76.5 x 6.8 x 4.7m (251 x 22.31 x 15.42ft)
Commissioned: 30 April 1940
Armament: 22 torpedoes (4 bow/2 stern tubes); 1 x 10.5cm (4.1in), 1 x 3.7cm (1.5in) and 1 x 2cm (0.8in) guns

▲ U-123

Type IXB

One of the most successful U-boats of the war, U-123 under her three Knight's Cross-winning commanders sank 42 merchant ships totalling 219,924 GRT, one auxiliary warship of 3209 GRT and the British submarine P615.

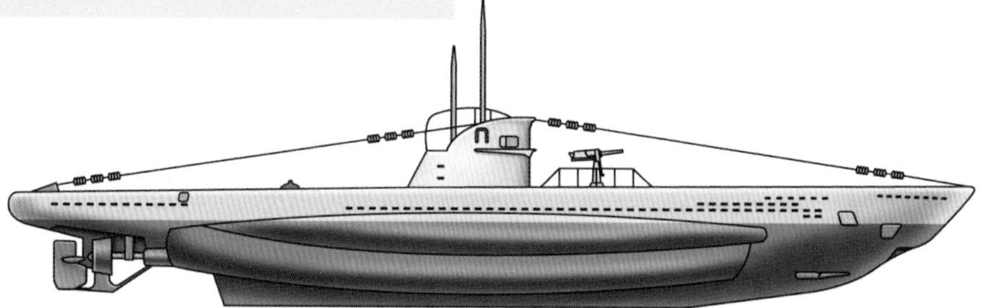

Specifications

Crew: 25
Powerplant: Diesel/electric
Max Speed: 23.5/13.7km/hr (12.7/7.4kt) s/d
Surface Range: 6389km (3450nm)
Displacement: 319/370t (314/364 tons) s/d
Dimensions (length/beam/draught): 44 x 4.9 x 3.9m (144.4 x 16.8 x 12.8ft)
Commissioned: Jun 1940 – Jan 1941
Armament: 6 torpedoes (3 bow tubes); 1 x 2cm (0.8in) gun

▲ U-137 – U-152

Type IID

Many of the most successful U-boat captains got their first command experience aboard the small Type II coastal boats. The Type IID was the last variant to be built, and had a longer range than earlier boats.

U-30

Type VIIA

Launched in August 1936, U-30 was one of the first Type VII boats to enter service with the *Kriegsmarine* and would serve until the end of World War II.

On 3 September 1939, U-30 became notorious when she was responsible for the first U-boat sinking of the war. On patrol south of Rockall at the outbreak of war, U-30 torpedoed the 13,799-tonne (13,581-ton) passenger liner *Athenia* by mistake. Hitler had announced that passenger liners were not to be attacked. U-30's commander, Fritz-Julius Lemp, almost had his career wrecked by the scandal, but he persuaded Dönitz and the high command that he had made a genuine error: because the target was darkened and was zig-zagging, he took it to be an Armed Merchant Cruiser, or AMC, which would have made the vessel a valid target.

U-30 went on to make six combat patrols, sinking 15 merchant ships totalling over 82,300 tonnes (81,000 tons). She was the first U-boat to make use of the newly captured French bases, entering Lorient on 7 July 1940 after her fifth patrol. After one more patrol U-30 was transferred to the 24th Flotilla in the Baltic where she was used for torpedo training. Used in the last months of the war as a range boat and as a school boat for training new U-boat crewmen, U-30 was scuttled on 4 May 1945 in Kupfermühlen Bay. The wreck was broken up for scrap in 1948.

▲ **U-30 before the war**

U-30 is seen here along with other *Flottille Salzwedel* boats at Hamburg in December 1937, en route to their new base at Wilhelmshaven.

U-30 Commanders

Kptlt. Hans Cohausz *(Oct 1936 – Oct 1938)*	Oblt. Kurt Baberg *(Apr 1941 – Mar 1942)*
Kptlt. Hans Pauckstadt *(Feb 1938 – Aug 1938)*	Oblt. Hermann Bauer *(Mar 1942 – Oct 1942)*
Kptlt. Fritz-Julius Lemp *(Nov 1938 – Sep 1940)*	Kptlt. Franz Saar *(Oct 1942 – Dec 1942)*
Kptlt. Robert Prützmann *(Sep 1940 – Mar 1941)*	Oblt. Ernst Fischer *(May 1943 – Dec 1943)*
Kptlt. Paul-Karl Loeser *(Apr 1941 – Apr 1941)*	Oblt. Ludwig Fabricius *(Dec 1943 – Dec 1944)*
Kptlt. Hubertus Purkhold *(Apr 1941 – Apr 1941)*	Oblt. Günther Schimmel *(Jan 1945 – Jan 1945)*

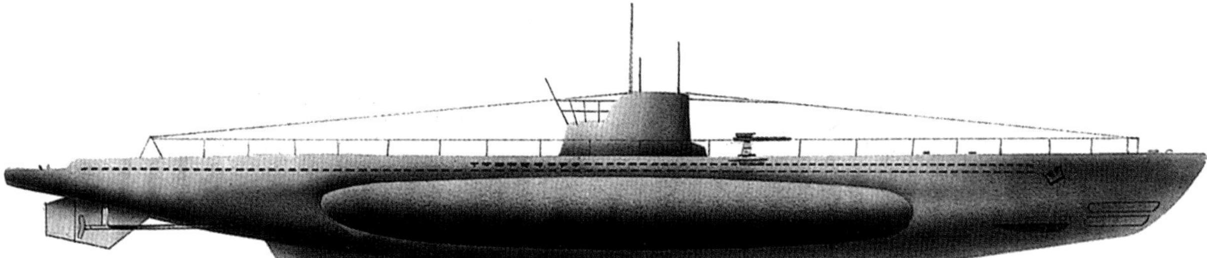

Specifications

Crew: 44
Powerplant: Diesel/electric
Max Speed: 29.6/14.8km/hr (16/8kt) s/d
Surface Range: 7964km (4300 nm)
Displacement: 636/757t (626/745 tons) s/d
Dimensions (length/beam/draught): 64.5 x 5.8 x 4.4m (211.6 x 19 x 14.4ft)
Commissioned: 8 Oct 1936
Armament: 11 torpedoes (4 bow/1 stern tubes); 1 x 8.8cm (3.5in) and 1 x 2cm (0.8in) guns

▲ **U-30**

Type VIIA

Much more capable than the tiny Type II boats known to their crews as 'canoes', the Type VII was to bear the brunt of the *U-Bootwaffe*'s war. U-30 was one of the earliest Type VIIs to enter service, commissioning in October 1936.

U-30 TIMETABLE		
Patrol Dates	**Operational Area**	**Ships Sunk**
22 Aug 1939 – 27 Sep 1939	Southwestern approaches	3
9 Dec 1939 – 14 Dec 1939	W of British Isles	0
23 Dec 1939 – 17 Jan 1940	Mining in Irish Sea off Liverpool	5
11 Mar 1940 – 30 Mar 1940	Norway/Orkneys/Shetland	0
3 Apr 1940 – 4 May 1940	Norway	0
8 Jun 1940 – 24 Jul 1940	Wolfpack operations SW of Ireland	7
5 Aug 1940 – 27 Aug 1940	WNW of Rockall	2

U-106

Type IXB

One of the more successful U-boats of the war, U-106 was a Type IXB boat laid down at AG Weser in Bremen in November 1939 and commissioned in September 1940.

In 10 patrols, U-106 sank 21 Allied merchantmen totalling 132,540 GRT. However, on 23 October 1941, two days into the boat's fourth patrol, U-106 graphically illustrated the perils of North Atlantic operations. When the replacement watch opened the conning tower hatch, they found that all four members of the previous watch had been washed overboard in stormy seas.

In July 1942 U-106 suffered a further loss. Two days out of Lorient, it came under attack from a Czech-crewed Vickers Wellington of No. 311 Sqn RAF. The boat was damaged, the commander was wounded and the first officer was killed.

U-106 was sunk on 2 August 1943, northwest of Cape Ortegal, Spain. Damaged by a Canadian Wellington of No. 407 Sqn RCAF, the boat tried to rendezvous with some E-boats that would escort her back to base but was spotted by an RAF Sunderland of No. 228 Sqn, which was driven off by its gunners. However, an Australian Sunderland of No. 461 Sqn joined the fight and U-106 was sunk. Twenty-two of the crew died; 36 survivors were picked up by German torpedo boats.

U-106 Commanders

Kptlt. Jürgen Oesten *(Sep 1940 — Oct 1941)*
Kptlt. Hermann Rasch *(Oct 1941 – Apr 1943)*
Oblt. Wolf-Dietrich Damerow *(Jun 1943 – Aug 1943)*

▲ **Under attack**

A Type IXB boat, probably U-106, as seen from one of two attacking Short Sunderland flying boats just before sinking in the Bay of Biscay.

U-106 TIMETABLE		
Patrol Dates	**Operational Area**	**Ships Sunk**
4 Jan 1941 – 10 Feb 1941	NW of Rockall	2
26 Feb 1941 – 17 Jun 1941	Central Atlantic	8
11 Aug 1941 – 11 Sep 1941	SW of Ireland	0
21 Oct 1941 – 22 Nov 1941	North Atlantic	1
3 Jan 1942 – 22 Feb 1942	US Coast	5
15 Apr 1942 – 29 Jun 1942	Gulf of Mexico	5
25 Jul 1942 – 28 Jul 1942	Damaged by aircraft in Bay of Biscay	0
22 Sep 1942 – 26 Dec 1942	Gulf of St Lawrence/Central Atlantic	1
17 Feb 1943 – 2 Aug 1943	Azores/Canaries	0
19 Mar 1941 – 5 Apr 1941	Sunk off northern Spain	0

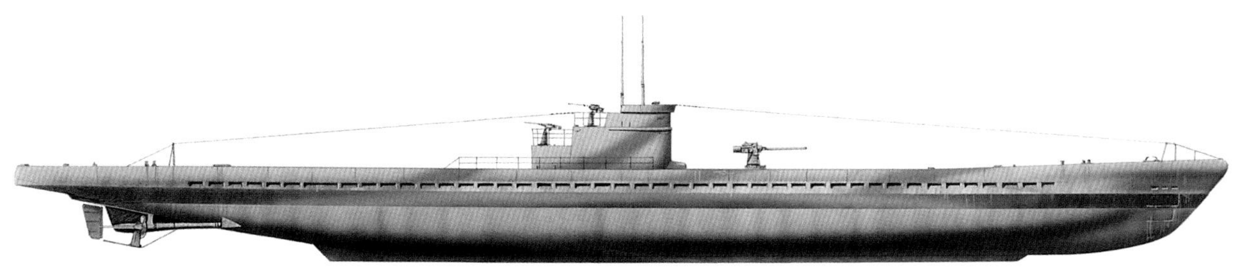

Specifications

Crew: 48–50

Powerplant: Diesel/electric

Max Speed: 33.7/13.5km/hr (18.2/7.3kt) s/d

Surface Range: 16,110km (8700nm)

Displacement: 1068/1197t (1051/1178 tons) s/d

Dimensions (length/beam/draught): 76.5 x 6.8 x 4.7m (251 x 22.31 x 15.42ft)

Commissioned: 30 April 1940

Armament: 22 torpedoes (4 bow/2 stern tubes); 1 x 10.5cm (4.1in), 1 x 3.7cm (1.5in) and 1 x 2cm (0.8in) guns

▲ **U-106**

Type IXB

Unlike the Type VII boats, many of the Type IXs, like U-106, retained their 8.8cm (3.5in) deck guns until late in the war. U-106 actually used her gun to sink the American tanker SS *Rochester* off the mouth of the Chesapeake in January 1942.

U-505

Type IXC

Laid down at Deutsche Werft, Hamburg, in June 1940, U-505 was commissioned on 28 August 1941 and served with the 2nd Flotilla from January 1942 until her capture on 4 June 1944.

U-505 MADE 12 PATROLS from 1 February 1942, sinking eight ships totalling 44,962 GRT. On 2 November 1942, the boat was attacked by a Lockheed Hudson of No. 53 Sqn RAF. The aircraft was shot down, but the boat was damaged and the second officer and a lookout were seriously wounded.

The commander of U-505, Kptlt. Peter Zschech, committed suicide while under a heavy depth charge attack on 24 October 1943. The first officer, *Oberleutnant* Paul Meyer, saved the boat and brought her back to port.

U-505 was captured at sea west of Africa on 4 June 1944, the first vessel taken as a prize on the high seas by the US Navy in the 20th century.

Specifications

Crew: 48–50

Powerplant: Diesel/electric

Max Speed: 33.9/13.5km/hr (18.3/7.3kt) s/d

Surface Range: 20,370km (11,000nm)

Displacement: 1138/1232t (1120/1232 tons) s/d

Dimensions (length/beam/draught): 76.8 x 6.8 x 4.7m (252 x 22.31 x 15.42ft)

Commissioned: 26 Aug 1941

Armament: 22 torpedoes (4 bow/2 stern tubes); 1 x 10.5cm (4.1in), 1 x 3.7cm (1.5in) and 1 x 2cm (0.8in) guns

▲ **U-505**

Type IXC

U-505 sailed three times on patrol in August 1943, returning each time after strange sounds were heard on diving. A number of French dockyard workers were arrested – suspected of sabotage – and shot by the Gestapo.

The capture was made by ships and aircraft of the US Navy Task Group 22.3, comprising the escort carrier USS *Guadalcanal* and the destroyer escorts USS *Pillsbury*, USS *Chatelain*, USS *Flaherty*, USS *Jenks* and USS *Pope*. Towed to the United States, U-505 is still in existence and is currently on display at the Chicago Museum of Science and Industry.

▶ U-boat captured

U-505 was one of the few German U-boats to be captured on the high seas. Taken off West Africa two days before D-Day, it was towed first to Bermuda.

U-505 Commanders

Korvkpt. Axel-Olaf Loewe *(Aug 1941 – Sep 1942)*
Kptlt. Peter Zschech *(Sep 1942 – Oct 1943)*
Oblt. Paul Meyer *(Oct 1943 – Nov 1943)*
Oblt. Harald Lange *(Nov 1943 – 4 Jun 1944)*

U-505 TIMETABLE

Patrol Dates	Operational Area	Ships Sunk
19 Jan 1942 – 3 Feb 1942	Transit around Britain from Kiel to Lorient	0
11 Feb 1942 – 7 May 1942	Central Atlantic off Freetown	4
7 Jun 1942 – 25 Aug 1942	Central Atlantic/Caribbean	3
4 Oct 1942 – 12 Dec 1942	Central Atlantic/Caribbean	1
1 Jul 1943 – 13 Jul 1943	Mechanical damage forced early return	0
1 Aug 1943 – 2 Aug 1943	Unidentifiable faults forced early return	0
14 Aug 1943 – 15 Aug 1943	Unidentifiable faults forced early return	0
21 Aug 1943 – 22 Aug 1943	Unidentifiable faults forced early return	0
18 Sep 1943 – 30 Sep 1943	Mechanical damage forced early return	0
9 Oct 1943 – 7 Nov 1943	Captain's suicide forced early return	0
25 Dec 1943 – 2 Jan 1944	Biscay, rescuing German warship survivors	0
16 Mar 1944 – 4 Jun 1944	Central Atlantic off Freetown	0

U-843

Type IXC/40

Laid down at AG Weser, Bremen, in April 1942, U-843 was commissioned in March 1943 and made her first operational patrol in October 1943.

By the time U-843 had completed her training and entered operational service, the Battle of the Atlantic had swung decisively in favour of the Allies. In place of the multiple sinkings made by earlier Type IX boats, U-843 managed to destroy only one Allied merchant vessel, west-southwest of Ascension Island on her way to join the *Monsun* boats operating in the Far East. After transferring to the 33rd Flotilla, U-843 returned from Batavia in the Dutch East Indies, carrying a cargo of zinc.

The boat never delivered her cargo. Reaching Bergen safely, U-843 headed for Kiel but was sunk on 9 April 1945 in the Kattegat, west of Gothenburg, by rockets from Mosquito fighter-bombers of Nos. 143, 235 and 248 Sqns RAF. Forty-four crewmen were killed and 12 survived.

U-843 Commanders

Kptlt. Oskar Herwartz *(Mar 1943 – Apr 1945)*

U-843 TIMETABLE		
Patrol Dates	**Operational Area**	**Ships Sunk**
7 Oct 1943 – 12 Oct 1943	Transit from Kiel to Trondheim	0
15 Oct 1943 – 15 Dec 1943	S of Greenland/SW of Ireland	0
19 Feb 1944 – 11 Jun 1944	Indian Ocean	1
Oct 1944	Transferred to 33. Flotille at Batavia	0
10 Dec 1944 – 3 Apr 1945	Transit from Far East to Bergen	0
6 Apr 1945 – 9 Apr 1945	Sunk in transit from Bergen to Germany	0

The *Laconia* incident

SEPTEMBER 1942

Far from being the bestial Nazis depicted by Hollywood, most U-boat commanders were scrupulous in their observance of the rules of war.

ON 12 SEPTEMBER 1942, U-156 under the command of Kptlt. Werner Hartenstein torpedoed a large target in the South Atlantic in position 05.05S, 11.38W. The vessel was the British liner *Laconia* (20,011 tonnes/19,695 tons), which sank at 23:23. The liner was carrying a 136-man crew, around 80 civilians – and 1800 Italian prisoners of war with 160 Polish guards.

Shortly after the sinking, the crew of U-156 heard Italian voices coming from those struggling in the water. Hartenstein immediately began rescue operations and radioed for assistance, both in code to nearby U-boats and in clear to be picked up by any other vessel. The U-boat commander promised not to attack any vessel coming to the rescue. By dawn, U-156 had picked up nearly 200 survivors and over the next hours had another 200 on tow in lifeboats.

Into attack

U-506 (Kptlt. Erich Würdemann) arrived on 15 September and continued rescue operations. The two boats were joined by U-507 under Korvkpt. Harro Schacht and the Italian submarine *Cappellini*. The boats headed for shore, filled like sardine cans with survivors and towing lifeboats.

On the morning of 16 September, the surfaced – and hence vulnerable – boats were attacked by an American B-24 Liberator bomber operating out of Ascension Island. On seeing the Red Cross flags, the pilot radioed his base asking for instructions. He was

Specifications

Crew: 48–50

Powerplant: Diesel/electric

Max Speed: 33.9/13.5km/hr (18.3/7.3kt) s/d

Surface Range: 20,370km (11,000nm)

Displacement: 1138/1252t (1120/1232 tons) s/d

Dimensions (length/beam/draught): 76.8 x 6.8 x 4.7m (252 x 22.31 x 15.42ft)

Commissioned: 26 Aug 1941

Armament: 22 torpedoes (4 bow/2 stern tubes); 1 x 10.5cm (4.1in), 1 x 3.7cm (1.5in) and 1 x 2cm (0.8in) guns

▲ **U-156**

Type IXC

U-156 was on its way to form part of the *Eisbar* wolfpack off the South African coast when it torpedoed the liner *Laconia*, carrying Italian prisoners of war. The boat's commander, Kptlt. Hartenstein, immediately began a rescue operation.

told to attack, and at 12:32 the U-boats were forced to cut loose the lifeboats and submerge. However, neutral Vichy French warships from Dakar arrived at that point, and most of those in the water were rescued. Once the U-boats were able to surface and unload their survivors, it was found that around 1500 of those travelling aboard the liner had been saved.

The *Laconia* incident became a scandalous rather than heroic incident because it prompted one of the most controversial orders Dönitz ever issued. Up until that time, U-boats had often helped the survivors of their victims with supplies, water – even directions to the nearest land. In what became known as the *Laconia* Order, Dönitz made it clear that from henceforth, U-boats were not to take part in any rescue operations; survivors were to be left in the sea to fend for themselves. The only exceptions were senior merchant officers, who might be interrogated for convoy information. Dönitz ended the order with the admonition to:

'Stay hard. Remember, the enemy does not care about women and children when he bombs Germany's towns and cities.'

This order was one of the key pieces of evidence used against Dönitz at Nuremberg in 1946, and some observers felt that he was simply being punished for being too efficient at his job. Dönitz eventually served over 11 years in prison.

Wolfpack *Eisbär*

August 1942

Against Admiral Dönitz's wishes, the *Kriegsmarine* high command ordered that a U-boat force be sent away from the main battlefield of the Atlantic to take the war to the Allies in distant waters.

Unlike many other wolfpacks, which tended to be ad hoc organizations of whichever boats happened to be in an operational area at the time, the *Eisbär* (Polar Bear) Group was a unit from the start. Four Type IXC boats – U-68, U-156, U-172 and U-504, all from the 2nd Flotilla at Lorient – sailed in company in August 1942, heading for South African waters. En route they attacked convoy SL 119 off the Spanish coast, sinking one vessel. The boats then operated independently on their way south, arranging to rendezvous in the South Atlantic.

U-156 sank the liner *Laconia* north of Ascension Island, setting in motion what was to become known as the *Laconia* Incident, but the boat was damaged by a subsequent air attack. U-159, already operating in the central Atlantic, was ordered to join up with the *Eisbär* boats as a replacement. After refuelling from the milchcow U-459 at a pre-arranged rendezvous well to the south of St Helena, the four boats reached their operational area off the Cape of Good Hope at the beginning of October.

Far from the main theatre of operations, merchant ships were still sailing independently. Over the next six weeks the *Eisbär* boats patrolled the South African coast from the Cape into the Indian Ocean as far north as Durban and between them sank 24 ships.

By mid-November most of the boats had used up their torpedoes and were ordered to return to Lorient. U-504 returned on 11 December, followed by U-68 on 12 December, U-172 on 27 December and U-159 on 5 January 1943. U-156 had returned with combat damage on 16 November.

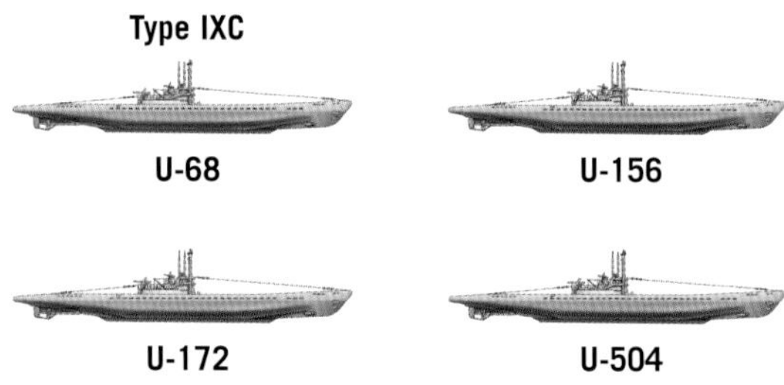

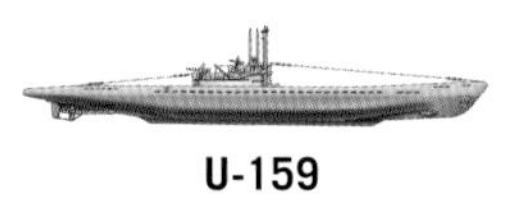

BOATS THAT SERVED WITH 2ND FLOTILLA (91 BOATS)

U-Boat	Type	Commissioned	Flotilla(s)	Patrols	Fate
U-25	IA	6-Apr-36	1 Apr 1936 – 1 Aug 1940	5 patrols. 7 ships sunk: total 33,209 GRT; 1 auxiliary warship sunk: total 17,046 GRT; 1 ship damaged: total 7638 GRT	Lost with all hands around 1 Aug 1940 in the North Sea north of Terchelling, probably in the minefield laid on 3 Mar by the destroyers HMS *Express*, HMS *Esk*, HMS *Icarus* and HMS *Impulsive*. 49 dead
U-26	IA	6-May-36	1 May 1936 – 1 Jul 1940	6 patrols. 11 ships sunk: total 48,645 GRT; 1 ship damaged: total 4871 GRT; 1 warship damaged: total 539t/530 tons	Scuttled 1 Jul 1940 southwest of Ireland after being heavily damaged by depth charges from the corvette HMS *Gladiolus* and bombs from an Australian Sunderland flying boat. 48 survivors – no casualties
U-27	VIIA	12-Aug-36	12 Aug 1936 – 20 Sep 1939	1 patrol. 2 ships sunk: total 624 GRT	Sunk 20 Sept 1939 west of Scotland by depth charges from the destroyers HMS *Fortune* and HMS *Forester*. 38 survivors – no casualties
U-28	VIIA	12-Sep-36	12 Sep 1936 – 9 Nov 1940	6 patrols. 11 ships sunk: total 42,252 GRT; 1 auxiliary warship sunk: total 4443 GRT; 1 ship a total loss: total 9577 GRT; 2 ships damaged: total 10,067 GRT	to 24. Flottille
U-29	VIIA	16-Nov-36	16 Nov 1936 – 1 Jan 1941	7 patrols. 11 ships sunk: total 62,765 GRT; 1 aircraft carrier (HMS *Courageous*) sunk: total 22,861t/22,500 tons	to 24. Flottille
U-30	VIIA	8-Oct-36	8 Oct 1936 – 30 Nov 1940	6 patrols. 15 ships sunk (including liner *Athenia*, first sinking of the war): total 86,165 GRT; 1 auxiliary warship sunk: total 325 GRT; 1 ship damaged: total 5642 GRT; 1 battleship (HMS *Barham*) damaged: total 31,599t/31,100 tons	to 24. Flottille
U-31	VIIA	28-Dec-36	28 Dec 1936 – 2 Nov 1940	7 patrols. 11 ships sunk: total 27,751 GRT; 2 auxiliary warships sunk: total 160 GRT; 1 battleship (HMS *Nelson*) damaged by a U-31-laid mine: total 34,495t/33,950 tons	Sunk with all hands 11 Mar 1940 in Jadebusen by RAF Blenheim bomber. 58 dead. Raised in Mar 1940, repaired and returned to service. Sunk again on 2 Nov 1940 NW of Ireland by depth charges from the destroyer HMS *Antelope*. 2 dead and 44 survivors
U-32	VIIA	15-Apr-37	15 Apr 1937 – 30 Oct 1940	9 patrols. 20 ships sunk (including largest ship sunk by U-boats, the 43,030t/42,350-ton liner *Empress of Britain*): total 116,836 GRT; 4 ships damaged: total 32,274 GRT; 1 warship damaged: total 8128t/8000 tons	Sunk 30 Oct 1940 northwest of Ireland by depth charges from the destroyers HMS *Harvester* and HMS *Highlander*. 9 dead and 33 survivors
U-33	VIIA	25-Jul-36	25 Jul 1936 – 12 Feb 1940	3 patrols. 10 ships sunk: total 19,261 GRT; 1 ship damaged beyond repair: total 3670 GRT	Sunk 12 Feb 1940 in the Firth of Clyde by depth charges from the minesweeper HMS *Gleaner*. 17 survivors, 25 dead
U-34	VIIA	12-Sep-36	12 Sep 1936 – 30 Sep 1940	7 patrols. 19 ships sunk: total 91,989 GRT; 3 warships sunk: total 2403t/2365 tons; 2 ships damaged: total 4957 GRT. Sank the Spanish submarine C-3 on 12 Dec 1936 while on neutrality patrol during the Spanish Civil War	to 21. Flottille
U-35	VIIA	3-Nov-36	3 Nov 1936 – 29 Nov 1939	3 patrols. 4 ships sunk: total 7850 GRT; 1 ship damaged: total 6014 GRT	Sunk 29 Nov 1939 in North Sea by depth charges from destroyers HMS *Kingston*, HMS *Icarus* and HMS *Kashmir*. 43 survivors – no casualties
U-36	VIIA	16-Dec-36	1 Sept 1939 – 4 Dec 1939 from U-Bootschulflottille	2 patrols. 2 ships sunk: total 2813 GRT; 1 ship damaged: total 1617 GRT	Sunk with all hands southwest of Kristiansand, torpedoed by the British submarine HMS *Salmon*. 40 dead
U-37	IX	4-Aug-38	1 Jan 1940 – 30 Apr 1941 from 6. Flottille	11 patrols. 53 ships sunk: total 200,125 GRT; 2 warships sunk: total 2443t/2404 tons; 1 ship damaged: total 9494 GRT. Second highest scoring U-boat in terms of numbers of vessels sunk	to 26. Flottille
U-38	IX	24-Oct-38	1 Jan 1940 – 30 Nov 1941 from 6. Flottille	11 patrols. 35 ships sunk: total 188,967 GRT; 1 ship damaged: total 3670 GRT	to 24. Flottille
U-41	IX	22-Apr-39	1 Jan 1940 – 5 Feb 1940 from 6. Flottille	3 patrols. 7 ships sunk: total 24,888 GRT; 1 ship damaged: total 8096 GRT	Sunk with all hands 5 Feb 1940 south of Ireland by depth charges from the destroyer HMS *Antelope*. 49 dead
U-43	IX	26-Aug-39	1 Jan 1940 – 30 Jul 1943 from 6. Flottille	14 patrols. 21 ships sunk: total 117,036 GRT; 1 ship a total loss: total 9131 GRT; 1 ship damaged: total 10,350 GRT	Sunk with all hands 30 Jul 1943 southwest of the Azores by a Fido homing torpedo from an Avenger of the escort carrier USS *Santee*. 55 dead
U-44	IX	4-Nov-39	1 Jan 1940 – 13 Mar 1940 from 6. Flottille	2 patrols. 8 ships sunk: total 30,885 GRT	Destroyed with all hands on or around 13 Mar 1940 by a mine laid by the destroyers HMS *Express*, HMS *Esk*, HMS *Icarus* and HMS *Impulsive*. 47 dead. Originally credited to depth charges from the destroyer HMS *Fortune*
U-64	IXB	16-Dec-39	16 Dec 1939 – 13 Apr 1940	1 patrol	Sunk 13 Apr 1940 near Narvik, Norway, by a bomb and machine-gun fire from a Swordfish floatplane of HMS *Warspite*. 8 dead and 38 survivors
U-65	IXB	15-Feb-40	15 Feb 1940 – 28 Apr 1941	6 patrols. 12 ships sunk: total 66,174 GRT; 3 ships damaged: total 22,490 GRT	Sunk with all hands 28 Apr 1941 in the North Atlantic southeast of Iceland by depth charges from the destroyer HMS *Douglas*. 50 dead. Originally credited to depth charges from the corvette HMS *Gladiolus*. That attack was actually on U-96 and inflicted no damage
U-66	IXC	2-Jan-41	2 Jan 1941 – 6 May 1944	9 patrols. 33 ships sunk: total 200,021 GRT; 2 ships damaged: total 22,674 GRT; 2 MTBs damaged: total 65t/64 tons	Sunk 6 May 1944 west of the Cape Verde Islands by depth charges and gunfire from Avengers and Wildcats of the escort carrier USS *Block Island*, and ramming by the destroyer escort USS *Buckley*. 24 dead and 36 survivors
U-67	IXC	22-Jan-41	22 Jan 1941 – 16 Jul 1943	7 patrols. 13 ships sunk: total 72,138 GRT; 5 ships damaged: total 29,726 GRT	Sunk 16 Jul 1943 in the Sargasso Sea by depth charges from an Avenger of VC-13 from the escort carrier USS *Core*. 48 dead and 3 survivors
U-68	IXC	11-Feb-41	11 Feb 1941 – 10 Apr 1944	10 patrols. 32 ships sunk: total 197,453 GRT; 1 auxiliary warship sunk: total 545 GRT	Sunk 10 Apr 1944 northwest of Madeira by depth charges and rockets from Avengers and Wildcats of the escort carrier USS *Guadalcanal*. 56 dead and 1 survivor
U-103	IXB	5-Jul-40	5 Jul 1940 – 1 Jan 1944	11 patrols. 45 ships sunk: total 237,596 GRT; 3 ships damaged: total 28,158 GRT	to 24. Flottille
U-104	IXB	19-Aug-40	19 Aug 1940 – 28 Nov 1940	1 patrol. 1 ship sunk: total 8240 GRT; 1 ship damaged: total 10,516 GRT	Missing with all hands on or after 28 Nov 1940 northwest of Ireland. May have struck a mine northwest of Tory Island. 49 dead. Previously credited to depth charges from the corvette HMS *Rhododendron* on 11 Nov 1940. That attack was actually against U-103 and inflicted no damage

BOATS THAT SERVED WITH 2ND FLOTILLA (91 BOATS)

U-Boat	Type	Commissioned	Flotilla(s)	Patrols	Fate
U-105	IXB	10-Sep-40	10 Sep 1940 – 2 Jun 1943	9 patrols. 22 ships sunk: total 123,924 GRT; 1 warship sunk: total 1571t/1546 tons	Sunk with all hands 2 Jun 1943 near Dakar by depth charges from a French Potez-CAMS 141 flying boat of *Flottille d'exploration* 4E, French Naval Air Force. 53 dead
U-106	IXB	24-Sep-40	24 Sep 1940 – 2 Aug 1943	10 patrols. 22 ships sunk: total 138,581 GRT; 2 ships damaged: total 12,634 GRT; 1 auxiliary warship damaged: total 8246 GRT; 1 battleship (HMS *Malaya*) damaged: total 31,599t/31,100 tons	Sunk 2 Aug 1943 northwest of Cape Ortegal, Spain, by depth charges from British and Australian Sunderland flying boats from Nos. 228 and 461 Sqns. 22 dead and 36 survivors
U-107	IXB	8-Oct-40	8 Oct 1940 – 18 Aug 1944	14 patrols. 37 ships sunk: total 207,375 GRT; 2 auxiliary warships sunk: total 10,411 GRT; 3 ships damaged: total 17,392 GRT; 1 auxiliary warship damaged: total 8246 GRT	Sunk with all hands 18 Aug 1944 in the Bay of Biscay west of La Rochelle by depth charges from a Sunderland of 201 Sqn. 58 dead. U-107 under Kptlt. Günther Hessler had previously completed the most successful patrol of the war, sinking 14 ships of 88,090 GRT around the Canaries and off Freetown
U-108	IXB	22-Oct-40	22 Oct 1940 – 31 Aug 1943	11 patrols. 25 ships sunk: total 118,722 GRT; 1 auxiliary warship sunk: total 16,644 GRT	to 8. Flottille
U-109	IXB	5-Dec-40	5 Dec 1940 – 4 May 1943	9 patrols. 12 ships sunk: total 79,969 GRT; 1 ship damaged: total 6548 GRT	Sunk with all hands 4 May 1943 south of Ireland by 4 depth charges from a Liberator of No. 86 Sqn RAF. 52 dead
U-110	IXB	21-Nov-40	21 Nov 1940 – 9 May 1941	2 patrols. 3 ships sunk: total 10,149 GRT; 2 ships damaged: total 8675 GRT	Captured on 9 May 1941 south of Iceland by the destroyers HMS *Bulldog*, HMS *Broadway* and the corvette HMS *Aubretia*. The boat was allowed to sink on 10 May to preserve the secret of her capture and the capture of an intact Enigma coding machine. 15 dead and 32 survivors
U-111	IXB	19-Dec-40	19 Dec 1940 – 4 Oct 1941	2 patrols. 4 ships sunk: total 24,176 GRT; 1 ship damaged: total 13,037 GRT	Sunk 4 Oct 1941 southwest of Tenerife by depth charges from the anti-submarine trawler HMS *Lady Shirley*. 8 dead and 44 survivors
U-116	XB	26-Jul-41	26 Jul 1941 – 31 Jan 1942	4 patrols. 1 ship sunk by mines: total 4284 GRT; 1 ship damaged by mines: total 7093 GRT	to 1. Flottille
U-117	XB	25-Oct-41	25 Oct 1941 – 31 Jan 1942	5 patrols. 2 ships damaged by mines: total 14,269 GRT	to 1. Flottille
U-122	IXB	30-Mar-40	30 Mar 1940 – 22 Jun 1940	2 patrols. 1 ship sunk: total 5911 GRT	Missing with all hands around 22 Jun 1940 in North Sea or the Bay of Biscay. Boat may have been lost in an underwater collision with the vessel *San Filipe* on 22 June, or by depth charges from the corvette HMS *Arabis* on 23 Jun. 49 dead
U-123	IXB	30-May-40	30 May 1940 – 1 Aug 1944	12 patrols. 42 ships sunk: total 219,924 GRT; 1 auxiliary warship sunk: total 3209 GRT; 1 warship sunk: total 694t/683 tons; 5 ships damaged: total 39,584 GRT; 1 auxiliary warship damaged: total 13,984 GRT	Taken out of service at Lorient, France, 17 Jun 1944. Scuttled 19 Aug 1944. Surrendered to France in 1945 and became the French submarine *Blaison*. Stricken 18 Aug 1959 as Q165
U-124	IXB	11-Jun-40	11 Jun 1940 – 2 Apr 1943	11 patrols. 46 ships sunk: total 219,178 GRT; 2 warships sunk: total 5868t/5775 tons; 4 ships damaged: total 30,067 GRT	Sunk with all hands 2 Apr 1943 west of Oporto by depth charges from the corvette HMS *Stonecrop* and the sloop HMS *Black Swan*. 53 dead
U-125	IXC	3-Mar-41	3 Mar 1941 – 6 May 1943	7 patrols. 17 ships sunk: total 82,873 GRT	Sunk with all hands 6 May 1943 east of Newfoundland: rammed by the destroyer HMS *Oribi* and finished off by gunfire from the corvette HMS *Snowflake*. 54 dead
U-126	IXC	22-Mar-41	22 Mar 1941 – 3 Jul 1943	6 patrols. 24 ships sunk: total 111,564 GRT; 2 ships damaged beyond repair: total 14,173 GRT; 5 ships damaged: total 37,501 GRT	Sunk with all hands 3 Jul 1943 northwest of Cape Ortegal, Spain, by depth charges from a British Wellington of No. 172 Sqn RAF. 55 dead
U-127	IXC	24-Apr-41	24 Apr 1941 – 15 Dec 1941	1 patrol	Sunk with all hands 15 Dec 1941 west of Gibraltar by depth charges from the Australian destroyer HMAS *Nestor*. 51 dead
U-128	IXC	12-May-41	12 May 1941 – 17 May 1943	6 patrols. 12 ships sunk: total 83,639 GRT	Sunk 17 May 1943 in the South Atlantic south of Pernambuco by gunfire from the US destroyers USS *Moffett*, USS *Jouett* and depth charges from two US Navy Mariner aircraft of Patrol Sqn VP-74. 7 dead and 47 survivors
U-129	IXC	21-May-41	1 Jul 1941 – 1 Jul 1944 from 4 Flottille	10 patrols. 29 ships sunk: total 143,748 GRT	Taken out of service at Lorient 4 Jul 1944. Scuttled 18 Aug 1944
U-130	IXC	11-Jun-41	1 Sep 1941 – 12 Mar 1943 from 4 Flottille	6 patrols. 21 ships sunk: total 127,608 GRT; 3 auxiliary warships sunk: total 34,407 GRT; 1 ship damaged: total 6986 GRT	Sunk with all hands 12 Mar 1943 west of the Azores by depth charges from the destroyer USS *Champlin*. 53 dead
U-131	VIIC	1-Jul-41	1 Nov 1941 – 17 Dec 1941 from 4 Flottille	1 patrol. 1 ship sunk: total 4016 GRT	Sunk 17 Dec 1941 northeast of Madeira by depth charges and gunfire from the escort destroyers HMS *Exmoor*, HMS *Blankney*, destroyer HMS *Stanley*, corvette HMS *Penstemon* and sloop HMS *Stork* and by depth charges from a Martlet aircraft of the escort carrier HMS *Audacity*. 47 survivors
U-153	IXC	19-Jul-41	1 Jun 1942 – 13 Jul 1942 from 4. Flottille	2 patrols. 3 ships sunk: total 16,186 GRT	Sunk with all hands 13 Jul 1942 near Panama by depth charges from the destroyer USS *Lansdowne*. 52 dead
U-154	IXC	2-Aug-41	1 Feb 1942 – 3 Jul 1944 from 4. Flottille	8 patrols. 10 ships sunk: total 49,288 GRT; 1 ship damaged beyond repair: total 8166 GRT; 2 ships damaged: total 15,771 GRT. One of its commanders, Oblt. Oskar Kusch, was executed on 12 May 1944 after being denounced by his former first officer for *Wehrkraftzersetzung* (sedition and defeatism)	Sunk with all hands 3 Jul 1944 west of Madeira by depth charges from the destroyer escorts USS *Inch* and USS *Frost*. 57 dead
U-156	IXC	4-Sep-41	1 Jan 1942 – 8 Mar 1943 from 4. Flottille	5 patrols. 20 ships sunk: total 97,205 GRT; 3 ships damaged: total 18,811 GRT; 1 warship damaged: total 1209t/1190 tons. On 12 Sep 1942 U-156 sank the liner *Laconia* west of Africa in what has become known as the *Laconia* Incident	Sunk with all hands at 13:15 on 8 Mar 1943 east of Barbados by depth charges from a US Navy Catalina of VP-53. 53 dead
U-157	IXC	15-Sep-41	1 Jun 1942 – 13 Jun 1942 from 4. Flottille	2 patrols. 1 ship sunk: total 6401 GRT	Sunk with all hands 13 Jun 1942 northeast of Havana by depth charges from the Coast Guard cutter USCG *Thetis*. 52 dead

BOATS THAT SERVED WITH 2ND FLOTILLA (91 BOATS)

U-Boat	Type	Commissioned	Flotilla(s)	Patrols	Fate
U-161	IXC	8-Jul-41	1 Jan, 1942 – 27 Sep 1943 from 4. Flottille	6 patrols. 13 ships sunk: total 60,407 GRT; 1 warship sunk: total 1148t/1130 tons; 1 ship damaged beyond repair: total 3305 GRT; 5 ships damaged: total 35,672 GRT; 1 warship damaged: total 5537t/5450 tons	Sunk with all hands 27 Sept 1943 in the South Atlantic near Bahia by depth charges from a US Navy Mariner aircraft of VP-74. 53 dead
U-162	IXC	9-Sep-41	1 Feb 1942 – 3 Sep 1942 from 4. Flottille	3 patrols. 14 ships sunk: total 82,027 GRT	Sunk 3 Sept 1942 near Trinidad by depth charges from the destroyers HMS *Vimy*, HMS *Pathfinder* and HMS *Quentin*. 2 dead and 49 survivors
U-168	IXC/40	10-Sep-42	1 Mar 1943 – 30 Sep 1944 from 4. Flottille	4 patrols. 2 ships sunk: total 6568 GRT; 1 auxiliary warship sunk: total 1440 GRT; 1 ship damaged: total 9804 GRT	to 33. Flottille
U-173	IXC	15-Nov-41	1 Jul 1942 – 16 Nov 1942	2 patrols. 1 auxiliary warship sunk: total 9359 GRT; 2 auxiliary warships damaged: total 18,713 GRT; 1 warship damaged: total 1656t/1630 tons	Sunk with all hands 16 Nov 1942 off Casablanca by depth charges from the destroyers USS *Woolsey*, USS *Swanson* and USS *Quick*. 57 dead
U-183	IXC/40	1-Apr-42	1 Oct 1942 – 30 Sep 1944 from 4. Flottille	6 patrols. 4 ships sunk: total 19,260 GRT; 1 ship damaged beyond repair: total 6993 GRT	to 33. Flottille
U-184	IXC/40	29-May-42	1 Nov 1942 – 21 Nov 1942 from 4. Flottille	1 patrol. 1 ship sunk: total 3192 GRT	Listed as missing with all hands 21 Nov 1942 in the North Atlantic east of Newfoundland. 50 dead. Loss previously attributed to a mid-Atlantic depth charge attack on 20 Nov 1942 by the Norwegian corvette *Potentilla*. That attack was probably against U-264 and inflicted no damage.
U-189	IXC/40	15-Aug-42	1 Apr 1943 – 23 Apr 1943 from 4. Flottille	1 patrol	Sunk with all hands 23 April 1943 east of Cape Farewell, Greenland, by depth charges from a Liberator aircraft of No. 120 Sqn RAF. 54 dead
U-190	IXC/40	24-Sep-42	1 Mar 1943 – 30 Sep 1944 from 4. Flottille	6 patrols. 1 ship sunk: total 7015 GRT; 1 warship sunk: total 599t/590 tons	to 33. Flottille
U-191	IXC/40	20-Oct-42	1 Apr 1943 – 23 Apr 1943 from 4. Flottille	1 patrol. 1 ship sunk: total 3025 GRT	Sunk with all hands 23 Apr 1943 southeast of Cape Farewell, Greenland, by depth charges from the destroyer HMS *Hesperus*. 55 dead
U-193	IXC/40	10-Dec-42	1 May 1943 – 31 Mar, 1944 from 4. Flottille	3 patrols. 1 ship sunk: total 10,172 GRT	to 10. Flottille
U-501	IXC	30-Apr-41	30 Apr 1941 – 10 Sep 1941	1 patrol. 1 ship sunk: total 2000 GRT	Sunk 10 Sep 1941 in the Straits of Denmark south of Angmagsalik, Greenland, by depth charges and ramming from the Canadian corvettes HMCS *Chambly* and HMCS *Moosejaw*. 11 dead and 37 survivors
U-502	IXC	31-May-41	31 May 1941 – 5 Jul 1942	4 patrols. 14 ships sunk: total 78,843 GRT; 2 ships damaged: total 23,797 GRT	Sunk with all hands 5 Jul 1942 in the Bay of Biscay west of La Rochelle by depth charges from a Wellington of No. 172 Sqn. 52 dead. This was the first successful use of Leigh Light equipment
U-503	IXC	10-Jul-41	10 Jul 1941 – 15 Mar 1942	1 patrol	Sunk with all hands 15 Mar 1942 southeast of Newfoundland by depth charges from a US Navy Lockheed PBO-1 Hudson of VP-82. 51 dead. This was the second U-boat sunk by the US Navy
U-504	IXC	30-Jul-41	1 Jan 1942 – 30 Jul 1943 from 4. Flottille	7 patrols. 15 ships sunk: total 74,959 GRT; 1 ship damaged beyond repair: total 7176 GRT	Sunk with all hands 30 Jul 1943 northwest of Cape Ortegal, Spain, by depth charges from the sloops HMS *Kite*, HMS *Woodpecker*, HMS *Wren* and HMS *Wild Goose*. 53 dead
U-505	IXC	26-Aug-41	1 Feb 1942 – 4 Jun 1944 from 4. Flottille	12 patrols. 8 ships sunk: total 44,962 GRT. Kptlt. Zschech committed suicide while under depth charge attack on 24 Oct 1943; the I WO, Meyer, brought the boat back to port	Captured at sea west of Africa on 4 Jun 1944 by US Navy Task Group 22.3 – escort carrier USS *Guadalcanal*, destroyer escorts USS *Pillsbury*, USS *Chatelain*, USS *Flaherty*, USS *Jenks* and USS *Pope*. 1 dead and 59 survivors. The boat survives and is currently on display at the Chicago Museum of Science and Industry
U-507	IXC	8-Oct-41	1 Mar 1942 – 13 Jan 1943	4 patrols. 19 ships sunk: total 77,144 GRT; 1 ship damaged: total 6561 GRT. Involved in the rescue of 1500 survivors of the *Laconia* in Sep 1942	Sunk with all hands 13 Jan 1943 in the South Atlantic northwest of Natal by depth charges from a US Navy PBY Catalina of VP-83. 55 dead (including one survivor from the merchant ship *Baron Dechmont*, sunk 3 Jan)
U-518	IXC	25-Apr-42	1 Oct 1942 – 31 Oct 1944 from 4. Flottille	7 patrols. 9 ships sunk: total 55,747 GRT; 3 ships damaged: total 22,616 GRT	to 33. Flottille
U-519	IXC	7-May-42	1 Nov 1942 – 31 Jan 1943 from 4. Flottille	2 patrols	Missing with all hands in the Bay of Biscay on or after 31 Jan 1943. 50 dead. May have been sunk by a Wellington of No. 172 Sqn RAF, which was shot down as it attacked an unidentified U-boat on 4 Feb 1943. Previously credited to a USAAF B-24 on 10 Feb, but that attack was actually against U-752
U-520	IXC	19-May-42	1 Oct 1942 – 30 Oct 1942 from 4. Flottille	1 patrol	Sunk with all hands 30 Oct 1942 east of Newfoundland by depth charges from a Canadian Douglas B-18 Digby aircraft of No. 10 Sqn RCAF. 53 dead
U-521	IXC	3-Jun-42	1 Oct 1942 – 2 Jun 1943 from 4. Flottille	3 patrols. 3 ships sunk: total 19,551 GRT; 1 auxiliary warship sunk: total 750 GRT	Sunk 2 Jun 1943 in the North Atlantic southeast of Baltimore by depth charges from the US patrol craft PC-565. 51 dead and 1 survivor
U-522	IXC	11-Jun-42	1 Oct 1942 – 23 Feb 1943	2 patrols. 7 ships sunk: total 45,826 GRT; 2 ships damaged: total 12,479 GRT	Sunk with all hands 23 Feb 1943 southwest of Madeira by depth charges from the sloop HMS *Totland*. 51 dead
U-531	IXC/40	28-Oct-42	1 Apr 1943 – 6 May 1943 from 4. Flottille	1 patrol	Sunk with all hands 6 May 1943 northeast of Newfoundland by depth charges from the destroyer HMS *Vedette*. 54 dead. Previously credited to destroyer HMS *Oribi* and corvette HMS *Snowflake*, but they probably sank U-125
U-532	IXC/40	11-Nov-42	1 Apr 1943 – 30 Sep 1944 from 4. Flottille	4 patrols. 8 ships sunk: total 46,895 GRT; 2 ships damaged: total 13,128 GRT	to 33. Flottille

BOATS THAT SERVED WITH 2ND FLOTILLA (91 BOATS)					
U-Boat	**Type**	**Commissioned**	**Flotilla(s)**	**Patrols**	**Fate**
U-534	IXC/40	23-Dec-42	1 Jun 1943 – 31 Oct 1944 from 4. Flottille	3 patrols	to 33. Flottille
U-536	IXC/40	13-Jan-43	1 Jun 1943 – 20 Nov 1943 from 4. Flottille	2 patrols. U-536 was involved in the attempt to pick up some of the top U-boat commanders held at Camp Bowmanville in Canada, but their escape attempt failed	Sunk 20 Nov 1943 northeast of the Azores by depth charges from the frigate HMS *Nene* and the corvettes HMCS *Snowberry* and HMCS *Calgary*. 38 dead and 17 survivors.
U-538	IXC/40	10-Feb-43	1 Nov 1943 – 21 Nov 1943 from 4. Flottille	1 patrol	Sunk with all hands 21 Nov 1943 southwest of Ireland by depth charges from the frigate HMS *Foley*. 55 dead
U-545	IXC/40	19-May-43	1 Dec 1943 – 10 Feb 1944 from 4. Flottille	1 patrol. 1 ship damaged: total 7359 GRT	Scuttled with heavy damage west of the Hebrides on 10 Feb 1944, after a depth charge attack by a Canadian Wellington of No. 407 Sqn (which was shot down by the boat) and another Wellington of No. 612 Sqn RAF. 56 survivors were rescued by U-714; 1 crewman was killed
U-547	IXC/40	16-Jun-43	1 Jan 1944 – 30 Sep 1944 from 4. Flottille	3 patrols. 2 ships sunk: total 8371 GRT; 1 auxiliary warship sunk: total 750 GRT	to 33. Flottille
U-548	IXC/40	30-Jun-43	1 Apr 1944 – 30 Sep 1944 from 4. Flottille	4 patrols. 1 warship sunk: total 1468t/1445 tons	to 33. Flottille
U-801	IXC/40	24-Mar-43	1 Nov 1943 – 17 Mar 1944 from 4. Flottille	2 patrols	Sunk 17 Mar 1944 near the Cape Verde Islands by Fido homing torpedo from Avengers of escort carrier USS *Block Island*, and by depth charges and gunfire from destroyer USS *Corry* and destroyer escort USS *Bronstein*. 10 dead and 47 survivors
U-802	IXC/40	12-Jun-43	1 Feb 1944 – 30 Nov 1944 from 4. Flottille	4 patrols. 1 ship sunk: total 1621 GRT	to 33. Flottille
U-821	VIIC	11-Oct-43	1 Nov 1943 – 31 Dec 1943 from 4. Flottille	Torpedo/underwater detection training	to 24. Flottille
U-841	IXC/40	6-Feb-43	1 Jul 1943 – 17 Oct 1943 from 4. Flottille	1 patrol	Sunk 17 Oct 1943 east of Cape Farewell, Greenland, by depth charges from the frigate HMS *Byard*. 27 dead and 27 survivors
U-842	IXC/40	1-Mar-43	1 Aug 1943 – 6 Nov 1943 from 4. Flottille	1 patrol	Sunk with all hands 6 Nov 1943 in the western North Atlantic by depth charges from the sloops HMS *Starling* and HMS *Wild Goose*. 56 dead
U-843	IXC/40	24-Mar-43	1 Nov 1943 – 30 Sep 1944 from 4. Flottille	4 patrols. 1 ship sunk: total 8261 GRT	to 33. Flottille
U-856	IXC/40	19-Aug-43	1 Mar 1944 – 7 Apr 1944 from 4. Flottille	1 patrol	Sunk 7 Apr 1944 east of New York by depth charges from destroyer USS *Champlin* and destroyer escort USS *Huse*. 27 dead and 28 survivors
U-858	IXC/40	30-Sep-43	1 May 1944 – 30 Sep 1944 from 4. Flottille	2 patrols	to 33. Flottille
U-868	IXC/40	23-Dec-43	1 Aug 1944 – 30 Sep 1944 from 4. Flottille	2 patrols. 1 warship sunk: total 683t/672 tons	to 33. Flottille
U-1223	IXC/40	6-Oct-43	1 Aug 1944 – 29 Dec 1944 from 4. Flottille	1 patrol. 1 warship damaged beyond repair: total 1392t/1370 tons; 1 ship damaged: total 7134 GRT	to 33. Flottille
U-1225	IXC/40	10-Nov-43	1 Jun 1944 – 24 Jun 1944 from 31. Flottille	1 patrol	Sunk with all hands 24 Jun 1944 northwest of Bergen by depth charges from a Consolidated Catalina of No. 162 Sqn RCAF
U-1226	IXC/40	24-Nov-43	1 Aug 1944 – 30 Sep 1944 from 31. Flottille	1 patrol	to 33. Flottille
U-1227	IXC/40	8-Dec-43	1 Aug 1944 – 31 Dec 1944 from 31. Flottille	1 patrol. 1 warship damaged beyond repair: total 1392t/1370 tons	to 33. Flottille
U-1228	IXC/40	22-Dec-43	1 Aug 1944 – 31 Oct 1944 from 31. Flottille	2 patrols. 1 warship sunk: total 914t/900 tons	to 33. Flottille
UA	Turkish	20-Sep-39	Apr 1941 – Dec 1941 from 7. Flottille	9 patrols. 7 ships sunk: total 40,706 GRT; 1 ship damaged: total 7524 tons	back to to 7. Flottille
UD-3	Dutch 0 21 class	8-Jun-41	Aug 1941 – Sep 1942 from 5. Flottille	3 patrols. 1 ship sunk: total 5041 GRT	to 10. Flottille

▶ U-boat pens

This photograph shows the inside of one of the U-boat pens on the French Atlantic coast. The thick concrete roofs of the pens allowed the U-boats to survive numerous air attacks by the RAF. The Type VIIA submarine on the left is probably U-30, identifiable from the dog emblem on the conning tower. The emblem represented the crew mascot 'Schnurzel', a dog who remained at the base while U-30 was on patrol.

3 Unterseebootsflottille

The 3rd U-boat Flotilla was founded on 4 October 1937 under the command of *Kapitänleutnant* Hans Eckermann and in its first incarnation existed until December 1939. It was refounded in March 1941, as the U-boat force fighting the Battle of the Atlantic expanded.

As with all of the early flotillas, the 3rd Flotilla was originally named after a notable U-boat commander of the Great War. Known as *U-Flottille* Lohs, it commemorated *Oberleutnant zur See* Johannes Lohs, who during World War I made 15 patrols in command of UC-75 and UB-57. He sank 76 ships for a total of 151,063 tonnes (148,677 tons), and he also destroyed the 1219-tonne (1200-ton) sloop HMS *Lavender*. Lohs was killed on 14 August 1918, when UB-57 was sunk by a mine.

The *Flottille* Lohs joined the 1st Flotilla at Kiel, followed by three more flotillas. The *Flottille* Wegener was to become the 7th Flotilla, the *Flottille* Hundius would be redesignated as the 6th Flotilla and the *Flottille* Emsmann became the 5th Flotilla.

Until the outbreak of war the eight Type IIB boats of the *Flottille* Lohs were mainly used for training: indeed, a number were in the process of being transferred to the *U-Ausbildungsflottille* (U-boat training school flotilla) at Danzig but became operational on the outbreak of hostilities. However, both the boats and the flotilla itself were too small to be operationally effective, and the *Flottille* Lohs was disbanded in December 1939.

Flotilla reborn

In January 1940 the organization of the German U-boat force underwent a radical restructuring. There were three main combat flotillas, the 1st and the 7th based at Kiel and the 2nd at Wilhelmshaven. The capture of the French Atlantic ports in the *Blitzkrieg* campaign of 1940 meant that the *Kriegsmarine*'s U-boat arm could now be based much closer to the main theatre of operations – the Atlantic Ocean to the west of the British Isles.

In 1940 and 1941, the three main combat flotillas were moved to new bases in France. However, the expansion of the U-boat war meant that three flotillas were not enough to control such an expanding force effectively. In March 1941 the 3rd U-boat Flotilla was recreated as an operational unit, and in September 1941 it was moved to La Pallice, France.

3rd Flotilla Base Locations

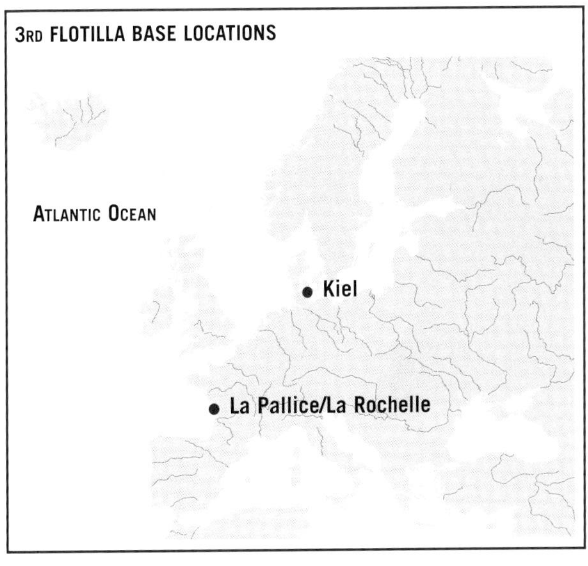

Chain of command

The restructuring of the U-boat arm in 1940 saw Karl Dönitz promoted to the rank of *Konteradmiral* and appointed *Befehlshaber der Unterseeboote Ops,* or Commander of U-boat Operations. Hans-Georg von Friedeburg was made BdU Org, or Commander of U-boat Organization. Beneath them, four Flag Officers for U-boats (*Führer des U-boote,* or FdU) were appointed, each responsible for a different

Commanders

Kptlt. Hans Eckermann *(Oct 1937 – Dec 1939)*
Korvkpt. Hans Rösing *(Mar 1941 – Jul 1941)*
Kptlt. Herbert Schultze *(Jul 1941 – Mar 1942)*
Kptlt. Heinz v. Reiche *(Mar 1942 – June 1942)*
Korvkpt. Richard Zapp *(June 1942 – Oct 1944)*

3RD FLOTILLA (1937–39, 1941–44)

Type	Boats ordered
Type IIB (to 1940)	8
Type IID	5
Type VIIB	1
Type VIIC	90
Captured/foreign	4

◀ **Captured U-boat**

U-570 was the first U-boat to be captured in the war, after she surrendered to an RAF Hudson of 269 Squadron on 27 August 1941.

operational area. The new 3rd Flotilla came under FdU *West*, based in Paris and later at Angers. By this time, the mainstay of the *U-bootwaffe* was the medium Type VII U-boat, and the first operational boats assigned to the new 3rd Flotilla were mostly Type VIICs, although four Type IIDs (longer-range Type IIs) served briefly in 1941.

French base

The base at La Pallice had originally been used as an alternative home port by the Italian boats located at Bordeaux from 1940. In April 1941 the *Kriegsmarine* decision to locate boats there saw the construction of bomb-proof fortified bunkers. The first two pens were finished in October 1941, and the first boat to arrive from Atlantic operations was U-82, which made port on 19 November 1941. The initial commander of the flotilla was Hans Rösing, an experienced U-boat man and one of a handful of *Reichsmarine* officers who had secretly served as crewmembers on foreign-built submarines between the wars.

Over 100 boats under 3 Flotilla command passed through La Pallice and the nearby base at La Rochelle over the next two and a half years. They mounted 161 combat patrols. Since the flotilla was formed after the first 'Happy Time' and with boats too short-ranged to operate off the US coast in the second 'Happy Time', few of its commanders were able to run up massive scores.

In August 1944 the last U-boats left La Pallice and La Rochelle for Norway as American troops drove southwards from Normandy, and the flotilla was disbanded in October 1944.

3RD FLOTILLA INSIGNIA

Fewer 3rd Flotilla boats carried the unit badge – the turtle – than was common in other units, which may be why it is not as well known as the Bull of the 7th Flotilla or the Laughing Swordfish of the 9th Flotilla.

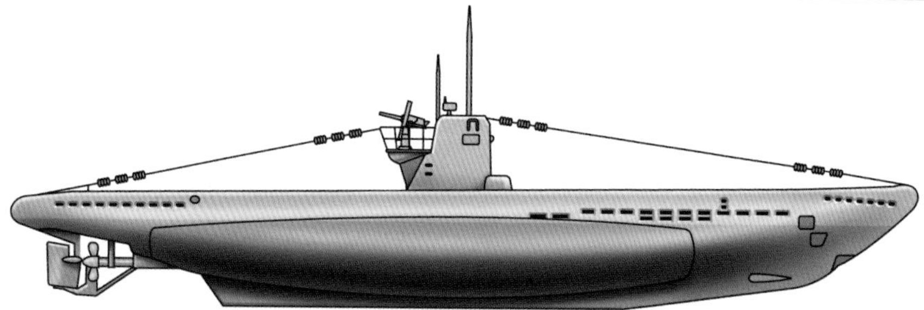

▲ **U-10**

Type IIB

In its first incarnation, the 3rd Flotilla operated a handful of small coastal boats like U-10. This boat had previously served with the 1st Flotilla, and was being used as a training boat until the outbreak of war, when it became operational.

Specifications

Crew: 25
Powerplant: Diesel/electric
Max Speed: 33/15.4km/hr (17.8/8.3kt) s/d
Surface Range: 3334km (1800nm)
Displacement: 283/334t (279/329 tons) s/d
Dimensions (length/beam/draught): 42.7 x 4.1 x 3.8m (140.1 x 13.5 x 12.5ft)
Commissioned: 21 Aug 1935
Armament: 6 torpedoes (3 bow tubes); 1 x 2cm (0.8in) gun

Star commanders

1939–45

Although boasting fewer of the top U-boat aces among its number than other, more well-known formations, the 3rd Flotilla did have several successful captains.

Korvettenkapitän Peter-Erich Cremer

Peter-Erich Cremer was born on 25 March 1911 in Metz, Lorraine. After studying law, he joined the *Reichsmarine* as part of Crew 32. He served with coastal artillery units and aboard destroyers before transferring to U-boats in August 1940.

In January 1941 Cremer commissioned the Type IID boat U-152 before moving on to command the Type VIIC boat U-333. In eight patrols he sank six ships for a total of 26,873 GRT. On his third patrol he was seriously wounded and spent several months in hospital. Early in 1943 he served on Dönitz's staff before returning to U-333. In 1944 Cremer commissioned the Type XXI 'Electro Boat' U-2519, but made no patrols. In the last days of the war he commanded a tank-destroyer battalion in the fight for Hamburg.

After the war, Cremer made a successful career in business, and wrote a memoir of his time with U-333. He died on 5 July 1992 in Hamburg.

Kapitänleutnant Heinz-Otto Schultze

Heinz-Otto Schultze was born on 13 September 1915 in Kiel, the son of World War I U-boat ace Otto Schultze. He joined the Navy with Crew 34. After training with surface ships, he entered the U-boat arm in May 1937 and served for two years aboard U-31. After some command experience aboard the Type II school boats U-9 and U-141, Schultze was given command of the new Type VIIC boat U-432, which was commissioned in April 1941. He left the boat in February 1942 and in March he joined the 12th Flotilla, where he took command of the new long-range Type IXD2 boat U-849.

In the course of seven patrols with U-432, Schultze sank 19 ships totalling 64,769 GRT, for which he was awarded the Knight's Cross. He died on 25 November 1943 when U-849, en route for the Indian Ocean on her first patrol, was attacked and sunk with all hands in the South Atlantic by a US Navy Liberator flying out of Ascension Island.

STAR COMMANDERS

Commander	Patrols	Ships Sunk
Korvettenkapitän Peter-Erich Cremer	8	6
Kapitänleutnant Heinz-Otto Schultze	8	19
Korvettenkapitän Helmut Möhlmann	8	5

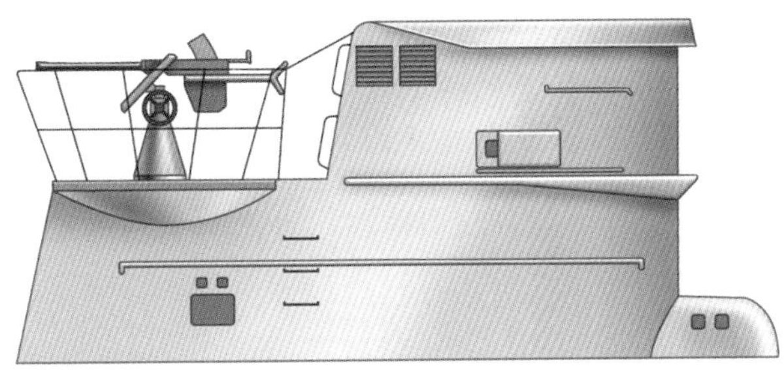

▲ **Type VIIB conning tower**

One of the problems with early Type VII boats was the rather cramped conditions on the bridge. There was little room for a full four-man bridge watch, and the 2cm (0.8in) gun mount had to be widened to make room for its crew. One of the modifications introduced with the Type VIIC boat was the enlargement of the tower by 6cm (2.4in) in width and 30cm (12in) in length.

Korvettenkapitän Helmut Möhlmann

Born on 25 June 1913 in Kiel, Helmut Möhlmann joined the Navy with Crew 33. He served on the light cruiser *Nürnberg* and aboard the torpedo boat (light escort destroyer) *Luchs*. In April 1940 he transferred to the U-boat force. His first command was the school boat U-143, but he moved on to the Type VIIC boat U-571 in May 1941.

Möhlmann made eight patrols in the North Atlantic and the Arctic, sinking five ships totalling 33,511 GRT and damaging three more. He left the boat in May 1943 for a course at the Naval Academy at Berlin, going on to serve on the staff of BdU. From December 1944, he was the commander of the 14th Flotilla at Narvik, Norway. After the surrender, he spent more than four months in captivity. He died on 12 April 1977 at Prien am Chiemsee.

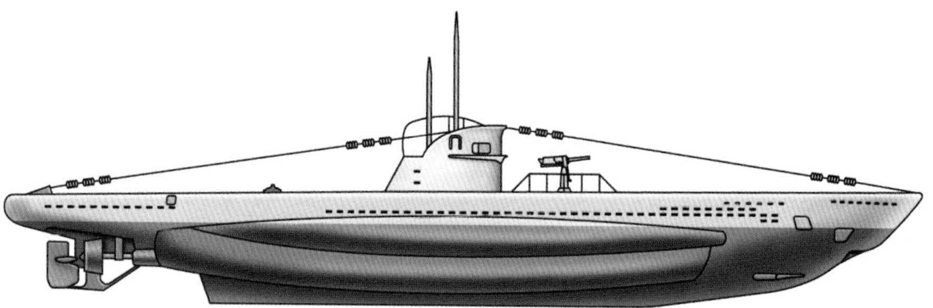

Specifications

Crew: 25
Powerplant: Diesel/electric
Max Speed: 23.5/13.7km/hr (12.7/7.4kt) s/d
Surface Range: 6389km (3450nm)
Displacement: 319/370t (314/364 tons) s/d
Dimensions (length/beam/draught): 44 x 4.9 x 3.9m (144.4 x 16.8 x 12.8ft)
Commissioned: Jun 1940 – Jan 1941
Armament: 6 torpedoes (3 bow tubes); 1 x 2cm (0.8in) gun

▲ **U-141**

Type IID

U-141 was a training boat, whose first commander was Heinz-Otto Schultze. It briefly served as a combat boat with 3 Flotilla, mounting four patrols in 1941, during which it sank three ships and damaged another.

◀ **Krupp workshops**

Type II and Type VII U-boats undergo service checks in the docks at Krupp's Germania shipyard in Kiel, 1939. Krupp were Nazi Germany's largest steelmaker, and were consequently involved in the production of many of the *Kriegsmarine*'s U-boats.

U-333

Type VIIC

U-333 had a varied career after it was commissioned out of the Nordseewerke yard at Emden in August 1941, making 11 patrols before being destroyed in the English Channel in 1944.

On its first patrol, U-333 sank three ships before encountering the German blockade runner *Spreewald*. The *Spreewald* was disguised as a Norwegian freighter, and was waiting to rendezvous with U-575 to be escorted into a Biscay port. However, the blockade runner was in the wrong position and was sunk in error by U-333.

On its fourth patrol, U-333 fought an epic battle with the British corvette HMS *Crocus* on 6 October 1942. Rammed twice, the U-boat lost three men dead (including the first officer) and several men wounded, including its commander, Cremer. The boat was heavily damaged and limped back to base with help of a replacement first officer, Kptlt. Lorenz

U-333 Commanders

Kptlt. Peter-Erich Cremer *(Aug 1941 – Oct 1942)*
Kptlt. Helmut Kandzior *(Oct 1942 – Oct 1942)*
Kptlt. Lorenz Kasch *(Oct 1942 – Nov 1942)*
Oblt. Werner Schwaff *(Nov 1942 – May 1943)*
Korvkpt. Peter-Erich Cremer *(May 1943 – Jul 1944)*
Kptlt. Hans Fiedler *(Jul 1944 – Jul 1944)*

Kasch, from the U-107. The boat was directed to meet with the milchcow U-459, which had a doctor aboard to treat the wounded. On the way back to La Pallice U-333 was attacked by HMS *Graph*, the former U-570 which had been captured by the British, but the German boat managed to evade all four torpedoes fired in the encounter. Cremer then spent three months in hospital.

On its sixth patrol, U-333 shot down a Leigh-Light Wellington, but not before the British bomber dropped four depth charges, which damaged the boat. On its eighth patrol, U-333 narrowly avoided being sunk by a destroyer, and snapped its periscope while surfacing under the British ship. On its tenth patrol, U-333 was stuck on the bottom while avoiding depth charges.

U-333 was sunk with all hands on 31 July 1944 to the west of the Scilly Isles by depth charges from Royal Navy warships – the sloop HMS *Starling* and the frigate HMS *Loch Killin*.

THREE LITTLE FISHES EMBLEM

The emblem of U-333 was chosen by its first commander, Peter-Erich Cremer. The 'Three Little Fishes' were suitably nautical, and the number was selected to reflect that of the U-boat.

▲ **U-333**

Type VIIC

U-333 was one of a number of boats newly equipped with a *Schnorchel* which were sent to try to interrupt the flow of supplies across the Channel after the Normandy invasion. It was the first boat to be sunk by the Squid ahead-throwing mortar.

Specifications

Crew: 44
Powerplant: Diesel/electric
Max Speed: 31.5/14.1km/hr (17/7.6kt) s/d
Surface Range: 12,040km (6500nm)
Displacement: 773/879t (761/865 tons) s/d
Dimensions (length/beam/draught): 67.1 x 6.2 x 4.8m (220.1 x 20.34 x 15.75ft)
Commissioned: 6 Feb 1941
Armament: 14 torpedoes (4 bow/1 stern tubes); 1 x 3.7cm (1.5in) and 2 x twin 2cm (0.8in) guns

U-333 TIMETABLE

Patrol Dates	Operational Area	Ships Sunk
27 Dec 1941 – 9 Feb 1942	Transit from Kiel to La Pallice via N Atlantic	3
30 Mar 1942 – 26 May 1942	US coast off Florida	3
11 Aug 1942 – 24 Aug 1942	Central Atlantic – returmed after damage	0
1 Sep 1942 – 23 Oct 1942	Central Atlantic – returned damaged	0
20 Dec 1942 – 2 Feb 1943	North Atlantic	0
5 Feb 1943 – 13 Apr 1943	North Atlantic	1
2 June 1943 – 31 Aug 1943	Central Atlantic	0
21 Oct 1943 – 1 Dec 1943	Off Spanish coast – returned damaged	0
10 Feb 1944 – 12 Feb 1944	North Atlantic, but returned with mechanical fault	0
14 Feb 1944 – 20 Apr 1944	North Atlantic	0
6 June 1944 – 13 June 1944	Channel invasion front	1
23 Jul 1944 – 31 Jul 1944	English Channel	0

U-570

Type VIIC

Laid down at the Blohm und Voss yard in Hamburg on 21 May 1940, U-570 was commissioned into the 3rd Flotilla in May of 1941. The boat set off on its only patrol on 23 August 1941.

The boat became famous because it was captured by the Royal Navy on 27 August 1941, south of Iceland. There were no casualties – all 44 members of the crew survived to be taken prisoner.

Captured on its first patrol

After leaving Trondheim, U-570 was ordered to patrol to the south of Iceland. The green crew were badly affected by the rough weather, and morale was low. While attempting to locate eastbound convoy HX 145, U-570 was spotted on the surface by an RAF Hudson of No. 269 Sqn, which dropped four depth charges before the boat could dive.

The inexperienced crew ran out on deck, waving white flags. The Hudson continued to circle until relieved by a Catalina of No. 209 Sqn. Before nightfall an anti-submarine trawler arrived, which was reinforced by two destroyers and three more trawlers overnight.

The boat was taken in tow and with difficulty was beached on Iceland at Thorlakshafn. U-570 was repaired and taken into service as HM Submarine *Graph* on 19 September 1941, becoming operational in September 1942. It was stricken on 20 March 1944 after running aground near Islay.

U-570 Commander

Kptlt. Hans-Joachim Rahmlow *(May 1941 – Aug 1941)*

Once in captivity, *Kapitänleutnant* Rahmlow and his first officer, Lt. Berndt, were considered to have displayed cowardice by their fellow prisoners. Berndt was killed in an escape attempt, while Rahmlow was ostracized by his fellows for the rest of the war.

▼ U-570 surface gun

Royal Navy personnel board U-570 after its capture. Type VIICs carried an 8.8cm (3.5in) gun. This was effective in dealing with smaller vessels not considered worth a torpedo, but it was of little use in attacking escorted convoys.

Specifications

Crew: 44
Powerplant: Diesel/electric
Max Speed: 31.5/14.1km/hr (17/7.6kt) s/d
Surface Range: 12,040km (6500nm)
Displacement: 773/879t (761/865 tons) s/d
Dimensions (length/beam/draught): 67.1 x 6.2 x 4.8m (220.1 x 20.34 x 15.75ft)
Commissioned: 6 Feb 1941
Armament: 14 torpedoes (4 bow/1 stern tubes); 1 x 8.8cm (3.5in) and 1x 2cm (0.8in) guns

▲ U-570

Type VIIC

The Type VIIC boats entered production from 1940. They were marginally longer than the preceding Type VIIB, the extra length being used to incorporate a larger control room to enable new sound-detection equipment to be fitted. This artwork shows U-570 in Royal Navy colours, after it became HM Submarine *Graph*.

U-571

Type VIIC

U-571 was laid down at the Blohm und Voss yard in Hamburg on 3 June 1940. The boat was commissioned under the command of Helmut Möhlmann on 22 May 1941.

The boat was assigned to 3rd Flottilla at Kiel, where it underwent working up training and from where it mounted its first patrol in Arctic waters. In October 1941, U-571 transferred from Kiel to 3rd Flotilla's French operating base at La Pallice. Under the command of *Kapitänleutnant* Helmut Möhlmann, U-571 went on seven patrols in the North Atlantic, off Gibraltar and in North American waters. Möhlmann transferred out of the boat in May 1943, going on to serve in staff positions. He was replaced by *Oberleutnant* Gustav Lüssow, who took the boat on her last two patrols into the Atlantic.

U-571 Commanders

Kptlt. Helmut Möhlmann (May 1941 – May 1943)

Oblt. Gustav Lüssow (May 1943 – 28 Jan 1944)

Fate

U-571 went on her last patrol in January 1944, when she joined the *Rügen* wolfpack that was dispersed widely in waters to the west of the British Isles. After unsuccesfully attacking a destroyer near Fastnet, U-571 was sunk with all hands on 28 January 1944 west of Ireland, by depth charges from an Australian Sunderland of No.461 Sqn.

U-571 TIMETABLE

Patrol Dates	Operational Area	Ships Sunk
18 Aug 1941 – 27 Aug 1941	Arctic waters off the Kola Peninsula	1
22 Oct 1941 – 26 Nov 1941	Transit to La Pallice via Newfoundland and the Azores	0
21 Dec 1941 – 27 Jan 1942	Off Gibraltar	0
10 Mar 1942 – 7 May 1942	Newfoundland/US Coast/Bermuda	3
11 Jun 1942 – 7 Aug 1942	W of Portugal/Carolina coast/Florida coast/Gulf of Mexico	2
3 Oct 1942 – 14 Nov 1942	Central Atlantic	0
22 Dec 1942 – 19 Feb 1943	Central Atlantic/SW of the Azores/W of Portugal	0
25 Mar 1943 – 1 May 1943	W of Biscay/S of Greenland/Newfoundland waters	0
8 Jun 1943 – 1 Sep 1943	Central Atlantic off W Africa	0
8 Jan 1944 – 28 Jan 1944	W of Ireland	0

Specifications

Crew: 44

Powerplant: Diesel/electric

Max Speed: 31.5/14.1km/hr (17/7.6kt) s/d

Surface Range: 12,040km (6500nm)

Displacement: 773/879t (761/865 tons) s/d

Dimensions (length/beam/draught): 67.1 x 6.2 x 4.8m (220.1 x 20.34 x 15.75ft)

Commissioned: 6 Feb 1941

Armament: 14 torpedoes (4 bow/1 stern tubes); 1 x 3.7cm (1.5in) and 2 x twin 2cm (0.8in) guns

▲ **U-571**

Type VIIC

Early in the war Type VII boats could only operate out to the centre of the Atlantic, but in 1942 commanders realised that by careful engine management they could mount patrols as far as the US coast and even the Caribbean. On U-571's fifth patrol it was refuelled by U-459 and reached as far as the Gulf of Mexico.

U-960

Type VIIC

U-960 saw extremes of service in less than a year of combat. From patrols to the edge of the Arctic ice, it was transferred to the warm waters of the Mediterranean.

Launched at Blohm und Voss, Hamburg, in December 1942, U-960 was commissioned on 28 January 1943. It mounted two minelaying patrols in Soviet waters before moving to Atlantic operations for three months. On 27 April 1944, U-960 set off for the Mediterranean, probably passing through the Straits of Gibraltar on the night of 14/15 May.

U-960 Commander

Oblt. Günther Heinrich *(Jan 1943 – May 1944)*

Fate

On 17 May, U-960 attacked the destroyer USS *Ellyson* off Oran. The destroyer had survivors on board from U-616, which had been destroyed only five hours before to the east of Cartagena. U-960's attack missed, and Allied anti-submarine forces immediately started a Swamp operation. This involved every available unit being vectored onto the possible position of the U-boat. Four American destroyers formed a line across the U-boat's predicted path, and once an aircraft made radar contact early on the 19th the nearest destroyers raced in to attack.

Forced to the surface, U-960 exchanged fire with first two and then four destroyers, until attacked by a Wellington and a Ventura. The boat dived, but depth charges from the USS *Niblack* again forced the boat to the surface, where the surviving crew abandoned U-960 as it sank.

U-960 TIMETABLE

Patrol Dates	Operational Area	Ships Sunk
3 Aug 1943 – 15 Aug 1943	Transit from Kiel to Narvik via Bergen	0
18 Aug 1943 – 1 Sep 1943	Minelaying patrol in Matochkin Strait	0
14 Sep 1943 – 10 Oct 1943	Minelaying/attack patrol in Soviet waters	2
14 Oct 1943 – 16 Oct 1943	Transit to Trondheim	0
4 Dec 1943 – 3 Feb 1944	Transit to La Pallice via N Atlantic	1
16 Feb 1944 – 18 Feb 1944	Returned with mechanical fault	0
19 Mar 1944 – 27 Mar 1944	Atlantic, but damaged by Mosquito attack	0
27 Apr 1944 – 19 May 1944	Transit to Mediterranean	0

Convoy TM 1

3 January 1943

Convoy TM 1 was a strategically important mission to supply fuel to the North African battle front. Escorted by four warships, the convoy was attacked by a wolfpack of 14 U-boats.

Operation *Torch* had taken place in November 1942. The Allied landings in Northwest Africa were intended to eliminate the Axis armies in Africa and to provide a jumping-off point for the planned invasion of Sicily. Fuel was a vital necessity, so it was decided that instead of loaded tankers sailing from the Caribbean up to Nova Scotia, then travelling in convoy to the UK before sailing on to Gibraltar, convoys would be formed at Trinidad and go directly to Gibraltar and thence to North Africa. TM 1 was to

CONVOY TM 1 BATTLE TIMETABLE	
Date	**Event**
29 Dec 1942	U-124 sights a part of the convoy heading for an assembly point
3 Jan 1943	U-514 locates the convoy and leaves one tanker abandoned and adrift. The hulk is sunk by U-105 three weeks later. Dönitz, realizing that such a large tanker convoy is likely to be heading direct for North Africa to support the victorious Allied offensives, orders his boats to ignore Convoy GUS 2, which a wolfpack had been preparing to attack, and to move instead against TM 1
4 Jan	Dönitz establishes Group *Delphin*, which with some other boats sets up a patrol line in the central Atlantic
8 Jan	U-381 sights the convoy. U-436, U-571 and U-575 head towards it. U-436 attacks in the evening, sinking a tanker and damaging another, before being damaged and driven off by the escort. U-571 and U-575 are unable to penetrate the screen
9 Jan	U-575 damages two tankers and newly arrived U-442 hits another. U-181 and U-134 are driven off, the latter damaged by depth charges. U-620 has also arrived, and shadows the convoy. At nightfall U-522 finishes off two damaged tankers, while U-442 and U-436 sink another. Meanwhile U-511 sinks an independent ship not belonging to the convoy
10 Jan	U-522 damages a tanker, which is given the *coup de grâce* by U-620
11 Jan	U-571 attacks but fails to sink the two surviving tankers
12 Jan	U-511 is driven off by the escort
13 Jan	The escort is reinforced by the destroyer HMS *Quentin* and the corvettes HMS *Penstemon* and *Samphire*. Air cover also arrives
14 Jan	The two surviving tankers arrive at Gibraltar

be the first of these direct fuel convoys. The Germans were fully aware of the importance of fuel convoys. U-124 spotted a small part of TM 1 headed eastwards, and when U-514 came across nine tankers Admiral Dönitz realized that a large fuel convoy was heading direct from the Caribbean oilfields to the battle theatre of North Africa.

The vital importance of the convoy was clear. Dönitz ordered a number of boats assembled to attack convoy GUS 2 to ignore that target and attempt to intercept the tankers. The U-boat C-in-C ordered the *Delphin* pack together with some independent boats, into a patrol line on the convoy's predicted route.

The convoy commander received a warning of U-boat activity based on direction-finding bearings on U-boat radio transmissions, but curiously ignored an instruction from the Submarine Tracking Room to re-route. As a result, the nine tankers ran straight into the patrol line, being sighted by U-381 on 8 January.

The opponents

The wolfpack *Delphin* consisted of 10 boats, including U-134 (Kptlt. Schendel), U-181 (Korvkpt. Lüth), U-381 (Kptlt. von Puckler und Limburg), U-436 (KptlLt. Seibicke), U-442 (Korvkpt. Hesse), U-511 (Kptlt. Schneewind), U-522 (Kptlt. Schneider), U-571 (Kptlt. Möhlmann), U-575 (Kptlt. Heydemann), and U-620 (Kptlt. Stein). They were reinforced by U-105 (Oblt. Nissen), U-124 (Korvkpt. Mohr), U-125 (Kptlt. Folkers) and U-514 (Kptlt. Auffermann). The convoy was escorted by Royal Navy Escort Group B5, which included the destroyer HMS *Havelock* and the corvettes HMS *Pimpernel*, HMS *Saxifrage* and HMS *Godetia*.

High toll

In two days of attacks, the U-boats succeeded in sinking seven out of nine tankers. However, the final attacks failed since by 12 January the escort had finally been reinforced by the destroyer HMS *Quentin* and the corvettes HMS *Penstemon* and HMS *Samphire*. The arrival of air cover ensured that the two remaining tankers finally arrived in Gibraltar on 14 January.

TM 1 suffered the highest percentage loss of any Atlantic convoy. Only two of the tankers eventually reached Gibraltar, the *Cliona* and the *Vanja*. On receiving the news of the convoy battle, the commander of *Panzerarmee Afrika*, General von Arnim, sent congratulations to Dönitz, thanking him for the substantial contribution the U-boats had made to the Axis battle for survival in the North African theatre.

Wolfpack group *Ritter*

FEBRUARY 1943

***Ritter* was one of three wolfpacks, along with the *Knappen* and *Neptun* groups, which were directed against convoy ON 166.**

Wolfpacks *Ritter*, *Knappen* and *Neptun* were sent to attack convoy ON 166. Located in the central Atlantic by the independently operating U-604 on 20 February 1943, ON 166's escorts drove off the shadowing boat before the wolfpacks could concentrate.

However, by the next day the U-boats were in position. Over the next five days, in a battle covering 1600km (1000 miles) right up to Newfoundland waters, ON 166 lost 14 ships totalling more than 88,000 GRT. At least three U-boats from the combined wolfpacks were sunk.

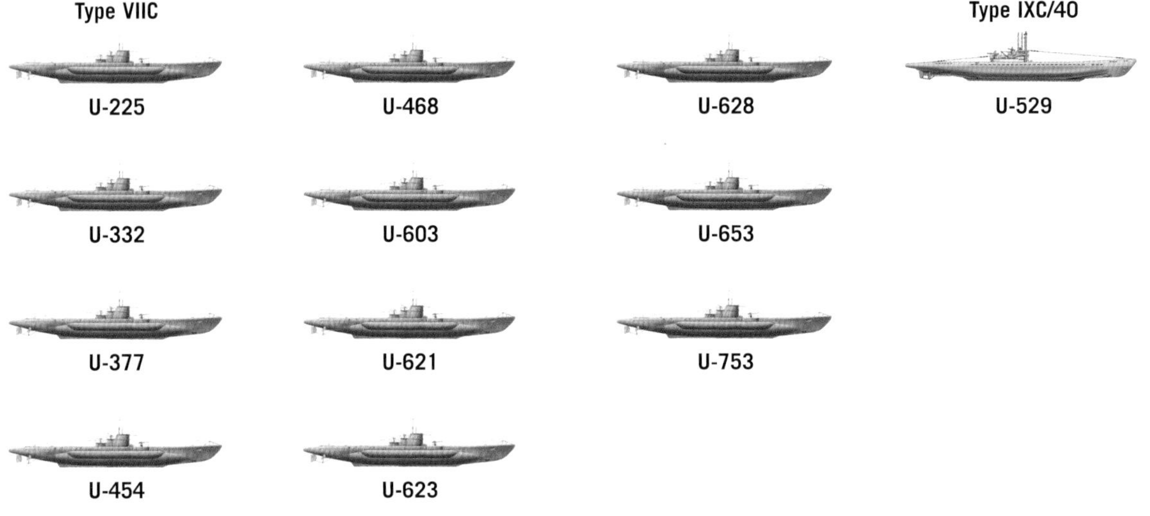

BOATS THAT SERVED WITH 3RD FLOTILLA (108 BOATS)

U-Boat	Type	Commissioned	Flotilla(s)	Patrols	Fate
U-10	IIB	9-Sep-35	4 Oct 1937 – 14 Apr 1939 from 1. Flottille	5 patrols. 2 ships sunk: total 6356 GRT	to U-Bootschulflottille
U-12	IIB	1-Sep-35	1 Sep 1935 – 8 Oct 1939	1 patrol	Sunk with all hands 8 Oct 1939 near Dover by a mine. 27 dead
U-14	IIB	18-Jan-36	18 Jan 1936 – 31 Oct 1939	6 patrols. 9 ships sunk: total 12,344 GRT	to U-Ausbildungsflottille
U-16	IIB	16-May-36	16 May 1936 – 25 Oct 1939	3 patrols. 1 ship sunk: total 3378 GRT; 1 auxiliary warship sunk: total 57 GRT	Sunk with all hands 25 Oct 1939 near Dover by depth charges from the ASW trawler HMS *Cayton Wyke* and the patrol vessel HMS *Puffin*. 28 dead
U-18	IIB	4-Jan-36	1 Sep 1939 – 1 Mar 1940 from 1. Flottille	14 patrols. 3 ships sunk: total 1985 GRT; 1 ship damaged: total 7745 GRT; 1 warship damaged: total 57t/56 tons	to U-Ausbildungsflottille
U-20	IIB	1-Feb-36	1 Feb 1936 – 31 Dec 1939	17 patrols. 14 ships sunk: total 37,669 GRT; 1 ship damaged beyond repair: total 844 GRT; 1 ship damaged: total 1846 GRT	to 1. Flottille
U-22	IIB	20-Aug-36	20 Aug 1936 – 31 Dec 1939	7 patrols. 6 ships sunk: total 7344 GRT; 2 auxiliary warships sunk: total 3633 GRT; 1 warship sunk: total 1497 GRT	to 1. Flottille
U-24	IIB	10-Oct-36	10 Oct 1936 – 17 Oct 1939	20 patrols. 1 ship sunk: total 961 GRT; 5 MTBs sunk: total 580 GRT; 1 ship a total loss: total 7886 GRT; 1 ship damaged: total 7661 GRT	to 1. Flottille
U-82	VIIC	14-May-41	14 May 1941 – 6 Feb 1942	3 patrols. 8 ships sunk: total 51,859 GRT; 1 warship sunk: total 1209t/1190 tons; 1 ship damaged: total 1999 GRT	Sunk with all hands 6 Feb 1942 north of the Azores by depth charges from the sloop HMS *Rochester* and the corvette HMS *Tamarisk*. The boat was attacking convoy OS 18 while returning from Operation *Drumbeat* off the US east coast. 45 dead

BOATS THAT SERVED WITH 3RD FLOTILLA (108 BOATS)

U-Boat	Type	Commissioned	Flotilla(s)	Patrols	Fate
U-85	VIIB	7-Jun-41	7 Jun 1941 – 14 Apr 1942	4 patrols. 3 ships sunk: total 15,060 GRT	Sunk with all hands 14 Apr 1942 off the US coast near Cape Hatteras by gunfire from the destroyer USS *Roper*. 46 dead. U-85 was the first of the Operation *Drumbeat* (*Paukenschlag*) U-boats to be sunk off the North American coast, three months after the campaign against American shipping started
U-132	VIIC	29-May-41	29 May 1941 – 4 Nov 1942	4 patrols. 8 ships sunk: total 32,964 GRT; 1 warship sunk: total 2252t/2216 tons; 1 ship damaged beyond repair: total 4367 GRT; 1 ship damaged: total 6690 GRT	U-132 and its crew probably died with its final victim on 4 Nov 1942; the ammunition ship *Hatimura* detonated in a massive explosion and U-132 was probably within the lethal radius. 47 dead. The sinking was originally attributed to RAF aircraft from No. 120 Sqn on 5 Nov 1942 southeast of Cape Farewell, Greenland. That attack was most likely against U-89, which was severely damaged
U-134	VIIC	26-Jul-41	1 Nov 1941 – 24 Aug 1943 from 5. Flottille	7 patrols. 3 ships sunk: total 12,147 GRT	Sunk with all hands 24 Aug 1943 in the North Atlantic near Vigo, Spain, by 6 depth charges from a Wellington of No. 179 Sqn RAF. 48 dead
U-138	IID	27-Jun-40	1 May 1941 – 18 Jun 1941 from 22. Flottille	5 patrols. 6 ships sunk: total 48,564 GRT; 1 ship damaged: total 6993 GRT	Sunk 18 Jun 1941 west of Cadiz by depth charges from destroyers HMS *Faulknor*, HMS *Fearless*, HMS *Forester*, HMS *Foresight* and HMS *Foxhound*. All 27 crew survived
U-141	IID	21-Aug-40	1 May 1941 – 30 Sept 1941 from 1. Flottille	4 patrols. 3 ships sunk: total 6801 GRT; 1 ship damaged: total 5133 GRT	to 21. Flottille
U-143	IID	18-Sep-40	1 Apr 1941 – 12 Sept 1941 from 22. Flottille	4 patrols. 1 ship sunk: total 1409 GRT	to 22. Flottille
U-146	IID	30-Oct-40	22 Jun 1941 – 31 Aug 1941 from 22. Flottille	2 patrols. 1 ship sunk: total 3496 GRT	to 22. Flottille
U-147	IID	11-Dec-40	Feb 1941 – 2 Jun 1941 from 22. Flottille	3 patrols. 3 ships sunk: total 8636 GRT	Sunk with all hands off Malin Head on 2 Jun 1941 by depth charges from destroyer HMS *Windermere* and corvette HMS *Periwinkle*. 26 dead
U-205	VIIC	3-May-41	3 May 1941 – 1 Nov 1941	11 patrols. 1 ship sunk: total 2623 GRT; 1 warship sunk: total 5537t/5450 tons	to 29. Flottille
U-206	VIIC	17-May-41	17 May 1941 – 30 Nov 1941	3 patrols. 2 ships sunk: total 3283 GRT; 1 warship sunk: total 940t/925 tons	Missing with all hands in the Bay of Biscay, west of St Nazaire, on about 30 Nov 1941. Possibly sunk in the minefield 'Beech' laid by RAF aircraft the previous year. 46 dead. Loss previously attributed to depth charges from a British Whitley aircraft of No. 502 Sqn; that attack is thought now to have been against U-71, which escaped without damage
U-212	VIIC	25-Apr-42	1 Nov 1943 – 21 Jul 1944 from 13. Flottille	15 patrols. 1 ship sunk: total 80 GRT	Sunk with all hands 21 Jul 1944 in the English Channel south of Brighton by depth charges from the frigates HMS *Curzon* and HMS *Ekins*. 49 dead
U-231	VIIC	14-Nov-42	1 May 1943 – 13 Jan 1944 from 5. Flottille (training)	3 patrols	Sunk 13 Jan 1944 northeast of the Azores by depth charges from a Vickers Wellington of No. 172 Sqn RAF. 7 dead and 43 survivors
U-241	VIIC	24-Jul-43	1 Apr 1944 – 18 May 1944 from 5. Flottille (training)	1 patrol	Sunk with all hands 18 May 1944 northeast of the Faroes by depth charges from a Catalina of No. 210 Sqn RAF. 51 dead
U-242	VIIC	14-Aug-43	1 Jun 1944 – 5 Jul 1944 from 5. Flottille (training)	7 patrols. 3 ships sunk: total 2595 GRT	to 5. Flottille
U-245	VIIC	18-Dec-43	1 Aug 1944 – 1 Oct 1944 from 5. Flottille (training)	3 patrols. 3 ships sunk: total 17,087 GRT	to 33. Flottille
U-246	VIIC	11-Jan-44	1 Aug 1944 – 30 Sep 1944 from 5. Flottille (training)	2 patrols	to 11. Flottille
U-257	VIIC	14-Jan-42	1 Oct 1942 – 24 Feb 1944 from 5. Flottille	6 patrols	Sunk 24 Feb 1944 in the North Atlantic by depth charges from the Canadian frigate HMCS *Waskesiu* and the British frigate HMS *Nene*. 30 dead and 19 survivors
U-258	VIIC	4-Feb-42	1 Sep 1942 – 20 May 1943 from 5. Flottille (training)	4 patrols. 1 ship sunk: total 6198 GRT	Sunk with all hands 20 May 1943 in the North Atlantic by depth charges from a Liberator of No. 120 Sqn RAF. 49 dead
U-259	VIIC	18-Feb-42	1 Sep 1942 – 15 Nov 1942 from 5. Flottille (training)	2 patrols	Sunk with all hands 15 Nov 1942 in the Mediterranean north of Algiers by depth charges from a Lockheed Hudson of No. 500 Sqn RAF. 48 dead
U-262	VIIC	15-Apr-42	1 Oct 1942 – 9 Nov 1944 from 5. Flottille (training)	10 patrols. 3 ships sunk: total 13,010 GRT; 1 warship sunk: total 940t/925 tons	to 33. Flottille
U-275	VIIC	25-Nov-42	1 Jun 1943 – 30 Sep 1944 from 8. Flottille	9 patrols. 1 ship sunk: total 4934 GRT; 1 warship sunk: total 1107t/1090 tons	to 11. Flottille
U-280	VIIC	13-Feb-43	1 Aug 1943 – 16 Nov 1943	1 patrol	Sunk with all hands 16 Nov 1943 southwest of Iceland by depth charges from a Liberator of No. 86 Sqn RAF. 49 dead
U-289	VIIC	10-Jul-43	1 Apr 1944 – 1 May 1944 from 8. Flottille	2 patrols. On 25 Apr 1944 U-289 landed 2 agents on Iceland.	to 13. Flottille
U-332	VIIC	7-Jun-41	7 Jun 1941 – 29 Apr 1943	7 patrols. 8 ships sunk: total 46,729 GRT; 1 ship damaged: total 5964 GRT	Sunk with all hands 29 Apr 1943 north of Cape Finisterre, Spain, by depth charges from a Liberator of No. 224 Sqn RAF. 45 dead. Previously the sinking was credited to an Australian Sunderland on 2 May 1943, but that probably sank U-465.
U-333	VIIC	25-Aug-41	1 Jan 1942 – 31 Jul 1944 from 5. Flottille	12 patrols. 7 ships sunk: total 32,107 GRT; 1 ship damaged: total 8327 GRT; 1 warship damaged: total 940t/925 tons	Sunk with all hands 31 Jul 1944 west of the Scilly Isles by depth charges from the sloop HMS *Starling* and the frigate HMS *Loch Killin*. 45 dead
U-334	VIIC	9-Oct-41	1 Mar 1942 – 30 Jun 1942 from 8. Flottille	8 patrols. 2 ships sunk: total 14,372 GRT	to 11. Flottille

BOATS THAT SERVED WITH 3RD FLOTILLA (108 BOATS)

U-Boat	Type	Commissioned	Flotilla(s)	Patrols	Fate
U-341	VIIC	28-Nov-42	1 Jun 1943 – 19 Sep 1943 from 8. Flottille	2 patrols	Sunk with all hands 19 Sep 1943 southwest of Iceland by depth charges from a Liberator of No. 10 Sqn RCAF. 50 dead
U-343	VIIC	26-Mar-43	1 Apr 1944 – 31 May 1944 from 8. Flottille	5 patrols. 1 warship sunk: total 1372t/1350 tons	to 11. Flottille
U-352	VIIC	28-Aug-41	28 Aug 1941 – 9 May 1942	3 patrols	Sunk 9 May 1942 southwest of Cape Hatteras by depth charges from the US Coast Guard cutter *Icarus*. 15 dead and 33 survivors
U-373	VIIC	22-May-41	22 May 1941 – 8 Jun 1944	15 patrols. 3 ships sunk: total 10,263 GRT	Sunk 8 Jun 1944 in the Bay of Biscay west of Brest by depth charges from a Liberator of No. 224 Sqn RAF. 4 dead and 47 survivors. The same aircraft also sank U-441 20 minutes later.
U-375	VIIC	19-Jul-41	1 Nov 1941 – 31 Dec 1941 from 5. Flottille	11 patrols. 9 ships sunk: total 16,847 GRT; 1 ship damaged b/r: total 6288 GRT; 1 warship damaged: total 2693t/2650 tons	to 29. Flottille
U-376	VIIC	21-Aug-41	1 Mar 1943 – 13 Apr 1943 from 11. Flottille	8 patrols. 2 ships sunk: total 10,146 GRT	Missing with all hands in the Bay of Biscay on or after 13 Apr 1943. 47 dead. Previously credited to a Wellington of No. 172 Sqn RAF on 10 Apr 1943 west of Nantes. The aircraft actually severely damaged U-465 in that attack
U-378	VIIC	30-Oct-41	1 Mar 1942 – 30 Jun 1942 from 8. Flottille	11 patrols. 1 warship sunk: total 1951t/1920 tons	to 11. Flottille
U-378	VIIC	30-Oct-41	1 May 1943 – 20 Oct 1943 from 11. Flottille	11 patrols. 1 warship sunk: total 1951t/1920 tons	Sunk with all hands 20 Oct 1943 in the North Atlantic by depth charges and gunfire from US Navy Avengers and Wildcats of the escort carrier USS *Core*. 48 dead
U-384	VIIC	18-Jul-42	1 Jan 1943 – 19 Mar 1943 from 5. Flottille	2 patrols. 2 ships sunk: total 13,407 GRT	Sunk with all hands 19 Mar 1943 southwest of Iceland by depth charges from a B-17 Fortress of No. 206 Sqn RAF. 47 dead. Previously credited to a Sunderland the next day, but that attack was actually against U-631 and caused no damage
U-391	VIIC	24-Apr-43	1 Oct 1943 – 13 Dec 1943 from 5. Flottille	1 patrol	Sunk with all hands 13 Dec 1943 in the Bay of Biscay northwest of Cape Ortegal by depth charges from a Liberator of No. 53 Sqn. 51 dead
U-398	VIIC	18-Dec-43	1 Aug 1944 – 31 Oct 1944 from 5. Flottille	2 patrols	to 33. Flottille
U-402	VIIC	21-May-41	21 May 1941 – 13 Oct 1943	8 patrols. 14 ships sunk: total 70,434 GRT; 1 auxiliary warship sunk: total 602 GRT; 3 ships damaged: total 28,682 GRT	Sunk with all hands 13 Oct 1943 in the central North Atlantic by a Fido acoustic torpedo dropped by a US Navy Avenger of the escort carrier USS *Card*. 50 dead
U-431	VIIC	5-Apr-41	5 Apr 1941 – 31 Dec 1941	16 patrols. 7 ships sunk: total 9752 GRT; 1 auxiliary warship sunk: total 313 GRT; 2 warships sunk: total 3605t/3548 tons; 1 ship damaged beyond repair: total 6415 GRT; 1 ship damaged: total 3560 GRT; 1 warship damaged: total 457t/450 tons	to 29. Flottille
U-432	VIIC	26-Apr-41	26 Apr 1941 – 11 Mar 1943	8 patrols. 19 ships sunk: total 64,769 GRT; 1 warship sunk: total 1362t/1340 tons; 2 ships damaged: total 15,666 GRT	Sunk 11 Mar 1943 in the North Atlantic by depth charges and gunfire from the Free French corvette *Aconit*. 26 dead and 20 survivors
U-433	VIIC	24-May-41	24 May 1941 – 16 Nov 1941	2 patrols. 1 ship damaged: total 2215 GRT	Foundered on 16 Nov 1941 in the Mediterranean south of Malaga, Spain, after being damaged by depth charges and gunfire east of Gibraltar by the corvette HMS *Marigold*. 6 dead and 38 survivors
U-444	VIIC	9-May-42	1 Jan 1943 – 11 Mar 1943 from 8. Flottille	2 patrols	Sunk 11 Mar 1943 in the North Atlantic by ramming and depth charges from the destroyer HMS *Harvester* and the Free French corvette *Aconit*. 41 dead and 4 survivors
U-451	VIIC	3-May-41	3 May 1941 – 21 Dec 1941	4 patrols. 1 warship sunk: total 448t/441 tons	Sunk 21 Dec 1941 near Tangier by depth charges from a Royal Navy Swordfish of No. 812 Sqn. 44 dead and 1 survivor
U-452	VIIC	29-May-41	29 May 1941 – 25 Aug 1941	1 patrol	Sunk with all hands 25 Aug 1941 southeast of Iceland by depth charges from the anti-submarine trawler HMS *Vascama* and from a Catalina of No. 209 Sqn RAF. 42 dead
U-458	VIIC	12-Dec-41	1 Jul 1942 – 31 Oct 1942 from 8. Flottille	7 patrols. 2 ships sunk: total 7584 GRT	to 29. Flottille
U-466	VIIC	17-Jun-42	1 Jan 1943 – 31 Mar 1944 from 5. Flottille	5 patrols	to 29. Flottille
U-468	VIIC	12-Aug-42	1 Feb 1943 – 11 Aug 1943 from 5. Flottille	3 patrols. 1 ship sunk: total 6537 GRT	Sunk 11 Aug 1943 near Bathurst by depth charges from a Liberator of No. 200 Sqn RAF, which was shot down. 44 dead and 7 survivors. The pilot of the Liberator, Flying Officer Lloyd Trigg RNZAF, was awarded a posthumous Victoria Cross based on the testimony of the surviving officers of the U-boat
U-469	VIIC	7-Oct-42	1 Mar 1943 – 25 Mar 1943 from 5. Flottille	1 patrol	Sunk with all hands 25 Mar 1943 south of Iceland by depth charges from a Flying Fortress of No. 206 Sqn RAF. 47 dead
U-476	VIIC	28-Jul-43	1 Apr 1944 – 25 May 1944	1 patrol	Badly damaged northwest of Trondheim 24 May 1944 by depth charges from a Catalina of No. 210 Sqn RAF which killed 34. Scuttled the next day by torpedoes from U-990. U-990 rescued 21 of the crew, but was itself sunk by a Liberator a few hours later. 19 of the rescued crewmen survived and two died
U-478	VIIC	8-Sep-43	1 Jun 1944 – 30 Jun 1944 from 5. Flottille	1 patrol	Sunk with all hands 30 Jun 1944 northeast of the Faroes by depth charges from a Canso (Canadian-built PBY Catalina) of No. 162 Sqn RCAF and a Liberator of No. 86 Sqn RAF. 52 dead

BOATS THAT SERVED WITH 3RD FLOTILLA (108 BOATS)

U-Boat	Type	Commissioned	Flotilla(s)	Patrols	Fate
U-483	VIIC	22-Dec-43	1 Aug 1944 – 4 Sep 1944 from 5. Flottille	2 patrols. 1 warship damaged beyond repair: total 1321t/1300 tons	to 11. Flottille
U-484	VIIC	19-Jan-44	1 Aug 1944 – 9 Sep 1944 from 5. Flottille	1 patrol	Sunk with all hands 9 Sept 1944 northwest of Ireland by depth charges from the corvette HMS *Porchester Castle* and the frigate HMS *Helmsdale*. 52 dead
U-553	VIIC	23-Dec-40	1 Dec 1942 – 20 Jan 1943 from 7. Flottille	10 patrols. 13 ships sunk: total 64,612 GRT; 2 ships damaged: total 15,273 GRT	Missing with all hands in the central North Atlantic in Jan 1943. The boat sent its last message on 20 Jan 1943, reporting: '*Sehrohr unklar*' (Periscope unclear). 47 dead
U-567	VIIC	24-Apr-41	24 Apr 1941 – 31 Oct 1941	3 patrols. 2 ships sunk: total 6809 GRT	to 7. Flottille
U-568	VIIC	1-May-41	1 May 1941 – 31 Dec 1941	5 patrols. 1 ship sunk: total 6023 GRT; 2 warships sunk: total 1880t/1850 tons; 1 warship damaged: total 1656t/1630 tons	to 29. Flottille
U-569	VIIC	8-May-41	8 May 1941 – 22 May 1943	9 patrols. 1 ship sunk: total 984 GRT; 1 ship damaged: total 4458 GRT	Scuttled 22 May 1943 in the North Atlantic after being badly damaged by depth charges from a pair of Grumman Avengers of the escort carrier USS *Bogue*. 21 dead and 25 survivors
U-570	VIIC	15-May-41	15 May 1941 – 27 Aug 1941	1 patrol	Captured by the Royal Navy on 27 Aug 1941 south of Iceland, after being damaged by a Lockheed Hudson of No. 269 Sqn RAF. 44 survivors – no casualties. Repaired and taken into service as HM Submarine *Graph* on 19 Sep 1941, becoming operational in Sep 1942. Taken out of service in Feb 1944. Stricken on 20 Mar 1944 after running aground near Islay. Broken up
U-571	VIIC	22-May-41	22 May 1941 – 28 Jan 1944	11 patrols. 5 ships sunk: total 33,511 GRT; 2 ships damaged beyond repair: total 13,658 GRT; 1 ship damaged: total 11,394 GRT	Sunk with all hands 28 Jan 1944 west of Ireland by depth charges from an Australian Sunderland of No. 461 Sqn. 52 dead
U-572	VIIC	29-May-41	29 May 1941 – 3 Aug 1943	9 patrols. 6 ships sunk: total 19,323 GRT; 1 ship damaged: total 6207 GRT	Sunk with all hands 3 Aug 1943 in the Caribbean northeast of Trinidad by depth charges from a Martin Mariner of US Navy Patrol Squadron VP-205. 47 dead. Former commander Kptlt. Heinz Hirsacker was the only U-boat captain to be found guilty of cowardice in the face of the enemy. He committed suicide on 24 Apr 1943, shortly before his scheduled execution
U-573	VIIC	5-Jun-41	5 Jun 1941 – 31 Dec 1941	4 patrols. 1 ship sunk: total 5289 GRT	to 29. Flottille
U-596	VIIC	13-Nov-41	1 Jul 1942 – 18 Nov 1942 from 8. Flottille	12 patrols. 12 ships sunk: total 41,411 GRT; 1 warship sunk: total 250t/246 tons; 2 ships damaged: total 14,180 GRT	to 29. Flottille
U-600	VIIC	11-Dec-41	1 Aug 1942 – 25 Nov 1943 from 5. Flottille	6 patrols. 5 ships sunk: total 28,600 GRT; 3 ships damaged: total 19,230 GRT	Sunk with all hands 25 Nov 1943 north of Punta Delgada by depth charges from the frigates HMS *Bazely* and HMS *Blackwood*. 54 dead
U-611	VIIC	26-Feb-42	1 Oct 1942 – 8 Dec 1942 from 5. Flottille	1 patrol	Sunk with all hands 8 Dec 1942 southeast of Cape Farewell by depth charges from a Liberator of No. 120 Sqn RAF. 45 dead. Previously credited to a US Navy PBY Catalina on 10 Dec, but that attack was probably against U-609, which was undamaged
U-613	VIIC	12-Mar-42	1 Nov 1942 – 23 Jul 1943 from 8. Flottille	4 patrols. 2 ships sunk: total 8087 GRT	Sunk with all hands 23 Jul 1943 south of the Azores by depth charges from the destroyer USS *George E. Badger*. 48 dead
U-615	VIIC	26-Mar-42	1 Sep 1942 – 7 Aug 1943 from 8. Flottille	4 patrols. 4 ships sunk: total 27,231 GRT	Scuttled after being damaged in one of the longest battles between a U-boat and aircraft. From the night of 5/6 Aug to 7 Aug, U-615 was attacked by 6 US Navy Mariners and 1 Ventura. U-615's battle let many other U-boats in the Caribbean come to the surface and escape to the east. 4 dead and 43 survivors
U-619	VIIC	23-Apr-42	1 Oct 1942 – 5 Oct 1942 from 5. Flottille	1 patrol. 2 ships sunk: total 8723 GRT	Sunk with all hands 5 Oct 1942 southwest of Iceland, by 4 depth charges from a Hudson of No. 269 Sqn RAF. 44 dead. Previously credited to destroyer HMS *Viscount* on 15 Oct 1942, but that attack almost certainly sank U-661.
U-620	VIIC	30-Apr-42	1 Oct 1942 – 13 Feb 1943 from 8. Flottille	2 patrols. 1 ship sunk: total 6983 GRT	Sunk with all hands 13 Feb 1943 northwest of Lisbon by depth charges from a Catalina of No. 202 Sqn RAF. 47 dead. Another Catalina was credited with sinking U-620 the next day, but it probably targeted U-381 and caused no damage
U-625	VIIC	4-Jun-42	1 Oct 1942 – 31 Oct 1942 from 8. Flottille	9 patrols. 3 ships sunk: total 18,751 GRT; 2 auxiliary warships sunk: total 939 GRT	to 11. Flottille
U-630	VIIC	9-Jul-42	1 Apr 1943 – 6 May 1943 from 5. Flottille	1 patrol. 2 ships sunk: total 14,894 GRT	Sunk with all hands 6 May 1943 northeast of Newfoundland by depth charges from the destroyer HMS *Vidette*. 47 dead. Previously credited to a Catalina of No. 5 Sqn RCAF on 4 May 1943 south of Greenland, which actually damaged U-209
U-635	VIIC	13-Aug-42	1 Apr 1943 – 5 Apr 1943 from 5. Flottille	1 patrol. 1 ship sunk: total 9365 GRT; 1 ship damaged: total 5529 GRT	Sunk with all hands 5 Apr 1943 southwest of Iceland by depth charges from a Liberator of No. 210 Sqn RAF. 47 dead. Previously credited to depth charges from the frigate HMS *Tay*, which attacked U-306 the same day and inflicted no damage
U-645	VIIC	22-Oct-42	1 May 1943 – 24 Dec 1943 from 5. Flottille	3 patrols. 2 ships sunk: total 12,788 GRT	Sunk with all hands 24 Dec 1943 northeast of the Azores by depth charges from the destroyer USS *Schenck*. 55 dead

BOATS THAT SERVED WITH 3RD FLOTILLA (108 BOATS)					
U-Boat	**Type**	**Commissioned**	**Flotilla(s)**	**Patrols**	**Fate**
U-652	VIIC	3-Apr-41	3 Apr 1941 – 31 Dec 1941	8 patrols. 2 ships sunk: total 8152 GRT; 1 auxiliary warship sunk: total 558 GRT; 2 warships sunk: total 2784t/2740 tons; 2 ships damaged: total 9918 GRT; 1 auxiliary warship damaged: total 10,917 GRT	to 29. Flottille. U-652 fought an inconclusive duel with the destroyer USS *Greer* on 4 Sep 1941 – three months before the US declaration of war
U-657	VIIC	8-Oct-41	1 Mar 1942 – 30 Jun 1942 from 8. Flottille	7 patrols. 1 ship sunk: total 5196 GRT	to 8. Flottille
U-661	VIIC	12-Feb-42	1 Oct 1942 – 15 Oct 1942 from 5. Flottille	1 patrol. 1 ship sunk: total 3672 GRT	Sunk with all hands 15 Oct 1942 in the North Atlantic, rammed by destroyer HMS *Viscount*. 44 dead. Credited to a 120 Sqn Liberator, but the bomber probably depth-charged U-615 causing no damage
U-671	VIIC	3-Mar-43	1 May 1944 – 5 Aug 1944 from 5. Flottille	2 patrols	Sunk 5 Aug 1944 south of Brighton by depth charges from the frigate HMS *Stayner* and the escort destroyer HMS *Wensleydale*. 47 dead and 5 survivors
U-677	VIIC	20-Sep-43	1 Jun 1944 – 1 Jul 1944 from 5. Flottille	1 patrol	to 23. Flottille
U-701	VIIC	16-Jul-41	16 Jul 1941 – 7 Jul 1942	3 patrols. 5 ships sunk: total 25,390 GRT; 3 aux warships sunk: total 1429 GRT; 1 warship sunk: total 864 GRT; 4 ships damaged: total 37,093 GRT; 1 warship damaged: total 1209t/1190 tons	Sunk 7 Jul 1942 in American waters near Cape Hatteras by depth charges from a Lockheed Hudson of the 396th US Army Bomb Sqn. 39 dead and 7 survivors
U-706	VIIC	16-Mar-42	1 Oct 1942 – 3 Aug 1943 from 3. Flottille	5 patrols. 3 ships sunk: total 18,650 GRT	Damaged 3 Aug 1943 northwest of Cape Ortegal, Spain, by depth charges from a Handley-Page Hampden of No. 415 Sqn RCAF. Finished off by a B-24 of the USAAF's 4th A/S Sqn. 42 dead and 4 survivors
U-712	VIIC	5-Nov-42	1 Nov 1943 – 31 Dec 1943 from 8. Flottille	No patrols	to 21. Flottille
U-719	VIIC	27-Jul-43	1 May 1944 – 26 Jun 1944 from 5. Flottille	1 patrol	Sunk with all hands 26 Jun 1944 northwest of Ireland by depth charges from the destroyer HMS *Bulldog*. 52 dead
U-734	VIIC	5-Dec-42	1 Aug 1943 – 9 Feb 1944	2 patrols	Sunk with all hands 9 Feb 1944 southwest of Ireland by depth charges from the sloops HMS *Wild Goose* and HMS *Starling*. 49 dead
U-752	VIIC	24-May-41	24 May 1941 – 23 May 1943	7 patrols. 6 ships sunk: total 32,358 GRT; 2 auxiliary warships sunk: total 1134 GRT; 1 ship damaged: total 4799 GRT	Sunk 23 May 1943 in the North Atlantic by rockets from a Fairey Swordfish of the escort carrier HMS *Archer*. 29 dead and 17 survivors
U-753	VIIC	18-Jun-41	18 Jun 1941 – 13 May 1943	7 patrols. 3 ships sunk: total 23,117 GRT; 2 ships damaged: total 6908 GRT	Sunk with all hands 13 May 1943 in the North Atlantic by depth charges from corvette HMCS *Drumheller*, frigate HMS *Lagan* and from a Sunderland of No. 423 Sqn RCAF. 47 dead
U-760	VIIC	15-Oct-42	1 May 1943 – 8 Sep 1943 from 8. Flottille	2 patrols	Attacked and damaged off Cape Finisterre by a Wellington of No. 179 Sqn RAF. Retreated to Vigo in Spain where, unable to make repairs in the 24 hours allowed by international law, the boat was interned. Handed over to the British 23 Jul 1945 and sunk in Operation *Deadlight* on 13 Dec 1945
U-763	VIIC	13-Mar-43	1 Nov 1943 – 30 Sep 1944 from 8. Flottille	4 patrols. 1 ship sunk: total 1499 GRT	to 33. Flottille
U-952	VIIC	10-Dec-42	1 May 1943 – 31 Jan 1944 from 5. Flottille	5 patrols. 2 ships sunk: total 13,374 GRT; 1 warship sunk: total 940t/925 tons; 1 ship damaged: total 7176 GRT	to 29. Flottille
U-953	VIIC	17-Dec-42	1 Jun 1943 – 14 Oct 1944 from 5. Flottille	10 patrols. 1 ship sunk: total 1927 GRT	to 33. Flottille
U-957	VIIC	7-Jan-43	1 Aug 1943 – 31 Dec 1943 from 5. Flottille	6 patrols. 2 ships sunk: total 7353 GRT; 2 warships sunk: total 614t/604 tons	to 11. Flottille
U-960	VIIC	28-Jan-43	1 Aug 1943 – 19 May 1944 from 5. Flottille	5 patrols. 2 ships sunk: total 9656 GRT; 1 auxiliary warship sunk: total 611 GRT	Sunk 19 May 1944 northwest of Algiers by destroyers USS *Niblack* and USS *Ludlow* and by Wellingtons and Venturas of Nos. 36 and 500 Sqns RAF. 31 dead and 20 survivors
U-970	VIIC	25-Mar-43	1 Mar 1944 – 7 Jun 1944 from 5. Flottille	2 patrols	Sunk 7 Jun 1944 west of Bordeaux by depth charges from a Sunderland of No. 228 Sqn RAF. 38 dead and 14 survivors
U-971	VIIC	1-Apr-43	1 Jun 1944 – 24 Jun 1944	1 patrol	Sunk 24 Jun 1944 in the Channel north of Brest by depth charges from destroyers HMS *Eskimo* and HMCS *Haida* and by depth charges from a Czech Liberator of No. 311 Sqn RAF. 1 dead and 51 survivors
U-975	VIIC	29-Apr-43	1 Jan 1944 – 1 Jul 1944 from 5. Flottille	1 patrol	to 23. Flottille
U-978	VIIC	12-May-43	1 Aug 1944 – 4 Sep 1944 from 5. Flottille	2 patrols. 1 ship damaged beyond repair: total 7176 GRT	to 11. Flottille
U-992	VIIC	2-Aug-43	1 Mar 1944 – 31 May 1944 from 5. Flottille	8 patrols. 1 warship damaged beyond repair: total 1077t/1060 tons	to 11. Flottille
U-993	VIIC	19-Aug-43	1 Mar 1944 – 4 Oct 1944 from 5. Flottille	3 patrols	Destroyed at Bergen on 4 Oct 1944 during an RAF air raid. 2 crew killed
UB	British S class	30-Nov-40	May 1941 – 31 Jul 1941 from 1. Flottille	No patrols; used as trials boat	Used as a trials boat. Decommissioned 31 Jul 1941. Scuttled at Kiel 3 May 1945
UD-1	British H class	21-Nov-40	May 1941 – Aug 1941 from 1. Flottille	Trials boat	to 5. Flottille
UD-3	Dutch O 21 class	8-Jun-41	Jun 1941 – Jul 1941	Trials boat	Launched 1 May 1940 as the O 25 at Wilton Feyenoord shipyard in Schiedam. Taken over by the German Navy on 14 May 1940. Completed and commissioned 8 Jun 1941. Transferred to 5. Flottille
UD-4	Dutch O 21 class	28-Jan-41	May 1941 – Jul 1941 from 1. Flottille	Trials boat	to 5. Flottille

5 Unterseebootsflottille

The 5th U-boat Flotilla, *U-Flottille* Emsmann, was founded on 1 December 1938 under the command of one of the few experienced U-boat officers serving with the *Kriegsmarine*, *Kapitänleutnant* Hans Rudolf Rösing.

THE FLOTILLA WAS NAMED in honour of a U-boat ace of World War I, *Oberleutnant* Hans Joachim Emsmann. Emsmann commanded the boats UB-5, UB-10, UB-40 and UB-116. On 10 patrols, he sank 27 ships totalling 9369 tonnes (9221 tons). He was killed on 28 October 1918, when UB-116 struck a mine while attempting to break into the Royal Navy fleet anchorage at Scapa Flow, a feat achieved more successfully 21 years later by *Kaptänleutnant* Prien.

The *U-Flottille* Emsmann was part of the expansion of the *U-bootwaffe*'s organization which took place in the late 1930s, in accordance with the Anglo-German Naval Treaty of 1935. Since by treaty the tonnage of submarines allowed to be built was limited, the 5th Flotilla was never more than six boats strong, and the boats on strength were the smaller and less capable Type IIC coastal submarines.

Most of the boats were still in training at the outbreak of war, but they were rushed into operational service, making numerous short patrols in the North Sea and off the British coast. However, the flotilla was disbanded at the end of 1939, most of its boats being assigned to the 1st Flotilla. The 5th Flotilla was resurrected as a training unit in 1941.

Commander

Kpt. z. S. Hans Rudolf Rösing

(Dec 1938 – Dec 1939)

5TH FLOTILLA BASE LOCATION

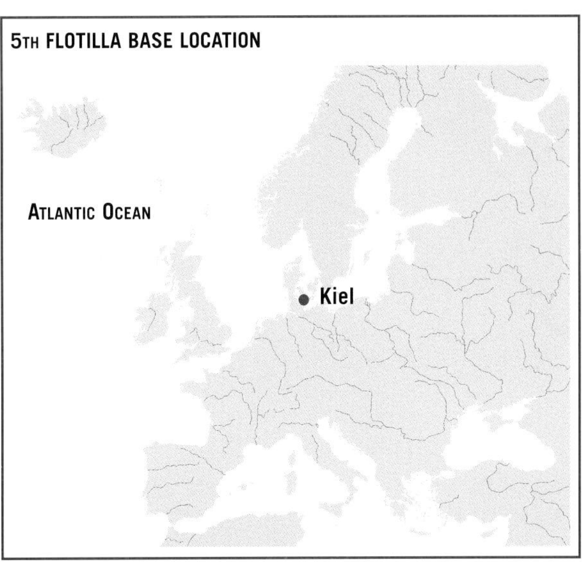

Kapitän zur See Hans Rudolf Rösing

Hans Rudolf Rösing was born on 28 September 1905 in Wilhelmshaven, and joined the interwar *Reichsmarine* in Crew 24. He commanded U-11, U-35, U-10 and U-48, sinking 12 ships totalling 60,702 GRT in just two patrols in the last-mentioned boat, for which he was awarded the Knight's Cross.

Rösing was one of a handful of German officers who secretly served aboard foreign-built submarines between the wars. This was the only way that the *Reichsmarine*, hampered by the terms of the Treaty of Versailles, could gain any submarine experience. He commissioned the Type IIB boat U-11 in September 1935. Although it was primarily a training boat, Rösing commanded a patrol to the Azores in 1937.

In 1938 he became the first and only commander of the *Flottille* Emsmann, later redesignated as the 5th Flotilla. On its disbandment he took command of the highly successful 7th Flotilla in January 1940, making two patrols in U-48.

From September 1940 to February 1941, he served as liaison officer with the Italian submarine force in Bordeaux. From March to August 1941, Rösing was commander of the 3rd Flotilla. In July 1942, he became the FdU *West*, where he was responsible for all U-boats stationed in France. After the surrender, Rösing spent more than a year as a POW. In 1956 Hans Rudolf Rösing joined the *Bundesmarine*, retiring in 1965 as *Konteradmiral*.

5TH FLOTILLA INSIGNIA

U-boat insignia varied from the overtly military through humorous to personal emblems of the commander. Many had an underwater theme, the rarely seen 5th Flotilla's insignia being a seahorse.

In 1966 he was decorated for his postwar achievements with the *Bundesverdienstkreuz* (Federal Merit Cross). Rösing died on 16 December 2004 at Kiel, aged 99.

U-59

U-59 was a Type IIC boat and was laid down on 5 October 1937 at Deutsche Werke, Kiel. It was commissioned on 4 March 1939 under the command of *Oberleutnant* Harald Jürst, who was promoted to *Kapitänleutnant* soon after. The boat was assigned to the 5th Flotilla, where it underwent combat training until the outbreak of war. The boat then became operational, mounting four patrols before being transferred to 1 Flotilla on 1 January 1940.

▲ **Type IIC conning tower**

The hatch is open on this Type IIC conning tower. The periscope housing can be seen immediately behind the open hatch. The commander would have stood at the front-right of the tower, next to the voice tube.

U-59 Commanders

Kptlt. Harald Jürst *(Mar 1939 – Jul 1940)*
Joachim Matz *(Jul 1940 – Nov 1940)*
Kptlt. Baron Siegfried von Forstner *(Nov 1940 – Apr 1941)*
Oblt. Günter Gretschel *(Apr 1941 – Dec 1941)*
Oblt. Günter Poser *(Dec 1941 — Jul 1942)*
Oblt. Karl-Heinz Sammler *(Jul 1942 – Jun 1943)*
Oblt. Hans-Jürgen Schley *(Jun 1943 – Jun 1944)*
Ltn. Herbert Walther *(Jul 1944 – Apr 1945)*

At the outbreak of war, U-59 was part of a patrol line southwest of Norway. On its second patrol, the boat sank two fishing boats and an anti-submarine trawler off the Orkney Islands. The third patrol saw U-59 laying mines in shallow waters off Great Yarmouth, Norfolk. The mines sank a minesweeper and a small coastal vessel. On her last patrol with 5th Flotilla, in December 1939, U-59 sank three vessels totalling more than 4000 GRT. The boat returned to Kiel, where she bacame part of the 1st Flotilla, the 5th Flotilla having been disbanded.

U-59 continued to serve as a combat boat to the end of 1940. Under the command of Joachim Matz and Baron Siegfried von Forstner, the boat made a further nine patrols, the combined totals of its successes with the 5th and 1st Flotillas reaching 16 ships sunk for a total of 29,514 GRT, along with two auxiliary warships sunk, and two ships totalling nearly 13,000 GRT damaged.

School boat

In January 1941, as most of the Type II boats were withdrawn from general combat roles, U-59 was transferred to the 22nd Flotilla at Gotenhafen in the Baltic, becoming a school boat where new U-boat crewmen received initial training. It was transferred to the 19th Flotilla in July 1944. U-59 was finally scuttled in the Kiel Arsenal on 3 May 1945.

BOATS THAT SERVED WITH 5TH FLOTILLA (7 BOATS)

U-Boat	Type	Commissioned	Flotilla(s)	Patrols	Fate
U-56	IIC	26-Nov-38	26 Nov 1938 – 31 Dec 1939 (training and combat)	12 patrols. 3 ships sunk: total 8860 GRT; 1 auxiliary warship sunk: total 16,923 GRT; 1 ship damaged: total 3829 GRT	to 1. Flottille
U-57	IIC	29-Dec-38	29 Dec 1938 – 31 Dec 1939 (training and combat)	11 patrols. 11 ships sunk: total 48,053 GRT; 1 auxiliary warship sunk: total 8240 GRT; 1 ship damaged beyond repair: total 10,191 GRT; 2 ships damaged: total 10,403 GRT	to 1. Flottille
U-58	IIC	4-Feb-39	4 Feb – 31 Dec 1939 (training and combat)	12 patrols. 6 ships sunk: total 16,148 GRT; 1 auxiliary warship sunk: total 8401 GRT	to 1. Flottille
U-59	IIC	4-Mar-39	4 Mar – 31 Dec 1939 (training and combat)	13 patrols. 16 ships sunk: total 29,514 GRT; 2 auxiliary warships sunk: total 864 GRT; 1 ship damaged beyond repair: total 4943 GRT; 1 ship damaged: total 8009 GRT	to 1. Flottille
U-60	IIC	22-Jul-39	22 Jul – 31 Dec 1939 (training)	9 patrols. 3 ships sunk: total 7561 GRT; 1 ship damaged: total 15,434 GRT	to 1. Flottille
U-61	IIC	12-Aug-39	12 Aug – 31 Dec 1939 (training)	10 patrols. 5 ships sunk: total 19,668 GRT; 1 ship damaged: total 4434 GRT	to 1. Flottille
U-62	IIC	21-Dec-39	21 – 31 Dec 1939 (training)	5 patrols. 1 ship sunk: total 4581 GRT; 1 warship sunk: total 1372t/1350 tons	to 1. Flottille

6 Unterseebootsflottille

The 6th U-boat Flotilla, *U-Flottille* Hundius, was founded at Kiel on 1 October 1938 under the command of Korvkpt. Werner Hartmann. The first dedicated long-range flotilla, it was equipped with early examples of the new, large Type IX boats then entering service.

THE NEW FLOTILLA WAS named in commemoration of *Kapitänleutnant* Paul Hundius, who in World War I commanded UB-16, UC-47 and UB-103. On 20 patrols, he sank 67 ships totalling 96,809 tonnes (95,280 tons). He was killed on 16 September 1918, when his boat was sunk by depth charges.

German prewar planning called for a balanced force of U-boats, comprising small Type IIs, medium Type VIIs and large Type IX boats. The Type IXs began to commission in 1938 and 1939, and were assigned to the newly formed *U-Flottille* Hundius.

At around 1016 tonnes (1000 tons), the Type IX had been built as a result of a *Kriegsmarine* study of potential operations against the two major potential enemies, Britain and France. The Type IX design was developed to enable German interdiction of sea lines of communication in the Mediterranean, along the Atlantic coast and as far south as West Africa.

6TH FLOTILLA BASE LOCATIONS

Commanders

Korvkpt. Werner Hartmann *(Oct 1938 – Dec 1939)*
Korvkpt. Wilhelm Schulz *(Aug 1941 – Jan 1942)*
Korvkpt. Carl Emmermann *(Nov 1943 – Aug 1944)*

Operations

The Type IX boats of the *U-Flottille* Hundius quickly completed their training and moved to Wilhelmshaven for operations on the outbreak of war. Three of the eight boats were lost before the flotilla was disbanded in December 1939. U-39 was depth-charged and sunk on 14 September, northwest of Ireland. All 44 crew survived the first U-boat loss of the war. U-40 was sunk by mines on 13 October, with only three of the 48 crew being picked up. U-42 was sunk on the same day, southwest of Ireland, by depth charges from the destroyers HMS *Imogen* and HMS *Ilex*. Twenty of the 46 crew survived.

6TH FLOTILLA INSIGNIA

Originally carried by Otto von Bülow's U-404, the 6th Flotilla emblem was a U-boat silhouette over a stylized Viking ship prow. It may have also been used by the 23rd Flotilla under von Bülow's command.

6TH FLOTILLA (1939 AND 1941–44)

Type	Boats assigned
Type IXA	8
Type VIIB	1
Type VIIC	81
Type VIIC/41	1

Rebirth of the flotilla

The flotilla was refounded as the 6th Flotilla in July 1941 at Danzig. During the first months of its existence, its crews were under training in the Baltic, but in February 1942 the flotilla was moved as a combat-capable unit to St Nazaire in France. Since it was primarily tasked with Atlantic operations, it was largely equipped with Type VIIC boats.

The approach of Allied armies after the invasion of Normandy meant that the Atlantic bases had to be abandoned. Surviving 6th Flotilla boats were transferred to Norway in August 1944 and the unit was disbanded.

Star commanders

1941–45

The first incarnation of the 6th Flotilla did not last long enough for any ace commanders to emerge, but from 1941 the reformed flotilla was in action in the hotbed of the North Atlantic.

Korvettenkapitän Carl Emmermann

Carl Emmermann was born on 6 March 1915 in Hamburg. He joined the Navy with Crew 34. For some years he was training officer at the *Marineschule* Mürwik, but with the outbreak of war he transferred to the U-boat arm. In November 1940 he served aboard U-A, a large boat being built for Turkey but taken over by the *Kriegsmarine* in 1939.

In November 1941 Emmermann's first command was the Type IXC boat U-172. He completed five patrols – in the Caribbean, with the wolfpack *Eisbär* in South African waters, and in the North and South Atlantic. He sank 26 ships totalling 152,778 GRT. On his fifth and last patrol, he rescued half the crew of U-604, which had been scuttled after air attacks. He became commander of the 6th Flotilla in November 1943, before going on to head the test unit for the new Type XXIII boat. He ended the war in command of a naval infantry battalion in Hamburg. Emmermann survived the war and died in March 1990.

Korvettenkapitän Otto von Bülow

Otto von Bülow was born on 16 October 1911 in Wilhelmshaven. He joined the *Reichsmarine* with Crew 30. After initial service aboard a pre-dreadnought and a pocket battleship, he transferred to U-boats in April 1940. After gaining command experience with the training boat U-9, he commissioned U-404 in August 1941.

In five patrols Bülow sank 14 ships of 71,450 GRT as well as the Royal Navy destroyer HMS *Veteran.* He attacked the escort carrier HMS *Biter*, thinking it was the USS *Ranger*, and claimed it sunk after hearing four explosions. In the event all four were premature detonations. Even so, he was awarded the Knight's Cross with Oak Leaves. Bülow then commanded a training flotilla and one of the new Type XXI boats.

After the war, he joined the *Bundesmarine*, eventually commanding a destroyer squadron. Otto von Bülow died on 5 January 2006, aged 94.

STAR COMMANDERS

Commander	Patrols	Ships Sunk
Korvettenkapitän Carl Emmermann	5	26
Korvettenkapitän Otto von Bülow	5	15

ARMOURED GAUNTLET EMBLEM

This armoured gauntlet emblem probably refers to the 15th-century knight Götz von Berlichingen, who lost his hand in combat and had an iron fist attached in its place. U-586 and U-2527 used the insignia.

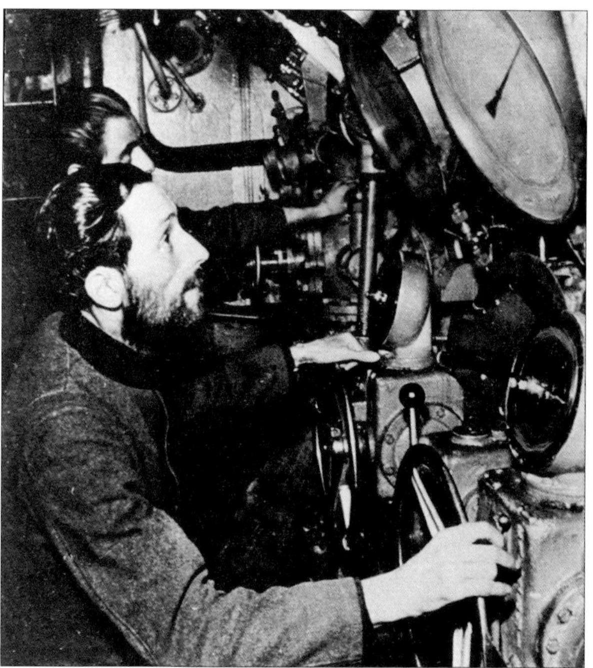

▲ **Keeping watch**

Crew at their stations monitor instumentation. Conditions in the U-boats were cramped and uncomfortable, ranging from stuffy tropical humidity to freezing Arctic temperatures, depending on the location of the boat.

U-37

Type IX

U-37's long career saw the boat become the second highest scoring U-boat of the war in terms of numbers of vessels sunk.

The boat was built at Germania Werft in Kiel. It was laid down in March 1937 and entered service in August 1938, the first Type IX to be commissioned. It served with the *U-Flottille* Hundius for the first months of the war, before the long-range boats were transferred to the 2nd Flotilla and the Hundius Flotilla was disbanded.

One of the most successful submarines in history, U-37 made 11 patrols under four commanders in two years, sinking 53 merchant ships totalling 200,000 GRT. On its second patrol, U-37 carried the tactical commander in the first attempt to mount a controlled, coordinated wolfpack operation. On its third patrol, U-37 landed two agents on the Irish coast in Donegal.

U-37 was removed from active service in May 1941, becoming a training boat in the Baltic for the rest of the war. It was scuttled on 8 May 1945 in Sonderburg Bay.

U-37 Commanders

Kptlt. Heinrich Schuch *(Aug 1938 – Sep 1939)*
Korvkpt. Werner Hartmann *(Sep 1939 – May 1940)*
Kptlt. Victor Oehrn *(May 1940 – Oct 1940)*
Kptlt. Asmus Nicolai Clausen *(Oct 1940 – May 1941)*
Kptlt. Ulrich Folkers *(May 1941 – Nov 1941)*
Kptlt. Gustav Janssen *(Nov 1941 – Jun 1942)*
Kptlt. Albert Lauzemis *(Jul 1942 – Jan 1943)*
Kptlt. Hinrich Kelling *(Jan 1943 – Nov 1943)*
Oblt. Peter Gerlach *(Nov 1943 – Jan 1944)*
Oblt. Wolfgang Seiler *(Jan 1944 – Dec 1944)*
Kptlt. Eberhard von Wenden *(Dec 1944 – May 1945)*

Specifications

Crew: 48–55
Powerplant: Diesel/electric
Max Speed: 33.7/14.3km/hr (18.2/7.7kt) s/d
Surface Range: 15,000km (8100nm)
Displacement: 1049/1172t (1032/1153 tons) s/d
Dimensions (length/beam/draught): 76.5 x 6.5 x 4.7m (251 x 21.33 x 15.42ft)
Commissioned: 4 Aug 1938
Armament: 22 torpedoes (4 bow/2 stern tubes); 1 x 10.5cm (4.1in), 1 x 3.7cm (1.5in) and 1 x 2cm (0.8in) guns

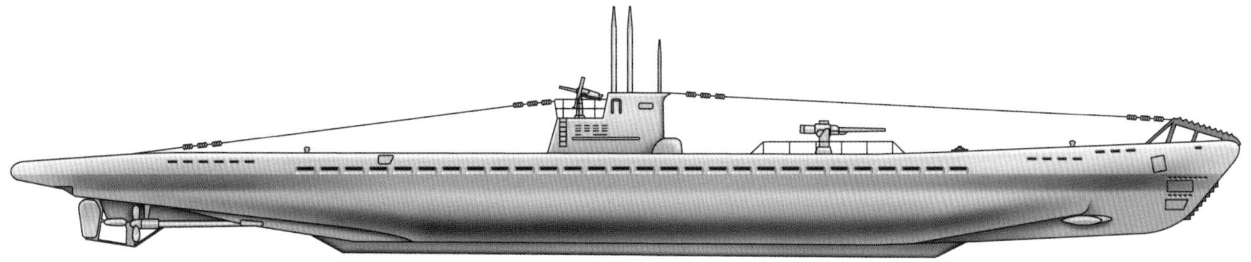

▲ **U-37**

Type IX

Although the Type IX was designed as a long-range boat, early examples like U-37 did not have the reach of later variants. Even so, the boat was highly successful in the Atlantic. On her fifth patrol, under the command of Kptlt. Victor Oehrn, U-37 sank 10 ships totalling more than 40,000 tonnes (39,368 tons), eight of them in the space of just seven days.

U-37 TIMETABLE

Patrol Dates	Operational Area	Ships Sunk
19 Aug 1939 – 15 Sep 1939	W of the Iberian Peninsula	0
5 Oct 1939 – 8 Nov 1939	Central Atlantic	8
28 Jan 1940 – 27 Feb 1940	SW of Ireland	8
30 Mar 1940 – 18 Apr 1940	Escorting raider Faroes/Shetlands	3
15 May 1940 – 9 Jun 1940	NW of Cape Finisterre	10
1 Aug 1940 – 12 Aug 1940	Transit from Wilhemshaven to Lorient	1
17 Aug 1940 – 30 Aug 1940	W of the British Isles	6
24 Sep 1940 – 22 Oct 1940	W of the British Isles	6
28 Nov 1940 – 7 Jan 1941	W of Spain/W of Africa	6
30 Jan 1941 – 18 Feb 1941	Central Atlantic off Freetown	3
27 Feb 1941 – 22 Mar 1941	North Atlantic	2

U-87

TYPE VIIB

Built by Flenderwerft at Lübeck, U-87 was commissioned into the 6th Flotilla in August 1941, and after a period of training with the flotilla went on her first patrol in December of that year.

U-87'S FIVE patrols accounted for five ships totalling 38,014 GRT. Early in 1942, Hitler feared an Allied landing in Norway, and ordered Dönitz to divert boats from the Atlantic. U-87 was one of the boats used to set up a patrol line west of the Faroes. She was sunk with all hands on 4 March 1943, west of Oporto, by depth charges from HMCS *Shediac* and HMCS *St. Croix*.

U-87 TIMETABLE

Patrol Dates	Operational Area	Ships Sunk
24 Dec 1941 – 30 Jan 1942	Transit from Kiel to La Pallice	2
22 Feb 1942 – 27 Mar 1942	Norwegian Sea	0
19 May 1942 – 8 Jul 1942	Minelaying and patrol off Boston	2
31 Aug 1942 – 20 Nov 1942	N of Cape Verde Islands	1
9 Jan 1943 – 4 Mar 1943	Azores/Canaries	0

U-87 Commander

Kptlt. Joachim Berger *(Aug 1941 – Mar 1943)*

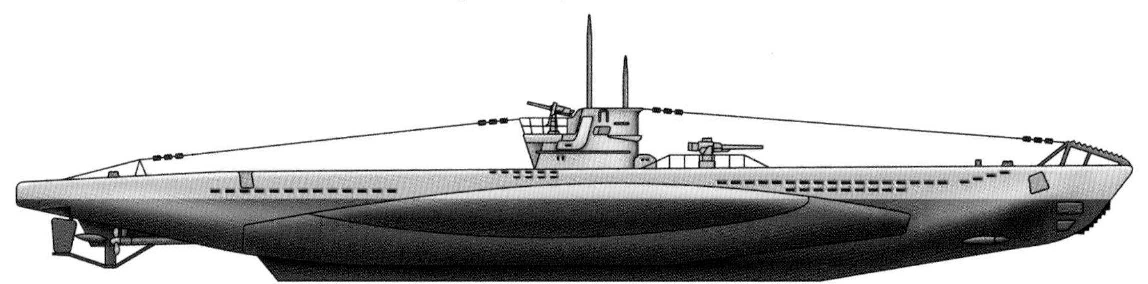

Specifications

Crew: 44
Powerplant: Diesel/electric
Max Speed: 31.9/14.8km/hr (17.2/8kt) s/d
Surface Range: 12,040km (6500nm)
Displacement: 765/871t (753/857 tons) s/d
Dimensions (length/beam/draught): 66.5 x 6.2 x 4.7m (218.1 x 20.34 x 15.4ft)
Commissioned: 19 Aug 1941
Armament: 14 torpedoes (4 bow/1 stern tubes); 1 x 8.8cm (3.5in) and 1 x 2cm (0.8in) guns

▲ **U-87**

Type VIIB

U-87 entered service with the kind of armament typical of Type VII boats before the rise of Allied air power forced a change. The main gun was an 8.8cm (3.5in) artillery piece, with a 2cm (0.8in) AA gun mounted on the conning tower.

U-404

TYPE VIIC

Commanded by Otto von Bülow, U-404 was commissioned in August 1941 and became operational in December, in time to take part in U-boat operations against the United States.

U-404'S FIRST PATROL was as part of the *Schlei* wolfpack operating west of Rockall, but the boats were ordered home early to prepare for operations off the US east coast.

On its second patrol, the boat initially operated off the Canadian coast before moving south to operate off New Jersey. The inexperienced crew did well, sinking four ships, although one was actually a

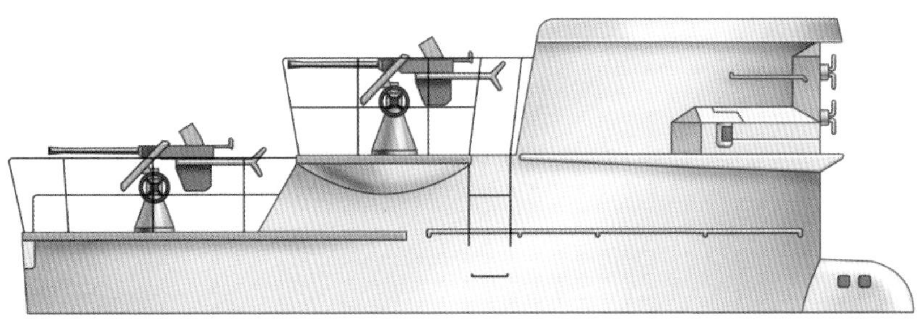

◀ Type VIIC 'winter garden' conning tower

Adding extra anti-aircraft guns meant increasing the size of the turret of the Type VIIC. Bridge Conversion II saw the addition of a 'winter garden' platform abaft the conning tower. The unreliable 2cm (0.8in) C/30 guns were replaced by improved C/38 weapons, based on an Army Flak gun.

U-404 TIMETABLE

Patrol Dates	Operational Area	Ships Sunk
17 Jan 1942 – 1 Feb 1942	Transit from Kiel to St Nazaire	0
14 Feb 1942 – 4 Apr 1942	Central Atlantic/US coast	4
6 May 1942 – 14 Jul 1942	US Atlantic coast/Bermuda	6 + 1 destroyer
23 Aug 1942 – 13 Oct 1942	W of Ireland/off Newfoundland	1
21 Dec 1942 – 6 Feb 1943	N Atlantic	0
21 Mar 1943 – 3 May 1943	S of Greenland	3
24 Jul 1943 – 28 Jul 1943	Transit through Biscay	0

U-404 Commander

Korvkpt. Otto von Bülow *(Aug 1941 – Jul 1943)* Oblt. Adolf Schönberg *(Jul 1943 – Jul 1943)*

Chilean neutral and should not have been attacked. The next patrol, off New York, initially offered no targets, but when the boat moved south to Bermuda she sank seven vessels.

On 25 April 1943, on her sixth patrol, U-404 fired four torpedoes at a carrier identified as the USS *Ranger*. Hearing four explosions, Korvpt. Otto von Bülow claimed to have sunk the ship.

However, the target was actually the escort carrier HMS *Biter*. The explosions were a consequence of premature detonations and caused no damage.

Nevertheless, the Supreme Command of the Armed Forces announced the sinking, and von Bülow was awarded Oak Leaves to the Knight's Cross. The *Führer der Unterseeboote* was not as certain, and later disallowed the claim.

Fate

U-404 was sunk with all hands on 28 July 1943 in the Bay of Biscay northwest of Cape Ortegal by depth charges from two USAAF B-24s of the 4th A/S Sqn and from a Liberator of No. 224 Sqn RAF. All 51 crew were killed in the attack.

Specifications

Crew: 44
Powerplant: Diesel/electric
Max Speed: 31.5/14.1km/hr (17/7.6kt) s/d
Surface Range: 12,040km (6500nm)
Displacement: 773/879t (761/865 tons) s/d
Dimensions (length/beam/draught): 67.1 x 6.2 x 4.8m (220.1 x 20.34 x 15.75ft)
Commissioned: 6 Feb 1941
Armament: 14 torpedoes (4 bow/1 stern tubes); 1 x 2cm (0.8in) quad and 2 x 2cm (0.8in) guns

▲ U-404

Type VIIC

By 1942, the threat posed by Allied convoy escorts and aircraft meant that U-boats rarely had a chance to use their main gun, and heavier AA protection was necessary. Soon the big gun would be removed in favour of more AA guns.

U-757

Type VIIC

Laid down at the *Kriegsmarine-Werft* in Wilhelmshaven, U-757 was commissioned in February 1942 and after operational training with the 6th Flotilla was ready for combat in September.

Like most boats that entered service in the later stages of the war, U-757 had little chance of running up the huge scores typical of earlier years. In five patrols, she sank only two ships. On her third patrol, U-757 was damaged when the ammunition ship she had just torpedoed, exploded. On her fourth patrol, an explosion aboard the boat forced her early return. On 8 January 1944 in the North Atlantic southwest of Ireland, on her fifth patrol, U-757 was sunk with all hands by depth charges from the frigate HMS *Bayntun* and the corvette HMCS *Camrose*. All 49 crew were killed.

U-757 Commander

Korvkpt. Friedrich Deetz *(Feb 1942 – Jan 1944)*

Specifications

Crew: 44

Powerplant: Diesel/electric

Max Speed: 31.5/14.1km/hr (17/7.6kt) s/d

Surface Range: 12,040km (6500nm)

Displacement: 773/879t (761/865 tons) s/d

Dimensions (length/beam/draught): 67.1 x 6.2 x 4.8m (220.1 x 20.34 x 15.75ft)

Commissioned: 6 Feb 1941

Armament: 14 torpedoes (4 bow/1 stern tubes); 1 x 8.8cm (3.5in) quad and 2 x 2cm (0.8in) guns

▲ **U-757**

Type VIIC

U-757 spent most of its operational career in the central Atlantic, mounting patrols from the waters west of Ireland to as far south as the Azores. Late in 1943, the boat had to abandon four patrols because of mechanical faults.

Convoy ON 127

9 September 1942

ON 127 was a westbound convoy travelling across the North Atlantic from Britain to Canada. It consisted of 32 merchant ships, protected by an inexperienced Canadian escort group.

ON 127 was escorted by the Canadian Escort Group C4, which comprised the destroyers HMCS *St. Croix* and HMCS *Ottawa* and the corvettes HMCS *Amherst*, HMCS *Arvida*, HMCS *Sherbrooke* and the British corvette HMS *Celandine.*

The attack on ON 127 achieved considerable success at very little cost to the U-boat force. Unusually, every boat involved in the operation actually used their weapons in the battle – all too often, many of the boats deployed in such an attack never made contact with a target. The Germans were helped by the poor tactics used by the Canadian escorts. Lacking radar and the latest direction-finding equipment, the escorts made extensive use of

'Snowflake' illuminating rockets. However, instead of lighting up the U-boats on the surface, all the pyrotechnics achieved was to ruin the night vision of the Allied lookouts while at the same time letting every U-boat within miles know the exact location of their targets. Attacked by the *Vorwarts* wolfpack, the convoy lost seven ships plus the destroyer HMCS *Ottawa,* and several merchantmen were damaged.

CONVOY ON 127 BATTLE TIMETABLE

Date	Event
9 Sep	Convoy is sighted by U-584. U-Boat command orders wolfpack *Vorwarts* to concentrate and attack. Group *Vorwarts* was made up of 12 boats – U-91, U-92, U-96, U-211, U-218, U-380, U-404, U-407, U-411, U-584, U-594 and U-608
10 Sep	U-584 loses contact during the night, but it is regained at about noon when U-96 sights the merchantmen and their escorts. U-96 makes a submerged daylight attack, sinking 2 ships and damaging a tanker. As the other *Vorwarts* group boats arrive through the night, they mount a series of attacks. U-659 damages a tanker. U-608, attacking about the same time, does not score any hits
11 Sep	U-404 and U-218 each damage a tanker, while U-92 and U-594 mount unsuccessful attacks. U-584 finishes off the tanker previously hit by U-659. During the day, U-96 uses its gun to sink a Portuguese trawler that had lost contact with the convoy
12 Sep	The wolfpack continues to press home its attacks through the night of 11/12 September. U-380 makes an unsuccessful attack while U-404 damages a tanker. U-92 takes a shot at the escorting destroyer *Ottawa* but misses. U-584 sinks a ship, while U-211 damages 2 more. Both are finished off by U-608. The escorts have little success against the wolfpack, only U-659 sustaining any damage, which is not serious enough to stop the boat returning to its French base
13 Sep	As the night of 12/13 September closes in, the U-boats again press home their attacks, but only U-407 and U-594 make contact with the main body of the convoy and both fail to hit any targets. U-594 sinks a straggler as daylight breaks, and U-91 sinks the destroyer *Ottawa*. U-411 launches a torpedo at one of the corvettes but misses, and U-92 loses contact with the convoy. The U-boats now break off the attack: during the night the escort has been reinforced by the British destroyer HMS *Witch* and the American destroyer USS *Annapolis*, and the convoy has now come within range of aircraft based in Newfoundland

Wolfpacks *Falke, Habicht* & *Haudegen*

JANUARY 1943

There is a perception that the *Kriegsmarine*'s U-boat wolfpacks were fearsome hunters of the deep, homing in on every merchantman crossing the Atlantic in convoy and sinking Allied vessels at will.

This was far from the case, as the boats in the large *Falke* and *Habicht* groups discovered in the winter of 1942/43, when the Battle of the Atlantic approached its climax.

The *Falke* and *Habicht* groups were formed to the west of Ireland at the end of 1942. With 29 boats available, the two groups could have wreaked considerable destruction on even the most heavily defended convoy.

However, Ultra codebreakers and high-frequency direction-finding equipment meant that the Allies knew almost as much about U-boat deployments as did their commanders in France, and convoys were routed around known U-boat concentrations.

Missed contact

Nothing having crossed the U-boat patrol line, both groups were ordered westwards in an attempt to intercept eastbound ON convoys. The boats were combined into a new group, known as *Haudegen,* which covered almost 480km (300 miles) of sea southeast of Cape Farewell, Greenland. Several convoys were sighted by independent boats, and small groups of *Haudegen* boats were detached to try to intercept Convoys SG 19, HX 223 and SC 118. In spite of the large force of U-boats deployed, none were able to make contact with any of the convoys, in part because of Allied evasion tactics, but also due to the atrocious weather experienced in the North Atlantic in January.

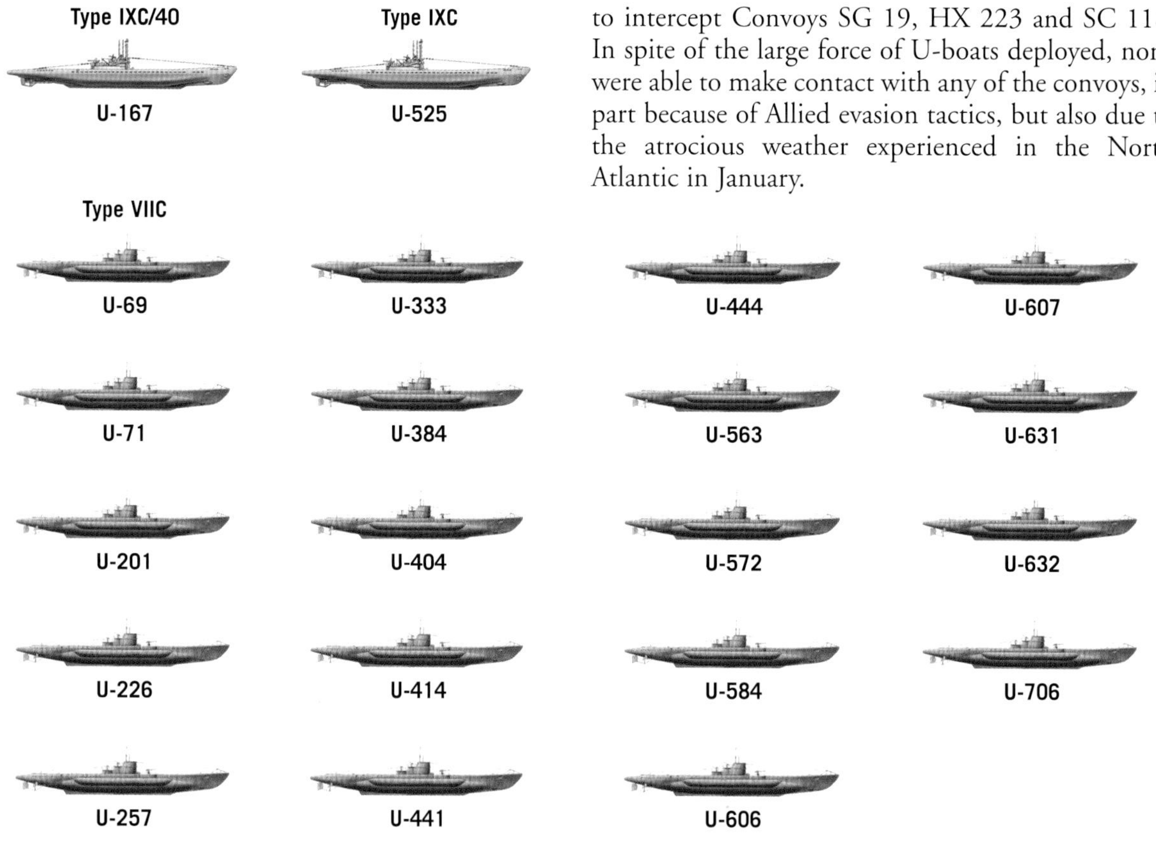

BOATS THAT SERVED WITH 6TH FLOTILLA (91 BOATS)

U-Boat	Type	Commissioned	Flotilla(s)	Patrols	Fate
U-37	IX	4-Aug-38	1 Apr 1938 – 31 Dec 1939	11 patrols. 53 ships sunk: total 200,125 GRT; 2 warships sunk: total 2443t/2404 tons; 1 ship damaged: total 9494 GRT. Second highest scoring U-boat in terms of numbers of vessels sunk	to 2. Flottille
U-38	IX	24-Oct-38	24 Oct 1938 – 31 Dec 1939	11 patrols. 35 ships sunk: total 188,967 GRT; 1 ship damaged: total 3670 GRT	to 2. Flottille
U-39	IX	10-Dec-38	10 Dec 1938 – 14 Sep 1939	1 patrol	Depth-charged and sunk 14 Sept 1939 northwest of Ireland by the destroyers HMS *Faulknor*, HMS *Foxhound* and HMS *Firedrake*. No casualties – 44 survivors. First U-boat sunk in the war
U-40	IX	11-Feb-39	11 Feb 1939 – 13 Oct 1939	2 patrols	Sunk by mines 13 Oct 1939 in the English Channel. 45 dead and 3 survivors
U-41	IX	22-Apr-39	22 Apr 1939 – 31 Dec 1939	3 patrols. 7 ships sunk: total 24,888 GRT; 1 ship damaged: total 8096 GRT	to 2. Flottille
U-42	IX	15-Jul-39	15 Jul 1939 – 13 Oct 1939	1 patrol. 1 ship damaged: total 4803 GRT	Sunk 13 Oct 1939 southwest of Ireland by depth charges from the destroyers HMS *Imogen* and HMS *Ilex*. 26 dead and 20 survivors
U-43	IX	26-Aug-39	26 Aug 1939 – 31 Dec 1939	14 patrols. 21 ships sunk: total 117,036 GRT; 1 ship a total loss: total 9131 GRT; 1 ship damaged: total 10,350 GRT	to 2. Flottille
U-44	IX	4-Nov-39	4 Nov 1939 – 31 Dec 1939	2 patrols. 8 ships sunk: total 30,885 GRT	to 2. Flottille
U-87	VIIB	19-Aug-41	19 Aug 1941 – 4 Mar 1943	5 patrols. 5 ships sunk: total 38,014 GRT	Sunk with all hands 4 Mar 1943 west of Oporto by depth charges from the Canadian warships HMCS *Shediac* and HMCS *St. Croix*. 49 dead
U-136	VIIC	30-Aug-41	30 Aug 1941 – 11 Jul 1942	3 patrols. 5 ships sunk: total 23,649 GRT; 2 warships sunk: total 1880t/1850 tons; 1 ship damaged: total 8955 GRT	Sunk with all hands 11 Jul 1942 in Atlantic west of Madeira by the Free French destroyer *Léopard*, the frigate HMS *Spey* and the sloop HMS *Pelican*. 45 dead
U-209	VIIC	11-Oct-41	11 Oct 1941 – 30 Jun 1942	7 patrols. 4 ships sunk: total 1356 GRT	to 11. Flottille
U-223	VIIC	6-Jun-42	1 Feb 1943 – 31 Oct 1943 from 8. Flottille (training)	6 patrols. 2 ships sunk: total 12,556 GRT; 1 warship sunk: total 1966t/1935 tons; 1 ship damaged beyond repair: total 4970 GRT; 1 warship damaged beyond repair: total 1321t/1300 tons	to 29. Flottille

BOATS THAT SERVED WITH 6TH FLOTILLA (91 BOATS)					
U-Boat	**Type**	**Commissioned**	**Flotilla(s)**	**Patrols**	**Fate**
U-226	VIIC	1-Aug-42	1 Jan 1943 – 6 Nov 1943 from 5. Flottille (training)	3 patrols. 1 ship sunk: total 7134 GRT	Sunk with all hands 6 Nov 1943 in the North Atlantic east of Newfoundland by depth charges from the British sloops HMS *Starling*, HMS *Woodcock* and HMS *Kite*. 51 dead
U-228	VIIC	12-Sep-42	1 Mar 1943 – 5 Oct 1944 from 5. Flottille (training)	6 patrols	Stricken at Bergen, Norway, 5 Oct 1944 and broken up
U-229	VIIC	3-Oct-42	1 Mar 1943 – 22 Sep 1943 from 5. Flottille (training)	3 patrols. 2 ships sunk: total 8352 GRT; 1 ship damaged: total 3670 GRT	Sunk with all hands 22 Sep 1943 in the North Atlantic southeast of Cape Farewell, Greenland, by the destroyer HMS *Keppel*. 50 dead
U-251	VIIC	20-Sep-41	20 Sep 1941 – 30 Jun 1942	9 patrols. 2 ships sunk: total 11,408 GRT	to 11. Flottille
U-252	VIIC	4-Oct-41	4 Oct 1941 – 14 Apr 1942	1 patrol. 1 ship sunk: total 1355 GRT. A spy was landed on Iceland on this boat's only patrol	Sunk with all hands 14 Apr 1942 southwest of Ireland by depth charges from the sloop HMS *Stork* and the corvette HMS *Vetch*. 44 dead
U-253	VIIC	21-Oct-41	1 Sep 1942 – 25 Sep 1942 from 8. Flottille	1 patrol	Sunk with all hands 25 Sep 1942 northwest of Iceland, probably by a British mine. 45 dead. Previously credited to a British Catalina, but that was probably an ineffective attack against U-255
U-260	VIIC	14-Mar-42	1 Oct 1942 – 31 Oct 1944 from 8. Flottille (training)	9 patrols. 1 ship sunk: total 4893 GRT	to 33. Flottille
U-261	VIIC	28-Mar-42	1 Sep 1942 – 15 Sep 1942	1 patrol	Sunk with all hands 15 Sep 1942 west of the Shetlands by depth charges from an Armstrong-Whitworth Whitley of No. 58 Sqn RAF. 43 dead
U-264	VIIC	22-May-42	1 Nov 1942 – 19 Feb 1944	5 patrols. 3 ships sunk: total 16,843 GRT	Sunk 19 Feb 1944 in the North Atlantic by depth charges from the sloops HMS *Woodpecker* and HMS *Starling*. No casualties – 52 survivors
U-269	VIIC	19-Aug-42	1 Nov 1943 – 25 Jun 1944 from 11. Flottille	5 patrols	Sunk 25 Jun 1944 in the Channel southeast of Torquay by depth charges from the frigate HMS *Bickerton*. 13 dead and 39 survivors
U-270	VIIC	5-Sep-42	1 Apr 1943 – 13 Aug 1944	6 patrols. 1 warship damaged beyond repair: total 1392t/1370 tons	Stricken 1 Jul 1944 after extensive damage from British Wellington and Fortress aircraft. Recommissioned early Aug. Sunk on 13 Aug 1944 in the Bay of Biscay west of La Rochelle by depth charges from an Australian Sunderland of No. 461 Sqn RAAF. No casualties – 71 survivors
U-277	VIIC	21-Dec-42	1 Jun 1943 – 31 Oct 1943 from 8. Flottille	5 patrols	to 13. Flottille
U-290	VIIC	24-Jul-43	1 May 1944 – 31 Jul 1944 from 8. Flottille	3 patrols	to 11. Flottille
U-308	VIIC	23-Dec-42	1 Jun 1943 – 4 Jun 1943 from 8. Flottille	1 patrol	Sunk with all hands 4 Jun 1943 northeast of the Faroes, torpedoed by the submarine HMS *Truculent*. 44 dead
U-312	VIIC	21-Apr-43	1 Dec 1943 – 31 Dec 1943 from 8. Flottille	12 patrols	to 11. Flottille
U-335	VIIC	17-Dec-41	1 Aug 1942 – 3 Aug 1942 from 8. Flottille	1 patrol	Sunk 3 Aug 1942 northeast of the Faroes, torpedoed by the submarine HMS *Saracen*. 43 dead and 1 survivor
U-337	VIIC	6-May-42	1 Jan 1943 – 3 Jan 1943 from 5. Flottille	1 patrol	Missing with all hands in the North Atlantic on or after 3 Jan 1943. 47 dead. Previously listed as sunk 15 Jan 1943 by depth charges from a Flying Fortress of No. 206 Sqn RAF. That attack was against U-632, which escaped without damage
U-340	VIIC	16-Oct-42	1 May 1943 – 2 Nov 1943 from 8. Flottille	3 patrols	Sunk 2 Nov 1943 near Tangier by depth charges from the sloop HMS *Fleetwood*, the destroyers HMS *Active* and HMS *Witherington* and a Wellington of No. 179 Sqn RAF. 1 dead and 48 survivors
U-356	VIIC	20-Dec-41	20 Dec 1941 – 27 Dec 1942	2 patrols. 3 ships sunk: total 13,649 GRT; 1 ship damaged: total 7051 GRT	Sunk with all hands 27 Dec 1942 north of the Azores by depth charges from the destroyer HMCS *St. Laurent* and corvettes HMCS *Chilliwack*, HMCS *Battleford* and HMCS *Napanee*. 46 dead
U-357	VIIC	18-Jun-42	1 Dec 1942 – 26 Dec 1942 from 8. Flottille	1 patrol	Sunk 26 Dec 1942 northwest of Ireland by depth charges from the destroyers HMS *Hesperus* and HMS *Vanessa*. 36 dead and 6 survivors
U-376	VIIC	21-Aug-41	21 Aug 1941 – 30 Jun 1942	8 patrols. 2 ships sunk: total 10,146 GRT	to 11. Flottille
U-377	VIIC	2-Oct-41	2 Oct 1941 – 30 Jun 1942	12 patrols	to 11. Flottille
U-380	VIIC	22-Dec-41	1 Sep 1942 – 30 Nov 1942 from 5. Flottille	12 patrols. 2 ships sunk: total 14,063 GRT; 1 ship damaged beyond repair: total 7178 GRT; 1 ship damaged: total 7191 GRT	to 29. Flottille
U-385	VIIC	29-Aug-42	1 Mar 1944 – 11 Aug 1944 from 5. Flottille	3 patrols	Sunk 11 Aug 1944 in the Bay of Biscay west of La Rochelle by depth charges from the sloop HMS *Starling* and from an Australian Sunderland of No. 461 Sqn. 1 dead and 42 survivors
U-386	VIIC	10-Oct-42	1 May 1943 – 19 Feb 1944	4 patrols. 1 ship sunk: total 1997 GRT	Sunk 19 Feb 1944 in the North Atlantic by depth charges from the frigate HMS *Spey*. 33 dead and 16 survivors
U-404	VIIC	6-Aug-41	6 Aug 1941 – 28 Jul 1943	7 patrols. 14 ships sunk: total 71,450 GRT; 1 warship sunk: total 1138t/1120 tons; 2 ships damaged: total 16,689 GRT	Sunk with all hands 28 Jul 1943 in Biscay northwest of Cape Ortegal by depth charges from 2 USAAF B-24s of the 4th A/S Sqn and from a Liberator of No. 224 Sqn RAF. 51 dead
U-405	VIIC	17-Sep-41	1 Mar 1943 – 1 Nov 1943 from 11. Flottille	11 patrols. 2 ships sunk: total 11,841 GRT	Sunk with all hands 1 Nov 1943 in the North Atlantic by ramming, small-arms fire and depth charges from the destroyer USS *Borie*. 49 dead

BOATS THAT SERVED WITH 6TH FLOTILLA (91 BOATS)

U-Boat	Type	Commissioned	Flotilla(s)	Patrols	Fate
U-411	VIIC	18-Mar-42	1 Sep 1942 – 13 Nov 1942 from 8. Flottille	2 patrols	Sunk with all hands 13 Nov 1942 west of Gibraltar by depth charges from a Hudson of No. 500 Sqn RAF. 46 dead. The destroyer HMS *Wrestler* had been credited with sinking this boat on 15 Nov 1942, but she actually sank U-98
U-414	VIIC	1-Jul-42	1 Jan 1943 – 30 Apr 1943 from 8. Flottille	3 patrols. 1 ship sunk: total 5979 GRT; 1 ship damaged: total 7134 GRT	to 29. Flottille
U-417	VIIC	26-Sep-42	1 Jun 1943 – 11 Jun 1943 from 8. Flottille	1 patrol	Sunk with all hands 11 Jun 1943 southeast of Iceland by depth charges from a Boeing Fortress of No. 206 Sqn RAF. 46 dead
U-436	VIIC	27-Sep-41	1 Sep 1942 – 26 May 1943 from 11. Flottille	8 patrols. 6 ships sunk: total 36,208 GRT; 2 ships damaged: total 15,575 GRT	Sunk with all hands 26 May 1943 west of Cape Ortegal by depth charges from the frigate HMS *Test* and the corvette HMS *Hyderabad*. 47 dead
U-437	VIIC	25-Oct-41	25 Oct 1941 – 5 Oct 1944	13 patrols	Damaged by British bombs at Bergen, Norway, 4 Oct 1944 and stricken 5 Oct 1944. Broken up in 1946
U-445	VIIC	30-May-42	1 Nov 1942 – 24 Aug 1944 from 8. Flottille	9 patrols	Sunk with all hands 24 Aug 1944 in the Bay of Biscay west of St Nazaire by depth charges from the frigate HMS *Louis*. 52 dead
U-456	VIIC	18-Sep-41	18 Sep 1941 – 30 Jun 1942	11 patrols. 6 ships sunk: total 31,528 GRT; 1 auxiliary warship sunk: total 251 GRT; 1 warship (HMS *Edinburgh*) damaged: total 11,685t/11,500 tons	to 11. Flottille
U-457	VIIC	5-Nov-41	5 Nov 1941 – 30 Jun 1942	Training	to 11. Flottille
U-465	VIIC	20-May-42	1 Oct 1942 – 2 May 1943 from 8. Flottille	4 patrols	Sunk with all hands 2 May 1943 north of Cape Finisterre by depth charges from an Australian Sunderland of No. 461 Sqn. 48 dead. Originally credited to another Australian Sunderland five days later, but that attack caused major damage to U-663
U-477	VIIC	18-Aug-43	1 Jun 1944 – 3 Jun 1944 from 5. Flottille	1 patrol	Sunk with all hands 3 Jun 1944 west of Trondheim, Norway, by depth charges from a Catalina of No. 162 Sqn RCAF. 51 dead
U-585	VIIC	28-Aug-41	28 Aug 1941 – 30 Mar 1942	3 patrols	Sunk with all hands 30 Mar 1942 north of Murmansk by a loose mine from a German minefield. 44 dead. Originally thought to have been sunk 29 Mar 1942 by the destroyer HMS *Fury*, which in fact attacked U-378 and caused no damage
U-586	VIIC	4-Sep-41	4 Sep 1941 – 30 Jun 1942	12 patrols. 2 ships sunk: total 12,716 GRT; 1 ship damaged: total 9057 GRT	to 29. Flottille
U-586	VIIC	4-Sep-41	1 Oct 1943 – 29 Feb 1944 from 13. Flottille	12 patrols. 2 ships sunk: total 12,716 GRT; 1 ship damaged: total 9057 GRT	to 11. Flottille
U-587	VIIC	11-Sep-41	11 Sep 1941 – 27 Mar 1942	2 patrols. 4 ships sunk: total 22,734 GRT, 1 auxiliary warship sunk: total 655 GRT	Sunk with all hands 27 Mar 1942 in the North Atlantic by depth charges from the escort destroyers HMS *Grove* and HMS *Aldenham* and the destroyers HMS *Volunteer* and HMS *Leamington*. 42 dead
U-588	VIIC	18-Sep-41	18 Sep 1941 – 31 Jul 1942	4 patrols. 7 ships sunk: total 31,492 GRT; 1 ship damaged: total 7460 GRT	Sunk with all hands 31 Jul 1942 in the North Atlantic by depth charges from the corvette HMCS *Wetaskiwin* and destroyer HMCS *Skeena*. 46 dead
U-589	VIIC	25-Sep-41	25 Sep 1941 – 30 Jun 1942	8 patrols. 1 ship sunk: total 2847 GRT; 1 auxiliary warship sunk: total 417 GRT	to 11. Flottille
U-590	VIIC	2-Oct-41	2 Oct 1941 – 9 Jul 1943	5 patrols. 1 ship sunk: total 5228 GRT; 1 ship damaged: total 5464 GRT	Sunk with all hands 9 Jul 1943 off the mouth of the Amazon by depth charges from a US Navy PBY Catalina aircraft of VP-94. 45 dead
U-591	VIIC	9-Oct-41	9 Oct 1941 – 30 Jun 1942	8 patrols. 4 ships sunk: total 19,932 GRT; 1 ship damaged: total 5701 GRT	to 11. Flottille
U-592	VIIC	16-Oct-41	16 Oct 1941 – 30 Jun 1942	10 patrols. 1 ship sunk: total 3770 GRT	to 11. Flottille
U-592	VIIC	16-Oct-41	1 Mar 1943 – 31 Jan 1944 from 11. Flottille	10 patrols. 1 ship sunk: total 3770 GRT	Sunk with all hands 31 Jan 1944 southwest of Ireland by depth charges from the sloops HMS *Starling*, HMS *Wild Goose* and HMS *Magpie*. 49 dead
U-598	VIIC	27-Nov-41	1 Jul 1942 – 23 Jul 1943 from 8. Flottille	4 patrols. 2 ships sunk: total 9295 GRT; 1 ship damaged: total 6197 GRT	Sunk 23 Jul 1943 in the South Atlantic near Natal by depth charges from two US Navy Liberators of VB-107. 43 dead and 2 survivors
U-608	VIIC	5-Feb-42	1 Sep 1942 – 10 Aug 1944 from 5. Flottille	10 patrols. 4 ships sunk: total 35,539 GRT	Sunk 10 Aug 1944 off La Rochelle by depth charges from the sloop HMS *Wren* and a Liberator of No. 53 Sqn RAF. No casualties – 52 survivors
U-609	VIIC	12-Feb-42	1 Aug 1942 – 7 Feb 1943	4 patrols. 2 ships sunk: total 10,288 GRT	Sunk with all hands 7 Feb 1943 in the North Atlantic by depth charges from the Free French corvette *Lobelia*. 47 dead
U-610	VIIC	19-Feb-42	1 Oct 1942 – 8 Oct 1943 from 5. Flottille	5 patrols. 4 ships sunk: total 21,273 GRT; 1 ship damaged: total 9551 GRT	Sunk with all hands 8 Oct 1943 in the North Atlantic by depth charges from a Sunderland of No. 423 Sqn RCAF. 51 dead
U-614	VIIC	19-Mar-42	1 Feb 1943 – 29 Jul 1943 from 8. Flottille	3 patrols. 1 ship sunk: total 5730 GRT	Sunk with all hands 29 Jul 1943 northwest of Cape Finisterre by depth charges from a Wellington of No. 172 Sqn RAF. 49 dead
U-616	VIIC	2-Apr-42	1 Jan 1943 – 31 May 1943 from 8. Flottille	9 patrols. 2 warships sunk: total 2216t/2181 tons; 2 ships damaged: total 17,754 GRT	to 29. Flottille
U-623	VIIC	21-May-42	1 Dec 1942 – 21 Feb 1943 from 8. Flottille	2 patrols	Sunk with all hands 21 Feb 1943 in the Atlantic by depth charges from a Liberator of No. 120 Sqn RAF. 46 dead

BOATS THAT SERVED WITH 6TH FLOTILLA (91 BOATS)

U-Boat	Type	Commissioned	Flotilla(s)	Patrols	Fate
U-626	VIIC	11-Jun-42	1 Nov 1942 – 15 Dec 1942 from 5. Flottille	1 patrol	Missing with all hands on or after 14 Dec 1942. May have been sunk 15 Dec 1942 in the North Atlantic by depth charges from the US Coast Guard cutter *Ingham*. 47 dead
U-627	VIIC	18-Jun-42	1 Oct 1942 – 27 Oct 1942 from 5. Flottille	1 patrol	Sunk with all hands 27 Oct 1942 south of Iceland by depth charges from a Boeing B-17 Flying Fortress of No. 206 Sqn RAF. 44 dead
U-640	VIIC	17-Sep-42	1 May 1943 – 14 May 1943 from 5. Flottille	1 patrol	Sunk with all hands 14 May 1943 east of Cape Farewell by depth charges from a US Navy PBY Catalina of Patrol Squadron VP-84. 49 dead. Loss previously credited to depth charges from the frigate HMS *Swale* on 17 May 1943, which actually sank U-657
U-642	VIIC	1-Oct-42	1 Mar 1943 – 30 Nov 1943 from 5. Flottille	4 patrols. 1 ship sunk: total 2125 GRT	to 29. Flottille
U-648	VIIC	12-Nov-42	1 May 1943 – 23 Nov 1943 from 5. Flottille	4 patrols	Sunk with all hands 23 Nov 1943 northeast of the Azores by the frigates HMS *Bazely*, HMS *Blackwood* and HMS *Drury*. 50 dead. Other attacks thought to have been against U-648 actually targetted U-424, U-714 and U-843. None caused any damage
U-655	VIIC	11-Aug-41	11 Aug 1941 – 24 Mar 1942	1 patrol	Sunk with all hands 24 Mar 1942 in the Barents Sea, rammed by minesweeper HMS *Sharpshooter*. 45 dead
U-658	VIIC	5-Nov-41	1 Aug 1942 – 30 Oct 1942 from 8. Flottille	2 patrols. 3 ships sunk: total 12,146 GRT; 1 ship damaged: total 6466 GRT	Sunk with all hands 30 Oct 1942 east of Newfoundland by depth charges from a Lockheed Hudson of No. 145 Sqn RCAF. 48 dead
U-666	VIIC	26-Aug-42	1 Mar 1943 – 10 Feb 1944 from 5. Flottille	4 patrols. 1 warship sunk: total 1392t/1370 tons; 1 ship damaged: total 5234 GRT	Missing with all hands in the North Atlantic on or after 10 Feb 1944. 51 dead. Previously credited to aircraft from the escort carrier HMS *Fencer*, now thought to have been attacking a false target
U-668	VIIC	16-Nov-42	1 Apr 1944 – 31 May 1944 from 5. Flottille	6 patrols	to 13. Flottille
U-672	VIIC	6-Apr-43	1 Oct 1943 – 18 Jul 1944 from 5. Flottille	4 patrols	Sunk 18 Jul 1944 north of Guernsey by depth charges from frigate HMS *Balfour*. No casualties – 52 survivors
U-673	VIIC	8-May-43	1 Jun 1944 – 20 Jun 1944 from 5. Flottille	5 patrols	to 13. Flottille
U-673	VIIC	8-May-43	1 Aug 1944 – 24 Oct 1944 from 13. Flottille	5 patrols	Collided with U-382, ran aground and wrecked 24 Oct 1944 north of Stavanger. Raised 9 Nov 1944. Surrendered to Norway in 1945 and broken up
U-675	VIIC	14-Jul-43	1 May 1944 – 24 May 1944 from 5. Flottille	1 patrol	Sunk with all hands 24 May 1944 west of Alesund, Norway, by depth charges from a Short Sunderland of No. 4 Sqn RAF. 51 dead
U-680	VIIC	23-Dec-43	1 Aug 1944 – 30 Sep 1944 from 31. Flottille	4 patrols	to 11. Flottille
U-703	VIIC	16-Oct-41	16 Oct 1941 – 30 Jun 1942	13 patrols. 5 ships sunk: total 29,523 GRT; 1 auxiliary warship sunk: total 559 GRT; 1 warship sunk: total 1900t/1870 tons	to 11. Flottille
U-705	VIIC	30-Dec-41	1 Aug 1942 – 3 Sep 1942	1 patrol. 1 ship sunk: total 3279 GRT	Sunk with all hands 3 Sep 1942 west of Brest by depth charges from an Armstrong Whitworth Whitley of No. 77 Sqn RAF. 45 dead
U-742	VIIC	1-May-43	1 Apr 1944 – 31 May 1944 from 8. Flottille	2 patrols	to 13. Flottille
U-756	VIIC	30-Dec-41	30 Dec 1941 – 1 Sep 1942	1 patrol	Sunk with all hands 1 Sep 1942 in the North Atlantic by the corvette HMCS *Morden*. 43 dead. Previously credited to a US Navy Catalina the same day, which actually damaged U-91
U-757	VIIC	28-Feb-42	28 Feb 1942 – 8 Jan 1944	5 patrols. 2 ships sunk: total 11,313 GRT	Sunk with all hands 8 Jan 1944 southwest of Ireland by depth charges from the frigate HMS *Bayntun* and corvette HMCS *Camrose*. 49 dead
U-758	VIIC	5-May-42	5 May 1942 – 14 Oct 1944	7 patrols. 2 ships sunk: total 13,989 GRT	to 33. Flottille
U-766	VIIC	30-Jul-43	1 Mar 1944 – 21 Aug 1944 from 8. Flottille	5 patrols	Unable to put to sea 21 Aug 1944 at La Pallice. Surrendered to France and was commissioned into French service as the *Laubie* in 1947. Renamed Q335 and stricken 11 Mar 1963
U-964	VIIC	18-Feb-43	1 Oct 1943 – 16 Oct 1943 from 5. Flottille	1 patrol	Sunk 16 Oct 1943 southwest of Iceland by depth charges from a Liberator of No. 86 Sqn RAF. 47 dead and 3 survivors
U-967	VIIC	11-Mar-43	1 Oct 1943 – 29 Feb 1944 from 5. Flottille	3 patrols. 1 warship sunk: total 1321t/1300 tons	to 29. Flottille
U-972	VIIC	8-Apr-43	1 Dec 1943 – 1 Jan 1944 from 5. Flottille	1 patrol	Missing with all hands Jan 1944. 49 dead. May have been sunk by one of its own acoustic homing torpedoes
U-981	VIIC	3-Jun-43	1 Dec 1943 – 12 Aug 1944 from 5. Flottille	3 patrols	Sunk 12 Aug 1944 at La Rochelle by an air-laid mine and by depth charges from a Handley Page Halifax of No. 502 Sqn RAF. 12 dead and 40 survivors
U-982	VIIC	10-Jun-43	1 Feb 1944 – 1 Jul 1944 from 5. Flottille	1 patrol	to 24. Flottille
U-986	VIIC	1-Jul-43	1 Mar 1944 – 17 Apr 1944 from 5. Flottille	1 patrol	Usually recorded as sunk with all hands 17 Apr 1944 southwest of Ireland by depth charges from the destroyer HMS *Swift* and Canadian sub-chaser HMCS *PC-619*. 50 dead. However, that is far north of the return route to Lorient, and there is doubt about its fate
U-999	VIIC/41	21-Oct-43	1 Jun 1944 – 30 Jun 1944 from 5. Flottille	1 patrol	to 24. Flottille

7 Unterseebootsflottille

Last of the prewar U-boat flotillas to be formed, the 7th Flotilla was established as the *U-bootflottille* Wegener on 25 June 1938 at Kiel. After offically becoming the 7th Flotilla, the unit was transferred to St Nazaire over the autumn of 1940 and into 1941.

THE FLOTILLA WAS NAMED after Kptlt. Bernd Wegener, who commanded U-27 during World War I. On 10 patrols he sank 29 ships, becoming famous after his death on 19 August 1915. U-27 was sunk by the Q-ship *Barolong*, and the crew of the British vessel caused an international incident when they killed 10 of the survivors of U-27 in what became known as the *Barolong* Incident.

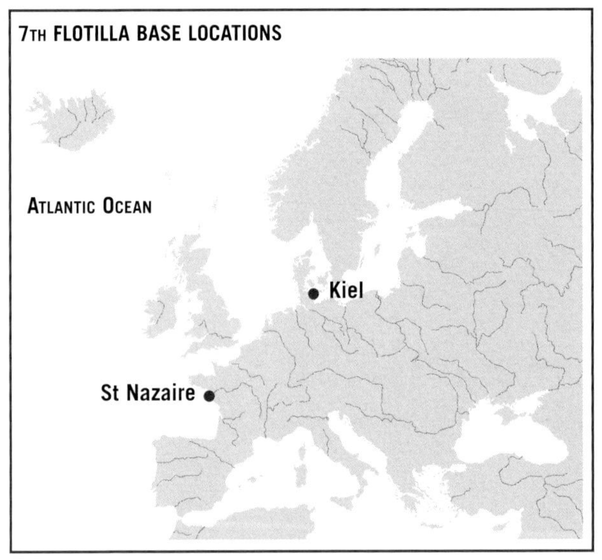

French success

Once established in France, the 7th Flotilla amassed a combat record second to none. It was home to many of the most successful aces. The first boat of the

7TH FLOTILLA BASE LOCATIONS

▼ U-47 crew

Gunther Prien and the crew of U-47 pose on deck after their triumphant return from sinking the battleship *Royal Oak* at Scapa Flow in the Orkneys.

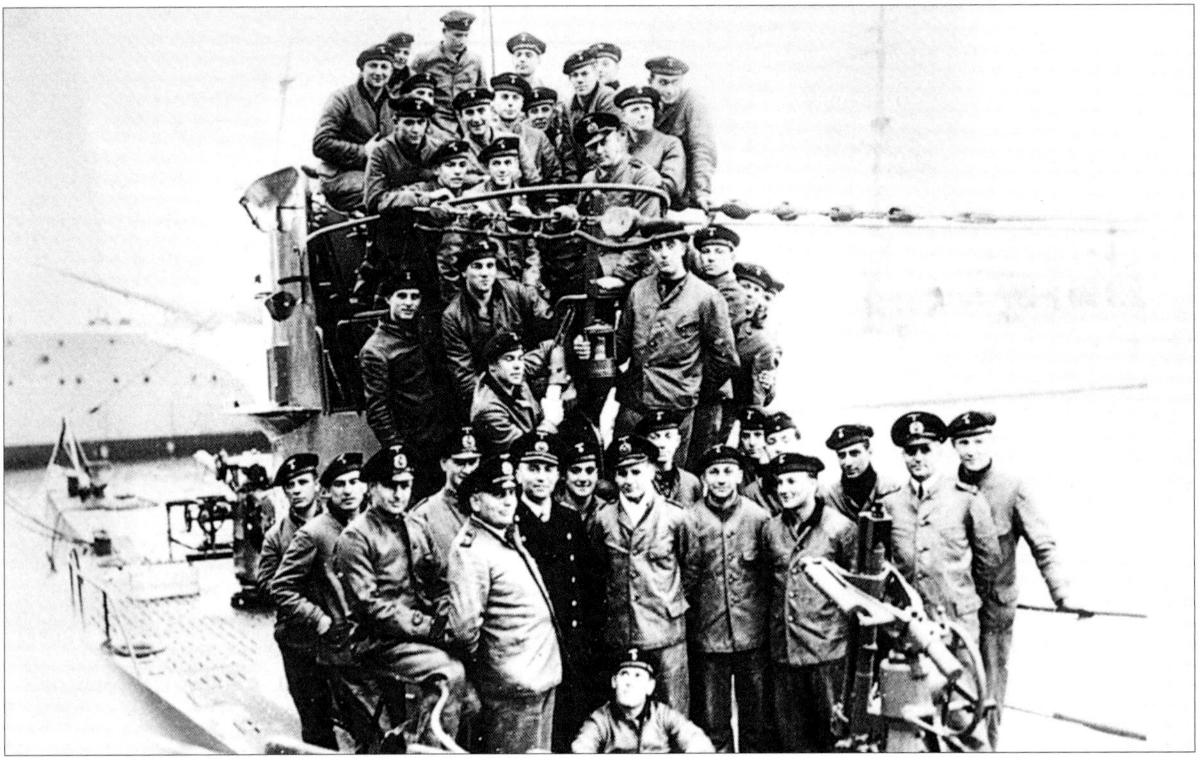

7TH FLOTILLA INSIGNIA

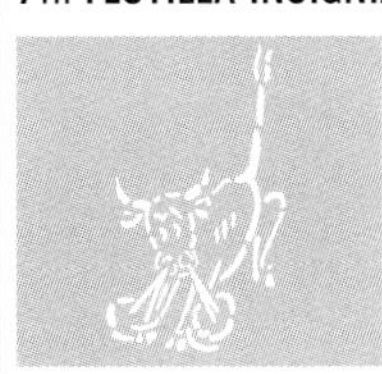

The 'Snorting Bull' was originally the emblem of U-47, after Gunther Prien's nickname of 'the Bull'. Designed by Engelbert Endrass, it was later selected as the 7th Flotilla's insignia.

Commanders

Korvkpt. Ernst Sobe *(Jun 1939 – Dec 1939)*
Korvkpt. Hans Rudolf Rösing *(Jan 1940 – May 1940)*
Kptlt. Herbert Sohler *(May 1940 – Sep 1940)*
Korvkpt. Herbert Sohler *(Sep 1940 – Feb 1944)*
Korvkpt. Adolf Piening *(Mar 1944 – May 1945)*

7TH FLOTILLA

Type	Boats assigned
Type VIIB	19
Type VIIC	89
Type VIIC/41	1
Type U-A	1

flotilla to reach St Nazaire, on 29 September 1940, was U-46, commanded by future U-boat ace Engelbert Endrass. St Nazaire boats of the 6th and 7th Flotillas mounted 388 operational patrols between the end of 1940 and the summer of 1944.

Allied advances after the invasion of Normandy meant that most boats left for Norway in August and September 1944. The 7th Flotilla was disbanded in August 1944. Many of the unit's shore-based personnel were unable to escape, however, and they were used as ground troops defending the *Festung* Saint-Nazaire, which remained in German hands until the end of the war.

Only one boat remained at the base. Engineering problems meant that U-255 had been unable to sail for Norway. However, it was repaired by base personnel and went on a last minelaying patrol near Les Sables d'Olonne in April 1945 under the flotilla's last commander, Korvkpt. Piening. U-255 finally left St Nazaire on 7 May 1945 and surrendered five days later at sea.

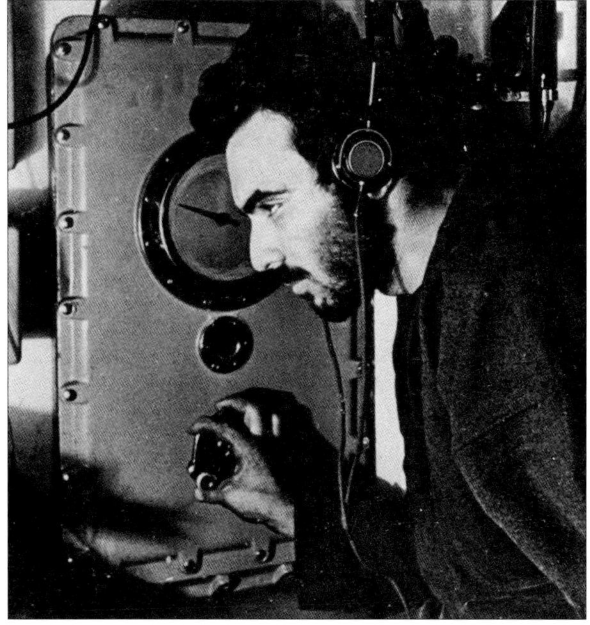

▶ Radio operator

The strict control maintained by the high command over operational U-boats meant that the *Funkers*, or radio operators, were vital members of any boat's crew.

Star commanders

1939–45

The 7th Flotilla was the most successful U-boat formation of the war, numbering many of the highest-scoring commanders and boats in history in its ranks.

Fregattenkapitän Otto Kretschmer

The son of a teacher, Otto Kretschmer was the top submarine ace of World War II. Born at Heidau in Silesia, he spent eight months in England before joining the German Navy in 1930. In 1936 he transferred to the U-boat arm, commanding his first boat in 1937. As a wartime U-boat captain in U-23 and U-99, he sank 44 ships totalling 266,629 GRT. His motto on operations was 'One torpedo … one ship'. He was awarded the Knight's Cross with Oak Leaves on 4 November 1940, adding the Swords while in captivity on 26 December 1941. On 17

March 1941, in a running battle with the destroyer HMS *Walker*, U-99 was forced to the surface by depth charges. Kretschmer was captured and with him 39 out of his crew of 43. After the war, Kretschmer entered the West German *Bundesmarine*, where he served with distinction, retiring with the rank of *Flotillenadmiral* in September 1970. He died in an accident on 5 August 1998 in Bavaria.

Korvettenkapitän Gunther Prien

Prien was the U-boat ace who became one of the Third Reich's earliest war heroes. On the night of 13/14 October 1939, Prien took the Type VII U-boat U-47 into the heavily defended Royal Navy base at Scapa Flow in the Orkneys. Penetrating the minefields and anti-submarine nets, he launched two torpedo attacks on HMS *Royal Oak*. The battleship sank in 15 minutes, and 24 officers and 800 men were killed. Prien made a skilful surface escape. He was awarded the Knight's Cross – the first to any U-boat commander – and each member of his crew received the Iron Cross (Second Class).

Born in Thuringia, Prien was a merchant seaman before joining the German Navy in 1934. He transferred to U-boats in 1935, and by the outbreak of war was in command of U-47. Described by William L. Shirer as 'clean-cut, cocky, a fanatical Nazi and obviously capable', he was one of the most successful of all U-boat commanders, sinking over 180,000 tonnes (177,158 tons) of British shipping in 18 months. He was awarded Oak Leaves in October

▲ U-boat ace

He was not the highest-scoring ace, but Prien's feat at Scapa Flow early in the war meant that he became the most famous of all U-boat commanders.

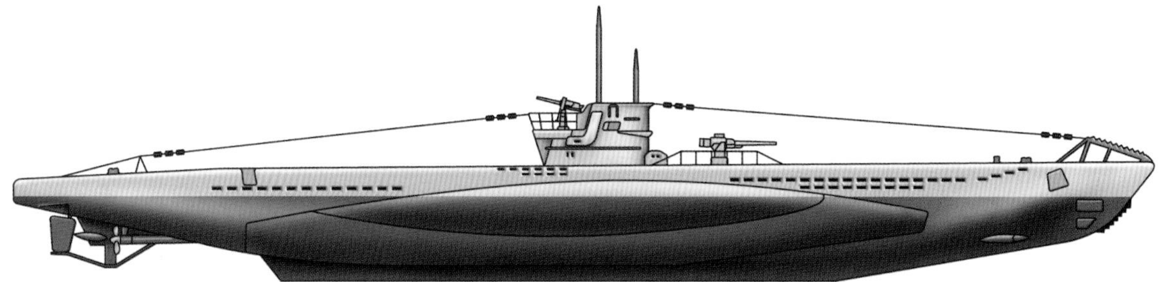

Specifications

Crew: 44
Powerplant: Diesel/electric
Max Speed: 31.9/14.8km/hr (17.2/8kt) s/d
Surface Range: 12,040km (6500nm)
Displacement: 765/871t (753/857 tons) s/d
Dimensions (length/beam/draught): 66.5 x 6.2 x 4.7m (218.1 x 20.34 x 15.4ft)
Commissioned: 17 Dec 1938
Armament: 14 torpedoes (4 bow/1 stern tubes); 1 x 8.8cm (3.5in) and 1 x 2cm (0.8in) guns

▲ U-47

Type VIIB

Launched on 29 October 1938, U-47 was commanded for its entire existence by Gunther Prien. The boat was always assigned to the Wegener Flotilla, which later became the 7th U-boat Flotilla.

1940. Prien was killed in action on the night of 7/8 March 1941, when U-47 was thought to have been sunk by the British destroyer HMS *Wolverine*. However, recent research indicates that the destroyer actually attacked U-A and that U-47 was lost to unknown causes.

STAR COMMANDERS		
Commander	**Patrols**	**Ships Sunk**
Fregattenkapitän Otto Kretschmer	16	44
Kapitänleutnant Joachim Schepke	14	36
Fregattenkapitän Erich Topp	12	35
Korvettenkapitän Gunther Prien	10	31

Fregattenkapitän Erich Topp

The third-highest scoring commander after Kretschmer and Lüth, Erich Topp sank 35 ships (200,629 tonnes/197,460 tons) in 12 patrols in U-57 and U-552. Topp began his naval career with Crew 34 and joined the U-boat force in October 1937. After four patrols commanding U-57, he transferred to U-552, known as the 'Red Devil' boat after Topp's personal emblem. Topp scored most of his successes in the North Atlantic against convoys and off the North American coast. After commanding the 27th Tactical Training Flotilla, Topp commissioned the 'Electro' boats U-3010 and U-2513. After the war, Topp served in the *Bundesmarine*, retiring in 1969 as a *Konteradmiral*. He died on 26 December 2005.

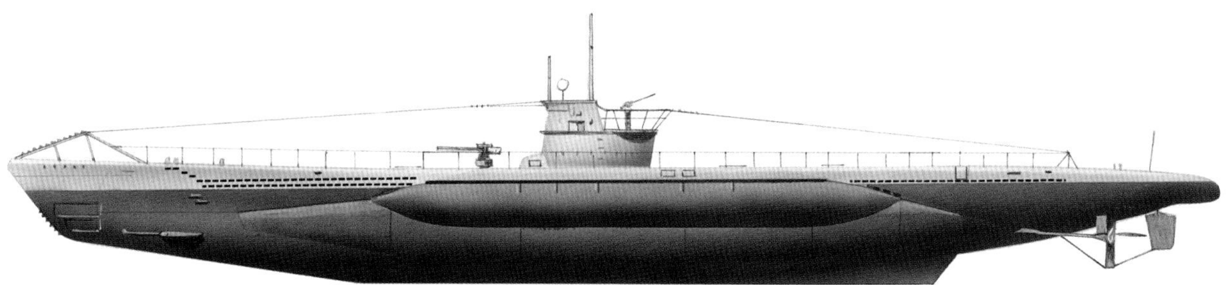

Specifications

Crew: 44
Powerplant: Diesel/electric
Max Speed: 31.9/14.8km/hr (17.2/8kt) s/d
Surface Range: 12,040km (6500nm)
Displacement: 765/871t (753/857 tons) s/d
Dimensions (length/beam/draught): 66.5 x 6.2 x 4.7m (218.1 x 20.34 x 15.4ft)
Commissioned: 18 Apr 1940
Armament: 14 torpedoes (4 bow/1 stern tubes); 1 x 8.8cm (3.5in) and 1 x 2cm (0.8in) guns (1941)

▲ U-99

Type VIIB

U-99 was the third boat commanded by Otto Kretschmer. In it, the top-scoring ace of the war sank 36 out of the 44 vessels he destroyed between September 1939 and his capture in March 1941.

Specifications

Crew: 44
Powerplant: Diesel/electric
Max Speed: 31.5/14.1km/hr (17/7.6kt) s/d
Surface Range: 12,040km (6500nm)
Displacement: 773/879t (761/865 tons) s/d
Dimensions (length/beam/draught): 67.1 x 6.2 x 4.8m (220.1 x 20.34 x 15.75ft)
Commissioned: 4 Dec 1940
Armament: 14 torpedoes (4 bow/1 stern tubes); 1 x 8.8cm (3.5in) and 1 x 2cm (0.8in) guns

▲ U-552

Type VIIC

Erich Topp commissioned U-552 in December 1940. The boat served with the 7th Flotilla until 1944, with Topp in command until August 1942. Under Topp and his successor Klaus Popp, U-552 sank 29 merchant ships of some 163,529 GRT.

U-48

Type VIIB

The most successful U-boat of World War II, U-48 was launched on 5 March 1939 and commissioned into the *Flottille* Wegener, later the 7th Flotilla, on 22 April.

Under the successive commands of Knight's Cross winners Herbert Schultze, Hans Rudolf Rösing and Heinrich Bleichrodt, U-48 sank more ships of a greater tonnage than any other submarine in World War II. On 12 patrols, the boat accounted for 51 merchant ships totalling 306,875 GRT, as well as sinking a Royal Navy sloop and damaging three ships for a total of 20,480 GRT. On its last mission in support of the *Bismarck*, U-48 joined in the search for survivors when the battleship was sunk, spending four days looking but with no success.

From June 1941 to 1945, U-48 was with the 26th and 21st Flotillas as a training boat. Decommissioned in October 1943, U-48 was used as a non-operational instructional platform by the 3. *Unterseeboots-lehrdivision* (a training school known until 1940 as an *Unterseebootsschule*) at Neustadt. At the end of the war, the boat was still at Neustadt, where it was scuttled on 3 May 1945.

U-48 Commanders

Kptlt. Herbert Schultze *(Apr 1939 – May 1940)*
Korvkpt. Hans Rudolf Rösing *(May 1940 – Sep 1940)*
Kptlt. Heinrich Bleichrodt *(Sep 1940 – Dec 1940)*
Oblt. Diether Todenhagen *(Sep 1940 – Oct 1940)*
Kptlt. Herbert Schultze *(Dec 1940 – Jul 1941)*
Oblt. Siegfried Atzinger *(Aug 1941 – Sep 1942)*

U-48
Type VIIB
A standard Type VIIB boat, U-48 used her 8.8cm (3.5in) gun to sink a number of her victims, especially on early patrols.

U-48 TIMETABLE

Patrol Dates	Operational Area	Ships Sunk
19 Aug 1939 – 17 Sep 1939	W of Biscay	3
4 Oct 1939 – 25 Oct 1939	W of Finsterre	5
20 Nov 1939 – 20 Dec 1939	Orkneys/Channel approaches	4
24 Jan 1940 – 26 Feb 1940	Channel approaches	4
3 Apr 1940 – 20 Apr 1940	Norway	0
26 May 1940 – 29 June 1940	WNW of Finisterre	7
7 Aug 1940 – 28 Aug 1940	WSW of Rockall	5
8 Sep 1940 – 25 Sep 1940	W of British Isles	8
5 Oct 1940 – 27 Oct 1940	NW of Rockall	7
20 Jan 1941 – 27 Feb 1941	S of Iceland	2
17 Mar 1941 – 8 Apr 1941	S of Iceland	5
22 May 1941 – 21 June 1941	W of St Nazaire (supporting *Bismarck*)/N of the Azores/central Atlantic	0
June 1941 – 1945	Served wth 26 and 21 Flotillas as a training boat	
Oct 1943	Decommissioned: used by 3 ULD	
3 May 1945	Scuttled at Neustadt	

U-76

TYPE VIIB

Although a small number of boats under ace commanders were running up large scores in 1940 and 1941, most boats, like U-76, had less spectacular careers.

COMMISSIONED IN DECEMBER 1940 after being built by Bremer Vulkan, Vegesack, U-76 under the command of *Oberleutnant* Friederich von Hippel spent a shorter time than average in working up to combat standards. Normally, this could take up to six months, but U-76 went on its first patrol on 19 March 1941. After sinking a merchantman, the boat closed with Convoy SC 26. The boat was abandoned and sank after being forced to surface by depth charge attacks from the destroyer HMS *Wolverine* and the sloop HMS *Scarborough*. One crewman was killed; 42

U-76 Commander

Oblt. Friederich von Hippel *(Dec 1940 – Apr 1941)*

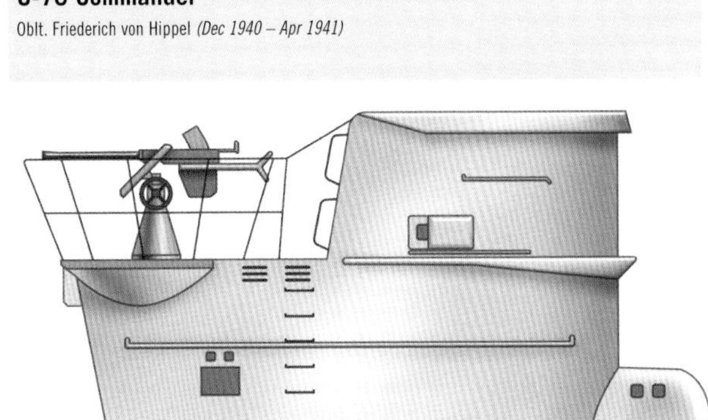

▲ Type VIIB AA conversion

In an attempt to increase the anti-aircraft defences of the Type VIIB boats without being forced to completely rebuild the conning tower, U-84 was fitted with a raised AA platform for an extra 2cm (0.8in) C/38 gun behind the bridge. This was not as effective as the 'winter garden' conversion, and the experiment proceeded no further.

U-76 TIMETABLE

Patrol Dates	Operational Area	Ships Sunk
19 Mar 1941 – 5 Apr 1941	Central N Atlantic	1
5 Apr 1941	Boat was abandoned and sank after being forced to the surface by depth-charge attacks from destroyer HMS *Wolverine* and sloop HMS *Scarborough*. 1 crewman killed; 42 captured	

Specifications

Crew: 44

Powerplant: Diesel/electric

Max Speed: 31.9/14.8km/hr (17.2/8kt) s/d

Surface Range: 12,040km (6500nm)

Displacement: 765/871t (753/857 tons) s/d

Dimensions (length/beam/draught): 66.5 x 6.2 x 4.7m (218.1 x 20.34 x 15.4ft)

Commissioned: 3 Dec 1940

Armament: 14 torpedoes (4 bow/1 stern tubes); 1 x 8.8cm (3.5in) and 1 x 2cm (0.8in) guns

▲ U-76

Type VIIB

Although U-boats were not as fast as front-line warships, they could easily outpace merchant convoys. U-76 spent three days of her only patrol shadowing Convoy SC 26, although she was unable to mount any successful attacks.

U-553

Type VIIC

Laid down at Blohm und Voss, Hamburg, in November 1939, U-553 was launched on 7 November 1940 and commissioned into the 7th Flotilla in December of that year.

After four months working up at Kiel, U-553 set off for the flotilla's operational base in France. The boat went on to amass a respectable score. Commanded by *Korvettenkapitän* Karl Thurmann, U-553 sank 13 ships for a total of 64,612 GRT in its 10 sorties, and damaged two more vessels totalling 15,273 GRT.

In two years with the 7th Flotilla, the boat operated in the North Atlantic, off Canada and down the US east coast. It was at about this time that Type VII commanders discovered that by careful regulation of engine speed they could stretch endurance more than had originally been expected, and the boat made one patrol as far south as the Caribbean.

The boat went missing in January 1943, after sending a last message saying 'Periscope unclear'.

U-553 Commander

Korvkpt. Karl Thurmann *(Dec 1940 – Jan 1943)*

U-553 TIMETABLE

Patrol Dates	Operational Area	Ships Sunk
13 Apr 1941 – 2 May 1941	Transit from Kiel to St Nazaire	0
7 June 1941 – 19 Jul 1941	Azores/Newfoundland Bank	2
7 Aug 1941 – 16 Sep 1941	SW of Iceland	0
7 Oct 1941 – 22 Oct 1941	N Atlantic SE of Cape Farewell	3
1 Jan 1942 – 3 Feb 1942	Canadian waters	2
19 Apr 1942 – 24 June 1942	Canadian waters. Attacked several times, sustained damage	3
19 Jul 1942 – 17 Sep 1942	N Atlantic/Caribbean	4
November 1942	Transferred to 3rd Flotilla	
23 Nov 1942 – 18 Dec 1942	N Atlantic	1
16 Jan 1943 – 22 Jan 1943	W of Ireland	0
20 Jan 1943	Last communication from U-553	
22 Jan 1943	Declared lost with all hands to unknown causes. 47 dead	

▲ U-553

Type VIIC

By 1943 the anti-aircraft armament of U-boats was increasing dramatically to meet an equally increased threat. Firepower was greatly enhanced by the fitting of the Flakvierling quadruple 2cm (0.8in) anti-aircraft mounting.

Specifications

Crew: 44

Powerplant: Diesel/electric

Max Speed: 31.5/14.1km/hr (17/7.6kt) s/d

Surface Range: 12,040km (6500nm)

Displacement: 773/879t (761/865 tons) s/d

Dimensions (length/beam/draught): 67.1 x 6.2 x 4.8m (220.1 x 20.34 x 15.75ft)

Commissioned: 23 Dec 1940

Armament: 14 torpedoes (4 bow/1 stern tubes); 1 x 2cm (0.8in) quad and 2 x twin 2cm (0.8in) guns

Attack on convoy SC 7

October 1940

SC 7 was one of the first convoys to suffer heavily from an effective wolfpack attack, and its terrible stuggle for life showed that the U-boat was a real threat to Britain's survival.

On the night of 21 September 1940, HX 72, a fast convoy consisting of 41 merchantmen, was attacked and 11 vessels were sunk. The commodore of the convoy was sure at least two U-boats had taken part in the attack. The senior officer of the escorts agreed. There was a suggestion that U-boats were beginning to coordinate their attacks. Slow convoy SC 7 was to put the matter beyond doubt.

The Canadian port of Sydney saw the gathering of a motley collection of ships, and convoy SC 7 got under way in the first week of October 1940. SC 7 was not expected to make more than 15km/hr (8kt) – in fact, some of the ships were so old and decrepit that they struggled to make 9km/hr (5kt).

Slaughter begins

In the early hours of 16 October, one of the stragglers was attacked. The convoy's single escort, the sloop HMS *Scarborough*, could do nothing. Late that night, the watch on the bridge of U-48 spotted the moonlit silhouette of a ship. As the boat closed, it became clear it was part of a convoy, a large one, weakly protected. U-48 sent a message to Lorient giving the convoy's course and speed. Five boats were ordered to close with the convoy and attack. U-48 went in first, sinking the 9650-tonne (9500 ton) tanker *Languedoc*. Two minutes later, the freighter *Scoresby* was hit.

CONVOY SC 7 BATTLE TIMETABLE

Date	Event
4/5 Oct	Departs Sydney, Cape Breton Island – 35 ships
16 Oct	One straggler sunk
17 Oct	One straggler sunk. Convoy spotted by U-48 – 2 ships sunk. U-46, U-99, U-100, U-123 vectored to intercept
18 Oct	7 ships sunk, 4 damaged
19 Oct	9 ships sunk
20 Oct	15 surviving ships of convoy reach Liverpool

The escort, now reinforced by sloops HMS *Leith*, HMS *Fowey* and corvettes HMS *Bluebell* and HMS *Heartsease*, spent a good deal of the 17th rounding up ships. The convoy was spread over 30km (18 miles) of ocean, and some ships did not even know there had been an attack.

But it was to be a brief respite. U-48 was shadowing SC 7 when it was forced to dive by a Sunderland flying boat, but it had passed enough information to ensure the convoy would be

Specifications

Crew: 44
Powerplant: Diesel/electric
Max Speed: 31.9/14.8km/hr (17.2/8kt) s/d
Surface Range: 12,040km (6500nm)
Displacement: 765/871t (753/857 tons) s/d
Dimensions (length/beam/draught): 66.5 x 6.2 x 4.7m (218.1 x 20.34 x 15.4ft)
Commissioned: 30 May 1940
Armament: 14 torpedoes (4 bow/1 stern tubes); 1 x 8.8cm (3.5in) and 1 x 2cm (0.8in) guns (1941)

▲ U-100

Type VIIB

Joachim Schepke rivalled Gunther Prien in his popularity with Germany's Propaganda Ministry. His piratical appearance masked a capable commander who with U-3, U-19 and U-100 sank 36 ships in just 18 months..

intercepted by U-38, U-46, U-100 and U-99, the last three commanded by ace commanders Endrass, Schepke and Kretschmer. SC 7 was just the second convoy to be attacked by a wolfpack.

On 18 October seven ships were torpedoed and sunk, including the iron ore ship SS *Creekirk*, bound for Cardiff, Wales. With her heavy cargo, she sank like a stone, taking all 36 crew members with her. October 19 1940 was the blackest day of all, with the wolfpack sinking nine ships, including the SS *Empire Brigand* with her cargo of trucks. She went down with six of her crew. Other casualties were the commodore's ship, SS *Assyrian*, and the SS *Fiscus* with its cargo of steel ingots. The convoy lost 20 ships out of 35, of which seven fell to Kretschmer's U-99. The total tonnage lost was 80,869 tonnes (79,592 tons).

The arrival in the vicinity of Convoy HX 79 diverted the wolfpack and they went on to sink 14 more ships from that convoy, making a total of 34 ships destroyed in 48 hours. No U-boats were lost.

Wolfpack group *West*

June 1941

Formed in June 1941 from Type VII boats, mostly from 7th Flotilla and 1st Flotilla, together with a number of larger Type IX boats from 2nd Flotilla, the *West* group gathered southeast of the Newfoundland Bank. However, even in summer it was hard to find targets in the North Atlantic.

On 20 June, the group spread out northeastwards, forming a widely spaced line in the centre of the North Atlantic. No convoys were encountered, but a number of independently sailing merchantmen were sunk. On 24 June, U-203 (not part of the *West* group) sighted the westbound convoy OB 336 to the south of Greenland. OB convoys were outward bound to North America, and OB 336, consisting of 24 ships, had sailed from Liverpool. Taking a chance when offered, U-203 made an attack and sank two

▼ **Scanning the horizon**

Well protected against the ocean spray, the crew of a U-boat search for potential prey in the North Atlantic, summer 1941.

vessels. U-77, U-101, U-108, U-553 and U-558 of Group *West* were ordered to intercept and closed to shadow the convoy. However, the submarines lost the merchant vessels in fog – always a possibility in these waters, whatever the season – before any more could be sunk.

Late in June, Group *West*, together with some independent boats, was ordered eastwards after a Focke-Wulf Fw 200 Condor aircraft sighted Convoy OG 66 about 500km (290nm) west of Ireland. The OG convoys were routed from Britain to Gibraltar and West Africa, and the 55 ships of OG 66 had left Liverpool on 24 June. Further aircraft sightings were made on 30 June and 1 July, but the wolfpack was unable to close because of poor visibility caused by fog and bad weather.

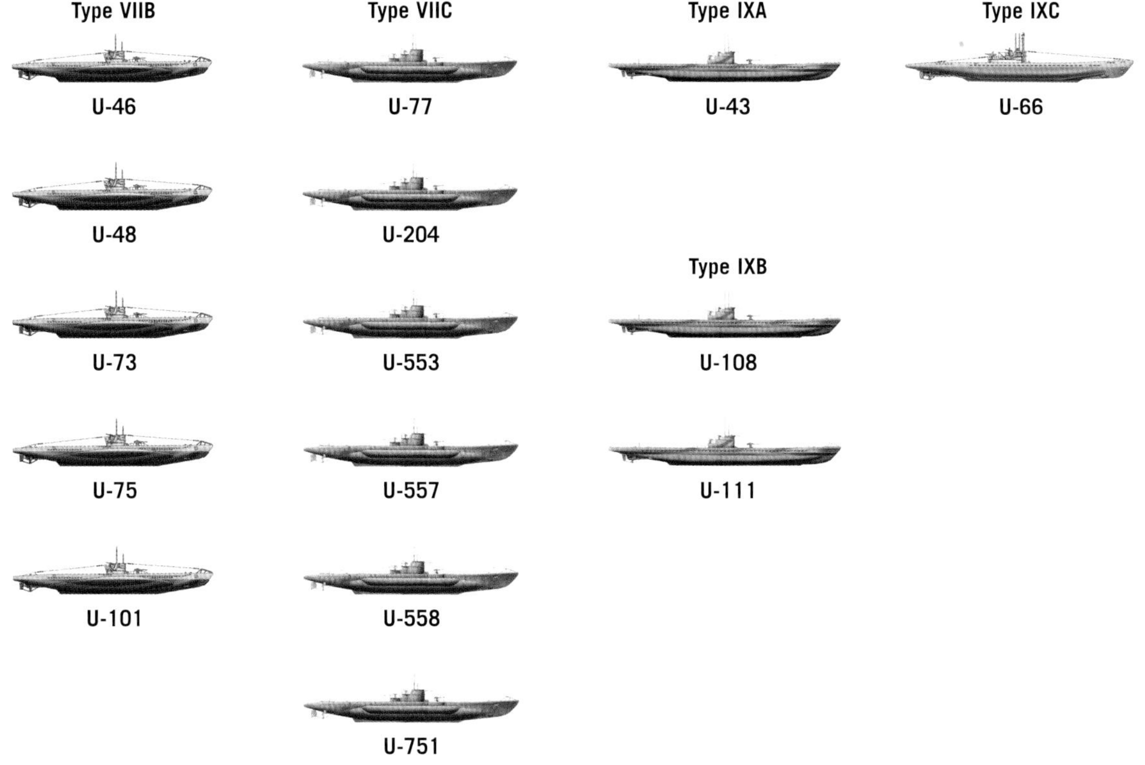

BOATS THAT SERVED WITH 7TH FLOTILLA (110 BOATS)

U-Boat	Type	Commissioned	Flotilla(s)	Patrols	Fate
U-45	VIIB	25-Jun-38	25 Jun 1938 – 14 Oct 1939	2 patrols. 2 ships sunk: total 19,313 GRT	Sunk with all hands 14 Oct 1939 southwest of Ireland by depth charges from the destroyers HMS *Inglefield*, HMS *Ivanhoe* and HMS *Intrepid*. 38 dead
U-46	VIIB	2-Nov-38	2 Nov 1938 – 1 Sep 1941	13 patrols. 21 ships sunk: total 90,408 GRT; 2 auxiliary warships sunk: total 35,284 GRT; 1 ship a total loss: total 2080 GRT; 4 ships damaged: total 25,491 GRT	to 26. Flottille
U-47	VIIB	17-Dec-38	17 Dec 1938 – 7 Mar, 1941	10 patrols. 30 ships sunk: total 162,768 GRT; 1 battleship (HMS *Royal Oak*) sunk: total 29,618t/29,150 tons; 8 ships damaged: total 62,751 GRT	Missing with all hands 7 Mar 1941 in North Atlantic near the Rockall Banks. 45 dead. Previously recorded fate is probably an error: destroyer HMS *Wolverine* claimed to have sunk U-47 on 8 Mar 1941 after depth-charge attacks, but the *Wolverine* actually attacked Eckermann's U-A. U-47 may have hit a mine, or possibly fallen to an attack by corvettes HMS *Camellia* and HMS *Arbutus*
U-48	VIIB	22-Apr-39	22 Apr 1939 – 30 Jun 1941	12 patrols. 51 ships sunk: total 306,875 GRT; 1 warship sunk: total 1077t/1060 tons; 3 ships damaged: total 20,480 GRT. Most successful submarine of World War II both in terms of tonnage and numbers of ships sunk	to 26. Flottille
U-49	VIIB	12-Aug-39	12 Aug 1939 – 15 Apr 1940	4 patrols. 1 ship sunk: total 4258 GRT	Sunk 15 Apr 1940 near Narvik, Norway, by depth charges from the British destroyers HMS *Fearless* and HMS *Brazen*. 1 dead and 41 survivors

BOATS THAT SERVED WITH 7TH FLOTILLA (110 BOATS)					
U-Boat	**Type**	**Commissioned**	**Flotilla(s)**	**Patrols**	**Fate**
U-50	VIIB	12-Dec-39	12 Dec 1939 – 6 Apr 1940	2 patrols. 4 ships sunk: total 16,089 GRT	Destroyed with all hands 6 April 1940 by mines laid by destroyers HMS *Express*, HMS *Esk*, HMS *Icarus* and HMS *Impulsive* 3 March 1940. 44 dead. Previously the loss was attributed to an attack by the destroyer HMS *Hero* 10 April 1940; but this was most probably against a false target
U-51	VIIB	6-Aug-38	6 Aug 1938 – 20 Aug 1940	4 patrols. 5 ships sunk: total 26,296 GRT; 1 auxiliary warship sunk: total 4724 GRT	Sunk with all hands 20 Aug 1940 in the Bay of Biscay west of Nantes, France, by a torpedo from the submarine HMS *Cachalot*. 43 dead
U-52	VIIB	4-Feb-39	4 Feb 1939 – 31 May 1941	8 patrols. 13 ships sunk: total 56,333 GRT	to 26. Flottille
U-53	VIIB	24-Jun-39	24 Jun 1939 – 23 Feb 1940	3 patrols. 7 ships sunk: total 27,316 GRT; 1 ship damaged: total 8022 GRT	Sunk with all hands 23 Feb 1940 in the North Sea, Orkney waters, by depth charges from the destroyer HMS *Gurkha*. 42 dead
U-54	VIIB	23-Sep-39	23 Sept 1939 – 20 Feb 1940	1 patrol	Missing with all hands 20 Feb 1940 in the North Sea, position unknown. 41 dead. The boat was possibly lost to mines laid by the destroyers HMS *Ivanhoe* and HMS *Intrepid* early in Jan 1940
U-55	VIIB	21-Nov-39	21 Nov 1939 – 30 Jan 1940	1 patrol. 6 ships sunk: total 15,853 GRT	Sunk 30 Jan 1940 in the English Channel southwest of the Scilly Isles by depth charges from the destroyer HMS *Whitshed*, the sloop HMS *Fowey*, the French destroyers *Valmy* and *Guépard*, and by depth charges from a British Sunderland aircraft of No. 228 Sqn. 1 dead and 41 survivors
U-69	VIIC	2-Nov-40	2 Nov 1940 – 17 Feb 1943 (front boat)	11 patrols. 16 ships sunk: total 67,500 GRT; 1 ship damaged beyond repair: total 5445 GRT; 1 ship damaged: total 4887 GRT	Sunk with all hands 17 Feb 1943 in the North Atlantic east of Newfoundland by depth charges from the British destroyer HMS *Fame*. 46 dead. Originally thought to have been sunk by destroyer HMS *Viscount*. That attack actually sank U-201
U-70	VIIC	23-Nov-40	23 Nov 1940 – 7 Mar 1941	1 patrol. 1 ship sunk: total 820 GRT; 3 ships damaged: total 20,484 GRT	Sunk 7 Mar 1941 southeast of Iceland, in position 60.15N, 14.00W, by British corvettes HMS *Camellia* and HMS *Arbutus*. 20 dead and 25 survivors
U-71	VIIC	14-Dec-40	14 Dec 1940 – 31 May 1943	10 patrols. 5 ships sunk: total 38,894 GRT	to 24. Flottille
U-73	VIIB	31-Oct-40	31 Oct 1940 – 30 Nov 1941	8 patrols. 4 ships sunk: total 24,694 GRT; 1 warship sunk: total 940t/925 tons; 1 ship damaged: total 97 GRT; 1 auxiliary warship damaged: total 11,402 GRT	to 29. Flottille
U-75	VIIB	19-Dec-40	19 Dec 1940 – 1 Oct 1941	5 patrols. 7 ships sunk: total 37,884 GRT; 2 warships sunk: total 756t/744 tons	to 23. Flottille
U-76	VIIB	3-Dec-40	3 Dec 1940 – 5 Apr 1941	1 patrol. 2 ships sunk: total 7290 GRT	Sunk 5 Apr 1941 south of Iceland by depth charges from the destroyer HMS *Wolverine* and the sloop HMS *Scarborough*. 1 dead and 42 survivors
U-77	VIIC	18-Jan-41	18 Jan 1941 – 31 Dec 1941	12 patrols. 14 ships sunk: total 31,186 GRT; 1 warship sunk: total 1067t/1050 tons; 1 ship damaged beyond repair: total 5222 GRT; 2 ships damaged: total 5384 GRT; 2 warships damaged: total 2926t/2880 tons	to 23. Flottille
U-88	VIIC	15-Oct-41	1 May 1942 – 30 Jun 1942 from 8. Flottille	3 patrols. 2 ships sunk: total 12,304 GRT	to 11. Flottille
U-93	VIIC	30-Jul-40	30 Jul 1940 – 15 Jan 1942	7 patrols. 8 ships sunk: total 43,392 GRT	Sunk 15 Jan 1942 in North Atlantic by the destroyer HMS *Hesperus*. 6 dead and 40 survivors
U-94	VIIC	10-Aug-40	10 Aug 1940 – 28 Aug 1942	10 patrols. 26 ships sunk: total 141,853 GRT; 1 ship damaged: total 8022 GRT	Sunk in the Caribbean Sea on 28 Aug 1942 by depth charges from a US Navy Catalina from patrol squadron VP-92, followed by ramming by the Canadian corvette HMCS *Oakville*. 19 dead and 26 survivors
U-95	VIIC	31-Aug-40	31 Aug 1940 – 28 Nov 1941	7 patrols. 8 ships sunk: total 28,415 GRT; 4 ships damaged: total 27,916 GRT	Sunk 28 Nov 1941 off the Spanish coast southwest of Almeria by the Dutch submarine HrMs *O 21*. 35 dead and 12 survivors
U-96	VIIC	14-Sep-40	14 Sep 1940 – 31 Mar 1943	11 patrols. 27 ships sunk: total 181,206 GRT; 1 ship damaged beyond repair: total 8888 GRT; 4 ships damaged: total 33,043 GRT	To 24. Flottille. Lothar-Günther Buchheim joined U-96 for one patrol as a war correspondent, which provided material for the best-selling novel, TV series and film *Das Boot* (*The Boat*)
U-97	VIIC	28-Sep-40	28 Sep 1940 – 31 Oct 1941	13 patrols. 15 ships sunk: total 64,404 GRT; 1 auxiliary warship sunk: total 6833 GRT; 1 ship damaged: total 9718 GRT	to 23. Flottille
U-98	VIIC	12-Oct-40	12 Oct 1940 – 15 Nov 1942	9 patrols. 10 ships sunk: total 48,878 GRT; 1 auxiliary warship sunk: total 10,549 GRT; 1 warship damaged: total 188t/185 tons	Sunk with all hands 15 Nov 1942 in North Atlantic west of Gibraltar, in position 36.09N, 07.42W, by depth charges from the British destroyer HMS *Wrestler*. 46 dead
U-99	VIIB	18-Apr-40	18 Apr 1940 – 17 Mar 1941	8 patrols. 35 ships sunk: total 198,218 GRT; 3 auxiliary warships sunk: total 46,440 GRT; 5 ships damaged: total 37,965 GRT; 1 ship taken as prize: total 2136 GRT	Scuttled 17 Mar 1941 southeast of Iceland after being depth-charged by the British destroyer HMS *Walker*. 3 dead and 40 survivors
U-100	VIIB	30-May-40	30 May 1940 – 17 Mar 1941	6 patrols. 25 ships sunk: total 135,614 GRT; 1 ship damaged beyond repair: total 2205 GRT; 4 ships damaged: total 17,229 GRT	Sunk 17 Mar 1941 southeast of Iceland after being rammed and depth-charged by the destroyers HMS *Walker* and HMS *Vanoc*. U-100 was the first U-boat sunk after being located on the surface in poor visibility by radar. 38 dead and 6 survivors
U-101	VIIB	11-Mar-40	11 Mar 1940 – 28 Feb 1942	10 patrols. 22 ships sunk: total 112,618 GRT; 1 warship sunk: total 1209t/1190 tons; 2 ships damaged: total 9113 GRT	to 26. Flottille

BOATS THAT SERVED WITH 7TH FLOTILLA (110 BOATS)

U-Boat	Type	Commissioned	Flotilla(s)	Patrols	Fate
U-102	VIIB	27-Apr-40	27 Apr 1940 – 1 Jul 1940	1 patrol. 1 ship sunk: total 5219 GRT	Sunk with all hands 1 Jul 1940 southwest of Ireland by depth charges from the destroyer HMS *Vansittart*. 43 dead. Originally thought to have been lost to unknown causes in the Bay of Biscay on or after 30 Jun 1940
U-133	VIIC	5-Jul-41	5 Jul 1941 – 31 Dec 1941	3 patrols. 1 warship sunk: total 1951t/1920 tons	to 23. Flottille
U-135	VIIC	16-Aug-41	1 Dec 1941 – 15 Jul 1943 from 5. Flottille	7 patrols. 3 ships sunk: total 21,302 GRT; 1 ship damaged: total 4762 GRT	Sunk 15 Jul 1943 in the Atlantic by the sloop HMS *Rochester*, the corvettes HMS *Mignonette* and HMS *Balsam* and a US Navy PBY Catalina of Patrol Squadron VP-92. 5 dead and 41 survivors
U-207	VIIC	7-Jun-41	7 Jun 1941 – 11 Sep 1941	1 patrol. 2 ships sunk: total 9727 GRT	Sunk with all hands 11 Sep 1941 in the Straits of Denmark by depth charges from the destroyers HMS *Leamington* and HMS *Veteran*. 41 dead
U-221	VIIC	9-May-42	1 Sep 1942 – 27 Sep 1943 from 5. Flottille (training)	5 patrols. 11 ships sunk: total 69,589 GRT; 1 ship damaged: total 7197 GRT	Sunk with all hands 27 Sep 1943 southwest of Ireland by depth charges from a Handley-Page Halifax of No. 58 Sqn RAF. 50 dead
U-224	VIIC	20-Jun-42	1 Nov 1942 – 13 Jan 1943 from 5. Flottille (training)	2 patrols. 2 ships sunk: total 9535 GRT	Sunk 13 Jan 1943 in the Mediterranean west of Algiers by ramming and depth charges from the corvette HMCS *Ville de Quebec*. 45 dead and 1 survivor
U-227	VIIC	22-Aug-42	1 Apr 1943 – 30 Apr 1943 from 5. Flottille (training)	1 patrol	Sunk with all hands 30 Apr 1943 north of the Faroes by depth charges from an Australian Hampden aircraft of No. 455 Sqn. 49 dead
U-255	VIIC	29-Nov-41	1 Dec 1943 – 1 Sep 1944 from 13. Flottille	15 patrols. 10 ships sunk: total 47,529 GRT; 1 warship sunk: total 1219t/1200 tons; 1 ship damaged b/r: total 7191 GRT	to 13. Flottille
U-265	VIIC	6-Jun-42	1 Feb 1943 – 3 Feb 1943	1 patrol	Sunk with all hands 3 Feb 1943 south of Iceland by depth charges from a Boeing B-17 Flying Fortress of No. 220 Sqn RAF. 46 dead
U-266	VIIC	24-Jun-42	1 Jan 1943 – 15 May 1943 from 8. Flottille	2 patrols. 4 ships sunk: total 16,089 GRT	Sunk with all hands 15 May 1943 in the North Atlantic by depth charges from a Halifax of No. 58 Sqn RAF. 47 dead. Previously credited to a No. 86 Sqn Liberator, but that attack was against U-403 and did no damage
U-267	VIIC	11-Jul-42	1 Feb 1943 – 1 Oct 1944 from 8. Flottille	7 patrols. Last boat to leave the U-boat base at St Nazaire on 23 Sep 1944	to 33. Flottille
U-274	VIIC	7-Nov-42	1 Aug 1943 – 23 Oct 1943 from 8. Flottille	2 patrols	Sunk with all hands 23 Oct 1943 southwest of Iceland by depth charges from the destroyers HMS *Duncan* and HMS *Vidette*, and a Liberator of No. 224 Sqn RAF. 48 dead
U-278	VIIC	16-Jan-43	1 Oct 1943 – 31 Dec 1943 from 8. Flottille	7 patrols. 1 ship sunk: total 7177 GRT; 1 warship sunk: total 1839t/1810 tons	to 11. Flottille
U-281	VIIC	8-May-43	1 Aug 1943 – 9 Nov 1944 from 8. Flottille	4 patrols	to 33. Flottille
U-285	VIIC	15-May-43	1 Aug 1944 – 30 Sep 1944 from 8. Flottille	3 patrols	to 11. Flottille
U-300	VIIC/41	29-Dec-43	1 Aug 1944 – 30 Sep 1944 from 8. Flottille	4 patrols. 2 ships sunk: total 7559 GRT; 1 ship damaged beyond repair: total 9551 GRT; 1 ship damaged: total 7176 GRT	to 11. Flottille
U-303	VIIC	7-Jul-42	1 Jan 1943 – 31 Mar 1943 from 8. Flottille	2 patrols. 1 ship sunk: total 4959 GRT	to 29. Flottille
U-310	VIIC	24-Feb-43	1 Aug 1944 – 4 Sep 1944 from 8. Flottille	6 patrols. 2 ships sunk: total 14,395 GRT	to 13. Flottille
U-338	VIIC	25-Jun-42	1 Mar 1943 – 21 Sep 1943 from 8. Flottille	3 patrols. 4 ships sunk: total 21,927 GRT; 1 ship damaged: total 7134 GRT	Missing with all hands in the North Atlantic on or after 20 Sep 1943. 51 dead. Previously recorded as having been sunk 20 Sep 1943 southwest of Iceland by a homing torpedo from a Liberator of No. 120 Sqn RAF. That attack was probably against U-386, and caused no damage
U-342	VIIC	12-Jan-43	1 Mar 1944 – 17 Apr 1944	2 patrols	Sunk with all hands 17 Apr 1944 southwest of Iceland by depth charges from a Catalina of No. 162 Sqn RCAF. 51 dead
U-358	VIIC	15-Aug-42	1 Feb 1943 – 1 Mar 1944 from 8. Flottille	6 patrols. 4 ships sunk: total 17,753 GRT; 1 warship sunk: total 1211t/1,192 tons	Sunk 1 Mar 1944 north of the Azores by depth charges and gunfire from the frigates HMS *Gould*, HMS *Affleck*, HMS *Gore* and HMS *Garlies*. 50 dead and 1 survivor
U-359	VIIC	5-Oct-42	1 Mar 1943 – 26 Jul 1943 from 8. Flottille	3 patrols	Sunk with all hands 26 Jul 1943 in the Caribbean south of Santo Domingo by depth charges from a US Navy Mariner of VP-32. 47 dead. Previously credited to another VP-32 Mariner on 28 Jul, but that attack actually destroyed U-159
U-364	VIIC	3-May-43	1 Nov 1943 – 31 Jan 1944 from 5. Flottille	2 patrols	Probably sunk with all hands 29 Jan 1944 in the Bay of Biscay by depth charges from a Halifax of No. 502 Sqn RAF. 49 dead. Originally loss was attributed to a Wellington of No. 172 Sqn RAF. That attack was probably against U-608, which shot down the aircraft before it could drop its charges
U-381	VIIC	25-Feb-42	1 Oct 1942 – 19 May 1943 from 5. Flottille	3 patrols	Missing with all hands south of Greenland on or after 9 May 1943, when the boat reported for the last time. 47 dead. Previously thought to have been sunk 19 May 1943 southeast of Cape Farewell, Greenland, by depth charges from the destroyer HMS *Duncan* and the corvette HMS *Snowflake*. That attack was actually against two boats, U-304 and U-636, and caused minor damage

BOATS THAT SERVED WITH 7TH FLOTILLA (110 BOATS)

U-Boat	Type	Commissioned	Flotilla(s)	Patrols	Fate
U-382	VIIC	25-Apr-42	1 Oct 1942 – 31 Oct 1944 from 5. Flottille	6 patrols. 1 ship damaged: total 9811 GRT	to 33. Flottille
U-387	VIIC	24-Nov-42	1 Jul 1943 – 31 Oct 1943 from 5. Flottille	15 patrols	to 13. Flottille
U-390	VIIC	13-Mar-43	1 Dec 1943 – 5 Jul 1944 from 5. Flottille	4 patrols. 1 auxiliary warship sunk: total 545 GRT; 1 ship damaged: total 7934 GRT	Sunk 5 Jul 1944 in the mouth of the Seine by depth charges from the destroyer HMS *Wanderer* and the frigate HMS *Tavy*. 48 dead and 1 survivor
U-397	VIIC	20-Nov-43	1 Jun 1944 – 30 Jun 1944 from 5. Flottille	No patrols	to 23. Flottille
U-403	VIIC	25-Jun-41	1 Sep 1941 – 30 Jun 1942 from 5. Flottille	7 patrols. 2 ships sunk: total 12,946 GRT	to 11. Flottille
U-406	VIIC	22-Oct-41	1 May 1942 – 18 Feb 1944 from 8. Flottille	11 patrols. 1 ship sunk: total 7452 GRT; 3 ships damaged: total 13,285 GRT	Sunk 18 Feb 1944 in the North Atlantic by depth charges from the frigate HMS *Spey*. 12 dead and 45 survivors
U-410	VIIC	23-Feb-42	1 Sep 1942 – 31 May 1943 from 5. Flottille	7 patrols. 7 ships sunk: total 47,244 GRT; 2 warships sunk: total 7006t/6895 tons; 1 ship damaged beyond repair: total 3722 GRT; 1 ship damaged: total 7134 GRT	to 29. Flottille
U-427	VIIC	2-Jun-43	1 Jun 1944 – 31 Jul 1944 from 8. Flottille	5 patrols	to 11. Flottille
U-434	VIIC	21-Jun-41	21 Jun 1941 – 18 Dec 1941	1 patrol	Sunk 18 Dec 1941 north of Madeira by depth charges from the escort destroyer HMS *Blankney* and the destroyer HMS *Stanley*. 2 dead and 42 survivors
U-436	VIIC	27-Sep-41	1 Feb 1942 – 30 Jun 1942 from 5. Flottille	8 patrols. 6 ships sunk: total 36,208 GRT; 2 ships damaged: total 15,575 GRT	to 11. Flottille
U-442	VIIC	21-Mar-42	1 Oct 1942 – 12 Feb 1943 from 5. Flottille	2 patrols. 4 ships sunk: total 25,417 GRT	Sunk with all hands 12 Feb 1943 west of Cape St Vincent by depth charges from a Hudson of No. 48 Sqn RAF. 48 dead
U-448	VIIC	1-Aug-42	1 Feb 1943 – 14 Apr 1944 from 8. Flottille	5 patrols	Sunk 14 Apr 1944 northeast of the Azores by depth charges from the frigate HMCS *Swansea* and the sloop HMS *Pelican*. 9 dead and 42 survivors
U-449	VIIC	22-Aug-42	1 May 1943 – 24 Jun 1943 from 8. Flottille	1 patrol	Sunk with all hands on 24 Jun 1943 northwest of Cape Ortegal, Spain, by depth charges from the sloops HMS *Wren*, HMS *Woodpecker*, HMS *Kite* and HMS *Wild Goose*. 49 dead
U-453	VIIC	26-Jun-41	26 Jun 1941 – 31 Dec 1941	17 patrols. 9 ships sunk: total 23,289 GRT; 1 warship sunk: total 848t/835 tons; 1 warship damaged beyond repair: total 1732t/1705 tons; 2 ships damaged: total 16,610 GRT	to 29. Flottille
U-454	VIIC	24-Jul-41	1 Nov 1941 – 1 Aug 1943 from 5. Flottille	10 patrols. 1 ship sunk: total 557 GRT; 1 warship sunk: total 1900t/1870 tons; 1 ship damaged: total 5395 GRT	Sunk at 14:00 1 Aug 1943 in the Bay of Biscay northwest of Cape Ortegal by depth charges from an Australian Sunderland of No. 10 Sqn. 32 dead and 14 survivors
U-455	VIIC	21-Aug-41	1 Jan 1942 – 29 Feb 1944 from 5. Flottille	10 patrols. 3 ships sunk: total 17,685 GRT	to 29. Flottille
U-551	VIIC	7-Nov-40	7 Nov 1940 – 23 Mar 1941	1 patrol	Sunk with all hands 23 Mar 1941 southeast of Iceland by depth charges from the ASW trawler HMS *Visenda*. 45 dead
U-552	VIIC	4-Dec-40	4 Dec 1940 – 30 Apr 1944	15 patrols. 29 ships sunk: total 163,529 GRT; 2 auxiliary warships sunk: total 747 GRT; 1 warship sunk (USS *Reuben James*, the first US warship sunk in WWII – 6 weeks before declaration of war): total 1209t/1190 tons; 3 ships damaged: total 26,910 GRT	to 22. Flottille
U-553	VIIC	23-Dec-40	23 Dec 1940 – 30 Nov 1942	10 patrols. 13 ships sunk: total 64,612 GRT; 2 ships damaged: total 15,273 GRT	to 3. Flottille
U-567	VIIC	24-Apr-41	1 Nov 1941 – 21 Dec 1941 from 3. Flottille	3 patrols. 2 ships sunk: total 6809 GRT	Sunk with all hands 21 Dec 1941 northeast of the Azores by depth charges from the sloop HMS *Deptford* and the corvette HMS *Samphire*. 47 dead
U-575	VIIC	19-Jun-41	19 Jun 1941 – 13 Mar 1944	10 patrols. 8 ships sunk: total 36,106 GRT; 1 warship sunk: total 1031t/1015 tons; 1 ship damaged: total 12,910 GRT	Sunk 13 Mar 1944 north of the Azores by depth charges from the frigate HMCS *Prince Rupert*, the destroyer USS *Hobson*, the destroyer escort USS *Haverfield*, a Wellington of No. 172 Sqn RAF, 2 Flying Fortresses of Nos. 206 and 220 Sqns RAF and a Grumman Avenger of VC-95 of the escort carrier USS *Bogue*. 18 dead and 37 survivors
U-576	VIIC	26-Jun-41	26 Jun 1941 – 15 Jul 1942	5 patrols. 4 ships sunk: total 15,450 GRT; 2 ships damaged: total 19,457 GRT	Sunk with all hands 15 Jul 1942 off Cape Hatteras by depth charges from 2 US Navy Kingfisher seaplanes of VS-9. Boat may also have been rammed by MV *Unicoi* which had previously hit the boat with its deck gun. 45 dead
U-577	VIIC	3-Jul-41	3 Jul 1941 – 31 Dec 1941	3 patrols	to 29. Flottille
U-578	VIIC	10-Jul-41	1 Sep 1941 – 6 Aug 1942 from 5. Flottille	5 patrols. 4 ships sunk: total 23,635 GRT; 1 warship sunk: total 1107t/1090 tons	Missing with all hands in the Bay of Biscay on or after 6 Aug 1942. 49 dead. Previously credited to depth charges from a Czech-crewed Wellington of No. 311 Sqn RAF, which caused minor damage to U-135
U-581	VIIC	31-Jul-41	1 Dec 1941 – 2 Feb 1942 from 5. Flottille	2 patrols. 1 auxiliary warship sunk: total 364 GRT	Sunk 2 Feb 1942 southwest of the Azores by the destroyer HMS *Westcott*. 4 dead and 41 survivors
U-593	VIIC	23-Oct-41	1 Mar 1942 – 31 Oct 1942 from 8. Flottille	16 patrols. 9 ships sunk: total 38,290 GRT; 3 warships sunk: total 2949t/2902 tons; 1 ship damaged b/r: total 8426 GRT; 1 warship damaged b/r: total 1651t/1625 tons; 1 ship damaged: total 4853 GRT; 1 warship damaged: total 1651t/1625 tons	to 29. Flottille
U-594	VIIC	30-Oct-41	1 Mar 1942 – 4 Jun 1943 from 8. Flottille	5 patrols. 2 ships sunk: total 14,390 GRT	Sunk with all hands 4 Jun 1943 west of Gibraltar by rockets from a Hudson of No. 48 Sqn RAF. 50 dead

BOATS THAT SERVED WITH 7TH FLOTILLA (110 BOATS)

U-Boat	Type	Commissioned	Flotilla(s)	Patrols	Fate
U-602	VIIC	29-Dec-41	1 Oct 1942 – 31 Dec 1942 from 5. Flottille	4 patrols. 1 warship damaged beyond repair: total 1565t/1540 tons	to 29. Flottille
U-607	VIIC	29-Jan-42	1 Aug 1942 – 13 Jul 1943 from 5. Flottille	5 patrols. 4 ships sunk: total 28,937 GRT; 2 ships damaged: total 15,201 GRT	Sunk 13 Jul 1943 in the Bay of Biscay northwest of Cape Ortegal by depth charges from a Sunderland of No. 228 Sqn RAF. 45 dead and 7 survivors
U-617	VIIC	9-Apr-42	1 Sep 1942 – 30 Nov 1942 from 5. Flottille	7 patrols. 8 ships sunk: total 25,879 GRT; 1 auxiliary warship sunk: total 810 GRT; 2 warships sunk: total 3759t/3700 tons	to 29. Flottille
U-618	VIIC	16-Apr-42	1 Sep 1942 – 14 Aug 1944 from 5. Flottille	10 patrols. 3 ships sunk: total 15,788 GRT	Sunk with all hands 14 Aug 1944 west of St Nazaire by depth charges from frigates HMS *Duckworth* and HMS *Essington* and a Liberator of No. 53 Sqn RAF. 61 dead
U-624	VIIC	28-May-42	1 Oct 1942 – 7 Feb 1943 from 8. Flottille	2 patrols. 5 ships sunk: total 39,855 GRT; 1 ship damaged: total 5432 GRT	Sunk with all hands 7 Feb 1943 in the North Atlantic by depth charges from a B-17 Flying Fortress of No. 220 Sqn RAF. 45 dead
U-641	VIIC	24-Sep-42	1 Mar 1943 – 19 Jan 1944	4 patrols	Sunk with all hands 19 Jan 1944 southwest of Ireland by depth charges from corvette HMS *Violet*. 50 dead
U-647	VIIC	5-Nov-42	1 Jun 1943 – 28 Jul 1943 from 5. Flottille	1 patrol	Missing with all hands on or after 28 Jul 1943 north of the Shetland Islands, position unknown, possibly mined. 48 dead
U-650	VIIC	26-Nov-42	1 May 1943 – 30 Sep 1944 from 5. Flottille	7 patrols	to 11. Flottille
U-662	VIIC	9-Apr-42	1 Oct 1942 – 21 Jul 1943 from 5. Flottille	4 patrols. 3 ships sunk: total 18,609 GRT; 1 ship damaged: total 7174 GRT	Sunk 21 Jul 1943 in the mouth of the Amazon by depth charges from a US Navy PBY Catalina of VP-94. 44 dead and 3 survivors
U-667	VIIC	21-Oct-42	1 Jun 1943 – 25 Aug 1944 from 5. Flottille	5 patrols. 1 ship sunk: total 7176 GRT; 2 warships sunk: total 1190t/1171 tons; 1 warship damaged b/r: total 1680t/1653 tons	Sunk with all hands 25 Aug 1944 in the Bay of Biscay near La Rochelle by a mine. 45 dead
U-678	VIIC	25-Oct-43	1 Jun 1944 – 7 Jul 1944 from 5. Flottille	1 patrol	Sunk with all hands 7 Jul 1944 southwest of Brighton by depth charges from the destroyers HMCS *Ottawa* and HMCS *Kootenay* and corvette HMS *Statice*. 52 dead
U-702	VIIC	3-Sep-41	1 Mar 1942 – 3 Apr 1942 from 5. Flottille	1 patrol	Missing with all hands after 3 Apr 1942 in the North Sea. In 1987 a wreck that had struck a mine was found during oil exploration off Norway, and may be U-702
U-704	VIIC	18-Nov-41	1 Jul 1942 – 1 Apr 1943 from 8. Flottille	5 patrols. 1 ship sunk: total 6942 GRT	to 21. Flottille
U-707	VIIC	1-Jul-42	9 Dec 1942 – 9 Nov 1943 from 8. Flottille	3 patrols. 2 ships sunk: total 11,811 GRT	Sunk with all hands 9 Nov 1943 east of Azores by depth charges from a Fortress of No. 220 Sqn RAF. 51 dead
U-708	VIIC	24-Jul-42	1 Oct 1943 – 1 Feb 1944 from 8. Flottille	No patrols	to 5. Flottille
U-710	VIIC	2-Sep-42	1 Apr 1943 – 24 Apr 1943 from 5. Flottille	1 patrol	Sunk with all hands 24 Apr 1943 south of Iceland by depth charges from a Flying Fortress of No. 206 Sqn RAF. 49 dead
U-714	VIIC	10-Feb-43	1 Aug 1943 – 10 Nov 1944 from 5. Flottille	6 patrols. 1 ship sunk: total 1226 GRT; 1 auxiliary warship sunk: total 425 GRT	to 33. Flottille
U-751	VIIC	31-Jan-41	31 Jan 1941 – 17 Jul 1942	7 patrols. 5 ships sunk: total 21,412 GRT; 1 warship sunk: total 11,177t/11,000 tons; 1 ship damaged: total 8096 GRT	Sunk with all hands 17 Jul 1942 northwest of Cape Ortegal, Spain, by depth charges from an Armstrong Whitworth Whitley and an Avro Lancaster of Nos. 61 and 502 Sqns RAF. 48 dead
U-765	VIIC	19-Jun-43	1 Apr 1944 – 6 May 1944 from 8. Flottille	1 patrol	Sunk 6 May 1944 in the North Atlantic by depth charges from 2 Swordfish flying from escort carrier HMS *Vindex*, and from frigates HMS *Bickerton*, HMS *Bligh* and HMS *Aylmer*. 37 dead and 11 survivors
U-962	VIIC	11-Feb-43	1 Aug 1943 – 8 Apr 1944 from 5. Flottille	2 patrols	Sunk with all hands 8 Apr 1944 NW of Finisterre by depth charges from sloops HMS *Crane* and HMS *Cygnet*. 50 dead
U-969	VIIC	24-Mar-43	1 Oct 1943 – 29 Feb 1944 from 5. Flottille	3 patrols. 2 ships damaged beyond repair: total 14,352 GRT	to 29. Flottille
U-974	VIIC	22-Apr-43	1 Nov 1943 – 19 Apr 1944 from 5. Flottille	1 patrol	Sunk 19 Apr 1944 off Stavanger, Norway, torpedoed by Norwegian submarine HNoMS *Ula*. 42 dead and 8 survivors
U-976	VIIC	5-May-43	1 Nov 1943 – 25 Mar 1944 from 5. Flottille	2 patrols	Sunk 25 Mar 1944 near St Nazaire by gunfire from two Mosquitoes of No. 248 Sqn RAF. 4 dead and 49 survivors
U-980	VIIC	27-May-43	1 Jun 1944 – 11 Jun 1944 from 5. Flottille	1 patrol	Sunk with all hands 11 Jun 1944 northwest of Bergen by depth charges from a Catalina of No. 162 Sqn RCAF. 52 dead
U-985	VIIC	24-Jun-43	1 Jan 1944 – 15 Nov 1944 from 5. Flottille	3 patrols. 1 ship sunk: total 1735 GRT	Damaged by a German mine in Norwegian waters. Stricken 15 Nov 1944. Captured at Kristiansand May 1945. Broken up
U-988	VIIC	15-Jul-43	1 Jun 1944 – 29 Jun 1944 from 5. Flottille	1 patrol. 1 ship sunk: total 2385 GRT; 1 ship damaged beyond repair: total 7058 GRT; 1 warship damaged beyond repair: total 940t/925 tons	Thought to have been sunk 29 Jun 1944 west of Guernsey by depth charges from frigates HMS *Domett*, HMS *Cooke*, HMS *Essington*, HMS *Duckworth*, and a Liberator of No. 244 Sqn. 50 dead. However, boat may have been sunk 11 days earlier by a Polish Wellington of No. 304 Sqn.
U-994	VIIC	2-Sep-43	1 Jun 1944 – 5 Jul 1944 from 5. Flottille	1 patrol	to 5. Flottille
U-1004	VIIC/41	16-Dec-43	1 Aug 1944 – 31 Oct 1944 from 31. Flottille	2 patrols. 1 ship sunk: total 1313 GRT; 1 warship sunk: total 996 GRT	to 11. Flottille
U-1191	VIIC	9-Sep-43	1 May 1944 – 12 Jun 1944 from 8. Flottille	1 patrol	Missing with all hands on or after 12 Jun 1944 in the English Channel. 50 dead
U-1192	VIIC	23-Sep-43	1 May 1944 – 31 Jul 1944 from 8. Flottille	1 patrol	to 24. Flottille
U-A	Turkish	20-Sep-39	Sep 1939 – Mar 1941 and Dec 1941 – Aug 1942	9 patrols. 7 ships sunk: total 40,706 GRT	Former Turkish *Badiray*. Second of 4 boats ordered from Germaniawerft. When war broke out she was commissioned into the German Navy. Given the U-A designation on 21 Sep 1939. To 2. Flottille Apr–Dec 1941

9 Unterseebootsflottille

The first combat flotilla to be founded after the outbreak of war, the 9th Flotilla was established in the autumn of 1941. After the organization of the unit had been settled, it was transferred to Brest at the beginning of 1942, where it would play its part in the Battle of the Atlantic.

BREST WAS ONE OF the first French bases to be used by U-boats, and was home to the 1st U-boat Flotilla as well as the 9th. The base was captured by the 5th Panzer Division in June 1940, and it quickly became clear that any plans to operate U-boats from it would have to be delayed: the retreating British had destroyed most of the port's facilities.

Urgent repair work began immediately, and within two months the first U-boat, U-85, had arrived for repairs. By the autumn of 1940, the port was fully operational. However, it became evident that any U-boats using the port would be vulnerable to air attack, and in January 1941 construction work began on the massive concrete U-boat pens that would become characteristic of such bases.

The bunkers were built on a huge scale. Five 'wet' pens could each accommodate up to three boats. Ten 'dry' pens were also built, in which single boats could be dry-docked for major repairs. Boats began using the pens from the autumn of 1941, although the facility was not completed until the summer of 1942.

Massive protection

The bunkers were subject to Allied air attack from the moment construction began. They were a massive target, more than 333m (1093ft) by 192m (630ft), but more than 80 large-scale raids during the war caused very little damage. Even when nine 'Tallboy' six-tonne (5.9-ton) bombs scored direct hits in August 1944, only five penetrated the 6m (20ft) of concrete on the roof, and caused no damage either to the interior or to the U-boats berthed there.

The 9th Flotilla was commanded by two of the U-boat arm's most respected aces. Jürgen Oesten commanded U-61, U-106 and U-861 in a career that would take him from the Arctic to the Far East. He was the first commander of the 9th Flotilla, leaving to become *U-Boot-Admiralstabsoffizier* with the *Admiral Nordmeer*, where he had a major part to play in directing the U-boat war in Arctic waters. When Oesten arrived at Brest he discovered that there were

Commanders

Kptlt. Jürgen Oesten *(Oct 1941 – Feb 1942)*

Korvkpt. Heinrich Lehmann-Willenbrock *(May 1942 – Sep 1944)*

9TH FLOTILLA INSIGNIA

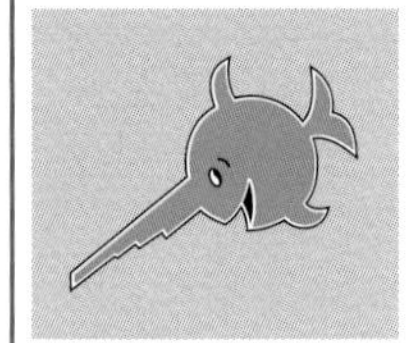

The 9th Flotilla's 'Laughing Swordfish' was famous. Originally the emblem of Heinrich Lehmann-Willenbrock's U-96, it became the flotilla's insignia when the ace commander took over the unit from Jürgen Oesten.

▼ The sinking of U-744

This photograph shows two of the seven Canadian escorts that combined to destroy U-744 in the North Atlantic on 6 March 1944. Twelve U-boat crewmen were killed and another 40 captured.

9TH FLOTILLA	
Type	**Boats assigned**
Type VIIC	73
Type VIIC/41	5
Type VIID	6

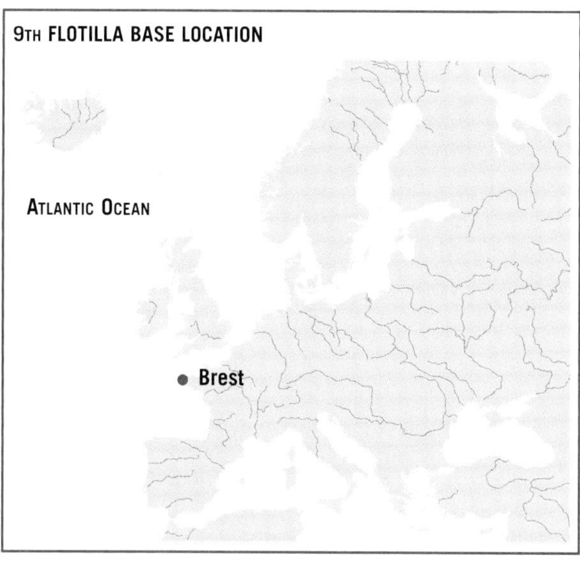

no facilities available for his crew, all of the prewar French barracks having been taken by the 1st Flotilla. Eventually he found a partially built hospital and helped by the *Organisation Todt* he completed this to house his crews.

He was succeeded as 9th Flotilla commander by Heinrich Lehmann-Willenbrock. The successful commander of U-96, Lehmann-Willenbrock was the model for *Der Alte*, the commander in Lothar-Günther Buchheim's best-selling *Das Boot*. As a *Sonderführer-Leutnant*, or War Correspondent, Buchheim accompanied U-96 on her seventh patrol, which provided the background for the book and the film and television series that followed.

Limited success

Brest was the third busiest of the U-boat bases in France, after Lorient and St Nazaire. Between them, the 1st and 9th Flotillas mounted 329 U-boat patrols between 28 August 1940 and 4 September 1944. However, having been formed after the end of the first 'Happy Time' the unit's boats did not run up the massive scores earlier commanders had achieved. Few boats sank more than three ships, and many did not survive their first patrol. The flotilla paid a considerable price for its participation in the Battle of the Atlantic: 54 out of the 84 boats which saw service were sunk by enemy action, the majority going down with all hands.

The last U-boat to leave Brest was U-256, commanded by the flotilla commander, Korvkpt. Lehmann-Willenbrock. It left the port on 4 September 1944, reaching Bergen in Norway on 17 October. Both the 1st and 9th Flotillas were disbanded as U-boat activity ceased. Brest was captured by the US Army on 21 September 1944 after a fierce month-long battle.

Specifications

Crew: 44
Powerplant: Diesel/electric
Max Speed: 31.5/14.1km/hr (17/7.6kt) s/d
Surface Range: 12,040km (6500nm)
Displacement: 773/879t (761/865 tons) s/d
Dimensions (length/beam/draught): 67.1 x 6.2 x 4.8m (220.1 x 20.34 x 15.75ft)
Commissioned: 6 Nov 1941
Armament: 14 torpedoes (4 bow/1 stern tubes); 1 x 8.8cm (3.5in) and 2 x 2cm (0.8in) guns (1942)

▲ U-595

Type VIIC

Destroyed on 14 November 1942 northeast of Oran by depth charges from Hudsons of No. 608 Sqn RAF, assisted by five more aircraft from the same squadron. The crew beached the boat on the Algerian shore: all 45 survived.

Star commanders

1941–44

Although the flotilla was led by two highly successful aces, wartime conditions by the time it was founded meant that it had fewer 'star' captains than earlier U-boat formations.

▲ **Concrete protection**

The massive concrete U-boat pens built by the *Organisation Todt* on the French Atlantic coast proved impervious to Allied air attack.

Fregattenkapitän Heinrich Lehmann-Willenbrock

Born on 11 December 1911 in Bremen, Heinrich Lehmann-Willenbrock joined the *Reichsmarine* as part of Crew 31. In April 1939, he transferred to the U-boat force. After one patrol in U-5, he commissioned U-96, in which he made eight patrols, sinking 24 ships totalling over 170,000 GRT. Lehmann-Willenbrock was the sixth highest scoring U-boat ace of the war. Commander of the 9th Flotilla from 1942, he took the last U-boat out of Brest in September 1944. After the war he worked as a salvage contractor and as master of several merchant ships. He died on 18 April 1986 at Bremen.

Oberleutnant zur See Heinz Sieder

Born 28 June 1920 in Munich, Sieder joined the *Kriegsmarine* as part of Crew 38. After active service aboard the battlecruiser *Scharnhorst,* he transferred to the U-boat arm in April 1941. He commissioned the Type VIIC U-boat U-984 in June 1943.

In January 1944, he was attached to the 9th Flotilla in Brest. He was awarded the Knight's Cross for a patrol at the end of June 1944, in which he torpedoed a British destroyer and four merchant vessels, damaging three beyond repair.

Sieder died on 20 August 1944, when U-984 was sunk with all hands west of Brest by depth charges from the Canadian destroyers HMCS *Ottawa*, *Kootenay* and *Chaudiere.*

Oberleutnant zur See Hermann Stuckmann

Born on 2 January 1921 in Wuppertal-Barmen, Stuckmann joined the *Kriegsmarine* soon after the beginning of the war in Class X/39. In July 1941, he was attached to the U-boat force and served as watch officer for more than a year on U-571 under the command of Kptlt. Helmut Möhlmann. In July 1943, he commissioned the Type VIIC boat U-316, which he commanded until May 1944 as a school boat in the Baltic. In May 1944, he took command of the combat boat U-621, which operated against the Allied landing ships in the English Channel in 1944. During these patrols he sank two landing ships. Stuckmann died when U-621 was sunk with all hands on 18 August 1944 in the Bay of Biscay near La Rochelle by depth charges from Canadian destroyers.

STAR COMMANDERS

Commander	Patrols	Ships Sunk
Fregkpt. Heinrich Lehmann-Willenbrock	10	24
Oblt. zur See Heinz Sieder	4	3
Oblt. zur See Hermann Stuckmann	3	1

U-210

Type VIIC

Built by Germania Werft at Kiel, U-210 was laid down in March 1941 and was launched in December. The boat was commissioned in February 1942.

After a period of working up with the 5th Flotilla in the Baltic, U-210 was transferred to the 9th Flotilla at Brest. The boat's first patrol started at Kiel and was intended to finish at its new base, but as happened to so many boats in the later stages of the war, things did not go according to plan. The boat set off from Kiel on 18 July 1942, heading for the Norwegian Sea, from where it would prepare for its foray out into the Atlantic.

On 29 July, U-210 was ordered to intercept Convoy ON 115, which had been located in the central Atlantic and was being shadowed by U-164. U-210 reached the convoy the next day, but an alert and efficient escort force ensured that no U-boat was able to press home an attack.

The boat was then ordered to join the *Pirat* wolfpack, which was then establishing a patrol line well ahead of ON 115 in the hope of re-establishing contact. On 2 August U-552 spotted the convoy to the east of Cape Race, and the wolfpack moved in to attack before the merchant ships could reach the Newfoundland Bank, where they would be within range of air cover from Canada. However, a thick fog which fell the next day – an ever-present hazard in these waters – meant that the attack had to be abandoned after two ships had been sunk.

U-210 was then ordered to join the *Steinbrinck* wolfpack patrolling about 645km (400 miles) to the northeast of Newfoundland in the path of Convoy SC 94. U-593 spotted the merchant ships on 5 August and U-210 closed on their position south of Cape Farewell. On 6 August, as U-210 approached the convoy submerged, it was located by the Canadian destroyer HMCS *Assiniboine*. An accurate depth-charge attack forced the boat to the surface, and the combatants engaged in a close-range gun battle, during which the U-boat commander, *Kapitänleutnant* Lemcke, was killed. The destroyer then rammed the U-boat, which sank leaving six dead. The 37 survivors were taken prisoner.

U-210 Commander

Kptlt. Rudolf Lemcke *(Feb 1942 – Aug 1942)*

U-210 TIMETABLE

Patrol Dates	Operational Area	Ships Sunk
18 Jul 1942 – 6 Aug 1942	North Atlantic	0

Specifications

Crew: 44

Powerplant: Diesel/electric

Max Speed: 31.5/14.1km/hr (17/7.6kt) s/d

Surface Range: 12,040km (6500 nm)

Displacement: 773/879t (761/865 tons) s/d

Dimensions (length/beam/draught): 67.1 x 6.2 x 4.8m (220.1 x 20.34 x 15.75ft)

Commissioned: 21 Feb 1942

Armament: 14 torpedoes (4 bow/1 stern tubes); 1 x 8.8cm (3.5in) and 2 x 2cm (0.8in) guns

▲ **U-210**

Type VIIC

A typical boat of the Type VIIC, which made up the largest single class of submarine ever built, U-210 nevertheless had no chance to use its weapons against enemy convoys in its short, one-patrol career.

U-256

Type VIIC

Commissioned as a standard Type VIIC at the end of November 1941, U-256 was one of a handful of boats converted as Flak platforms for use against Allied aircraft in the Bay of Biscay.

U-256 TIMETABLE		
Patrol Dates	**Operational Area**	**Ships Sunk**
28 Jul 1942 – 3 Sep 1942	Transit from Kiel to Lorient	0
4 Oct 1943 – 17 Nov 1943	Protecting tanker U-488 W of the Azores	0
25 Jan 1944 – 22 Mar 1944	W of Ireland/SW of Ireland	1
6 June 1944 – 8 June 1944	Channel invasion front	0
3 Sep 1944 – 17 Oct 1944	Transit from France to Bergen, Norway	0

U-256 Commanders

Kptlt. Odo Loewe *(Dec 1941 – Nov 1942)*
Wilhelm Brauel *(Aug 1943 – June 1944)*
Korvkpt. Heinrich Lehmann-Willenbrock *(Sep 1944 – Oct 1944)*

THE BOAT WAS BUILT at Bremer Vulkan and made its first combat patrol on its transfer from Kiel to 9th Flotilla at Brest. After pursuing Convoy SC 94 with the *Steinbrinck* wolfpack, U-256 joined the *Lohs* group west of Ireland. In the early hours of 25 August, the boat was damaged by depth charges while attacking Convoy ONS 122. Limping towards France and safety, U-256 was further damaged by an RAF Whitley bomber on 2 September. The damage was so bad that the boat was taken out of service in November 1942.

The submarine was converted to a Flak boat from May 1943, recommissioning as U-Flak 2 on 16 August 1943. In company with U-271, the boat left Lorient on 4 October 1943. Her mission was to rendezvous with and provide anti-aircraft protection for the milchcow U-488 to the west of the Azores.

On 31 October, U-256 was on the surface when she was detected by the destroyer USS *Borie*. Diving, the Flak boat was subjected to three depth-charge attacks which caused some damage. Evading her attacker, U-256 returned to Brest in November.

The Flak conversions had not been a great success, and U-256 was rebuilt as a conventional Type VIIC boat in December and January. Seriously damaged on a patrol in June 1944, U-256 was the last boat left in Brest as Allied armies approached from Norway. Repaired and equipped with a *Schnorchel* on her last patrol, she was captained by Korvkpt. Heinrich Lehmann-Willenbrock, the commander of the 9th Flotilla, on her last voyage from France to Norway. The boat was decommissioned for the final time on 23 October 1944 at Bergen.

▼ Type VIIC Flak boat conning tower

The increased Allied air threat prompted Admiral Dönitz to authorize the development of 'Flak boats'. These were Type VII boats with extensively modified conning towers, which carried heavy anti-aircraft armament. Two quad 2cm (0.8in) Flakvierlings were mounted, together with a 3.7cm (1.5in) Flak gun. Although the Flak boats achieved some success, they could still be swamped by Allied fighter-bombers like the Mosquito, and the enlarged tower adversely affected both dive times and underwater handling.

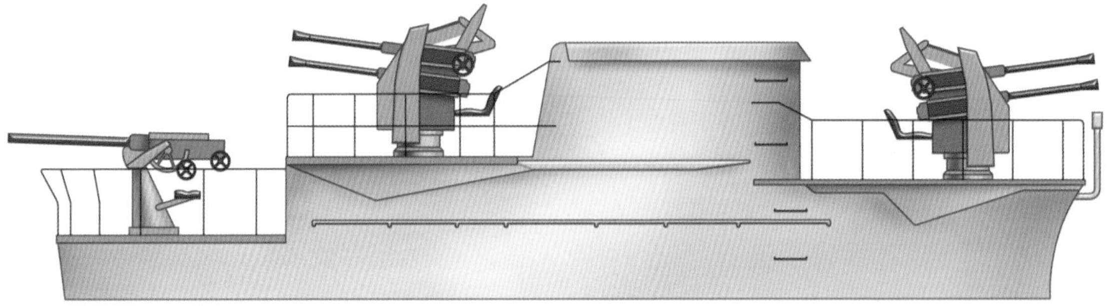

U-377

Type VIIC

Built at Howaldtswerke Kiel and commissioned in October 1941, U-377 had an active career in the Arctic and the Atlantic, but sank nothing in 12 patrols.

THE BOAT OPERATED with the 11th Flotilla against the PQ and QP convoys in the Arctic before transferring to the 9th Flotilla early in 1943. During the journey south, U-377 made the first penetration of British coastal waters for two years.

U-377 went missing with all 52 hands on or after 15 January 1944. The boat was originally thought to have been sunk on 17 January, southwest of Ireland, by depth charges from the destroyer HMS *Wanderer* and the frigate HMS *Glenarm*. However, there is a good chance that U-377 may have been sunk by one of its own acoustic (T5) homing torpedoes on 15 January. British codebreakers picked up at least two emergency messages from U-boats reporting damage from torpedo hits around that time, though there is no record that the signals were ever received by the *Kriegsmarine* or by FdU *West*. No Allied units made any report of attacking a U-boat on that day. One of the signals was probably from U-305 and the other is likely to have been from U-377.

U-377 Commanders

Kptlt. Otto Köhler *(Oct 1941 – Aug 1943)*
Oblt. Gerhard Kluth *(Aug 1943 – Jan 1944)*
Oblt. Ernst-August Gerke *(Sep 1943 – Oct 1943)*

U-377 TIMETABLE

Patrol Dates	Operational Area	Ships Sunk
14 Feb 1942 – 28 Feb 1942	Transit from Kiel to Norway	0
6 Mar 1942 – 19 Mar 1942	Arctic, S of Jan Mayen Is	0
22 Mar 1942 – 25 Mar 1942	Patrol from Narvik aborted	0
5 Apr 1942 – 19 Apr 1942	Off Kola Peninsula, USSR	0
25 May 1942 – 29 May 1942	Arctic against convoy PQ 16	0
31 May 1942 – 2 June 1942	Moved to Trondheim for repair	0
20 Nov 1942 – 25 Nov 1942	Transferred to Bergen	0
30 Jan 1943 – 18 Mar 1943	Transit to France via Orkney and N Atlantic	0
15 Apr 1943 – 7 June 1943	Central and western N Atlantic	0
26 Aug 1943 – 30 Aug 1943	Atlantic patrol aborted	0
6 Sep 1943 – 10 Oct 1943	S of Iceland/off Newfoundland	0
15 Dec 1943 – 15 Jan 1944	NE of the Azores/West of Portugal	0

Specifications

Crew: 44
Powerplant: Diesel/electric
Max Speed: 31.5/14.1km/hr (17/7.6kt) s/d
Surface Range: 12,040km (6500nm)
Displacement: 773/879t (761/865 tons) s/d
Dimensions (length/beam/draught): 67.1 x 6.2 x 4.8m (220.1 x 20.34 x 15.75ft)
Commissioned: 2 Oct 1941
Armament: 14 torpedoes (4 bow/1 stern tubes); 1 x 8.8cm (3.5in) and 2 x 2cm (0.8in) guns

▲ **U-377**

Type VIIC

U-377 landed at least two weather detachments on Spitzbergen on her Arctic patrols, and was assigned to several wolfpacks in the North Atlantic after transferring to the 9th Flotilla, but had no successes in attacking convoys.

Attack on convoy SC 94

August 1942

During the summer of 1942 U-boats returned to the Atlantic convoy routes after wreaking havoc amid the unprotected shipping on the American coast and in the Caribbean.

The convoy consisted of 36 ships, escorted by Canadian Escort Group C1 (destroyer HMCS *Assiniboine* and corvettes HMCS *Chilliwack* and HMCS *Orillia*) and three Royal Navy corvettes, HMS *Nasturtium*, HMS *Dianthus* and HMS *Primrose*. Originating at Halifax, the slow eastbound convoy had left Sydney, Cape Breton Island, on 31 July 1942.

Ranged against the convoy were the eight boats of Group *Steinbrinck* – U-71, U-210, U-379, U-454, U-593, U-597, U-607 and U-704. These were reinforced by a number of newly arrived boats, including U-174, U-176, U-254, U-256, U-438, U-595, U-605, U-660 and U-705.

U-boat attacks

On 6 August, the *Assiniboine* sighted a submarine on the surface and attacked her using gunfire. The submarine, which was U210, returned fire, setting the destroyer's bridge on fire. The submarine was unable to dive and, eventually, the destroyer decided to ram her, sinking the U-boat. However, *Assiniboine* was so severely damaged she had to put back to St Johns for repairs, denying the convoy escort its largest and most mobile asset.

A massive underwater explosion on 8 August caused several merchant crews to abandon their vessels. Most, however, realizing that their ships had not been torpedoed, reboarded their vessels. The explosion may have been from a munitions ship, one of five sunk in a very short period of time by U-176 and U-379.

The repeated attacks by the *Steinbrinck* boats signalled that the *U-Bootwaffe* was back in the Atlantic with a vengeance: SC 94 lost 11 out of its 36 ships before it could reach Britain and safety.

CONVOY SC 94 BATTLE TIMETABLE

Date	Event
5 Aug 1942	A group of 6 merchantmen and two escorts, separated from the convoy due to fog, are spotted by U-593. U-593 sinks one ship, and is then driven off by the escort, along with U-595 which had responded to U-593's sighting report
6 Aug	U-454 and U-595 try to penetrate the escort screen, but are severely damaged and have return to port. U-210 attacks but is sunk by the *Assiniboine*
7 Aug	The *Steinbrinck* wolfpack is reinforced by six of the newly arrived outbound boats. Eleven boats attack the convoy overnight and into 8 August, but all fail to hit a target
8 Aug	After midday, U-176 sinks three ships. An almost simultaneous attack by U-379 accounts for two more. This is the first serious attack on an Atlantic convoy since the previous year, most U-boat strength having been diverted to operations off the US coast and the Caribbean. The crews of some of the merchantmen panic, and three are abandoned simply through fear of being attacked. One of the drifting vessels is sunk by U-176
8/9 Aug	The Polish destroyer *Blyskawica* and the British destroyer HMS *Broke* reinforce the convoy escort. U-379 is sunk by HMS *Dianthus*. Aggressive patrolling by the escorts keeps the U-boats away from the convoy, only U-595 and U-607 being able to mount attacks, which are unsuccessful
9 Aug	Most of the escort has been drawn away from the convoy, pursuing a contact, but long-range aircraft are now able to reach the area and provide cover. U-174, U-254, U-256 and U-704 all launch attacks, but are unable to get close enough to achieve any success
10 Aug	U-597 launches an unsuccessful attack. However, bad planning leaves the convoy temporarily uncovered by aircraft, and while the escorts are still pursuing contacts far astern, U-438 sinks three ships and U-660 destroys another

Wolfpack group *Leuthen*

SEPTEMBER–OCTOBER 1943

In contrast to the situation the previous summer, the U-boats attacking convoys in the summer and autumn of 1943 did so at their peril.

NEVERTHELESS, ALTHOUGH the battle had swung in favour of the escorts, Dönitz could still mount some effective attacks on the convoy routes. On 20 September 1943, 14 boats on patrol in the North Atlantic were ordered to establish patrol line *Leuthen*, stretching south-southwest of Iceland. Their aim was to locate and attack any ONS convoys that might have been passing through the area. They were to be reinforced by a number of other boats, which had been refuelling north of the Azores.

However, as that group moved north, one of the *Leuthen* boats, U-341, was spotted on the surface and sunk by a Canadian Liberator just east of the planned patrol line, alerting Allied anti-submarine forces to the presence of U-boats.

Convoy attack

On 20 September, U-270 spotted westbound convoy ON 202 near Cape Farewell. The *Leuthen* boats were not yet in position, so they made best speed to attack the convoy, which had merged with convoy ONS 18 during the night. Five boats attacked the merchant ships, but most of the rest of the group targeted the escorts. The theory was that if the escort was sufficiently weakened, the U-boats would be free to attack the real target – the merchantmen. The U-boats claimed 10 destroyers sunk or damaged over the night of 20/21 September. In fact, three escorts were sunk and one was damaged.

Fog meant that the U-boats lost contact during 21 September. As it cleared in the afternoon of the 22nd, five boats regained contact and tried to attack, but were driven off. The operation was called off on 23 September as visibility again got worse and the convoy came under the protective umbrella of Newfoundland-based aircraft. In addition to the escort losses, six merchant ships had been lost and another damaged. U-229 and U-338 were sunk.

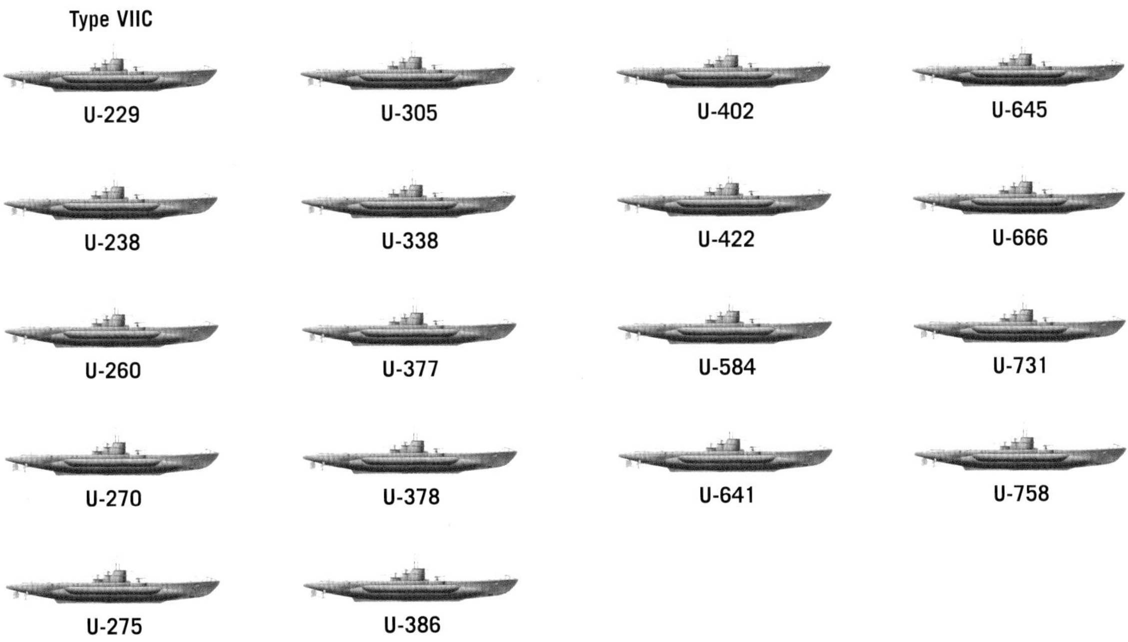

BOATS THAT SERVED WITH 9TH FLOTILLA (84 BOATS)

U-Boat	Type	Commissioned	Flotilla(s)	Patrols	Fate
U-89	VIIC	19-Nov-41	1 May 1942 – 12 May, 1943 from 8. Flottille	4 patrols. 4 ships sunk: total 13,815 GRT	Sunk with all hands 12 May 1943 in the North Atlantic by the destroyer HMS *Broadway*, the frigate HMS *Laganan* and an 811 Sqn Swordfish aircraft from the escort carrier HMS *Biter*. 48 dead
U-90	VIIC	20-Dec-41	1 Jul 1942 – 24 Jul 1942 from 8. Flottille	1 patrol	Sunk with all hands 24 Jul 1942 in the North Atlantic by the Canadian destroyer HMCS *St. Croix*. 44 dead
U-91	VIIC	28-Jan-42	1 Sep 1942 – 25 Feb 1944 from 5. Flottille	6 patrols. 4 ships sunk: total 26,194 GRT; 1 warship sunk: total 1307t/1375 tons	Sunk 26 Feb 1944 in the North Atlantic by the frigates HMS *Affleck*, HMS *Gore* and HMS *Gould*. 36 dead and 16 survivors
U-92	VIIC	3-Mar-42	1 Sep 1942 – 12 Oct 1944 from 5. Flottille	9 patrols. 2 ships sunk: total 17,612 GRT; 1 warship damaged b/r: total 1651t/1625 tons; 1 ship damaged: total 9348 GRT	Badly damaged 4 Oct 1944 in Bergen, Norway, by RAF bombs – decommissioned and scrapped
U-210	VIIC	21-Feb-42	1 Aug 1942 – 6 Aug 1942 from 5. Flottille (training)	1 patrol	Sunk 6 Aug 1942 in the North Atlantic south of Cape Farewell, Greenland, by ramming, depth charges and gunfire from the destroyer HMCS *Assiniboine*. 6 dead and 37 survivors
U-211	VIIC	7-Mar-42	1 Sep 1942 – 19 Nov 1943 from 5. Flottille (training)	5 patrols. 1 ship sunk: total 11,237 GRT; 1 warship sunk: total 1372t/1350 tons; 2 ships damaged: total 20,646 GRT	Sunk with all hands 19 Nov 1943 east of the Azores by depth charges from a Wellington aircraft of No. 179 Sqn RAF. 54 dead
U-213	VIID	30-Aug-41	1 May 1942 – 31 Jul 1942 from 1. Flottille	3 patrols. 1 special operation, landing an *Abwehr* agent on New Brunswick, Canada 14 May 1942	Sunk with all hands 31 Jul 1942 in the Atlantic east of the Azores by depth charges from the sloops HMS *Erne*, HMS *Rochester* and HMS Sandwich. 50 dead
U-214	VIID	1-Nov-41	1 May 1942 – 26 Jul 1944 from 5. Flottille (training)	11 patrols. 3 ships sunk: total 18,266 GRT; 1 warship sunk: total 1549t/1525 tons; 1 ship damaged: total 6507 GRT; 1 auxiliary warship damaged: total 10,552 GRT	Sunk with all hands 26 Jul 1944 in the English Channel southeast of Eddystone by depth charges from the frigate HMS *Cooke*. 48 dead
U-215	VIID	22-Nov-41	1 Jul 1942 – 3 Jul 1942 from 5. Flottille (training)	1 patrol. 1 ship sunk: total 7191 GRT	Sunk with all hands 3 Jul 1942 in the Atlantic east of Boston by depth charges from the anti-submarine trawler HMS *Le Tiger*. 48 dead
U-216	VIID	15-Dec-41	1 Sep 1942 – 20 Oct 1942	1 patrol. 1 ship sunk: total 4989 GRT	Sunk with all hands 20 Oct 1942 southwest of Ireland by 6 depth charges from a Liberator of No. 224 Sqn. 45 dead
U-217	VIID	31-Jan-42	1 Aug 1942 – 5 June 1943 from 5. Flottille (training)	3 patrols. 3 ships sunk: total 10,651 GRT	Sunk with all hands 5 Jun 1943 in mid-Atlantic by depth charges from Grumman TBF Avengers of the escort carrier USS *Bogue*. 50 dead
U-218	VIID	24-Jan-42	1 Sep 1942 – 30 Sep 1944 from 5. Flottille (training)	10 patrols. 3 ships sunk: total 698 GRT; 1 ship damaged: total 7361 GRT; 1 auxiliary warship damaged: total 7177 GRT	to 8. Flottille
U-230	VIIC	24-Oct-42	1 Feb 1943 – 30 Nov 1943 from 5. Flottille (training)	8 patrols. 1 ship sunk: total 2868 GRT; 3 warships sunk: total 3643t/3585 tons	to 29. Flottille
U-232	VIIC	28-Nov-42	1 May 1943 – 8 Jul 1943 from 5. Flottille (training)	1 patrol. On 24 Feb 1943, U-232 collided with and sank U-649 during training in the Bay of Danzig	Sunk with all hands 8 Jul 1943 west of Oporto by depth charges from a USAAF B-24. 46 dead
U-240	VIIC	3-Apr-43	1 Feb 1944 – 17 May 1944 from 5. Flottille (training)	1 patrol	Missing with all hands west of Norway after 17 May 1944. 50 dead. It was credited to depth charges from a Norwegian Sunderland of No. 330 Sqn RAF, but that target was probably U-668, which took no damage
U-244	VIIC	9-Oct-43	1 Aug 1944 – 31 Oct 1944	4 patrols	to 11. Flottille
U-248	VIIC	6-Nov-43	1 Aug 1944 – 31 Oct 1944 from 5. Flottille (training)	2 patrols	to 11. Flottille
U-254	VIIC	8-Nov-41	1 Aug 1942 – 8 Dec 1942 from 8. Flottille	3 patrols. 3 ships sunk: total 18,967 GRT	Sank 8 Dec 1942 southeast of Cape Farewell, Greenland, after a collision with U-221. 41 dead and 4 survivors
U-256	VIIC	18-Dec-41	1 Aug 1942 – 5 Oct 1944 from 8. Flottille (training)	5 patrols. 1 warship sunk: total 1321t/1300 tons	Heavily damaged 25 Aug 1942 and stricken in November 1942. Converted to U-Flak 2 in May 1943; commissioned for second time 16 Aug 1943. Converted back December 1943. Stricken 23 Oct 1944 in Bergen, Norway. Captured there and cannibalized
U-273	VIIC	21-Oct-42	1 May 1943 – 19 May 1943 from 8. Flottille	1 patrol	Sunk with all hands 19 May 1943 southwest of Iceland by depth charges from a Lockheed Hudson of No. 269 Sqn RAF. 46 dead
U-279	VIIC	3-Feb-43	1 Aug 1943 – 4 Oct 1943 from 8. Flottille	1 patrol. On its single patrol U-279 landed an agent on Iceland	Sunk with all hands southwest of Iceland 4 Oct 1943 by depth charges from a US Navy Ventura of VB-128. 48 dead. Originally credited to a British Liberator, which actually sank U-389
U-282	VIIC	13-Mar-43	1 Oct 1943 – 29 Oct 1943	1 patrol	Sunk with all hands 29 Oct 1943 southeast of Greenland by depth charges from the destroyers HMS *Vidette*, HMS *Duncan* and the corvette HMS *Sunflower*. 48 dead
U-283	VIIC	31-Mar-43	1 Feb 1944 – 11 Feb 1944 from 8. Flottille	1 patrol	Sunk with all hands 11 Feb 1944 southwest of the Faroes by depth charges from a Vickers Wellington of No. 407 Sqn RCAF. 49 dead
U-284	VIIC	14-Apr-43	1 Nov 1943 – 21 Dec 1943	1 patrol	Scuttled 21 Dec 1943 southeast of Greenland after severe sea damage. No casualties – 49 survivors. Entire crew rescued by U-629 and returned to Brest 5 Jan 1944
U-293	VIIC/41	8-Sep-43	1 Apr 1944 – 31 Jul 1944 from 8. Flottille	6 patrols. 1 warship damaged: total 1685t/1658 tons	to 11. Flottille
U-296	VIIC/41	3-Nov-43	1 Aug 1944 – 30 Sep 1944 from 8. Flottille	3 patrols	to 11. Flottille
U-302	VIIC	16-Jun-42	1 Nov 1943 – 6 Apr 1944 from 9. Flottille	10 patrols. 3 ships sunk: total 12,697 GRT	Sunk with all hands 6 Apr 1944 in the Atlantic northwest of the Azores by depth charges from the frigate HMS *Swale*. 51 dead
U-309	VIIC	27-Jan-43	1 Nov 1943 – 1 Oct 1944 from 11. Flottille	11 patrols. 1 ship damaged beyond repair: total 7219 GRT	to 33. Flottille
U-317	VIIC/41	23-Oct-43	1 June 1944 – 26 June 1944 from 4. Flottille	2 patrols	Sunk with all hands 26 June 1944 northeast of the Shetlands by depth charges from a Liberator of No. 86 Sqn RAF. 50 dead

BOATS THAT SERVED WITH 9TH FLOTILLA (84 BOATS)

U-Boat	Type	Commissioned	Flotilla(s)	Patrols	Fate
U-347	VIIC	7-Jul-43	1 Mar 1944 – 31 May 1944 from 8. Flottille	4 patrols	to 11. Flottille
U-348	VIIC	10-Aug-43	1 Apr 1944 – 11 Jul 1944 from 8. Flottille	9 (possibly as many as 15) patrols	to 8. Flottille
U-365	VIIC	8-Jun-43	1 Mar 1944 – 8 Jun 1944 from 5. Flottille	11 patrols. 1 ship sunk: total 7540 GRT, 3 warships sunk: total 1377t/1355 tons, 1 warship damaged: total 1737t/1710 tons	to 13. Flottille
U-377	VIIC	2-Oct-41	1 Mar 1943 – 15 Jan 1944 from 11. Flottille	12 patrols	Missing with all hands southwest of Ireland Sep 1944. 52 dead. May have been sunk by its own acoustic (T5) homing torpedo on 15 Jan
U-383	VIIC	6-June-42	1 Oct 1942 – 1 Aug 1943 from 8. Flottille	4 patrols. 1 ship sunk: total 423 GRT	Lost with all hands 1 Aug 1943 west of Brittany, probably as a result of severe damage by depth charges from a Sunderland of No. 228 Sqn RAF. 52 dead
U-388	VIIC	31-Dec-42	1 Jun 1943 – 20 Jun 1943 from 5. Flottille	1 patrol	Sunk with all hands 20 Jun 1943 southeast of Cape Farewell, Greenland, by depth charges from a US Navy PBY Catalina from Patrol Squadron VP-84. 47 dead
U-389	VIIC	6-Feb-43	1 Aug 1943 – 4 Oct 1943 from 5. Flottille	2 patrols	Sunk with all hands 4 Oct 1943 southwest of Iceland by depth charges from a Liberator of No. 120 Sqn RAF. 50 dead. Previously credited to a Hudson of No. 269 Sqn in Denmark Strait, but that attack on 5 Oct actually sank U-336
U-403	VIIC	25-Jun-41	1 Mar 1943 – 18 Aug 1943 from 11. Flottille	7 patrols. 2 ships sunk: total 12,946 GRT	Sunk with all hands 18 Aug 1943 off the West African coast near Dakar by depth charges from a French-crewed Wellington of No. 344 Sqn RAF. 49 dead. Previously credited to a Lockheed Hudson of No. 200 Sqn, which attacked with depth charges earlier the same day but inflicted only minor damage
U-407	VIIC	18-Dec-41	1 Sep 1942 – 30 Nov 1942 from 5. Flottille	12 patrols. 3 ships sunk: total 26,892 GRT; 1 ship damaged beyond repair: total 7176 GRT; 1 ship damaged: total 6207 GRT; 2 warships damaged: total 18,187t/17,900 tons	to 29. Flottille
U-408	VIIC	19-Nov-41	1 May 1942 – 30 Jun 1942 from 5. Flottille	3 patrols. 3 ships sunk: total 19,689 GRT	to 11. Flottille
U-409	VIIC	21-Jan-42	1 Sep 1942 – 30 Jun 1943 from 5. Flottille	6 patrols. 3 ships sunk: total 16,199 GRT; 1 ship damaged: total 7519 GRT	to 29. Flottille
U-412	VIIC	29-Apr-42	1 Oct 1942 – 22 Oct 1942 from 8. Flottille	1 patrol	Sunk with all hands 22 Oct 1942 northeast of the Faroes by depth charges from a Vickers Wellington of No. 179 Sqn RAF. 47 dead
U-421	VIIC	13-Jan-43	1 Nov 1943 – 31 Mar 1944 from 8. Flottille	2 patrols	to 29. Flottille
U-425	VIIC	21-Apr-43	1 Nov 1943 – 31 Dec 1943 from 8. Flottille	8 patrols	to 11. Flottille
U-438	VIIC	22-Nov-41	1 Aug 1942 – 6 May 1943 from 8. Flottille	4 patrols. 4 ships sunk: total 19,502 GRT; 1 ship damaged: total 5496 GRT	Sunk with all hands 6 May 1943 northeast of Newfoundland by depth charges from the sloop HMS *Pelican*. 48 dead
U-443	VIIC	18-Apr-42	1 Oct 1942 – 31 Dec 1942 from 8. Flottille	3 patrols. 3 ships sunk: total 19,435 GRT; 1 warship sunk: total 1104t/1087 tons	to 29. Flottille
U-447	VIIC	11-Jul-42	1 Mar 1943 – 7 May 1943 from 8. Flottille	2 patrols	Sunk with all hands 7 May 1943 west of Gibraltar by depth charges from 2 Lockheed Hudsons of No. 233 Sqn RAF. 48 dead
U-450	VIIC	12-Sep-42	1 Jun 1943 – 30 Nov 1943 from 8. Flottille	4 patrols	to 29. Flottille
U-473	VIIC	16-Jun-43	1 Jan 1944 – 6 May 1944 from 5. Flottille	2 patrols. 1 warship damaged beyond repair: total 1422t/1400 tons	Sunk 6 May 1944 southwest of Ireland by depth charges from the sloops HMS *Starling*, HMS *Wren* and HMS *Wild Goose*. 23 dead and 30 survivors
U-480	VIIC	6-Oct-43	1 Jun 1944 – 14 Oct 1944 from 5. Flottille	3 patrols. 2 ships sunk: total 12,846 GRT; 2 warships sunk: total 1803t/1775 tons	to 11. Flottille
U-482	VIIC	1-Dec-43	1 Aug 1944 – 30 Sep 1944 from 5. Flottille	2 patrols. 4 ships sunk: total 31,611 GRT; 1 warship sunk: total 1026t/1010 tons	to 11. Flottille
U-591	VIIC	9-Oct-41	1 Jun 1943 – 30 Jul 1943 from 11. Flottille	8 patrols. 4 ships sunk: total 19,932 GRT; 1 ship damaged: total 5701 GRT	Sunk 30 Jul 1943 in the South Atlantic near Pernambuco by depth charges from a US Navy Ventura of VB-127. 19 dead and 28 survivors
U-595	VIIC	6-Nov-41	1 Aug 1942 – 14 Nov 1942 from 8. Flottille	3 patrols	Destroyed 14 Nov 1942 northeast of Oran by depth charges from 2 Hudsons of No. 608 Sqn RAF, assisted by five more aircraft from the same squadron. The crew beached the badly damaged boat on the Algerian shore: all 45 survived
U-604	VIIC	8-Jan-42	1 Aug 1942 – 11 Aug 1943 from 5. Flottille	6 patrols. 6 ships sunk: total 39,891 GRT	Scuttled 11 Aug 1943 in the Atlantic just south of the equator after being damaged by depth charges from a US Navy Ventura of VB-129 and a PB4Y Liberator of VB-107. 14 dead. 31 survivors were picked up by U-185 and U-172, but 14 U-604 crewmen died when U-185 was subsequently sunk
U-605	VIIC	15-Jan-42	1 Aug 1942 – 31 Oct 1942 from 5. Flottille	3 patrols. 3 ships sunk: total 8409 GRT	to 29. Flottille
U-606	VIIC	22-Jan-42	1 Nov 1942 – 22 Feb 1943 from 11. Flottille	3 patrols. 3 ships sunk: total 20,527 GRT; 2 ships damaged: total 21,925 GRT	Sunk 22 Feb 1943 in the North Atlantic by depth charges from the Polish destroyer *Burza* and the US coastguard cutter *Campbell*. 36 dead and 11 survivors
U-621	VIIC	7-May-42	1 Oct 1942 – 18 Aug 1944 (as U-Flak 3 19 Aug 1943 – 1 Oct 1943) from 8. Flottille	10 patrols. 4 ships sunk: total 20,159 GRT; 1 auxiliary warship sunk: total 2938 GRT; 1 ship damaged: total 10,048 GRT; 1 warship damaged: total 1651t/1625 tons. Refitted as U-Flak 3 7 Jul 1943. Converted back later in the year	Sunk with all hands 18 Aug 1944 in the Bay of Biscay near La Rochelle by depth charges from the destroyers HMCS *Ottawa*, HMCS *Kootenay* and HMCS *Chaudiere*. 56 dead
U-631	VIIC	16-Jul-42	1 Jan 1943 – 17 Oct 1943 from 5. Flottille	3 patrols. 2 ships sunk: total 9136 GRT	Sunk 17 Oct 1943 southeast of Greenland by depth charges from the corvette HMS *Sunflower*

BOATS THAT SERVED WITH 9TH FLOTILLA (111 BOATS)

U-Boat	Type	Commissioned	Flotilla(s)	Patrols	Fate
U-633	VIIC	30-Jul-42	1 Mar 1943 – 10 Mar 1943 from 5. Flottille	1 patrol. 1 ship sunk: total 3921 GRT	Sunk with all hands 10 Mar 1943 in the North Atlantic, rammed by the British merchantman SS *Scorton*. 43 dead. Previously credited to a Flying Fortress of No. 220 Sqn on 7 Mar 1943, which actually unsuccessfullly attacked U-641
U-634	VIIC	6-Aug-42	1 Feb 1943 – 30 Aug 1943 from 5. Flottille	3 patrols. 1 ship sunk: total 7176 GRT	Sunk with all hands 30 Aug 1943 east of the Azores by depth charges from the sloop HMS *Stork* and the corvette HMS *Stonecrop*. 47 dead
U-638	VIIC	3-Sep-42	1 Feb 1943 – 5 May 1943 from 5. Flottille	2 patrols. 1 ship sunk: total 5507 GRT; 1 ship damaged: total 6537 GRT	Sunk with all hands 5 May 1943 northeast of Newfoundland by depth charges from HMS *Sunflower*. 44 dead. Previously credited to HMS *Loosestrife* the same day, an attack which actually sank U-192
U-659	VIIC	9-Dec-41	1 Sep 1942 – 4 May 1943 from 5. Flottille	5 patrols. 1 ship sunk: total 7519 GRT; 3 ships damaged: total 21,565 GRT	Sunk 4 May 1943 west of Cape Finisterre, after colliding with U-439. 44 dead and 3 survivors
U-660	VIIC	8-Jan-42	1 Aug 1942 – 31 Oct 1942 from 5. Flottille	3 patrols. 2 ships sunk: total 10,066 GRT; 2 ships damaged: total 10,447 GRT	to 29. Flottille
U-663	VIIC	14-May-42	1 Nov 1942 – 8 May 1943 from 11. Flottille	3 patrols. 2 ships sunk: total 10,924 GRT	Probably foundered with all hands 8 May 1943 west of Brest after being seriously damaged on 7 May by depth charges from an Australian Sunderland of No. 10 Sqn. 49 dead. Previously credited to a 58 Sqn Halifax, which most likely caused minor damage to U-124
U-664	VIIC	17-Jun-42	1 Nov 1942 – 9 Aug 1943 from 8. Flottille	5 patrols. 3 ships sunk: total 19,325 GRT	Sunk 9 Aug 1943 in the North Atlantic by depth charges from Avengers flying from the escort carrier USS *Card*. 7 dead and 44 survivors
U-709	VIIC	12-Aug-42	1 Mar 1943 – 1 Mar 1944 from 5. Flottille	5 patrols	Sunk with all hands 1 Mar 1944 north of the Azores by depth charges from the destroyer escorts USS *Thomas*, USS *Bostwick* and USS *Bronstein*. 52 dead
U-715	VIIC	17-Mar-43	1 Jun 1944 – 13 Jun 1944 from 5. Flottille	1 patrol	Sunk 13 Jun 1944 northeast of the Faroes by depth charges from a Canso (Canadian-built Catalina) of No. 162 Sqn RCAF. 36 dead and 16 survivors
U-739	VIIC	6-Mar-43	1 Nov 1943 – 31 Dec 1943 from 8. Flottille	8 patrols. 1 warship sunk: total 635t/625 tons	to 13. Flottille
U-744	VIIC	5-Jun-43	1 Dec 1943 – 6 Mar 1944 from 8. Flottille	2 patrols. 1 ship sunk: total 7359 GRT; 1 warship sunk: total 1651t/1625 tons; 1 warship damaged: total 1651t/1625 tons	Sunk 6 Mar 1944 in the North Atlantic. Damaged by torpedoes from destroyer HMS *Icarus*, then sunk by depth charges from HMS *Icarus*, destroyers HMCS *Chaudiere* and HMCS *Gatineau*, frigate HMCS *St. Catherines*, corvettes HMS *Kenilworth Castle*, HMCS *Fennel* and HMCS *Chilliwack*. 12 dead and 40 survivors
U-755	VIIC	3-Nov-41	1 Aug 1942 – 30 Nov 1942 from 5. Flottille	5 patrols. 1 ship sunk: total 928 GRT; 2 auxiliary warships sunk: total 2974 GRT	to 29. Flottille
U-759	VIIC	15-Aug-42	1 Feb 1943 – 15 Jul 1943 from 5. Flottille	2 patrols. 2 ships sunk: total 12,764 GRT	Sunk with all hands 15 Jul 1943 east of Jamaica by depth charges from a US Navy Mariner of VP-32. 47 dead. Previously credited to another VP-32 aircraft on 26 Jul 1943, which sank U-359
U-761	VIIC	3-Dec-42	1 Aug 1943 – 24 Feb 1944 from 8. Flottille	3 patrols	Damaged by British and American aircraft while trying to pass through the Straits of Gibraltar. Scuttled 24 Feb 1944 off Tangier to avoid being sunk by destroyers HMS *Anthony* and HMS *Wishart*. 9 dead and 48 survivors
U-762	VIIC	30-Jan-43	1 Aug 1943 – 8 Feb 1944	2 patrols	Sunk with all hands 8 Feb 1944 in the North Atlantic by depth charges from the sloops HMS *Woodpecker* and HMS *Wild Goose*. 51 dead
U-764	VIIC	6-May-43	1 Nov 1943 – 30 Sep 1944 from 8. Flottille	8 patrols. 1 ship sunk: total 638 GRT; 2 warships sunk: total 1723t/1696 tons	to 11. Flottille
U-771	VIIC	18-Nov-43	1 Jun 1944 – 31 Jul 1944 from 31. Flottille	2 patrols	to 11. Flottille
U-772	VIIC	23-Dec-43	1 Aug 1944 – 14 Oct 1944 from 31. Flottille	2 patrols	to 11. Flottille
U-951	VIIC	3-Dec-42	1 Jun 1943 – 7 Jul 1943 from 5. Flottille	1 patrol	Sunk with all hands 7 Jul 1943 northwest of Cape St Vincent by depth charges from a USAAF B-24 of the 1st A/S Sqn. 46 dead
U-954	VIIC	23-Dec-42	1 May 1943 – 19 May 1943 from 5. Flottille	1 patrol	Sunk with all hands 19 May 1943 southeast of Cape Farewell, Greenland, by depth charges from the frigate HMS *Jed* and the sloop HMS *Sennen*. 47 dead
U-955	VIIC	31-Dec-42	1 Apr 1944 – 7 Jun 1944	1 patrol. Landed 3 spies on Iceland 20 Apr 1944	Sunk with all hands 7 Jun 1944 N of Cape Ortegal by depth charges from a Sunderland of No. 201 Sqn RAF. 50 dead
U-966	VIIC	4-Mar-43	1 Aug 1943 – 10 Nov 1943 from 5. Flottille	1 patrol	Sunk 10 Nov 1943 near Cape Ortegal by depth charges from British, American and Czech aircraft. 8 dead and 42 survivors
U-979	VIIC	20-May-43	1 Aug 1944 – 14 Oct 1944 from 5. Flottille	3 patrols. 1 auxiliary warship sunk: total 348 GRT; 2 ships damaged: total 12,133 GRT	to 11. Flottille
U-984	VIIC	17-Jun-43	Jan 1944 – 20 Aug 1944 from 5. Flottille	4 patrols. 1 ship damaged: total 7240 GRT; 3 ships damaged beyond repair: total 21,550 GRT; 1 warship damaged beyond repair: total 1321t/1300 tons	Sunk with all hands 20 Aug 1944 west of Brest by depth charges from destroyers HMCS *Ottawa*, HMCS *Kootenay* and HMCS *Chaudiere*. 45 dead
U-989	VIIC	22-Jul-43	1 Feb 1944 – 30 Sep 1944 from 5. Flottille	5 patrols. 1 ship sunk: total 1791 GRT; 1 ship damaged: total 7176 GRT	to 33. Flottille
U-997	VIIC/41	23-Sep-43	1 May 1944 – 31 May 1944 from 5. Flottille	7 patrols. 1 ship sunk: total 1603 GRT; 1 warship sunk: total 107t/105 tons; 1 ship damaged: total 4287 GRT	to 13. Flottille
U-1165	VIIC/41	17-Nov-43	1 Jun 1944 – 1 Aug 1944 from 8. Flottille	4 patrols. 1 warship sunk: total 40t/39 tons	to 11. Flottille

10 Unterseebootsflottille

The 10th U-boat Flotilla was founded at Lorient on 15 January 1942 under the command of *Kapitänleutnant* Günther Kuhnke. From the start, the new flotilla was home to the long-range boats of the U-boat arm, supplementing and replacing those serving with the 2nd Flotilla.

The flotilla came into being just when the need for long-range boats became more pressing, after Japan attacked the US Pacific Fleet at Pearl Harbor and Hitler declared war on the United States in support of Germany's Tripartite Pact ally. Germany and Japan had already had some naval dealings.

As early as March 1941, Hitler had issued a directive in which the High Command was to freely offer military intelligence and technical information to the Japanese authorities. German merchant ships had been trapped in Japanese ports at the outbreak of war, and they were used as blockade runners over the next two years in an attempt to bring strategic materials home to Germany.

By 1942, merchant ships had little chance of getting supplies through the Allied blockade, and thoughts turned to using submarines to carry vital strategic materials. Admiral Dönitz was not in favour of diverting his U-boat force from where he saw the real battle was taking place – in the North Atlantic. However, Hitler was keen on using the U-boats in Asian waters, both to acquire strategic materials and to prey on British and Commonwealth trade in those distant waters. Part of his reasoning was that such attacks would force the Allies to dilute their escort strength to deal with the new threat.

▼ U-464

U-464 was sunk by a Catalina from the US Navy's VP-73 patrol squadron in August 1942. Two crew were killed and the remaining 53 rescued.

Commander

Korvkpt. Günther Kuhnke *(Jan 1942 – Oct 1944)*

10TH FLOTILLA BASE LOCATION

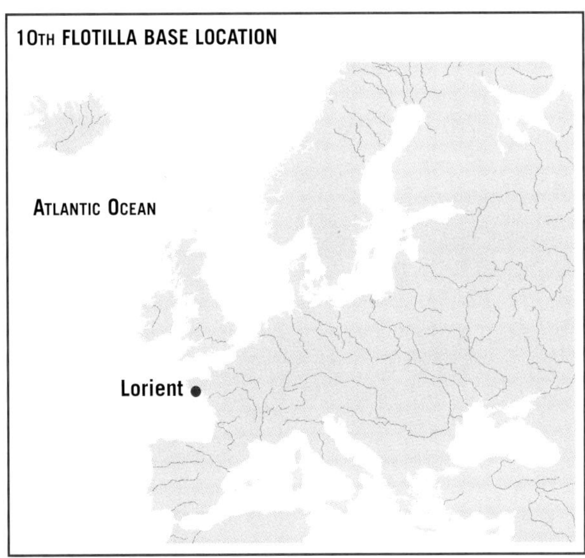

Much of the burden of those operations fell on the newly formed 10th Flotilla. Finding crews able to deal with the difficulties of operating in such strange and dangerous waters was not easy, but there were enough former merchant seamen with Far Eastern experience scattered through the U-boat arm to provide a core of experience, and a number of officers had served in those waters with blockade runners and armed merchant raiders in the first years of the war.

Atlantic operations

Missions to exotic locations in Southeast Asia were only part of the 10th Flotilla's remit – the bulk of unit's boats operated in the Atlantic, mounting patrols from Greenland through the central Atlantic and the Caribbean to the coasts of South America and Southern Africa. The 10th Flotilla also numbered many of the specialist Type XIV supply submarines, the so-called milchcows, in its inventory. These were used to extend the endurance of all kinds

10TH FLOTILLA	
Type	**Boats assigned**
Type IXC	26
Type IXC/40	41
Type IXD1	2
Type IXD2	4
Type XB	1
Type XIV	6

10TH FLOTILLA INSIGNIA

Overtly nationalistic or Nazi symbols were rare on U-boat insignia during World War II. The 9th Flotilla was the only unit that carried the *Balkenkreuz* more usually seen on aircraft or military vehicles.

of U-boats by providing refuelling, resupply and rearmament facilities in remote and unfrequented parts of the ocean.

The 10th Flotilla, like all French-based formations, had to leave its base in August 1944 as Allied armies smashed their way out of Normandy, advancing to threaten many of the bases along the Atlantic coast of France. Most surviving boats of the 10th Flotilla were transferred to Norway, although a number were assigned to the 33rd Flotilla and were based in the Far East.

Korvettenkapitän Kuhnke left Lorient with the last flotilla boat, U-853, on 27 August 1944 and reached Flensburg, Germany, on 14 October. The flotilla was officially disbanded that month.

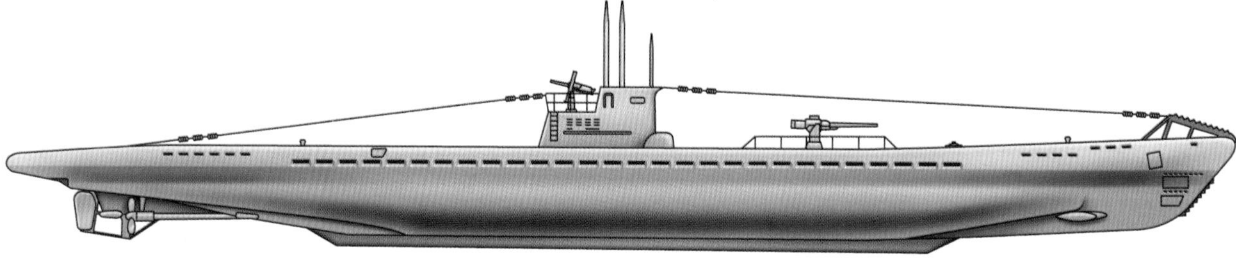

Specifications

Crew: 48–50
Powerplant: Diesel/electric
Max Speed: 33.9/13.5km/hr (18.3/7.3kt) s/d
Surface Range: 20,370km (11,000nm)
Displacement: 1138/1252t (1120/1232 tons) s/d
Dimensions (length/beam/draught): 76.8 x 6.8 x 4.7m (252 x 22.31 x 15.42ft)
Commissioned: 16 Oct 1941
Armament: 22 torpedoes (4 bow/2 stern tubes); 1 x 10.5cm (4.1in), 1 x 3.7cm (1.5in) and 1 x 2cm (0.8in) guns

▲ **U-160**

Type IXC

Commanded for three out of its four patrols by Knight's Cross holder Kptlt. Georg Lassen, U-160 served with the 10th Flotilla from March 1942 to July 1943. It sank 26 ships totalling more than 150,000 GRT before being tracked down and destroyed by aircraft from the escort carrier USS *Santee*.

Specifications

Crew: 53
Powerplant: Diesel/electric
Max Speed: 26.7/11.7km/hr (14.4/6.3kt) s/d
Surface Range: 17,220km (9300nm)
Displacement: 1688/1932t (1661/1901 tons) s/d
Dimensions (length/beam/draught): 67.1 x 9.4 x 6.5m (220.16 x 30.83 x 21.33ft)
Commissioned: 5 Mar 1942
Armament: 2 x 3.7cm (1.5in) and 1 x 2cm (0.8in) guns
Fuel load: 439t (432 tons)

▲ **U-462**

Type XIV

This submarine tanker refuelled at least 50 boats on her first four patrols, but was damaged by aircraft on patrols five and six. Spotted off Cape Ortegal on her way into the Atlantic on patrol seven, she was sunk by aircraft and warships.

Star commanders

1941–44

The long-range boats of the 10th U-boat Flotilla achieved a considerable amount of success in 1941 and 1942 and the unit boasted several high-scoring commanders.

Korvettenkapitän Adolf Cornelius Piening

Born on 16 September 1910 in Süderende, Tondern, Piening joined the *Reichsmarine* with Crew 30. After service on the pocket battleship *Deutschland* and in torpedo boats and minesweepers, he transferred to U-boats in October 1940. In August 1941 he took command of U-155. In four patrols he sank 25 ships totalling 126,664 GRT as well as the escort carrier HMS *Avenger* (14,733 tonnes/14,500 tons).

He took command of the 7th Flotilla in March 1944. He made his final patrol in April 1945, laying mines off St Nazaire in U-255. In 1956, Adolf Piening joined the *Bundesmarine*, serving for 13 years and retiring as a *Kapitän zur See*. He died on 15 May 1984 in Kiel.

Piening was famous for introducing the so-called 'Piening Route' (hugging the coast of France and Spain), which he invented as a means of evading marauding Allied aircraft in the open waters of the Bay of Biscay.

Korvettenkapitän Helmut Witte

Helmut Witte was born on 6 April 1915 in Bojendorf, Holstein. He joined the Navy with Crew 34. In July 1940, Witte transferred to the U-boat force from surface craft. After the usual training, he became an officer on the newly commissioned U-107 under Kptlt. Hessler. Before he left the boat in July 1941, he had taken part in the most successful patrol of the war, during which U-107 sank 14 ships totalling nearly 87,000 GRT.

Witte commissioned U-159 in October 1941 and operated in the waters off Panama on his second patrol. On his third patrol, U-159 was a part of the *Eisbär* group, which operated in the waters off Cape Town in September 1942. In four patrols, he sank 23 ships for a total of 119,684 GRT.

Witte left U-159 in June 1943, serving from then until the end of the war in several staff positions. He was promoted to *Korvettenkapitän* on 20 April 1945. Helmut Witte died on 3 October 2005 at Duisburg.

STAR COMMANDERS

Commander	Patrols	Ships Sunk
Korvettenkapitän Adolf Piening	8	25
Korvettenkapitän Helmut Witte	4	23
Korvettenkapitän Georg Lassen	4	26

Korvettenkapitän Georg Lassen

Born on 12 May 1915 in Berlin-Steglitz, Georg Lassen joined the Navy with Crew 35. For more than a year, he was I WO (*Erste Wacht Offizier*, or First Officer) aboard the successful U-29 commanded by *Kapitänleutnant* Otto Schuhart. They sank 11 ships for a total of 80,688 GRT as well as the 22,860-tonne (22,500-ton) aircraft carrier HMS *Courageous*. From January to September 1941, Kptlt. Georg Lassen was the commander of U-29, which at this time was a training boat in the 24th U-boat Flotilla.

On 16 October 1941, Lassen commissioned the Type IXC U-boat U-160, and on four patrols he sank 26 ships for a total of 156,082 GRT, damaging a further five ships totalling 34,419 GRT. On his first patrol as commander in March/April 1942, he sank or damaged six ships for a total of 43,560 GRT. On his last patrol, in South African waters, he sank or damaged six ships in less than five hours over the night of 3/4 March 1943 for a total of 41,076 GRT. Three days later he was awarded the Oak Leaves to the Knight's Cross.

Lassen left U-160 in May 1943, two months before the submarine was lost with all hands in the Atlantic, to become a tactics instructor at the 1st ULD (*U-Boot-Lehrdivision*).

CREW 37A EMBLEM

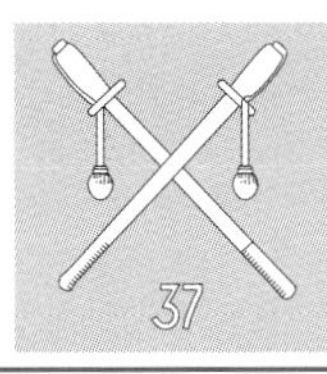

Kptlt. Hans-Jürgen Lauterbach-Emden, commander of the Type IXC/40 boat U-539, joined the *Kriegsmarine* with Crew 37A, and used his class insignia as a personal emblem on his first command.

U-459

TYPE XIV

In an attempt to extend the endurance of U-boats operating far out into the Atlantic, the *Kriegsmarine* developed a submarine tanker to support operational boats at sea.

U-459 WAS THE FIRST purpose-built 'milk cow', which were large boats designed to refuel combat boats at sea. They had no torpedo tubes but carried one 2cm (0.8in) and two 3.7cm (1.5in) AA guns for self-defence. The first of 10 such vessels commissioned between November 1941 and March 1943, U-459 set off on her first refuelling mission from Kiel in January 1942, returning to her new base at St Nazaire.

U-459 Commander

Korvkpt. Georg von Wilamowitz-Möllendorf *(Nov 1941 – Jul 1943)*

After suporting the *Eisbär* boats in October 1942, U-459 had to be refuelled herself by fellow milchcow U-462 in order to make it back to her next new base at Bordeaux, where the boat was transferred to the operational control of the 12th Flotilla.

Milchcow

On her third and fourth patrols, U-459 was used to support the *Eisbär* and *Seehund* wolfpack groups, made up from long-range Type IX boats on their way to operational areas off the coast of South Africa.

Air attack

The submarine was scuttled while heading out on her sixth patrol on 24 July 1943 near Cape Ortegal, Spain, after being badly damaged by two RAF Wellingtons from Nos. 172 and 547 Sqns. The first aircraft was shot down but crashed onto the boat's hull with only the rear gunner of the Wellington's crew surviving. A depth charge that landed on the deck was pushed

U-459 TIMETABLE

Patrol Dates	Operational Area	Boats Refuelled
29 Mar 1942 –15 May 1942	NE of Bermuda	15
6 June 1942 – 19 Jul 1942	W of the Azores	16
18 Aug 1942 – 4 Nov 1942	S of St Helena	11
20 Dec 1942 – 7 Mar 1943	S of St Helena	4
20 Apr 1943 – 3 June 1943	Central N Atlantic	17
22 Jul 1943 – 24 Jul 1943	Bay of Biscay	0

Specifications

Crew: 53

Powerplant: Diesel/electric

Max Speed: 26.7/11.7km/hr (14.4/6.3kt) s/d

Surface Range: 17,220km (9300nm)

Displacement: 1688/1932t (1661/1901 tons) s/d

Dimensions (length/beam/draught): 67.1 x 9.4 x 6.5m (220.16 x 30.83 x 21.33ft)

Commissioned: 15 Nov 1941

Armament: 2 x 3.7cm (1.5in) and 1 x 2cm (0.8in) guns

Fuel load: 439t (432 tons)

▲ **U-459**

Type XIV

Milchcows like U-459 had no offensive role, and carried no torpedoes or torpedo tubes. The only armament fitted was defensive, since refuelling operations had to be carried out on the surface where the boats were vulnerable to air attack.

overboard: however, it exploded, damaging the submarine's steering gear.

While going around in circles in an attempt to evade the aircraft, U-459 was attacked by the second Wellington. Nineteen crewmen were killed and 41 (including the rear gunner of the downed Wellington bomber) survived, to be picked up by the Polish destroyer *Orkan*.

U-506

Type IXC

In five patrols with the 10th Flotilla, U-506 sank 14 ships totalling more than 70,000 GRT. In July 1943 it was assigned to the *Monsun* group in Asia, but it was never to arrive.

U-506 took part in the operations to rescue survivors after the sinking of SS *Laconia* in September 1942 off West Africa. About 1500 men were saved by three U-boats, an Italian submarine and by Vichy French vessels from Dakar.

U-506 TIMETABLE

Patrol Dates	Operational Area	Ships Sunk
2 Mar 1942 – 25 Mar 1942	Transit from Kiel to Lorient via Heligoland	0
6 Apr 1942 – 15 June 1942	Florida/Gulf of Mexico	8
28 Jul 1942 – 7 Nov 1942	W African coast off Freetown	4
14 Dec 1942 – 8 May 1943	Central Atlantic/S Atlantic	2
6 Jul 1943 – 12 Jul 1943	Biscay, en route to the Far East	0

U-506 Commander

Kptlt. Erich Würdemann *(Sep 1941 – Jul 1943)*

Fate

U-506 was sunk on 12 July 1943 west of Vigo, Spain, by seven depth charges from a USAAF B-24 Liberator of A/S Sqn 1. Forty-eight crew were killed and six survived. This was one of the first boats detected using SC137 10cm (4in) radar, which the Germans could not detect.

About 15 men were seen in the water after the boat broke in two. The attacking pilot dropped a liferaft and a smoke flare to assist the surviving crew. Six men were picked up from the sea by a British destroyer on 15 July, three days after the sinking.

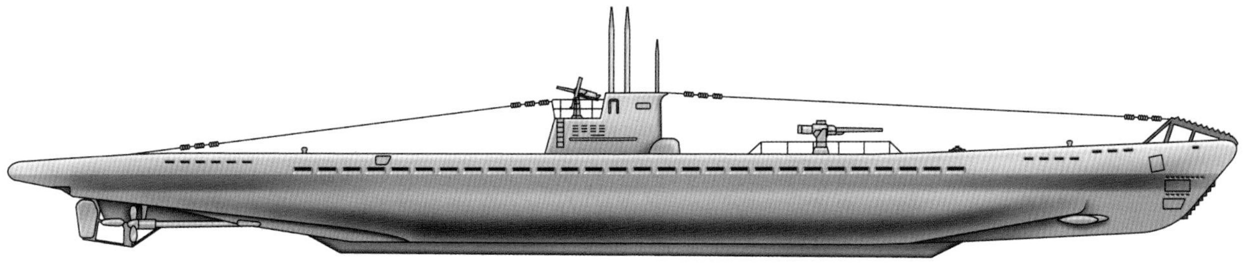

Specifications

Crew: 48–50

Powerplant: Diesel/electric

Max Speed: 33.9/13.5km/hr (18.3/7.3kt) s/d

Surface Range: 20,370km (11,000nm)

Displacement: 1138/1252t (1120/1232 tons) s/d

Dimensions (length/beam/draught): 76.8 x 6.8 x 4.7m (252 x 22.31 x 15.42ft)

Commissioned: 15 Sep 1941

Armament: 22 torpedoes (4 bow/2 stern tubes); 1 x 10.5cm (4.1in), 1 x 3.7cm (1.5in) and 1 x 2cm (0.8in) guns

▲ **U-506**

Type IXC

U-506 underwent working-up training with the 4th Flotilla in the Baltic before transferring to the 10th Flotilla at Lorient for operations. The boat spent her combat career in the central Atlantic and in American waters.

U-511

Type IXC

Laid down at Deutsche Werft, Hamburg, in February 1941, U-511 was launched in September and commissioned on 8 December of that year.

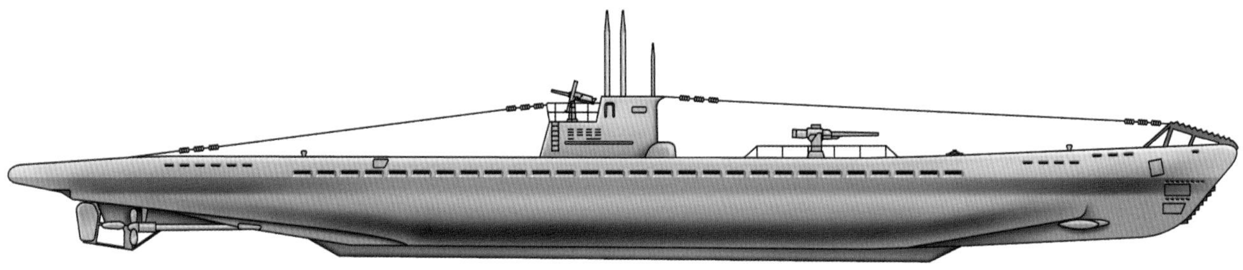

Specifications

Crew: 48–50
Powerplant: Diesel/electric
Max Speed: 33.9/13.5km/hr (18.3/7.3kt) s/d
Surface Range: 20,370km (11,000nm)
Displacement: 1138/1252t (1120/1232 tons) s/d
Dimensions (length/beam/draught): 76.8 x 6.8 x 4.7m (252 x 22.31 x 15.42ft)
Commissioned: 8 Dec 1941
Armament: 22 torpedoes (4 bow/2 stern tubes); 1 x 10.5cm (4.1in), 1 x 3.7cm (1.5in) and 1 x 2cm (0.8in) guns

▲ **U-511**
Type IXC
U-511 was one of a number of German Type IX boats that found their way into the service of the Imperial Japanese Navy in the last two years of the war. It was surrendered to the Americans in August 1945.

In the summer of 1942, while still working up in the Baltic the boat was detached to Peenemünde for use as a test platform in rocket experiments, possibly because Kptlt. Steinhoff's brother Dr Erich Steinhoff was a rocket scientist at Peenemünde at the time. A rack for six 30cm (11.8in) Wurfkörper 42 Spreng artillery rockets was fitted to the boat, missiles being launched successfully from the surface and submerged from as deep as 12m (39ft).

Although the experiments were technically successful, the U-boat staff did not proceed further with them. The rockets were not accurate enough to strike point targets such as ships. However, they might have functioned in a shore bombardment role had not the extra equipment on deck affected the boat's performance and handling underwater. The boat was assigned to the 10th Flotilla at Lorient from August 1942, and mounted four patrols, three in the central Atlantic and the Caribbean and one to the U-boat base at Penang in Malaya. The boat carried passengers on this trip, including the German Ambassador to Tokyo, the Japanese Naval Attaché in Berlin, and some German scientists and engineers.

Fate

The boat was handed over to a Japanese crew, who took it on to Kure. It was sold to Japan on 16 September 1943 and became the submarine RO-500. Surrendered in August 1945, it was scuttled off Maizuru by the US Navy on 30 April 1946.

U-511 Commanders

Kptlt. Friedrich Steinhoff *(Dec 1941 – Dec 1942)*
Kptlt. Fritz Schneewind *(Dec 1942 – Nov 1943)*

U-511 TIMETABLE

Patrol Dates	Operational Area	Ships Sunk
16 Jul 1942 – 29 Sep 1942	Transit from Kiel to Lorient via Caribbean	2
24 Oct 1942 – 28 Nov 1942	Off Moroccan Atlantic coast	0
31 Dec 1942 – 8 Mar 1943	Canaries/Azores/off Portuguese coast	1
10 May 1943 – 7 Aug 1943	Transit from Lorient to Penang	2

U-530

Type IXC/40

The Type IXC/40 was a marginally enlarged variant of the original Type IXC, with longer range and a more efficiently organized interior.

On 23 June 1944, on its way to the Caribbean, U-530 made a rendezvous west of the Cape Verde Islands with the Japanese submarine I-52. The huge Japanese boat (twice the tonnage of a Type IX) was heading for Europe with a cargo that included two tonnes (two tons) of gold plus other strategic materials. The German boat's mission was to supply the larger boat with a Naxos radar detector, two Naxos operators and a German navigator to help accomplish the last stage of its journey.

Unknown to the two Axis boats, Ultra intelligence had alerted the Allies to the rendezvous, and U-530 was being hunted by a US Navy task group led by the escort carrier USS *Bogue*. Immediately after making the transfer, U-530 headed for Trinidad, thus missing the attack made by Avengers from the *Bogue*. This was to be the last U-boat mission into the Caribbean. After the rendezvous, I-52 submerged but was located by newly developed sonobuoys. The Avengers dropped two depth bombs, followed by Fido homing torpedoes. Two underwater explosions marked the end of I-52.

On being told of the end of the war, the crew of U-530, then off the American coast, refused to follow Admiral Dönitz's instructions. Heading south, they surrendered in the Mar del Plata, Argentina, on 10 July 1945. The crew was interned and the boat transferred to the United States and used for trials. It was sunk as a target on 28 November 1947 by a torpedo from USS *Toro*.

U-530 Commanders

Kptlt. Kurt Lange *(Oct 1942 – Jan 1945)*

Oblt. Otto Wermuth *(Jan 1945 – Jul 1945)*

U-530 TIMETABLE

Patrol Dates	Operational Area	Ships Sunk
20 Feb 1943 – 22 Apr 1943	N Atlantic W of Ireland	2
29 May 1943 – 3 Jul 1943	SW of Canaries as a fuel tanker	0
27 Sep 1943 – 29 Sep 1943	Patrol aborted	0
3 Oct 1943 – 5 Oct 1943	Patrol aborted	0
17 Oct 1943 – 22 Feb 1944	Caribbean	1 damaged
22 May 1944 – 4 Oct 1944	Caribbean (last U-boat patrol in area)	0
3 Mar 1945 – 10 Jul 1945	US east coast	0

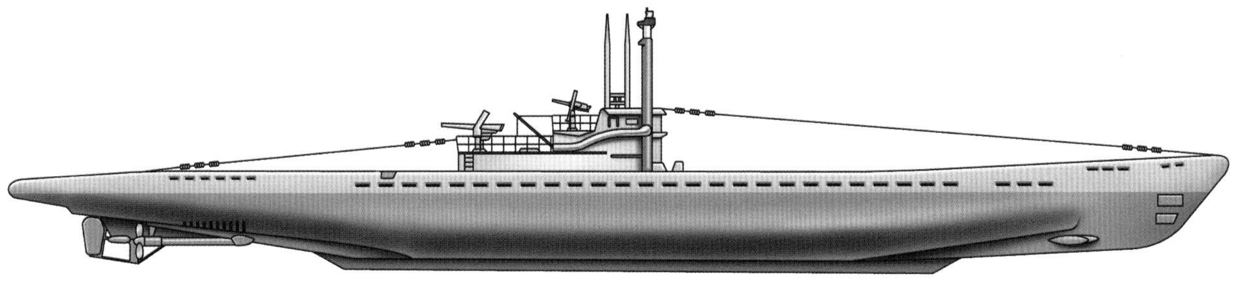

▲ **U-530**

Type IXC/40

U-530 made seven patrols under the control of the 10th Flotilla and the 33rd Flotilla, sinking just two merchant vessels totalling just over 12,000 GRT and damaging one more of 10,195 GRT.

Specifications

Crew: 48–50

Powerplant: Diesel/electric

Max Speed: 33.9/13.5km/hr (18.3/7.3kt) s/d

Surface Range: 20,370km (11,000nm)

Displacement: 1138/1252t (1120/1232 tons) s/d

Dimensions (length/beam/draught): 76.8 x 6.9 x 4.7m (252 x 22.6 x 15.42ft)

Commissioned: 14 Oct 1942

Armament: 22 torpedoes; 1 x 10.5cm (4.1in), 1 x 3.7cm (1.5in) and 1 x 2cm (0.8in) guns

Long-range operations
1941–45

Pre-war German planning had always envisaged the use of long-range submarines operating in concert with auxiliary cruisers or disguised merchant raiders in distant waters.

ADMIRAL KARL DÖNITZ WAS NOT in favour of the scheme, believing that the primary function of the U-boat was to sink enemy shipping. The best way to do that, he believed, was to operate where targets were most plentiful – on the convoy routes of the North Atlantic.

However, the *Oberkommando der Marine* (OKM, the Supreme Naval Command) had a wider view. By sending submarines farther afield, they could force the Royal Navy to stretch its anti-submarine assets over a much larger area. It would also force the introduction of the convoy system in the South Atlantic and the Indian Ocean, slowing the passage of war cargoes.

Initially, the long-range boats achieved considerable success. Author Bodo Herzog has listed the 16 most successful U-boats of November 1942, a particularly bad month for Allied shipping. Of the 16, only two were operating in the North Atlantic. Four were in the Caribbean, one was off the coast of West Africa, and no less than nine boats were successful in the South Atlantic and around the Cape of Good Hope.

Distant waters

Later, submarines were to operate even farther afield, making operational patrols in the Indian Ocean and in Southeast Asian waters. However, U-boats were still vulnerable in the early stages of a patrol. Many were lost to Allied aircraft as they traversed the lethal waters of the Bay of Biscay, while still more were destroyed by Allied hunter-killer groups deployed in the central Atlantic to block their passage as the boats moved south.

Replenishment of boats at sea
1941–44

Despite the development of the Type IX boats, long-range replenishment remained an issue for the *Kriegsmarine*.

EVEN THE LONG-RANGE Type IX boats lacked the endurance for extended operations in the South Atlantic and the Caribbean. Initially, they were to have been supported by supply ships, often disguised as neutral merchantmen. However, British success in cracking German naval codes meant that the locations of many supply rendezvous were known, especially after the capture of U-110 on 9 May 1941. In June 1941, nine out of ten supply ships were hunted down and sunk.

As a stop-gap, front-line boats were used as resupply platforms, but these could refuel or resupply only a handful of operational U-boats. The large Type XB minelayers were pressed into service as 'milk cows', or supply boats, and in 1941 these were joined by the purpose-designed Type XIV supply boat. Unarmed except for anti-aircraft defences, the Type XIVs could provide between 15 and 20 front-line boats with ammunition, fuel, water and food on a single patrol.

The first boat was U-459, which entered service with the 10th Flotilla on 1 April 1942. After some initial successes, the milchcows suffered the same fate as the surface supply vessels. Those that were not sunk in transit to their operational areas, far from the normal shipping lanes, were ruthlessly hunted down by Allied ships and aircraft, often operating on information provided by Ultra codebreakers.

BOATS THAT SERVED WITH 10TH FLOTILLA (82 BOATS)

U-Boat	Type	Commissioned	Flotilla(s)	Patrols	Fate
U-118	XB	6-Dec-41	1 Oct 1942 – 31 Oct 1942 from 4 Flottille	4 patrols. 3 ships sunk by mines: total 14,064 GRT; 1 warship sunk by mine: total 940t/925 tons; 2 ships damaged by mines: total 11,945 GRT	to 12. Flottille
U-155	IXC	23-Aug-41	1 Feb 1942 – 14 Aug 1944 from 4. Flottille	10 patrols. 25 ships sunk: total 126,664 GRT; 1 escort carrier (HMS *Avenger*) sunk: total 14,733t/14,500 tons; 1 auxiliary warship damaged: total 6736 GRT	to 33. Flottille
U-158	IXC	25-Sep-41	1 Feb 1942 – 30 Jun 1942 from 4. Flottille	2 patrols. 17 ships sunk: total 101,321 GRT 2 ships damaged: total 15,264 GRT	Sunk with all hands 30 Jun 1942 west of the Bermudas by depth charges from a US Navy Mariner of VP-74. 54 dead
U-159	IXC	4-Oct-41	1 May 1942 – 28 Jul 1943 from 4. Flottille	5 patrols. 23 ships sunk: total 119,684 GRT 1 ship damaged: total 265 GRT	Sunk with all hands 28 Jul 1943 south of Haiti by depth charges from a US Navy Mariner of VP-32. 53 dead. Previously credited to a Mariner from VP-32 on 15 Jul 1943 east of Jamaica.
U-160	IXC	16-Oct-41	1 Mar 1942 – 14 Jul 1943 from 4. Flottille	5 patrols. 26 ships sunk: total 156,082 GRT; 5 ships damaged: total 34,419 GRT	Sunk with all hands 14 Jul 1943 south of the Azores by a US Navy Avenger and Wildcats of the escort carrier USS *Santee*. 57 dead
U-163	IXC	21-Oct-41	1 Aug 1942 – 13 Mar 1943 from 4. Flottille	3 patrols. 3 ships sunk: total 15,011 GRT 1 warship damaged beyond repair: total 2032t/2000 tons	Sunk with all hands 13 Mar 1943 northwest of Cape Finisterre by depth charges from the Canadian corvette HMCS *Prescott*. 57 dead
U-164	IXC	28-Nov-41	1 Aug 1942 – 6 Jan 1943 from 4. Flottille	2 patrols. 3 ships sunk: total 8133 GRT	Sunk 6 Jan 1943 northwest of Pernambuco by depth charges from a US Navy Catalina of VP-83. 54 dead and 2 survivors
U-165	IXC	3-Feb-42	1 Sep 1942 – 27 Sep 1942 from 4. Flottille	1 patrol. 2 ships sunk: total 8396 GRT; 1 auxiliary warship sunk: total 358 GRT; 3 ships damaged: total 14,499 GRT; 1 auxiliary warship damaged: total 7252 GRT	Probably sunk with all hands 27 Sept 1942 in the Bay of Biscay west of Lorient by depth charges from a Czech-crewed Wellington of No. 311 Sqn RAF. 51 dead
U-166	IXC	23-Mar-42	1 Jun 1942 – 30 Jul 1942 from 4. Flottille	2 patrols. 4 ships sunk: total 7593 GRT	Sunk with all hands 30 Jul 1942 in the Gulf of Mexico by depth charges from the US Navy escort vessel PC-566. 52 dead. Originally thought to have been sunk by a single depth charge from a US Coast Guard J4F-1 aircraft, but that may have been an unsuccessful attack on U-171
U-167	IXC/40	4-Jul-42	1 Dec 1942 – 6 Apr 1943 from 4. Flottille	2 patrols. 1 ship sunk: total 4621 GRT; 1 ship damaged: total 7200 GRT	Scuttled 6 Apr 1943 near the Canary Islands after a depth charge attack by a Hudson aircraft of No. 233 Sqn the day before. All 50 crew members survived. It was raised in 1951 and transferred to Spain, where it was used commercially as an exhibit and as a film set
U-169	IXC/40	16-Nov-42	1 Mar 1943 – 27 Mar 1943 from 4. Flottille	1 patrol	Sunk with all hands 27 Mar 1943 south of Iceland by depth charges from a British B-17 Fortress. 54 dead
U-170	IXC/40	19-Jan-43	1 Jun 1943 – 31 Oct 1944 from 4. Flottille	4 patrols. 1 ship sunk: total 4663 GRT	to 33. Flottille
U-171	IXC	25-Oct-41	1 Jul 1942 – 9 Oct 1942 from 4. Flottille	1 patrol. 3 ships sunk: total 17,641 GRT	Sunk 9 Oct 1942 in the Bay of Biscay near Lorient by a mine. 22 dead and 30 survivors
U-172	IXC	5-Nov-41	1 May 1942 – 13 Dec 1943 from 4. Flottille	6 patrols. 26 ships sunk: total 152,778 GRT	Sunk 13 Dec 1943 in mid-Atlantic west of the Canary Islands after a 27-hour fight with Avenger and Wildcat aircraft of the escort carrier USS *Bogue* and by as many as 200 depth charges from the destroyers USS *George E. Badger*, USS *Clemson*, USS *Osmond Ingram* and USS *Du Pont*. 13 dead and 46 survivors
U-174	IXC	26-Nov-41	1 Aug 1942 – 27 Apr 1943	3 patrols. 5 ships sunk: total 30,813 GRT	Sunk with all hands 27 Apr 1943 south of Newfoundland by depth charges from a US Navy Ventura of VP-125. 53 dead
U-175	IXC	5-Dec-1941	1 Sep 1942 – 17 Apr 1943 from 4. Flottille	3 patrols. 10 ships sunk: total 40,619 GRT	Sunk 17 Apr 1943 southwest of Ireland by depth charges and gunfire from the US Coast Guard cutter USS *Spencer*. 13 dead and 41 survivors
U-176	IXC	15-Dec-41	1 Aug 1942 – 15 May 1943 from 4. Flottille	3 patrols. 10 ships sunk: total 45,850 GRT; 1 ship damaged: total 7457 GRT	Sunk with all hands 15 May 1943 northeast of Havana, by depth charges from the Cuban patrol boat CS 13 after being located by a US Navy OS2U-3 Kingfisher of VP-62. 53 dead
U-177	IXD2	14-Mar-42	1 Oct 1942 – 30 Nov 1942 from 4. Flottille	3 patrols. 14 ships sunk: total 87,388 GRT; 1 ship damaged: total 2588 GRT	to 12. Flottille
U-178	IXD2	14-Feb-42	1 Sep 1942 – 31 Oct 1942 from 4. Flottille	3 patrols. 13 ships sunk: total 87,030 GRT; 1 ship damaged: total 6348 GRT	to 12. Flottille
U-179	IXD2	7-Mar-42	1 Sep 1942 – 30 Sep 1942 from 4. Flottille	1 patrol. 1 ship sunk: total 6558 GRT	to 12. Flottille
U-180	IXD1	16-May-42	1 Feb 1943 – 1 Nov 1943 from 4. Flottille	2 patrols. 2 ships sunk: total 13,298 GRT	to 12. Flottille
U-181	IXD2	9-May-42	1 Oct 1942 – 31 Oct 1942	4 patrols. 27 ships sunk: total 138,779 GRT	to 12. Flottille
U-185	IXC/40	13-Jun-42	1 Nov 1942 – 24 Aug 1943 from 4. Flottille	3 patrols. 9 ships sunk: total 62,761 GRT; 1 ship damaged: total 6840 GRT	Sunk 24 Aug 1943 in mid-Atlantic by depth charges from 3 Avengers and Wildcats of the escort carrier USS *Core*. 29 dead and 22 survivors. 14 men who had been rescued from U-604 also died
U-186	IXC/40	10-Jul-42	1 Jan 1943 – 12 May 1943	2 patrols. 3 ships sunk: total 18,782 GRT	Sunk with all hands 12 May 1943 north of the Azores by depth charges from the destroyer HMS *Hesperus*. 53 dead
U-187	IXC/40	23-Jul-1942	1 Jan 1943 – 4 Feb 1943 from 4. Flottille	1 patrol	Sunk 4 Feb 1943 in the North Atlantic by depth charges from the destroyers HMS *Beverley* and HMS *Vimy*. 9 dead and 45 survivors
U-188	IXC/40	5-Aug-42	1 Feb 1943 – 20 Aug 1944 from 4. Flottille	3 patrols. 8 ships sunk: total 49,725 GRT; 1 warship sunk: total 1209t/1190 tons; 1 ship damaged: total 9977 GRT	Scuttled 20 Aug 1944 at the U-boat base in Bordeaux, unable to escape the Allied advance

BOATS THAT SERVED WITH 10TH FLOTILLA (82 BOATS)					
U-Boat	Type	Commissioned	Flotilla(s)	Patrols	Fate
U-192	IXC/40	16-Nov-42	1 May 1943 – 6 May 1943 from 4. Flottille	1 patrol	Sunk with all hands 6 May 1943 in the North Atlantic southeast of Cape Farewell by depth charges from the corvette HMS *Loosestrife*. 55 dead. Previously thought to have been sunk 5 May by depth charges from the corvette HMS *Pink*.
U-193	IXC/40	10-Dec-42	1 Apr 1944 – 23 Apr 1944 from 2. Flottille	3 patrols. 1 ship sunk: total 10,172 GRT	Missing with all hands on or after 23 Apr 1944 in the Bay of Biscay. 59 dead. Previously listed as sunk 28 Apr 1944 in the Bay of Biscay west of Nantes by depth charges from an RAF Wellington aircraft.
U-194	IXC/40	8-Jan-43	1 Jun 1943 – 24 Jun 1943 from 4. Flottille	1 patrol	Sunk with all hands 24 Jun 1943 in the North Atlantic southwest of Iceland by a homing torpedo from a US Navy PBY Catalina of VP-84. 54 dead.
U-195	IXD1	5-Sep-42	1 Apr 1943 – 1 Sep 1943 from 4. Flottille	3 patrols. 2 ships sunk: total 14,391 GRT 1 ship damaged: total 6797 GRT	to 12. Flottille
U-459	XIV	15-Nov-41	1 Apr 1942 – 31 Oct 1942 from 4. Flottille	6 resupply patrols	to 12. Flottille
U-460	XIV	24-Dec-41	1 Jul 1942 – 31 Oct 1942 from 4. Flottille	6 resupply patrols	to 12. Flottille
U-461	XIV	30-Jan-42	1 Jul 1942 – 31 Oct 1942 from 4. Flottille	6 resupply patrols	to 12. Flottille
U-462	XIV	5-Mar-42	1 Aug 1942 – 31 Oct 1942 from 4. Flottille	7 resupply patrols	to 12. Flottille
U-463	XIV	2-Apr-42	1 Aug 1942 – 31 Oct 1942 from 4. Flottille	5 resupply patrols	to 12. Flottille
U-464	XIV	30-Apr-42	1 Aug 1942 – 20 Aug 1942 from 4. Flottille	1 resupply patrol	Sunk 20 Aug 1942 southeast of Iceland by a US Navy PBY Catalina. 2 dead and 53 survivors
U-506	IXC	15-Sep-41	1 Feb 1942 – 12 Jul 1943 from 4. Flottille	5 patrols. 14 ships sunk: total 69,893 GRT; 1 ship damaged beyond repair: total 6821 GRT; 3 ships damaged: total 23,354 GRT. U-506 took part in the *Laconia* rescue operations in September 1942	Sunk 12 Jul 1943 west of Vigo, Spain, by 7 depth charges from a USAAF B-24 Liberator of A/S Sqn 1. 48 dead and 6 survivors. This was one of the first boats detected by centimetric airborne radar
U-508	IXC	20-Oct-41	1 Jul 1942 – 12 Nov 1943	6 patrols. 14 ships sunk: total 74,087 GRT	Sunk with all hands 12 Nov 1943 in the Bay of Biscay north of Cape Ortegal by depth charges from a US Navy Liberator of VB-103. 57 dead
U-509	IXC	4-Nov-41	1 Jul 1942 – 15 Jul 1943	4 patrols. 5 ships sunk: total 29,091 GRT; 1 ship damaged beyond repair: total 7129 GRT; 3 ships damaged: total 20,014 GRT	Sunk with all hands 15 Jul 1943 northwest of Madeira by aerial torpedoes from Grumman TBF/TBM Avengers of the escort carrier USS *Santee*. 54 dead
U-510	IXC	25-Nov-41	1 Aug 1942 – 30 Sep 1944 from 4. Flottille	7 patrols. 11 ships sunk: total 71,100 GRT; 1 auxiliary warship sunk: total 249 GRT; 3 ships damaged beyond repair: total 24,338 GRT; 8 ships damaged: total 53,289 GRT	to 33. Flottille
U-511	IXC	8-Dec-41	1 Aug 1942 – 1 Sep 1943	4 patrols. 5 ships sunk: total 41,373 GRT; 1 ship damaged: total 8773 GRT	Sold to Japan 16 Sep 1943 and became the Japanese submarine RO-500. Surrendered at Maizuru Aug 1945. Scuttled in Gulf of Maizuru by US Navy 30 Apr 1946
U-512	IXC	20-Dec-41	1 Sep 1942 – 2 Oct 1942 from 4. Flottille	1 patrol. 3 ships sunk: total 20,619 GRT	Sunk 2 Oct 1942 north of Cayenne by depth charges from an B-18A aircraft of US Army Bomb Sqn 99. 51 dead and 1 survivor (who spent 10 days adrift on a liferaft)
U-513	IXC	10-Jan-42	1 Sep 1942 – 19 Jul 1943 from 4. Flottille	4 patrols. 6 ships sunk: total 29,940 GRT; 2 ships damaged: total 13,177 GRT	Sunk 19 Jul 1943 in the South Atlantic southeast of Sao Francisco do Sul by depth charges from a US Navy Mariner of VP-74. 46 dead and 7 survivors
U-514	IXC	24-Jan-42	1 Sep 1942 – 8 Jul 1943 from 4. Flottille	4 patrols. 4 ships sunk: total 16,329 GRT; 2 ships damaged: total 13,551 GRT; 2 ships damaged beyond repair: total 8202 GRT	Sunk with all hands 8 Jul 1943 northeast of Cape Finisterre by rockets from a Liberator of No. 224 Sqn RAF. 54 dead
U-515	IXC	21-Feb-42	1 Sep 1942 – 9 Apr 1944 from 4. Flottille	7 patrols. 21 ships sunk: total 131,769 GRT; 2 auxiliary warships sunk: total 19,277 GRT; 1 ship damaged beyond repair: total 4668 GRT; 1 warship damaged beyond repair: total 1372t/1350 tons; 1 ship damaged: total 6034 GRT; 1 warship damaged: total 1951t/1920 tons	Sunk 9 Apr 1944 north of Madeira by rockets from Avenger and Wildcat aircraft of the escort carrier USS *Guadalcanal*, and by depth charges from the destroyer escorts USS *Pope*, USS *Pillsbury*, USS *Chatelain* and USS *Flaherty*. 16 dead and 44 survivors
U-516	IXC	21-Feb-42	1 Sep 1942 – 30 Sep 1944 from 4. Flottille	6 patrols. 16 ships sunk: total 89,385 GRT; 1 ship damaged: total 9687 GRT	to 33. Flottille
U-517	IXC	21-Mar-42	1 Sep 1942 – 21 Nov 1942 from 4. Flottille	2 patrols. 8 ships sunk: total 26,383 GRT; 1 warship sunk: total 914t/900 tons	Sunk 21 Nov 1942 southwest of Ireland by depth charges from Albacores of the fleet carrier HMS *Victorious*. 1 dead and 52 survivors
U-523	IXC	25-Jun-42	1 Feb 1943 – 25 Aug 1943 from 4. Flottille	4 patrols. 1 ship sunk: total 5848 GRT	Sunk 25 Aug 1943 west of Vigo, Spain, by depth charges from the destroyer HMS *Wanderer* and the corvette HMS *Wallflower*. 17 dead and 37 survivors
U-524	IXC	8-Jul-42	1 Dec 1942 – 22 Mar 1943 from 4. Flottille	2 patrols. 2 ships sunk: total 16,256 GRT	Sunk with all hands 22 Mar 1943 south of Madeira by depth charges from a B-24 Liberator of USAAF A/S Sqn 1. 52 dead
U-525	IXC/40	30-Jul-42	1 Jan 1943 – 11 Aug 1943 from 4. Flottille	3 patrols. 1 ship sunk: total 3454 GRT	Sunk with all hands 11 Aug 1943 northwest of the Azores by depth charges and torpedoes from aircraft of the escort carrier USS *Card*. 54 dead
U-526	IXC/40	12-Aug-42	1 Feb 1943 – 14 Apr 1943 from 4. Flottille	1 patrol	Sunk 14 Apr 1943 in the Bay of Biscay near Lorient by mines. 42 dead and 12 survivors
U-527	IXC/40	2-Sep-42	1 Feb 1943 – 23 Jul 1943 from 4. Flottille	2 patrols. 1 ship sunk: total 5242 GRT; 1 ship damaged: total 5848 GRT	Sunk 23 Jul 1943 south of the Azores by depth charges from Grumman Avengers of the escort carrier USS *Bogue*. 40 dead and 13 survivors
U-528	IXC/40	16-Sep-42	1 Apr 1943 – 11 May 1943 from 4. Flottille	1 patrol	Sunk 11 May 1943 southwest of Ireland by depth charges from a Handley Page Halifax of No. 58 Sqn RAF and from the sloop HMS *Fleetwood*. 11 dead and 45 survivors
U-529	IXC/40	30-Sep-42	1 Feb 1943 – 12 Feb 1943 from 4. Flottille	1 patrol	Missing with all hands on or after 12 Feb 1943 in the North Atlantic. 48 dead. Previously credited to a Liberator of No. 120 Sqn RAF, but that attack on 15 Feb 1943 most likely accounted for U-225

BOATS THAT SERVED WITH 10TH FLOTILLA (82 BOATS)

U-Boat	Type	Commissioned	Flotilla(s)	Patrols	Fate
U-530	IXC/40	14-Oct-42	1 Mar 1943 – 30 Sep 1944 from 4. Flottille	7 patrols. 2 ships sunk: total 12,063 GRT; 1 ship damaged: total 10,195 GRT	to 33. Flottille
U-533	IXC/40	25-Nov-42	1 May 1943 – 16 Oct 1943 from 4. Flottille	2 patrols	Sunk 16 Oct 1943 in the Gulf of Oman by depth charges from a Bisley (late-model Blenheim) of No. 244 Sqn RAF. 52 dead and 1 survivor
U-535	IXC/40	23-Dec-42	1 Jun 1943 – 5 Jul 1943 from 4. Flottille	1 patrol	Sunk with all hands 5 Jul 1943 northeast of Cape Finisterre by depth charges from a Liberator of No. 53 Sqn RAF. 55 dead
U-537	IXC/40	27-Jan-43	1 Aug 1943 – 30 Sep 1944 from 4. Flottille	3 patrols	to 33. Flottille
U-539	IXC/40	24-Feb-43	1 Jul 1943 – 30 Sep 1944 from 4. Flottille	3 patrols. 1 ship sunk: total 1517 GRT; 2 ships damaged: total 12,896 GRT. U-539 was the first *Schnorchel*-equipped U-boat to go on a combat patrol, 2 Jan 1944	to 33. Flottille
U-540	IXC/40	10-Mar-43	1 Oct 1943 – 17 Oct 1943 from 4. Flottille	1 patrol	Sunk with all hands 17 Oct 1943 east of Cape Farewell, Greenland, by depth charges from Liberators of Nos. 59 and 120 Sqns RAF. 55 dead
U-541	IXC/40	24-Mar-43	1 Nov 1943 – 31 Oct 1944 from 4. Flottille	4 patrols. 1 ship sunk: total 2140 GRT	to 33. Flottille
U-542	IXC/40	7-Apr-43	1 Oct 1943 – 28 Nov 1943 from 4. Flottille	1 patrol	Sunk with all hands 28 Nov 1943 north of Madeira by depth charges from a Leigh Light-equipped Wellington of No. 179 Sqn RAF. 56 dead. Often confused with an attack by another 179 Sqn Wellington on the same night, which actually caused minor damage to U-391
U-543	IXC/40	21-Apr-43	1 Nov 1943 – 2 Jul 1944 from 4. Flottille	2 patrols	Sunk with all hands 2 Jul 1944 southwest of Tenerife by depth charges and a Fido homing torpedo from Grumman Avengers flying from the escort carrier USS *Wake Island*. 58 dead
U-544	IXC/40	5-May-43	1 Nov 1943 – 16 Jan 1944 from 4. Flottille	1 patrol	Sunk with all hands 16 Jan 1944 northwest of the Azores by depth charges and rockets from Grumman Avenger aircraft of the escort carrier USS *Guadalcanal*. 57 dead
U-546	IXC/40	2-Jun-43	1 Jan 1944 – 9 Nov 1944 from 4. Flottille	3 patrols. 1 warship sunk: total 1200 tons	to 33. Flottille
U-549	IXC/40	14-Jul-43	1 Jan 1944 – 29 May 1944 from 4. Flottille	2 patrols. 1 warship sunk: total 9393 tons; 1 warship damaged: total 1321t/1300 tons	Sunk with all hands 29 May 1944 after sinking the escort carrier USS *Block Island* southwest of Madeira, by depth charges from the US destroyer escorts USS *Eugene E. Elmore* and USS *Ahrens*. 57 dead
U-550	IXC/40	28-Jul-43	1 Feb 1944 – 16 Apr 1944 from 4. Flottille	1 patrol. 1 ship sunk: total 11,017 GRT	Sunk 16 Apr 1944 in the North Atlantic east of New York by depth charges and gunfire from the destroyer escorts USS *Gandy*, USS *Joyce* and USS *Peterson*. 44 dead and 12 survivors
U-804	IXC/40	4-Dec-43	1 Jul 1944 – 30 Sep 1944 from 4. Flottille	2 patrols. 1 warship sunk: total 1321t/1300 tons	to 33. Flottille
U-844	IXC/40	7-Apr-43	1 Oct 1943 – 16 Oct 1943 from 4. Flottille	1 patrol	Sunk with all hands 16 Oct 1943 southwest of Iceland by depth charges from Liberators of Nos. 59 and 86 Sqns RAF. 53 dead
U-845	IXC/40	1-May-43	1 Jan 1944 – 10 Mar 1944 from 4. Flottille	1 patrol. 1 ship damaged: total 7039 GRT	Sunk 10 Mar 1944 in North Atlantic by depth charges from destroyers HMS *Forester* and HMCS *St. Laurent*, corvette HMCS *Owen Sound* and frigate HMCS *Swansea*. 10 dead and 45 survivors
U-846	IXC/40	29-May-43	1 Dec 1943 – 4 May 1944 from 4. Flottille	2 patrols	Sunk with all hands 4 May 1944 in the Bay of Biscay north of Cape Ortegal, Spain, by depth charges from a Vickers Wellington of No. 407 Sqn RCAF. 57 dead
U-853	IXC/40	25-Jun-43	1 Apr 1944 – 1 Oct 1944 from 4. Flottille	3 patrols. 1 ship sunk: total 5353 GRT; 1 warship sunk: total 437t/430 tons	to 33. Flottille
U-855	IXC/40	2-Aug-43	1 Apr 1944 – 11 Sep 1944 from 4. Flottille	1 patrol	Missing with all hands on or after 11 Sep 1944 west of Bergen while returning from a weather patrol. 56 dead. Possibly mined in the Iceland–Faroes barrage. Previously credited to a Liberator of No. 224 Sqn RAF on 24 Sep 1944, but that attack actually sank U-763
U-857	IXC/40	16-Sep-43	1 Jun 1944 – 30 Sep 1944 from 4. Flottille	3 patrols. 2 ships sunk: total 15,259 GRT; 1 ship damaged: total 6825 GRT	to 33. Flottille
U-865	IXC/40	25-Oct-43	1 Jul 1944 – 19 Sep 1944 from 4. Flottille	1 patrol	Missing with all hands after leaving Trondheim, Norway, 9 Sep 1944. 59 dead. Known to have had a faulty *Schnorchel* – may have contributed to loss.
U-866	IXC/40	17-Nov-43	1 Aug 1944 – 30 Sep 1944 from 4. Flottille	1 patrol	to 33. Flottille
U-1221	IXC/40	11-Aug-43	1 Jul 1944 – 30 Nov 1944 from 4. Flottille	1 patrol	to 33. Flottille
U-1222	IXC/40	1-Sep-43	10. Flottille 1 Mar 1944 – 11 Jul 1944 from 4. Flottille	1 patrol; no ships sunk or damaged	Sunk with all hands 11 Jul 1944 west of La Rochelle by depth charges from a Short Sunderland of No.201 Sqn RAF. 56 dead.
U-1229	IXC/40	13-Jan-44	10. Flottille 1 Aug 1944 – 20 Aug 1944 from 10. Flottille	1 patrol; no ships sunk or damaged.	Sunk 20 Aug 1944 off Newfoundland while en route to Maine to land an agent, by depth charges of the escort carrier USS *Bogue*. 18 dead and 41 survivors. To 33. Flott.
U-1230	IXC/40	26-Jan-44	10. Flottille 1 Aug 1944 – 30 Sep 1944 from 31. Flottille	No patrols	to U-Abwehrschule
UD-3	Dutch O 21 class	8-June-41	10. Flottille Oct 42 – Feb 43 from 2. Flottille	3 patrols; 1 ship sunk: total 5,041 GRT	

11 Unterseebootsflottille

The 11th Flotilla was founded on 15 May 1942 under the command of *Korvettenkapitän* Hans Cohausz. Based at Bergen in Norway, with boats operating from other ports stretching up beyond the Arctic Circle, the flotilla's primary mission was to interdict Allied supply lines to the USSR.

THE WESTERN ALLIES mounted a major effort to provide the USSR with war materials following the German invasion of Russia in June 1941. Seventy-eight convoys sailed between August 1941 and May 1945 with temporary pauses in the flow between July and September 1942, and March and November 1943. Early convoys sailed from Iceland, but after September 1942 they assembled at and sailed from Loch Ewe in Scotland. The route was around occupied Norway to the Soviet ports and was particularly dangerous due to the proximity of German air, submarine and surface forces and also because of the severe weather.

Outbound convoys carried the PQ designation while those returning to the Atlantic were known as QP or RA convoys. Hitler first began moving naval forces to Norway to forestall a potential invasion by the British, aimed at cutting German supplies of iron ore. However, having U-boats, destroyers, cruisers and capital ships in Norway meant that the *Kriegsmarine* had the chance to cut the flow of

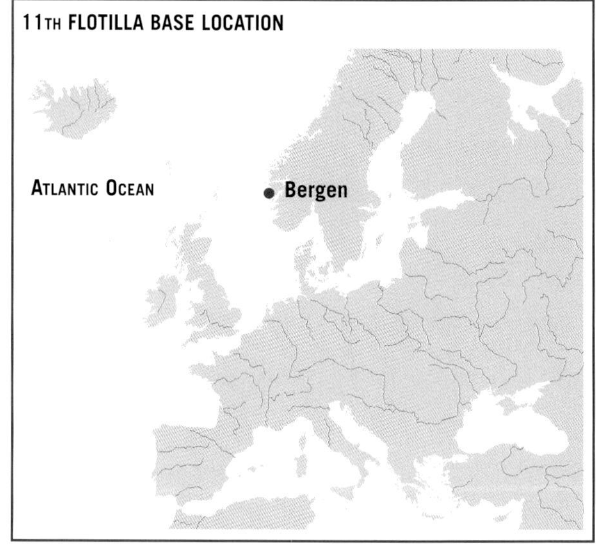

Debris

In the Barents Sea, a U-boat crew observe a patch of wreckage left behind by a recently destroyed US steamer.

Commanders

Fregkpt. Hans Cohausz *(May 1942 – Dec 1944)*

Fregkpt. Heinrich Lehmann-Willenbrock *(Dec 1944 – May 1945)*

11TH FLOTILLA INSIGNIA

Given that the 11th Flotilla's main operational area was in the Arctic, it is not surprising that the unit's insignia should depict a polar bear riding on the back of a surfaced U-boat.

9 FLOTILLA (1942–45)	
Type	**Boats assigned**
Type VIIC	121
Type VIIC/41	49
Type IXC/40	2
Type XB	1
Type XXI	6
Type XXIII	10

supplies from the United Kingdom and the United States to the Eastern Front.

In terms of numbers of ships sunk, the 11th Flotilla in Norway contributed little to the overall levels of U-boat successes, although there were occasional triumphs such as the massacre of Convoy PQ 17. Nevertheless, in combination with the *Luftwaffe,* its attacks forced the Allies to expend valuable resources in protecting the convoys. U-boats were also used to check on ice conditions and to set up weather stations on remote Arctic island groups. Submarines were even sent into the Siberian passage to try to intercept convoys coming from the Far East in the few months in summer when the passage was free of ice.

Following the Allied invasion of Normandy in 1944, Germany quickly lost the use of its ports in France, and the only area from which U-boats could set out on patrols into the Atlantic with relative safety was Norway. Most of the surviving boats from France were sent north. The original French-based U-boat flotillas were disbanded, and the boats were taken onto the strength of the Norwegian flotillas. From there they continued to mount patrols against both Arctic and Atlantic convoys.

The final act of the 11th Flotilla's existence came with the introduction into service of the new high-speed 'Electro boats', the Type XXI and Type XXIII. Several Type XXIIIs became operational, and the first operational Type XXI boat, U-2511, was under 11th Flotilla orders. The flotilla was disbanded in May 1945 when Germany surrendered.

Kapitänleutnant Reinhart Reche

Born on 13 December 1915, Reche joined the German Navy as part of Crew 34. He made two patrols on U-751 before being promoted to command his own boat. One of the few captains to achieve success in the north, he commanded U-255 on nine patrols in the Arctic and played a major part in the destruction of convoy PQ 17. Reche left U-255 for a staff appointment in June 1943.

After the war Reche, joined the *Bundesmarine* and from 1959 to 1961 commanded the submarine training unit. He retired in 1974 as a *Kapitän zur See*, and died on 3 March 1993.

Specifications

Crew: 14

Powerplant: Diesel/electric

Max Speed: 18.5/23.2km/hr (10/12.5kt) s/d

Surface Range: 2500km (1350nm)

Displacement: 236/260t (232/256 tons) s/d

Dimensions (length/beam/draught): 34.1 x 3 x 3.75m (112 x 10 x 12ft)

Commissioned: 10 Aug 1944

Armament: 2 torpedoes (2 bow tubes)

▲ **U-2326**

Type XXIII

The small Type XXIII boat had a short range and was lightly armed, but its high underwater speed made it a potentially deadly opponent in coastal waters. U-2326 survived the war, surrendering at Dundee on 14 May 1945.

U-218

Type VIID

U-218 was a Type VIID U-boat, a slightly lengthened version of the standard design with a section added aft of the conning tower intended to hold and dispense mines.

Laid down at Germania Werft, Kiel, in March 1941, U-218 was commissioned on 24 January 1942. On her fifth patrol at the beginning of August 1943, six of the boat's crewmen were wounded by machine-gun fire in an attack by an RAF Wellington. The boat having sustained damage, its mission to the Caribbean was aborted. On 4 November 1943, U-218 claimed to have sunk a sailing vessel off Trinidad, but the sinking has never been confirmed.

In June 1944 U-218 went on her first *Schnorchel*-equipped patrol. The *Schnorchel* was faulty and several crewmembers were taken ill with carbon-monoxide poisoning caused by diesel fumes. U-218 was to be transferred to Norway at the end of August 1944, but had to return to Kiel for a battery refit in October of that year. She returned to Norway for operations in March 1945.

U-218 was responsible for destroying the last British ship sunk as a result of the war. The steam fishing vessel *Kurd* went down on 10 July 1945, having struck a mine laid by the boat the previous August off Lizard Head.

U-218 Commanders

Kptlt. Richard Becker *(Jan 1942 – Aug 1944)*

Kptlt. Rupprecht Stock *(Aug 1944 – May 1945)*

U-218 TIMETABLE

Patrol Dates	Operational Area	Ships Sunk
25 Aug 1942 – 29 Sep 1942	Transit from Kiel to Brest	0
25 Oct 1942 – 21 Nov 1942	W of Ireland/Gibraltar	0
7 Jan 1943 – 10 Mar 1943	Canaries/Azores	0
18 Apr 1943 – 2 June 1944	N Atlantic	0
29 Jul 1943 – 6 Aug 1943	Minelaying off Trinidad	0
19 Sep 1943 – 8 Dec 1943	Minelaying in the Caribbean	0
12 Feb 1944 – 7 May 1944	Minelaying in the Caribbean	0
13 June 1944 – 9 Jul 1944	Minelaying in the Channel	0
10 Aug 1944 – 23 Sep 1944	Minelaying in the Channel	1
22 Mar 1945 – 8 May 1945	Minelaying in Clyde estuary	1

Fate

U-218 surrendered in Bergen, Norway, on 8 May 1945 and sank while under tow to the Operation *Deadlight* scuttling grounds on 4 December 1945.

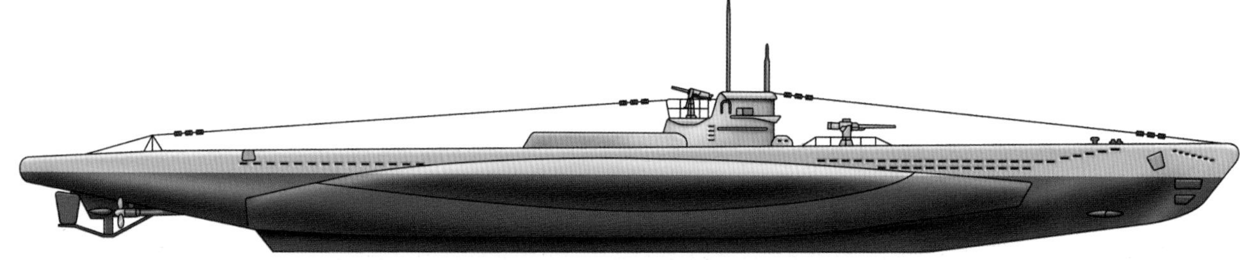

▲ **U-218**

Type VIID

Able to lay as many as 15 large ground mines, U-218 mounted 10 patrols between 1942 and the end of the war. Only two ships were sunk by its weapons, one in the Clyde estuary and one in the Channel after the end of the war.

Specifications

Crew: 44

Powerplant: Diesel/electric

Max Speed: 29.6/13.5km/hr (16/7.3kt) s/d

Surface Range: 8100km (4374nm)

Displacement: 980/1097t (965/1080 tons) s/d

Dimensions (length/beam/draught): 76.9 x 6.4 x 5m (252.3 x 21 x 16.4ft)

Commissioned: 24 Jan 1942

Armament: 14 torpedoes (4 bow/1 stern tubes); 15 mines; 1 x 8.8cm (3.5in) and 1 x 2cm (0.8in) guns

U-300

Type VIIC/41

Laid down at Bremer Vulkan, Vegesack, in April 1943, U-300 was commissioned in December of that year. It joined the 11th Flotilla in 1944.

U-300 TIMETABLE		
Patrol Dates	**Operational Area**	**Ships Sunk**
13 Jul 1944 – 17 Aug 1944	Hebrides/Iceland	0
4 Oct 1944 – 2 Dec 1944	S of Iceland	2
21 Jan 1945 – 22 Feb 1945	Off Gibraltar	0

After working up with the 8th Flotilla in the Baltic for more than six months, U-300 was assigned to the 7th Flotilla at St Nazaire. However, by the time the boat went on its first operational patrol in the Atlantic, the U-boat force was abandoning its French bases, and at the end of the patrol U-300 was ordered to make for Bergen, where it would join the 11th Flotilla. The boat mounted two patrols in British coastal waters, sinking four ships totalling 17,370 GRT.

Fate

Having been sent to patrol off Gibraltar, U-300 was sunk on 22 February 1945 west of Cadiz by depth charges from the minesweepers HMS *Recruit* and HMS *Pincher* and the armed yacht/minesweeper USS *Evadne*. Eleven crewmen died and 42 became POWs.

U-300 Commanders

Oblt. Fritz Hein *(Dec 1943 – Feb 1945)*

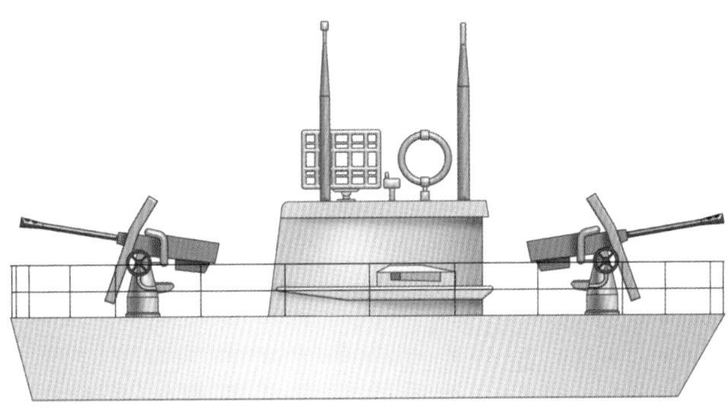

▲ **Type VII bridge conversion**

Designed to maximize anti-aircraft power, the Turm VII conversion carried two pairs of powerful 3.7cm (1.5in) Flak guns. Like the preceding Turm VII conversion, which was optimized for arctic operations, this alteration carried both forward-firing and aft-firing weaponry for better all-round protection. Had the war lasted longer, boats like U-300, a deep-diving Type VIIC/41, might well have been fitted with such armament. In any event, the boat was lost before conversion could take place.

▲ **U-300**

Type VIIC/41

Type VIIC/41 boats were virtually identical to other Type VIICs, but were constructed from thicker, stronger steel. This meant that they could dive more deeply than standard boats, and had more chance of avoiding depth charges.

Specifications

Crew: 44

Powerplant: Diesel/electric

Max Speed: 31.5/14.1km/hr (17/7.6kt) s/d

Surface Range: 12,040km (6500nm)

Displacement: 773/879t (761/865 tons) s/d

Dimensions (length/beam/draught): 67.2 x 6.2 x 4.8m (220.5 x 20.34 x 15.75ft)

Commissioned: 29 Dec 1943

Armament: 14 torpedoes (4 bow/1 stern tubes); 1 x 3.7cm (1.5in) and 2 x twin 2cm (0.8in) guns

U-486

Type VIIC

On her first patrol, U-486 sailed from Norway to the English Channel. She sent down three vessels in a notably successful combat debut at a time when few untried U-boats sank anything.

On 18 December 1944, U-486 sank the 6000 GRT *Silver Laurel*, sailing with Convoy BTC 10. Six days later, on the night of Christmas Eve, U-486 torpedoed the troopship SS *Leopoldville* in the English Channel just 8km (5 miles) from the port of Cherbourg, France. The *Leopoldville* was transporting 2235 soldiers of the US Army's 66th Infantry Division. The ship sank some two hours later.

So close to a major port, most of the passengers would normally have survived. However, everything that could go wrong with the rescue did go wrong. The escort commander, believing that the troopship could make port, ordered the escorts to hunt for the U-boat; calls for help were mishandled, rescue craft were slow to the scene and the weather was unfavourable.

When a secondary explosion hastened the vessel's sinking, 1000 troops were left in the freezing water. As many as 802 American soldiers died or were reported missing that night, together with 17 of the *Leopoldville*'s crew.

U-486 Commanders

Oblt. Gerhard Meyer *(Mar 1944 – Apr 1945)*

U-486 avoided the searching destroyers and frigates, and two days later she sank the frigate HMS *Capel*. Just 15 minutes later the boat damaged the frigate HMS *Affleck* beyond repair.

Fate

Despite being coated with Alberich anti-sonar material and equipped with a *Schnorchel*, U-486 was sunk with all 48 crew on 12 April 1945 northwest of Bergen, torpedoed by the Royal Navy submarine HMS *Tapir*. The U-boat had developed a *Schnorchel* problem, and was spotted by the British submarine, which was on patrol off the Norwegian ports, as U-486 surfaced on her way back into Bergen.

U-486 TIMETABLE

Patrol Dates	Operational Area	Ships Sunk
6 Nov 1944 – 20 Nov 1944	Transit from Kiel to Egersund	0
26 Nov 1944 – 15 Jan 1945	English Channel	3
9 Apr 1945 – 12 Apr 1945	British waters	0

Specifications

Crew: 44

Powerplant: Diesel/electric

Max Speed: 31.5/14.1km/hr (17/7.6kt) s/d

Surface Range: 12,040km (6500nm)

Displacement: 773/879t (761/865 tons) s/d

Dimensions (length/beam/draught): 67.1 x 6.2 x 4.8m (220.1 x 20.34 x 15.75ft)

Commissioned: 22 Mar 1944

Armament: 14 torpedoes (4 bow/1 stern tubes); 1 x 3.7cm (1.5in) and 2 x twin 2cm (0.8in) guns

▲ **U-486**

Type VIIC

Schnorchel-equipped U-boats entered service in large numbers in 1944. With the breathing device fitted, boats like U-486 could penetrate heavily defended waters with a reduced chance of being detected and destroyed.

U-2511

Type XXI

The best of the surviving U-boat commanders were assigned to the new, high-performance Type XXI submarines, but only a few of the many boats completed were ever declared operational.

On the evening of 3 May 1945, U-2511 set out from Bergen for her first and last patrol – the first operational mission by the revolutionary Type XXI *Elektroboot.*

Faster than any previous U-boat, with an integral *Schnorchel* allowing it to operate submerged as long as fuel and food held out, the Type XXI might have caused Allied escort forces some concern had it been available in any numbers. Fortunately very few were ready for action in the last days of the war, and none fired their weapons in anger. However, U-2511 came closest. Commanded by U-boat ace Adalbert Schnee, the boat was intended to patrol in the Caribbean, but on 4 May the captain received the cease-fire order that was to signal Germany's ultimate defeat.

A few hours later, north of the Faroes, U-2511 encountered a British task group. Schnee mounted a dummy attack on the heavy cruiser HMS *Norfolk*, approaching undetected to within 500m (547 yards).

U-2511 Commanders

Korvkpt. Adalbert Schnee *(Sep 1944 – May 1945)*

Having proved a point to himself and his crew, Schnee turned U-2511 away, increasing the boat's submerged speed to a fast 29.6km/hr (16kt) to make his escape. U-2511 returned to Bergen on 5 May 1945.

Fate

U-2511 was surrendered at Bergen in May 1945. It was transferred to Lisahally, Northern Ireland, on 14 June that year for Operation *Deadlight,* and was sunk as a naval gunfire target on 7 January 1946.

U-2511 TIMETABLE

Patrol Dates	Operational Area	Ships Sunk
16 Mar 1945 – 21 April 1945	Transit from Kiel to Bergen	0
3 May 1945 – 5 May 1945	Intended for the Caribbean	0

▲ **U-2511**

Type XXI

Korvkpt. Schnee spoke with some of the officers of HMS *Norfolk* after the surrender, who were shocked to learn that the U-boat ace had got his fully armed Type XXI boat to within 500m (547 yards) of their cruiser without being detected.

Specifications

Crew: 57

Powerplant: Diesel/electric

Max Speed: 28.9/32.6km/hr (15.6/17.6kt s/d

Surface Range: 11,150km (6021nm)

Displacement: 1647/1848t (1621/1819 tons) s/d

Dimensions (length/beam/draught): 76.7 x 6.6 x 6.3m (251.6 x 21.65 x 20.67ft)

Commissioned: 29 Sep 1944

Armament: 23 torpedoes (6 bow tubes); 2 x twin 2cm (0.8in) guns

Slaughter of PQ 17

27 June – 13 July 1942

The biggest convoy disaster of the war came when the British Admiralty overruled its commanders on the spot out of fear of a non-existent threat from German heavy units.

THIRTY-FIVE MERCHANTMEN LOADED with supplies set off into perilous Arctic waters on 27 June 1942. Convoy PQ 17 was carrying war matériel from Britain and the United States to the USSR. Through the course of 1942 on the northern route to Russia, Allied losses to German aircraft and U-boats had been increasing. In May PQ 16 had lost seven ships, but PQ 17 was the largest and most valuable convoy to date. The boost to Soviet supplies which had been provided by PQ 16 was noticeable in spite of the losses, which prompted the Germans to redouble their efforts to break the convoy route to Archangelsk and Murmansk. Operation *Rösselsprung* was set up, involving the assembly of powerful air, surface and submarine forces in northern Norway.

PQ 17 was provided with a large escort for the time. Close escort was provided by six destroyers, four corvettes and two anti-aircraft vessels. Nearby was the close-support force of four cruisers, three destroyers, two submarines and two tankers. Distant cover in case the convoy was attacked by heavy German units was provided by the Royal Navy Home

CONVOY PQ 17 BATTLE TIMETABLE

Date	Event
27 June 1942	At 16:00 the ships of convoy PQ 17 leave their anchorage in Hvalfjordur, Iceland, and head northwards. The convoy consists of 35 ships and is heavily loaded with 297 aircraft, 594 tanks, 4246 lorries and gun carriers and 158,503 tonnes (156,000 tons) of cargo. (This was enough to equip an army of 50,000 men and was valued at $700 million at the time.) Shortly after leaving, one ship runs aground and returns to port
29 June	The convoy encounters heavy drift ice. Four merchantmen are damaged, with one having to return to port. This leaves 33 ships en route to Russia
1 July	The convoy is spotted by U-255 and U-408. U-456 joins the other boats and begins tracking the convoy. Further reconnaissance information is provided by BV 138 flying boats of the *Luftwaffe*
2 July	A number of U-boats attempt attacks on the convoy, but to little effect. They are joined in the evening by the first in a series of *Luftwaffe* torpedo attacks
3 July	U-boats and *Luftwaffe* torpedo planes continue to attack without success. However, British intelligence receives reports that a powerful German surface force is leaving Norwegian waters and heading northwards. The Admiralty calculates that *Tirpitz*, *Hipper*, *Scheer* and *Lützow* would intercept the convoy on the evening of 4 July
4 July	Two ships are sunk by U-457 and U-334. At around 22:00, the British Admiralty, fearing that *Tirpitz* and her consorts are about to strike, and knowing that the battleships of the Home Fleet are too far away to intervene, orders the escorts to run westwards and for the convoy to scatter and proceed independently towards Russia
5 July	Even though the German surface forces have not left port, the scattered merchantmen are vulnerable to U-boats and air attack. The slaughter begins almost immediately. *Luftwaffe* aircraft sink six ships, while the U-boats account for a similar number (U-88 and U-703 sinking two each, while U-334 and U-456 sink the others)
6 July	Two more vessels are lost, one to the *Luftwaffe* and one to U-255
7 July	The *Luftwaffe* sinks another ship, while U-255, U-457 and U-355 account for three more
8 July	U-255 sinks her third ship
10 July	U-251 and U-376 each sink one merchantman
13 July	U-255 sinks a derelict merchant ship that has been adrift since being struck by *Luftwaffe* bombs on 5 July

Fleet, centred on the battleship HMS *Duke of York*, flying the flag of Admiral Tovey, and the powerful new 406mm (16in) fast battleship USS *Washington*.

Against this force Germany fielded U-88, U-251, U-255, U-334, U-355, U-376, U-456, U-457, U-657 and U-703, together with a substantial *Luftwaffe* force equipped with Heinkel He 111H (torp), Ju 88A-4, Heinkel He 115C, Blohm und Voss Bv 138 and Focke-Wulf Fw 200 Kondor aircraft. Lurking nearby in Norwegian fiords were the battleship *Tirpitz*, the pocket battleships *Scheer* and *Lützow*, and the heavy cruiser *Hipper*.

In all, 24 of the 35 merchant ships from PQ 17 were sunk. In addition to the loss of life, material losses were extremely heavy. The 144,805 tonnes (142,518 tons) of shipping that went down took with it 3350 motor vehicles, 430 tanks, 210 bombers and 100,910 tonnes (99,316 tons) of general cargo, which included radar sets and ammunition.

▲ **KMS *Tirpitz***

Battleship

The fear that the powerful battleship *Tirpitz* might attack the convoy caused the Admiralty to order PQ 17 to scatter. This left the merchantmen helpless against *Luftwaffe* torpedo planes and the *Kriegsmarine*'s U-boats.

The *Luftwaffe* had flown 202 sorties against the convoy, losing only five planes for the eight ships they sank. Three of the 11 surviving ships from PQ 17 were sunk on the return voyage from Russia in the next westbound convoy. One fell to U-255, becoming the boat's fifth victim.

The next convoy to do the northern route, PQ 18, sailed for Russia at the beginning of September, losing 13 ships (though three U-boats were sunk by the escorts). Convoy operations to Russia were suspended after the PQ 17 disaster and the losses to PQ 18 and were not resumed until JW 51 sailed in December 1942.

Specifications

Crew: 44

Powerplant: Diesel/electric

Max Speed: 31.5/14.1km/hr (17/7.6kt) s/d

Surface Range: 12,040km (6500nm)

Displacement: 773/879t (761/865 tons) s/d

Dimensions (length/beam/draught): 67.1 x 6.2 x 4.8m (220.1 x 20.34 x 15.75ft)

Commissioned: 29 Nov 1941

Armament: 14 torpedoes (4 bow/1 stern tubes); 1 x 3.7cm (1.5in) and 2 x twin 2cm (0.8in) guns

▲ **U-255**

Type VIIC

U-255 was a very successful U-boat, carrying out 15 patrols and sinking 10 ships for a total 47,529 GRT. The U-boat was eventually sunk with all hands on 15 May 1943 in the North Atlantic by depth charges from a Halifax of No. 58 Sqn RAF.

BOATS THAT SERVED WITH 11TH FLOTILLA (189 BOATS)					
U-Boat	**Type**	**Commissioned**	**Flotilla(s)**	**Patrols**	**Fate**
U-88	VIIC	15-Oct-41	1 Jul 1942 – 12 Sep, 1942 from 7. Flottille	3 patrols. 2 ships sunk: total 12,304 GRT	Sunk with all hands 12 Sep 1942 in the Arctic Ocean south of Spitzbergen by the destroyer HMS *Faulknor*. 46 dead
U-117	XB	25-Oct-41	15 Oct 1942 – 30 Nov 1942 from 1. Flottille	5 patrols. 2 ships damaged by mines: total 14,269 GRT	to 12. Flottille
U-209	VIIC	11-Oct-41	1 Jul 1942 – 28 Feb 1943 from 6. Flottille	7 patrols. 4 ships sunk: total 1356 GRT	to 1. Flottille
U-212	VIIC	25-Apr-42	1 Oct 1942 – 31 May 1943 from 8. Flottille (training)	15 patrols. 1 ship sunk: total 80 GRT	to 13. Flottille
U-218	VIID	24-Jan-42	1 Mar 1945 – 8 May 1945 from 8. Flottille	10 patrols. 2 ships sunk: total 552 GRT; 2 ships damaged: total 14,538 GRT; 1 auxiliary warship damaged: total 7177 GRT. Sank last British ship destroyed as result of the war: steam fishing vessel *Kurd* sunk 10 Jul 1945 by a minefield laid by U-218 the previous year off Lizard Head	Surrendered in Bergen, Norway, 8 May 1945. Sunk in Operation *Deadlight* 4 Dec 1945
U-244	VIIC	9-Oct-43	1 Nov 1944 – 8 May 1945	4 patrols	Surrendered at Lisahally, Northern Ireland, 14 May 1945. Sunk by naval gunfire after breaking cable while being towed out to the scuttling ground for Operation *Deadlight*
U-246	VIIC	11-Jan-44	1 Oct 1944 – 5 Apr 1945 from 3. Flottille	2 patrols	Missing with all hands Mar/Apr 1945 in the Irish Sea south of the Isle of Man. 48 dead. Sinking was credited to depth charges from the frigate HMS *Duckworth* off Land's End, but that attack probably sank U-1169
U-248	VIIC	6-Nov-43	1 Nov 1944 – 16 Jan 1945 from 9. Flottille	2 patrols	Sunk with all hands 16 Jan 1945 in the North Atlantic by depth charges from the destroyer escorts USS *Hayter*, USS *Otter*, USS *Varian* and USS *Hubbard*. 47 dead
U-251	VIIC	20-Sep-41	1 Jul 1942 – 31 May 1943 from 6. Flottille	9 patrols. 2 ships sunk: total 11,408 GRT	to 13. Flottille
U-255	VIIC	29-Nov-41	1 Jul 1942 – 31 May 1943 from 8. Flottille	15 patrols. 10 ships sunk: total 47,529 GRT; 1 warship sunk: total 1219t/1200 tons; 1 ship damaged b/r: total 7191 GRT	to 13. Flottille
U-269	VIIC	19-Aug-42	1 Apr 1943 – 31 Oct 1943 from 8. Flottille (training)	5 patrols	to 6. Flottille
U-275	VIIC	25-Nov-42	1 Oct 1944 – 10 Mar 1945 from 3. Flottille	9 patrols. 1 ship sunk: total 4934 GRT; 1 warship sunk: total 1107t/1090 tons	Sunk with all hands 10 Mar 1945 by a mine in the English Channel south of Newhaven. 48 dead
U-278	VIIC	16-Jan-43	1 Jan 1944 – 31 Aug 1944 from 7. Flottille	7 patrols. 1 ship sunk: total 7177 GRT; 1 warship sunk: total 1839t/1810 tons	to 13. Flottille
U-285	VIIC	15-May-43	1 Oct 1944 – 15 Apr 1945 from 7. Flottille	3 patrols	Sunk with all hands 15 Apr 1945 southwest of Ireland by depth charges from the frigates HMS *Grindall* and HMS *Keats*. 44 dead
U-286	VIIC	5-Jun-43	1 Aug 1944 – 4 Nov 1944 from 8. Flottille	4 patrols. 1 warship sunk: total 1168t/1150 tons	to 13. Flottille
U-286	VIIC	5-Jun-43	1 Mar 1945 – 29 Apr 1945 from 13. Flottille	4 patrols. 1 warship sunk: total 1168t/1150 tons	Sunk with all hands 29 Apr 1945 in the Arctic north of Murmansk by depth charges from the frigates HMS *Loch Insh*, HMS *Anguilla* and HMS *Cotton*. 51 dead
U-290	VIIC	24-Jul-43	1 Aug 1944 – 27 Aug 1944 from 6. Flottille	3 patrols	to 8. Flottille
U-293	VIIC/41	8-Sep-43	1 Aug 1944 – 4 Sep 1944 from 9. Flottille	6 patrols. 1 warship damaged: total 1685t/1658 tons	to 13. Flottille
U-294	VIIC/41	4-Oct-43	1 Aug 1944 – 5 Nov 1944 from 8. Flottille	5 patrols	to 13. Flottille
U-295	VIIC/41	20-Oct-43	1 Aug 1944 – 30 Sep 1944 from 8. Flottille	6 patrols. 1 warship damaged: total of 1168t/1150 tons	to 13. Flottille
U-296	VIIC/41	3-Nov-43	1 Oct 1944 – 12 Mar 1945 from 9. Flottille	3 patrols	Missing with all hands in the approaches to the North Channel on or after 12 Mar 1945. May have hit minefields T1 or T21 protecting the northern entrance to the Irish Sea. 42 dead
U-297	VIIC/41	17-Nov-43	1 Nov 1944 – 6 Dec 1944 from 8. Flottille	1 patrol	Sunk with all hands 6 Dec 1944 20km (12.4 miles) west of the Orkneys by depth charges from a Sunderland of No. 201 Sqn RAF. 50 dead. Previously listed missing in the Pentland Firth, but wreck found and identified May 2000
U-299	VIIC/41	15-Dec-43	1 Aug 1944 – 4 Nov 1944 from 8. Flottille	6 patrols	to 13. Flottille
U-300	VIIC/41	29-Dec-43	1 Oct 1944 – 22 Feb 1945 from 7. Flottille	3 patrols. 2 ships sunk: total 7559 GRT; 1 ship damaged beyond repair: total 9551 GRT; 1 ship damaged: total 7176 GRT	Sunk 22 Feb 1945 west of Cadiz by depth charges from minesweepers HMS *Recruit* and HMS *Pincher* and the armed yacht/minesweeper USS *Evadne*. 11 dead and 42 survivors
U-302	VIIC	16-Jun-42	1 Dec 1942 – 31 May 1943 from 8. Flottille	10 patrols. 3 ships sunk: total 12,697 GRT	to 13. Flottille
U-307	VIIC	18-Nov-42	1 May 1943 – 31 Oct 1943 from 8. Flottille	19 patrols. 1 ship sunk: total 411 GRT	to 13. Flottille
U-309	VIIC	27-Jan-43	1 Aug 1943 – 31 Oct 1943 from 8. Flottille	11 patrols. 1 ship damaged beyond repair: total 7219 GRT	to 9. Flottille
U-312	VIIC	21-Apr-43	1 Jan 1944 – 31 Aug 1944 from 6. Flottille	12 patrols	to 13. Flottille
U-313	VIIC	20-May-43	1 Jan 1944 – 14 Sep 1944 from 8. Flottille	14 patrols	to 13. Flottille
U-314	VIIC	10-Jun-43	1 Jan 1944 – 30 Jan 1944	2 patrols	Sunk with all hands 30 Jan 1944 in the Barents Sea southeast of Bear Island by depth charges from the destroyers HMS *Whitehall* and HMS *Meteor*. 49 dead
U-315	VIIC	10-Jul-43	1 Mar 1944 – 14 Sep 1944 from 8. Flottille	1 ship sunk: total 6996 GRT; 1 warship damaged beyond repair: total 1392t/1370 tons	to 13. Flottille

BOATS THAT SERVED WITH 11TH FLOTILLA (189 BOATS)

U-Boat	Type	Commissioned	Flotilla(s)	Patrols	Fate
U-318	VIIC/41	13-Nov-43	1 Aug 1944 – 4 Nov 1944 from 4. Flottille	8 patrols	to 13. Flottille
U-321	VIIC/41	20-Jan-44	1 Mar 1945 – 2 Apr 1945	2 patrols	Sunk with all hands 2 Apr 1945 southwest of Ireland by depth charges from a Polish Wellington of No. 304 Sqn. 41 dead
U-322	VIIC/41	5-Feb-44	1 Nov 1944 – 29 Dec 1944 from 4. Flottille	2 patrols. 1 ship sunk: total 5149 GRT; 2 ships damaged beyond repair: total 14,367 GRT	Sunk with all hands 29 Dec 1944 south of Weymouth by depth charges from the corvette HMCS *Calgary*. 52 dead. Previously thought to have been sunk 25 Nov 1944 west of the Shetlands by depth charges from the frigate HMS *Ascension*
U-324	VIIC/41	5-Apr-44	15 Mar 1945 – 8 May 1945 from 4. Flottille	No patrols	Surrendered at Bergen 8 May 1945. Broken up in Mar 1947
U-325	VIIC/41	6-May-44	1 Dec 1944 – 7 Apr 1945 from 4. Flottille	3 patrols	Missing with all hands on or after 7 Apr 1945 in the North Atlantic or on the southwest coast of Britain. 52 dead
U-326	VIIC/41	6-Jun-44	1 Mar 1945 – 25 Apr 1945 from 4. Flottille	1 patrol	Sunk with all hands 25 Apr 1945 west of Brittany in the Bay of Biscay by a homing torpedo from a US Navy PB4Y Liberator aircraft of VPB-103. 43 dead
U-327	VIIC/41	18-Jul-44	1 Feb 1945 – 27 Feb 1945 from 4. Flottille	3 patrols	Sunk with all hands 27 Feb 1945 in the western Channel by depth charges from the frigates HMS *Labuan*, HMS *Loch Fada* and the sloop HMS *Wild Goose*. But may have been sunk 3 Feb 1945 near Bergen by depth charges from the frigates HMS *Bayntun*, HMS *Braithwaite* and HMS *Loch Eck*. 46 dead
U-328	VIIC/41	19-Sep-44	2 May 1945 – 8 May 1945 from 4. Flottille	No patrols	Surrendered May 1945. Transferred to Scotland 30 May 1945 for Operation *Deadlight*. Sunk 30 Nov 1945
U-334	VIIC	9-Oct-41	1 Jul 1942 – 14 June 1943 from 3. Flottille	8 patrols. 2 ships sunk: total 14,372 GRT	Sunk with all hands 14 Jun 1943 southwest of Iceland by depth charges from the frigate HMS *Jed* and the sloop HMS *Pelican*. 47 dead
U-339	VIIC	25-Aug-42	1 Mar 1943 – 1 Apr 1943 from 8. Flottille	No patrols	to 22. Flottille
U-343	VIIC	26-Mar-43	1 Jun 1944 – 22 Aug 1944 from 3. Flottille	5 patrols. 1 warship sunk: total 1372t/1350 tons	Sunk with all hands 22 Aug 1944 in the Barents Sea northwest of Bear Island by depth charges from a Swordfish aircraft of the escort carrier HMS *Vindex*. 50 dead. Previously credited to the sloops HMS *Mermaid* and HMS *Peacock*, the frigate HMS *Loch Dunvegan* and the destroyer HMS *Keppel* on 24 Aug 1944. That attack actually sank U-354
U-347	VIIC	7-Jul-43	1 Jun 1944 – 17 Jul 1944 from 9. Flottille	4 patrols	Sunk with all hands 17 Jul 1944 west of Narvik by depth charges from a Liberator of No. 86 Sqn RAF. 49 dead. Originally credited to a Catalina that actually sank U-361
U-354	VIIC	22-Apr-42	15 Oct 1942 – 31 May 1943 from 1. Flottille	20 patrols. 1 ship sunk: total 7179 GRT; 1 warship sunk: total 1321t/1300 tons; 1 warship damaged beyond repair: total 11,603t/11,420 tons; 1 ship damaged: total 3771 GRT	to 13. Flottille
U-355	VIIC	29-Oct-41	1 Jul 1942 – 1 Apr 1944 from 5. Flottille	16 patrols. 1 ship sunk: total 5082 GRT	Missing with all hands in the Arctic while shadowing convoy JW 58 on or after 4 Apr 1944. 52 killed. Previously credited to the destroyer HMS *Beagle* and an Avenger from the escort carrier HMS *Tracker*. That attack damaged U-673
U-361	VIIC	18-Dec-42	1 Mar 1944 – 17 Jul 1944 from 8. Flottille	3 patrols	Sunk with all hands 17 Jul 1944 west of Narvik by depth charges from a Catalina of No. 210 Sqn RAF. 52 dead. Originally thought to have been sunk by a Liberator the same day, but that attack actually destroyed U-347
U-363	VIIC	18-Mar-43	1 Jun 1944 – 14 Sep 1944 from 8. Flottille	10 patrols	to 13. Flottille
U-376	VIIC	21-Aug-41	1 Jul 1942 – 28 Feb 1943 from 6. Flottille	8 patrols. 2 ships sunk: total 10,146 GRT	to 3. Flottille
U-377	VIIC	2-Oct-41	1 Jul 1942 – 28 Feb 1943 from 6. Flottille	12 patrols	to 9. Flottille
U-378	VIIC	30-Oct-41	1 Jul 1942 – 30 Apr 1943 from 3. Flottille	11 patrols. 1 warship sunk: total 1951t/1920 tons	to 3. Flottille
U-394	VIIC	7-Aug-43	1 Jun 1944 – 2 Sep 1944 from 1. Flottille	2 patrols	Sunk with all hands 2 Sep 1944 southeast of Jan Mayen island by rockets and depth charges from a Swordfish from the escort carrier HMS *Vindex* and from destroyers HMS *Keppel* and HMS *Whitehall* and sloops HMS *Mermaid* and HMS *Peacock*. 50 dead
U-396	VIIC	16-Oct-43	1 Oct 1944 – 23 Apr 1945 from 1. Flottille	5 patrols	Missing with all hands after the middle of Apr 1945 while returning from a weather-reporting patrol. 45 dead. Previously credited to an RAF Liberator on 23 Apr 1945 southwest of the Shetlands. This was probably against a false target
U-399	VIIC	22-Jan-44	1 Feb 1945 – 26 Mar 1945 from 5. Flottille	1 patrol. 1 ship sunk: total 362 GRT; 1 ship damaged beyond repair: total 7176 GRT	Sunk 26 Mar 1945 near Land's End by depth charges from the frigate HMS *Duckworth*. 46 dead and 1 survivor
U-400	VIIC	18-Mar-44	1 Nov 1944 – 15 Dec 1944 from 5. Flottille	1 patrol	Sunk with all hands on or after 15 Dec 1944, probably by a mine off Cornwall. 50 dead. Previously credited to the frigate HMS *Nyasaland* 17 Dec 1944, but that attack actually sank U-772
U-403	VIIC	25-Jun-41	1 Jul 1942 – 28 Feb 1943 from 7. Flottille	7 patrols. 2 ships sunk: total 12,946 GRT	to 9. Flottille
U-405	VIIC	17-Sep-41	1 Jul 1942 – 28 Feb 1943 from 1. Flottille	11 patrols. 2 ships sunk: total 11,841 GRT	to 6. Flottille

BOATS THAT SERVED WITH 11TH FLOTILLA (189 BOATS)

U-Boat	Type	Commissioned	Flotilla(s)	Patrols	Fate
U-408	VIIC	19-Nov-41	1 Jul 1942 – 5 Nov 1942 from 9. Flottille	3 patrols. 3 ships sunk: total 19,689 GRT	Sunk with all hands 5 Nov 1942 north of Iceland by depth charges from a US Navy PBY Catalina of VP-84. 45 dead
U-419	VIIC	18-Nov-42	1 Aug 1943 – 8 Oct 1943 from 8. Flottille	1 patrol	Sunk 8 Oct 1943 in the North Atlantic by depth charges from a Liberator of No. 86 Sqn RAF. 48 dead and 1 survivor
U-420	VIIC	16-Dec-42	1 Jul 1943 – 20 Oct 1943 from 8. Flottille	2 patrols	Missing with all hands after 20 Oct 1943 in the North Atlantic. 49 dead. Originally credited to a Liberator of No. 10 Sqn RCAF, which depth-charged a U-boat in the Atlantic on 26 Oct 1943, probably U-91, which was undamaged
U-425	VIIC	21-Apr-43	1 Jan 1944 – 14 Sep 1944 from 9. Flottille	8 patrols	to 13. Flottille
U-426	VIIC	12-May-43	1 Oct 1943 – 31 Oct 1943 from 8. Flottille	2 patrols. 1 ship sunk: total 6625 GRT	to 1. Flottille
U-427	VIIC	2-Jun-43	1 Aug 1944 – 4 Nov 1944 from 7. Flottille	5 patrols	to 13. Flottille
U-435	VIIC	30-Aug-41	1 Jul 1942 – 31 Jan 1943 from 1. Flottille	8 patrols. 9 ships sunk: total 53,712 GRT; 1 auxiliary warship sunk: total 2456 GRT; 3 warships sunk: total 869t/855 tons	to 1. Flottille
U-436	VIIC	27-Sep-41	1 Jul 1942 – 31 Aug 1942 from 7. Flottille	8 patrols. 6 ships sunk: total 36,208 GRT; 2 ships damaged: total 15,575 GRT	to 6. Flottille
U-456	VIIC	18-Sep-41	1 Jul 1942 – 30 Nov 1942 from 6. Flottille	11 patrols. 6 ships sunk: total 31,528 GRT; 1 auxiliary warship sunk: total 251 GRT; 1 warship (HMS *Edinburgh*) damaged: total 11,685t/11,500 tons	to 1. Flottille
U-457	VIIC	5-Nov-41	1 Jul 1942 – 16 Sep 1942 from 6. Flottille	3 patrols. 2 ships sunk: total 15,593 GRT; 1 ship damaged: total 8939 GRT	Sunk with all hands 16 Sep 1942 in the Barents Sea northeast of Murmansk by depth charges from the British destroyer HMS *Impulsive*. 45 dead
U-467	VIIC	15-Jul-42	1 Apr 1943 – 25 May 1943 from 5. Flottille	2 patrols	Sunk with all hands 25 May 1943 southeast of Iceland by a Fido homing torpedo from a US Navy PBY Catalina of Patrol Squadron VP 84. 46 dead
U-470	VIIC	7-Jan-43	1 Jul 1943 – 16 Oct 1943 from 5. Flottille	1 patrol	Sunk 16 Oct 1943 southwest of Iceland by depth charges from Liberators of Nos. 59 and 120 Sqns RAF. 46 dead and 2 survivors
U-472	VIIC	26-May-43	1 Jan 1944 – 4 Mar 1944 from 5. Flottille	1 patrol	Sunk 4 Mar 1944 in the Barents Sea southeast of Bear Island by naval gunfire and aerial rockets from the destroyer HMS *Onslaught* and Swordfish aircraft of the escort carrier HMS *Chaser*. 23 dead and 30 survivors
U-480	VIIC	6-Oct-43	15 Oct 1944 – 24 Feb 1945 from 9. Flottille	3 patrols. 2 ships sunk: total 12,846 GRT; 2 warships sunk: total 1803t/1775 tons	Sunk with all hands in the Channel some time in Feb 1945, probably in minefield Brazier D2. 48 dead. Previously credited to frigates HMS *Duckworth* and HMS *Rowley* 24 Feb 1945 southeast of Isles of Scilly. In fact they sank U-1208
U-482	VIIC	1-Dec-43	1 Oct 1944 – 16 Jan 1945 from 11. Flottille	2 patrols. 4 ships sunk: total 31,611 GRT; 1 warship sunk: total 1026t/1010 tons	Probably sunk with all hands 25 Nov 1944 west of the Shetlands by depth charges from frigate HMS *Ascension*. 48 dead. Previously recorded fates include loss to mines northwest of Malin Head around 7 Dec 1944 or to depth charges from sloops HMS *Peacock*, HMS *Starling*, HMS *Hart* and HMS *Amethyst* and frigate HMS *Loch Craggie* in the North Channel 16 Jan 1945
U-483	VIIC	22-Dec-43	5 Sep 1944 – 8 May 1945 from 3. Flottille	2 patrols. 1 warship damaged beyond repair: total 1321t/1300 tons	Surrendered at Trondheim. Transferred to Scotland 29 May 1945 for Operation *Deadlight*. Sunk 16 Dec 1945
U-485	VIIC	23-Feb-44	1 Nov 1944 – 8 May 1945 from 5. Flottille	2 patrols	Surrendered at Gibraltar 8 May 1945. Transferred to Scotland for Operation *Deadlight*. Sunk 8 Dec 1945
U-486	VIIC	22-Mar-44	1 Nov 1944 – 12 Apr 1945 from 5. Flottille	2 patrols. 2 ships sunk: total 17,651 GRT; 1 warship sunk: total 1102t/1085 tons; 1 warship damaged b/r: total 1102t/1085 tons	Sunk with all hands 12 Apr 1945 northwest of Bergen, torpedoed by the submarine HMS *Tapir*. 48 dead
U-586	VIIC	4-Sep-41	1 Jul 1942 – 31 May 1943 from 6. Flottille	12 patrols. 2 ships sunk: total 12,716 GRT; 1 ship damaged: total 9057 GRT	to 13. Flottille
U-589	VIIC	25-Sep-41	1 Jul 1942 – 14 Sep 1942 from 6. Flottille	8 patrols. 1 ship sunk: total 2847 GRT; 1 auxiliary warship sunk: total 417 GRT	Sunk with all hands 14 Sep 1942 in the Arctic Ocean southwest of Spitzbergen by depth charges from destroyer HMS *Onslow*, and from a Swordfish flying from the escort carrier HMS *Avenger*. 48 dead, including 4 *Luftwaffe* airmen the boat had rescued the previous day
U-591	VIIC	9-Oct-41	1 Jul 1942 – 31 May 1943 from 6. Flottille	8 patrols. 4 ships sunk: total 19,932 GRT; 1 ship damaged: total 5701 GRT	to 9. Flottille
U-592	VIIC	16-Oct-41	1 Jul 1942 – 28 Feb 1943 from 6. Flottille	10 patrols. 1 ship sunk: total 3770 GRT	to 6. Flottille
U-601	VIIC	18-Dec-41	1 Jul 1942 – 31 May 1943 from 5. Flottille	10 patrols. 3 ships sunk: total 8819 GRT	to 13. Flottille
U-606	VIIC	22-Jan-42	1 Sep 1942 – 31 Oct 1942 from 5. Flottille	3 patrols. 3 ships sunk: total 20,527 GRT; 2 ships damaged: total 21,925 GRT	to 9. Flottille
U-622	VIIC	14-May-42	2 Oct 1942 – 31 May 1943 from 8. Flottille	4 patrols	to 13. Flottille
U-625	VIIC	4-Jun-42	1 Nov 1942 – 31 May 1943 from 3. Flottille	9 patrols. 3 ships sunk: total 18,751 GRT; 2 auxiliary warships sunk: total 939 GRT	to 13. Flottille
U-629	VIIC	2-Jul-42	1 Dec 1942 – 31 Oct 1943 from 5. Flottille	11 patrols	to 1. Flottille
U-636	VIIC	20-Aug-42	1 Apr 1943 – 31 Oct 1943 from 5. Flottille	14 patrols. 1 ship sunk: total 7169 GRT	to 13. Flottille

BOATS THAT SERVED WITH 11TH FLOTILLA (189 BOATS)

U-Boat	Type	Commissioned	Flotilla(s)	Patrols	Fate
U-639	VIIC	10-Sep-42	1 Apr 1943 – 31 May 1943 from 5. Flottille	4 patrols	to 13. Flottille
U-644	VIIC	15-Oct-42	1 Apr 1943 – 7 Apr 1943 from 5. Flottille	1 patrol	Sunk with all hands 7 Apr 1943 northwest of Narvik, Norway, torpedoed by HM Submarine *Tuna*. 45 dead
U-646	VIIC	29-Oct-42	1 Apr 1943 – 17 May 1943 from 5. Flottille	2 patrols	Sunk with all hands 17 May 1943 southeast of Iceland by depth charges from a Hudson of No. 269 Sqn RAF. 46 dead
U-650	VIIC	26-Nov-42	1 Oct 1944 – 9 Dec 1944 from 7. Flottille	7 patrols	Missing with all hands in the North Atlantic or the Arctic Ocean on or after 9 Dec 1944. 47 dead
U-657	VIIC	8-Oct-41	1 Jul 1942 – 17 May 1943 from 3. Flottille	7 patrols. 1 ship sunk: total 5196 GRT	Sunk with all hands 17 May 1943 east of Cape Farewell by depth charges from the frigate HMS *Swale*. 47 dead. Previously credited to a torpedo from US Navy PBY Catalina of VP-82 on 14 May, which probably did attack U-657 but is unlikely to have damaged the boat
U-663	VIIC	14-May-42	1 Oct 1942 – 31 Oct 1942 from 5. Flottille	3 patrols; 2 ships sunk: total 10,924 GRT	to 9. Flottille
U-674	VIIC	15-Jun-43	1 Feb 1944 – 2 May 1944 from 5. Flottille	3 patrols	Sunk with all hands 2 May 1944 northwest of Narvik by rockets from a Swordfish of the escort carrier HMS *Fencer*. 49 dead
U-680	VIIC	23-Dec-43	1 Oct 1944 – 8 May 1945 from 6. Flottille	4 patrols	Surrendered at Wilhelmshaven 8 May 1945. Transferred to Scotland for Operation *Deadlight*. Sunk as a gunfire target 28 Dec 1945
U-681	VIIC	3-Feb-44	1 Nov 1944 – 10 Mar 1945 from 31. Flottille	1 patrol	Struck a rock 10 Mar 1945 while submerged near the Isles of Scilly; forced to surface near the Bishop Rock and spotted by a US Navy PB4Y Liberator of VPB-103. Sunk by depth charges. 11 dead and 38 survivors
U-682	VIIC	17-Apr-44	1 Dec 1944 – 1 Feb 1945 from 31. Flottille	No patrols	to 31. Flottille
U-683	VIIC	30-May-44	1 Jan 1945 – 20 Feb 1945 from 31. Flottille	1 patrol	Missing with all hands on or after 20 Feb 1945 southwest of Ireland or in the English Channel. 49 dead. Previously thought to have been sunk 12 Mar 1945 near Land's End by depth charges from the frigate HMS *Loch Ruthven* and the sloop HMS *Wild Goose*; those attacks probably targeted the wreck of U-247
U-703	VIIC	16-Oct-41	1 Jul 1942 – 31 May 1943 from 6. Flottille	13 patrols. 5 ships sunk: total 29,523 GRT; 1 auxiliary warship sunk: total 559 GRT; 1 warship sunk: total 1900t/1870 tons	to 13. Flottille
U-711	VIIC	26-Sep-42	1 Apr 1943 – 31 May 1943 from 5. Flottille	12 patrols. 1 ship sunk: total 7176 GRT; 1 warship sunk: total 940t/925 tons; 1 ship damaged: total 20 GRT	to 13. Flottille
U-713	VIIC	29-Dec-42	1 Jul 1943 – 31 Oct 1943 from 8. Flottille	5 patrols	to 13. Flottille
U-716	VIIC	15-Apr-43	1 Jan 1944 – 30 Sep 1944 from 5. Flottille	10 patrols. 1 ship sunk: total 7200 GRT	to 13. Flottille
U-722	VIIC	15-Dec-43	1 Oct 1944 – 27 Mar 1945 from 1. Flottille	3 patrols. 1 ship sunk: total 2190 GRT	Sunk with all hands 27 Mar 1945 in the North Atlantic off the Hebrides by depth charges from the frigates HMS *Fitzroy*, HMS *Redmill* and HMS *Byron*. 44 dead
U-735	VIIC	28-Dec-42	1 Aug 1944 – 28 Dec 1944 from 8. Flottille	No patrols	Sunk on 28 Dec 1944 in Oslo Fjord near Horten by British bombs. 39 dead and 1 survivor
U-764	VIIC	6-May-43	1 Oct 1944 – 8 May 1945 from 9. Flottille	8 patrols. 1 ship sunk: total 638 GRT; 2 warships sunk: total 1723t/1696 tons	Surrendered 14 May 1945 at Lisahally, Northern Ireland. Sunk 2 Feb 1946 in Operation *Deadlight*
U-771	VIIC	18-Nov-43	1 Aug 1944 – 30 Sep 1944 from 9. Flottille	2 patrols	to 13. Flottille
U-772	VIIC	23-Dec-43	15 Oct 1944 – 30 Dec 1944 from 9. Flottille	2 patrols	Sunk with all hands 17 Dec 1944 south of Cork by depth charges from frigate HMS *Nyasaland*. 48 dead. Previously credited to a Canadian Wellington south of Weymouth 30 Dec 1944, which was probably an ineffective attack against U-486
U-773	VIIC	20-Jan-44	1 Oct 1944 – 8 May 1945 from 1. Flottille	3 patrols	Surrendered at Trondheim 8 May 1945. Transferred to Scotland for Operation *Deadlight*. Sunk 8 Dec 1945.
U-774	VIIC	17-Feb-44	1 Feb 1945 – 8 Apr 1945 from 31. Flottille	1 patrol	Sunk with all hands 8 Apr 1945 southwest of Ireland by depth charges from the frigates HMS *Calder* and HMS *Bentinck*. 44 dead
U-775	VIIC	23-Mar-44	1 Nov 1944 – 8 May 1945 from 31. Flottille	2 patrols. 1 ship sunk: total 1926 GRT; 1 warship sunk: total 1321t/1300 tons; 1 ship damaged: total 6991 GRT	Surrendered at Trondheim, Norway, on 8 May 1945. Transferred to Scotland for Operation *Deadlight*. Sunk by gunfire 8 Dec 1945
U-778	VIIC	7-Jul-44	1 Mar 1945 – 8 May 1945 from 31. Flottille	1 patrol	Surrendered at Bergen 8 May 1945. Transferred to Scotland for Operation *Deadlight*. Foundered while on tow 4 Dec 1945 northeast of Inishtrahull
U-825	VIIC	4-May-44	1 Dec 1944 – 8 May 1945 from 8. Flottille	2 patrols. 1 ship damaged beyond repair: total 8262 GRT; 1 ship damaged: total 7198 GRT	Surrendered at Portland 10 May 1945. Transferred to Northern Ireland for Operation *Deadlight*. Sunk 3 Jan 1946
U-826	VIIC	11-May-44	1 Jan 1945 – 8 May 1945 from 8. Flottille	1 patrol	Surrendered at Loch Eriboll, Scotland, 11 May 1945. Sunk 1 Dec 1945 in Operation *Deadlight*
U-827	VIIC/41	25-May-44	1 Mar 1945 – 5 May 1945 from 8. Flottille	No patrols	Scuttled 5 May 1945 in Flensburg Fjord
U-867	IXC/40	12-Dec-43	1 Sep 1944 – 19 Sep 1944	1 patrol	Sunk with all hands 19 Sep 1944 northwest of Bergen by depth charges from a Liberator of No. 224 Sqn RAF. 60 dead
U-901	VIIC	29-Apr-44	15 Mar 1945 – 8 May 1945	1 patrol	Surrendered at Stavanger. Transferred to Northern Ireland 29 May 1945 for Operation *Deadlight*. Sunk 5 Jan 1946

BOATS THAT SERVED WITH 11TH FLOTILLA (189 BOATS)

U-Boat	Type	Commissioned	Flotilla(s)	Patrols	Fate
U-905	VIIC	8-Mar-44	1 Dec 1944 – 27 Mar 1945 from 31. Flottille	2 patrols	Sunk with all hands 27 Mar 1945 between the Hebrides and the Scottish mainland by depth charges from the frigate HMS *Conn*. 45 dead. Previously credited to a 120 Sqn Liberator 20 Mar 1945 southeast of Faroes, but this was probably a false target
U-907	VIIC	18-May-44	1 Dec 1944 – 8 May 1945 from 31. Flottille	2 patrols	Surrendered at Bergen. Transferred Scotland 29 May 1945 for Operation *Deadlight*. Sunk 7 Dec 1945
U-926	VIIC	29-Feb-44	15 Mar 1945 – 8 May 1945 from 4. Flottille	No patrols	Surrendered at Bergen, Norway, 8 May 1945. Taken into Norwegian service as HNMS *Kya*. Stricken 1962. One of only 3 U-boats left at Bergen after more than 30 boats were transferred to Scotland in late May and early Jun 1945
U-927	VIIC	27-Jun-44	1 Feb 1945 – 24 Feb 1945 from 4. Flottille	1 patrol	Sunk with all hands 24 Feb 1945 in the Channel southeast of Falmouth by depth charges from a Vickers Warwick of No. 179 Sqn RAF. 47 dead
U-956	VIIC	6-Jan-43	1 Jan 1944 – 30 Sep 1944 from 1. Flottille	13 patrols. 1 warship sunk: total 1209t/1190 tons; 1 ship damaged beyond repair: total 7176 GRT	to 13. Flottille
U-957	VIIC	7-Jan-43	1 Jan 1944 – 30 Sep 1944 from 3. Flottille	6 patrols. 2 ships sunk: total 7353 GRT; 2 warships sunk: total 614t/604 tons	to 13. Flottille
U-963	VIIC	17-Feb-43	1 Nov 1944 – 8 May 1945 from 1. Flottille	10 patrols	Scuttled 20 May 1945 on the Portuguese west coast. The crew was interned. 48 survivors
U-965	VIIC	25-Feb-43	1 Jan 1944 – 30 Sep 1944 from 5. Flottille	7 patrols	to 13. Flottille
U-978	VIIC	12-May-43	5 Sep 1944 – 8 May 1945 from 3. Flottille	2 patrols. 1 ship damaged beyond repair: total 7176 GRT. U-978 carried out the longest *Schnorchel* patrol of the war, 68 days submerged from Bergen, Norway, beginning 9 Oct 1944, returning 16 Dec	Transferred from Trondheim to Scotland 29 May 1945 for Operation *Deadlight*. Sunk 11 Dec 1945
U-979	VIIC	20-May-43	Oct 1944 – 24 May 1945 from 9. Flottille	3 patrols. 1 auxiliary warship sunk: total 348 GRT; 2 ships damaged: total 12,133 GRT	Scuttled 24 May 1945 at Amrum, Germany, after running aground
U-987	VIIC	8-Jul-43	1 Jun 1944 – 15 Jun 1944 from 1. Flottille	1 patrol	Sunk with all hands 15 Jun 1944 west of Narvik, torpedoed by the British submarine HMS *Satyr*. 53 dead
U-990	VIIC	28-Jul-43	1 Jan 1944 – 25 May 1944 from 5. Flottille	4 patrols. 1 warship sunk: total 1951t/1920 tons	Sunk 25 May 1944 west of Bodö by depth charges from a Liberator of No. 59 Sqn. 22 dead (including 2 rescued from U-476) and 51 survivors (including 18 from U-476)
U-991	VIIC	29-Jul-43	1 Sep 1944 – 8 May 1945 from 5. Flottille	1 patrol	Transferred from Bergen to Scotland 29 May 1945 for Operation *Deadlight*. Sunk 11 Dec 1945
U-992	VIIC	2-Aug-43	1 Jun 1944 – 30 Sep 1944 from 3. Flottille	8 patrols; 1 warship damaged beyond repair: total 1077t/1060 tons	to 13. Flottille
U-994	VIIC	2-Sep-43	1 Aug 1944 – 4 Nov 1944 from 5. Flottille	1 patrol	to 13. Flottille
U-1002	VIIC/41	30-Nov-43	1 Mar 1945 – 8 May 1945 from 31. Flottille	1 patrol	Transferred from Bergen to Scotland 30 May 1945 for Operation *Deadlight*. Sunk 13 Dec 1945
U-1003	VIIC/41	9-Dec-43	1 Sep 1944 – 23 Mar 1945 from 31. Flottille	2 patrols	Scuttled 23 Mar 1945 in the North Channel about 16km (10 miles) north of Malin Head after being rammed by the Canadian frigate HMCS *New Glasgow* 20 Mar 1945. 17 dead and 31 survivors
U-1004	VIIC/41	16-Dec-43	1 Nov 1944 – 8 May 1945 from 7. Flottille	2 patrols. 1 ship sunk: total 1313 GRT; 1 warship sunk: total 996t/980 tons	Transferred from Bergen to Scotland 30 May 1945 for Operation *Deadlight*. Sunk by gunfire 1 Dec 1945
U-1005	VIIC/41	30-Dec-43	1 Feb 1945 – 8 May 1945 from 31. Flottille	2 patrols	Transferred from Bergen to Scotland 30 May 1945 for Operation *Deadlight*. Foundered while under tow to the scuttling grounds 5 Dec 1945
U-1006	VIIC/41	11-Jan-44	1 Sep 1944 – 16 Oct 1944 from 11. Flottille	1 patrol	Sunk 16 Oct 1944 southeast of Faroes by depth charges from the frigate HMCS *Annan*. 6 dead and 44 survivors
U-1009	VIIC/41	10-Feb-44	1 Nov 1944 – 8 May 1945 from 31. Flottille	2 patrols	Surrendered 10 May 1945 at Loch Eriboll, Scotland. Sunk by naval gunfire in Operation *Deadlight* 16 Dec 1945
U-1010	VIIC/41	22-Feb-44	1 Apr 1945 – 8 May 1945	1 patrol	Surrendered 14 May 1945 at Loch Eriboll, Scotland. Sunk by gunfire in Operation *Deadlight* 7 Jan 1946
U-1014	VIIC/41	14-Mar-44	1 Jan 1945 – 4 Feb 1945 from 31. Flottille	1 patrol	Sunk with all hands 4 Feb 1945 in the Hebrides by depth charges from frigates HMS *Loch Scavaig*, HMS *Nyasaland*, HMS *Papua* and HMS *Loch Shin*. 48 dead
U-1017	VIIC/41	13-Apr-44	1 Nov 1944 – 29 Apr 1945 from 31. Flottille	2 patrols. 2 ships sunk: total 10,604 GRT	Possibly sunk 29 Apr 1945 northwest of Ireland by depth charges from a Liberator of No. 120 Sqn RAF. 34 dead. It might have been U-398: both boats disappeared at about the same time
U-1018	VIIC/41	24-Apr-44	1 Dec 1944 – 27 Feb 1945 from 31. Flottille	1 patrol. 1 ship sunk: total 1317 GRT	Sunk 27 Feb 1945 south of Penzance by depth charges from the frigate HMS *Loch Fada*. 51 dead and 2 survivors
U-1019	VIIC/41	4-May-44	1 Dec 1944 – 8 May 1945 from 31. Flottille	1 patrol	Transferred from Trondheim to Scotland 29 May 1945 for Operation *Deadlight*. Sunk by gunfire 7 Dec 1945
U-1020	VIIC/41	17-May-44	1 Dec 1944 – Jan 1945? from 31. Flottille	1 patrol	Missing with all hands in the North Sea after leaving Horten 22 Nov 1944. 52 dead
U-1021	VIIC/41	25-May-44	1 Dec 1944 – 30 Mar 1945 from 31. Flottille	1 patrol	Missing with all hands south of the Bristol Channel on or after 14 Mar 1945. 43 dead. Probably sunk in British-laid minefield A1 or ZME 25
U-1022	VIIC/41	7-Jun-44	1 Feb 1945 – 8 May 1945 from 31. Flottille	1 patrol. 1 ship sunk: total 1392 GRT; 1 auxiliary warship sunk: total 328 GRT	Transferred from Bergen to Scotland 30 May 1945 for Operation *Deadlight*. Sunk 29 Dec 1945
U-1023	VIIC/41	15-Jun-44	1 Mar 1945 – 8 May 1945 from 31. Flottille	1 patrol. 1 warship sunk: total 340t/335 tons; 1 ship damaged: total 7345 GRT	Surrendered 10 May 1945 at Weymouth. Sunk in Operation *Deadlight* 7 Jan 1946

BOATS THAT SERVED WITH 11TH FLOTILLA (189 BOATS)

U-Boat	Type	Commissioned	Flotilla(s)	Patrols	Fate
U-1024	VIIC/41	28-Jun-44	1 Feb 1945 – 12 Apr 1945 from 31. Flottille	1 patrol. 1 ship damaged beyond repair: total 7176 GRT; 1 ship damaged: total 7200 GRT	Captured 12 Apr 1945 in the Irish Sea south of Isle of Man by the frigates HMS *Loch Glendhu* and HMS *Loch More*. Foundered while on tow 13 Apr 1945. 9 dead and 37 survivors
U-1051	VIIC	4-Mar-44	1 Jan 1945 – 26 Jan 1945 from 5. Flottille	1 patrol. 1 ship sunk: total 1152 GRT; 1 warship a total loss: total 1321t/1300 tons	Sunk with all hands 26 Jan 1945 south of Isle of Man, by ramming and depth charges from frigates HMS *Aylmer*, HMS *Calder*, HMS *Bentinck* and HMS *Manners*. 47 dead. Previously credited to the frigates HMS *Tyler*, HMS *Keats* and HMS *Bligh* in St George's Channel 27 Jan 1945 but they actually sank U-1172
U-1053	VIIC	12-Feb-44	1 Nov 1944 – 15 Feb 1945 from 5. Flottille	2 patrols	Sank with all hands plus some dockyard personnel in a diving accident 15 Feb 1945 near Bergen. 45 dead
U-1055	VIIC	8-Apr-44	1 Dec 1944 – 23 Apr 1945 from 5. Flottille	2 patrols. 4 ships sunk: total 19,413 GRT	Missing with all hands on or after 23 Apr 1945 in Atlantic or Channel. 49 dead. Originally credited to a US Navy PBY off Brest, but the boat destroyed was probably U-1107
U-1058	VIIC	10-Jun-44	1 Jan 1945 – 8 May 1945 from 5. Flottille	2 patrols	Surrendered at Lough Eribol, Northern Ireland 10 May 1945. Awarded to the USSR and became Soviet submarine S-82 in Nov 1945
U-1063	VIIC/41	8-Jul-44	1 Mar 1945 – 15 Apr 1945 from 5. Flottille	1 patrol	Sunk 15 Apr 1945 west of Land's End by depth charges from the frigate HMS *Loch Killin*. 29 dead and 17 survivors
U-1064	VIIC/41	29-Jul-44	1 Feb 1945 – 8 May 1945 from 5. Flottille	1 patrol. 1 ship sunk: total 1564 GRT	Transferred from Trondheim to Loch Ryan 29 May 1945. Awarded to the USSR and became Soviet submarine S-83 in Nov 1945
U-1104	VIIC/41	15-Mar-44	1 Feb 1945 – 8 May 1945 from 8. Flottille	1 patrol	Transferred from Bergen to Scotland 30 May 1945 for Operation *Deadlight*. Sunk by gunfire 1 Dec 1945
U-1107	VIIC/41	8-Aug-44	16 Feb 1945 – 30 Apr 1945 from 8. Flottille	1 patrol. 2 ships sunk: total 15,209 GRT	Sunk 30 Apr 1945 west of Brest by retro bombs from a US Navy PBY of VP-63. 37 dead and 10+ survivors. Previously credited to a US Navy Liberator, which actually sank U-326
U-1109	VIIC/41	31-Aug-44	16 Feb 1945 – 8 May 1945 from 8. Flottille	2 patrols	Transferred from Norway to Northern Ireland 31 May 1945 for Operation *Deadlight*. Sunk 6 Jan 1946 by submarine torpedoes
U-1163	VIIC/41	6-Oct-43	1 Aug 1944 – 30 Sep 1944 from 8. Flottille	4 patrols. 1 ship sunk: total 433 GRT	to 13. Flottille
U-1165	VIIC/41	17-Nov-43	1 Aug 1944 – 8 May 1945 from 9. Flottille	4 patrols; 1 warship sunk: total 40t/39 tons	Transferred from Narvik to Scotland 19 May 1945 for Operation *Deadlight*. Sunk 30 Dec 1945
U-1169	VIIC/41	9-Feb-44	1 Feb 1945 – 29 Mar 1945 from 8. Flottille	1 patrol	Sunk with all hands 29 Mar 1945 in the English Channel south of Lizard Point, by depth charges from the frigate HMS *Duckworth*. 49 dead. Previously thought to have hit a mine 5 Apr, but the boat sunk was U-242
U-1171	VIIC/41	22-Mar-44	1 Mar 1945 – 8 May 1945 from 8. Flottille	No patrols	Transferred from Stavanger to Scotland 29 May 1945. Used by the Royal Navy as submarine N 19. Broken up in 1949
U-1172	VIIC/41	20-Apr-44	1 Dec 1944 – 27 Jan 1945 from 8. Flottille	1 patrol. 1 ship sunk: total 1599 GRT; 1 ship damaged: total 7429 GRT; 1 warship (escort carrier HMS *Thane*) damaged: total 11,583t/11,400 tons	Sunk with all hands 27 Jan 1945 in St George's Channel by depth charges from frigates HMS *Tyler*, HMS *Keats* and HMS *Bligh*. 52 dead. Previously credited to frigates HMS *Aylmer*, HMS *Calder*, HMS *Bentinck* and HMS *Manners*, which actually sank U-1051
U-1195	VIIC	4-Nov-43	1 Jan 1945 – 7 Apr 1945 from 5. Flottille	1 patrol. 2 ships sunk: total 18,614 GRT	Sunk 7 Apr 1945 in the English Channel by depth charges from the destroyer HMS *Watchman*. 32 dead and 18 survivors
U-1199	VIIC	23-Dec-43	10 Nov 1944 – 21 Jan 1945 from 1. Flottille	2 patrols. 1 ship damaged beyond repair: total 7176 GRT	Sunk 21 Jan 1945 near the Scilly Isles by depth charges from the destroyer HMS *Icarus* and the corvette HMS *Mignonette*. 48 dead and 1 survivor
U-1200	VIIC	5-Jan-44	1 Sep 1944 – 11 Nov 1944 from 8. Flottille	1 patrol	Sunk with all hands 11 Nov 1944 south of Ireland by depth charges from corvettes HMS *Pevensey Castle*, HMS *Lancaster Castle*, HMS *Porchester Castle* and HMS *Kenilworth Castle*. 53 dead
U-1202	VIIC	27-Jan-44	1 Sep 1944 – 8 May 1945 from 8. Flottille	2 patrols. 1 ship sunk: total 7176 GRT	Stricken at Bergen 10 May 1945. Surrendered to Britain. Transferred to Norway in Oct 1948. Became the Norwegian submarine KNM *Kinn* 1 Jul 1951. Stricken 1 June 1961. Broken up at Hamburg in 1963
U-1203	VIIC	10-Feb-44	1 Dec 1944 – 8 May 1945 from 8. Flottille	1 patrol. 1 auxiliary warship sunk: total 580 GRT	Transferred from Trondheim to Scotland 29 May 1945 for Operation *Deadlight*. Sunk 8 Dec 1945
U-1206	VIIC	16-Mar-44	1 Feb 1945 – 14 Apr 1945 from 8. Flottille	1 patrol	Sank in a diving accident 14 Apr 1945 off Peterhead, Scotland. 4 dead and 46 survivors
U-1208	VIIC	6-Apr-44	1 Jan 1945 – 27 Feb 1945 from 8. Flottille	1 patrol. 1 ship sunk: total 1644 GRT	Sunk with all hands 27 Feb 1945 southeast of Isles of Scilly by depth charges from frigates HMS *Duckworth* and HMS *Rowley*. 49 dead. Sinking previously credited to sloop HMS *Amethyst* south of Ireland, but that attack destroyed U-1276
U-1209	VIIC	13-Apr-44	1 Nov 1944 – 18 Dec 1944 from 8. Flottille	1 patrol	Ran into Wolf Rock near the Scilly Isles and was scuttled 18 Dec 1944. 9 dead and 44 survivors
U-1231	IXC/40	9-Feb-44	1 Sep 1944 – 30 Sep 1944 from 31. Flottille	2 patrols	to 33. Flottille
U-1272	VIIC/41	28-Jan-44	1 Mar 1945 – 8 May 1945 from 8. Flottille	1 patrol	Transferred from Bergen to Scotland 30 May 1945 for Operation *Deadlight*. Sunk 8 Dec 1945

BOATS THAT SERVED WITH 11TH FLOTILLA (189 BOATS)

U-Boat	Type	Commissioned	Flotilla(s)	Patrols	Fate
U-1273	VIIC/41	16-Feb-44	1 Feb 1945 – 17 Feb 1945 from 8. Flottille	Training	Sunk 17 Feb 1945 by a mine in Oslofjord near Horten. 43 dead and 8 survivors
U-1276	VIIC/41	6-Apr-44	1 Nov 1944 – 20 Feb 1945 from 8. Flottille	1 patrol. 1 warship sunk: total 940t/925 tons	Sunk with all hands 20 Feb 1945 south of Waterford, Ireland, by depth charges from the sloop HMS *Amethyst*. 49 dead
U-1277	VIIC/41	3-May-44	1 Feb 1945 – 8 May 1945 from 8. Flottille	1 patrol	Scuttled 3 Jun 1945 off Capo de Mundo near Oporto, Portugal. No casualties – 47 survivors. Crew paddled ashore in rubber dinghies and were interned before being handed over to the British. Eventually released from POW camp in 1948
U-1278	VIIC/41	31-May-44	1 Dec 1944 – 17 Feb 1945 from 8. Flottille	1 patrol	Sunk with all hands 17 Feb 1945 northwest of Bergen by depth charges from the frigates HMS *Bayntun* and HMS *Loch Eck*. 48 dead
U-1279	VIIC/41	5-Jul-44	1 Feb 1945 – 3 Feb 1945 from 8. Flottille	1 patrol	Sunk with all hands 3 Feb 1945 northwest of Bergen by depth charges from the frigates HMS *Bayntun*, HMS *Braithwaite* and HMS *Loch Eck*. 48 dead
U-1302	VIIC/41	25-May-44	1 Jan 1945 – 7 Mar 1945 from 4. Flottille	1 patrol. 3 ships sunk: total 8386 GRT	Sunk with all hands 7 Mar 1945 in St George's Channel by depth charges from the frigates HMCS *La Hulloise*, HMCS *Strathadam* and HMCS *Thetford Mines*. 48 dead
U-2321	XXIII	12-Jun-44	1 Feb 1945 – 8 May 1945 from 32. Flottille	1 patrol. 1 ship sunk: total 1406 GRT	Surrendered at Kristiansand Süd, Norway. Taken to Loch Ryan 29 May 1945 for Operation *Deadlight*. Sunk 27 Nov 1945 by naval gunfire
U-2322	XXIII	1-Jul-44	1 Feb 1945 – 8 May 1945 from 32. Flottille	2 patrols. 1 ship sunk: total 1317 GRT	Surrendered at Stavanger, Norway. Taken to Loch Ryan 31 May 1945 for Operation *Deadlight*. Sunk 27 Nov 1945 by naval gunfire
U-2324	XXIII	25-Jul-44	1 Feb 1945 – 8 May 1945 from 32. Flottille	2 patrols	Surrendered at Stavanger, Norway. Taken to Loch Ryan 29 May 1945 for Operation *Deadlight*. Sunk 27 Nov 1945 by naval gunfire
U-2325	XXIII	3-Aug-44	1 Feb 1945 – 8 May 1945 from 32. Flottille	No patrols	Surrendered at Kristiansand Süd, Norway. Taken to Loch Ryan 29 May 1945 for Operation *Deadlight*. Sunk 28 Nov by naval gunfire
U-2326	XXIII	10-Aug-44	1 Feb 1945 – 8 May 1945 from 32. Flottille	2 patrols	Surrendered at Dundee, Scotland, 14 May 1945. Became the British submarine N 35. Transferred to France in 1946. Sank 6 Dec 1946 at Toulon in an accident. Raised and broken up
U-2328	XXIII	25-Aug-44	1 Apr 1945 – 8 May 1945 from 32. Flottille	No patrols	Surrendered at Bergen, Norway. Taken to Loch Ryan 30 May 1945 for Operation *Deadlight*. Took on water and sank while on tow to scuttling grounds 27 Nov 1945
U-2329	XXIII	1-Sep-44	15 Mar 1945 – 8 May 1945 from 32. Flottille	1 patrol	Surrendered at Stavanger, Norway. Taken to Loch Ryan in Jun 1945 for Operation *Deadlight*. Sunk 28 Nov 1945 by naval gunfire
U-2330	XXIII	7-Sep-44	16 Mar 1945 – 3 May 1945 from 32. Flottille	No patrols	Scuttled 3 May 1945 at Kiel
U-2334	XXIII	21-Sep-44	1 Apr 1945 – 8 May 1945 from 32. Flottille	No patrols	Surrendered at Kristiansand Süd, Norway. Taken to Loch Ryan 29 May 1945 for Operation *Deadlight*. Sunk 28 Nov 1945 by naval gunfire
U-2335	XXIII	27-Sep-44	1 Apr 1945 – 8 May 1945 from 32. Flottille	No patrols	Surrendered at Kristiansand Süd, Norway. Taken to Loch Ryan 29 May 1945 for Operation *Deadlight*. Sunk 28 Nov 1945 by naval gunfire
U-2502	XXI	19-Jul-44	1 Mar 1945 – 8 May 1945 from 31. Flottille	No patrols	Surrendered with 11th Flotilla. Taken from Oslo 3 Jun to N Ireland for Operation *Deadlight*. Sunk 2 Jan 1946
U-2503	XXI	1-Aug-44	1 Apr 1945 – 4 May 1945 from 31. Flottille	No patrols	Damaged en route from Kiel to Norway by rockets from Mosquitoes of Nos. 236 and 254 Sqns RAF. Beached on Danish coast and scuttled 4 May 1945. 13 dead
U-2506	XXI	31-Aug-44	1 Apr 1945 – 8 May 1945 from 31. Flottille	No patrols	Transferred from Bergen to Lisahally, Northern Ireland for Operation *Deadlight*. Sunk 5 Jan 1946
U-2511	XXI	29-Sep-44	15 Mar 1945 – 8 May 1945 from 31. Flottille	1 patrol. First operational mission by a Type XXI boat	Surrendered at Bergen May 1945. Transferred to Northern Ireland 14 Jun 1945 for Operation *Deadlight*. Sunk 7 Jan 1946 by naval gunfire.
U-2513	XXI	12-Oct-44	1 Apr 1945 – 8 May 1945 from 31. Flottille	No patrols	Surrendered at Horten 8 May 1945 and moved to Northern Ireland. Transferred to United States in Aug 1945 and used for trials. Sunk 7 Oct 1951 west of Key West, Florida, in rocket tests
U-3008	XXI	19-Oct-44	1 Apr 1945 – 8 May 1945 from 4. Flottille	Preparing for first patrol in last days of war	Transferred from Wilhelmshaven to Loch Ryan 21 Jun 1945. Transferred to United States for trials Aug 1945. Sunk after demolition tests in May 1954. Broken up at Puerto Rico

12 Unterseebootsflottille

Long-range U-boats had originally been assigned to the 2nd Flotilla, but as that unit became more involved in the main battle in the Atlantic, new Type IXs and supply boats were assigned to the 10th Flotilla before many transferred to the 12th Flotilla.

THE 12TH FLOTILLA WAS FOUNDED on 15 October 1942 under the command of *Korvettenkapitän* Klaus Scholtz. It was assigned to the U-boat base at Bordeaux, originally home to the Italian flotilla that had been participating (not very successfully) in the Battle of the Atlantic.

The first German U-boat to arrive at its new base in Bordeaux was U-178, which made port on 9 January 1943. Most of the long-range boats from the 10th Flotilla, which had been operating in the South Atlantic and the Indian Ocean, were transferred and the 12th Flotilla also took over the remaining large Italian submarines in the base after the Italian armistice in 1943. The base also saw a number of large Japanese boats arrive from the Far East, bringing diplomatic and military personnel.

During August 1944, most of the boats still in European waters left the base for Flensburg. The last two boats to leave Bordeaux were U-534 and U-857, which sailed on 25 August 1944.

The flotilla was disbanded in August 1944. Those members of the unit unable to hitch a ride on the boats attempted to make their way back to Germany overland under Fregkpt. Scholtz but on 11 September 1944 were captured by US troops.

12TH FLOTILLA (1942–44)

Type	Boats assigned
Type VIIF	3
Type IXD	24
Type XB	6
Type XIV	9
Type UIT	5

▲ **'Milk cow' under attack**

A Type XB boat on a resupply operation off the Cape Verde Islands in the summer of 1943 is attacked by Avengers and Wildcats of a US Navy escort carrier.

Commander

Fregkpt. Klaus Scholtz *(Oct 1942 – Aug 1944)*

12TH FLOTILLA INSIGNIA

The insignia of a wolf's head over a U-boat silhouette was mounted over a globe showing Eurasia, all within a black 'U' for U-boat. Few 12th Flotilla boats actually carried the unit insignia.

12TH FLOTILLA BASE LOCATION

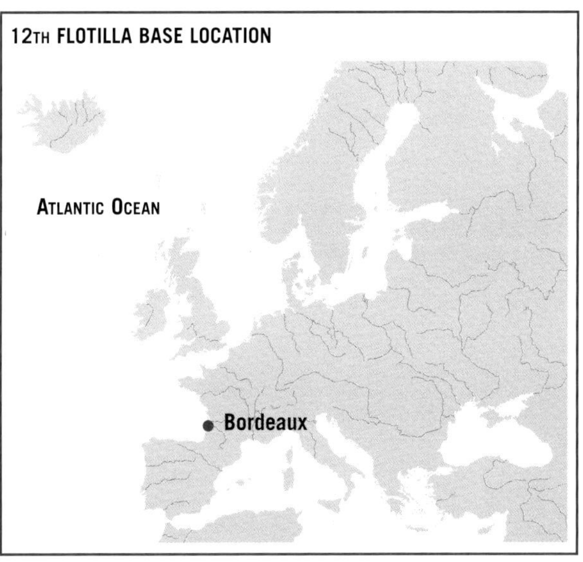

Star commanders
1942–44

By the time the 12th Flotilla was established, the time for running up massive scores in distant waters had gone, as Allied intelligence and countermeasures made the U-boat task harder.

Kapitän zur See Werner Hartmann

Werner Hartmann was born on 11 December 1902 in the Harz Mountains. He joined the *Reichsmarine* not long after World War I with Crew 21. After command experience aboard light destroyers, he transferred to the U-boat arm in 1935. In U-26, he operated in Spanish waters during the Civil War.

On the outbreak of war, Hartmann was commander of U-37 of the 2nd U-boat Flotilla. In October 1939 he led the first attempt to direct a wolfpack from U-37, but Admiral Dönitz found that control from a land base was more effective. Hartmann then served in staff positions and training commands before going back to sea.

In November 1942, he took over U-198, one of the large Type IXD2 boats, and completed the third longest patrol of the war. Leaving Kiel in March 1943, U-198 operated off the eastern coast of South Africa, returning to Bordeaux on 24 September after 201 days at sea. In 1944, he became U-boat commander in the Mediterranean.

In his operational career of four patrols, Hartmann sank 26 ships for a total of 115,338 GRT. He joined the *Bundesmarine* when it was formed in the 1950s. He died on 26 April 1963.

Korvettenkapitän Eitel-Friedrich Kentrat

Born on 11 September 1906 in Stahlheim, Kentrat joined the *Reichsmarine* with Crew 28. Although not one of the highest-scoring commanders – only seven ships sunk for a total of 42,433 GRT in nine patrols – he became famous while commanding U-196 for carrying out the longest submarine combat patrol of the war.

U-196 left Kiel on 13 March 1943 and reached Bordeaux on 23 October 1943, after 225 days at sea, during which Kentrat took the boat into the Indian Ocean. The next patrol was also long, lasting more than five months.

Kentrat left U-196 in Penang in August 1944 to take command of the German naval detachment at Kobe in Japan, and also spent time with the Naval Attache in Tokyo. He returned to Germany, after more than two years in Allied captivity, in October 1947. He died on 9 January 1974, at Bad Schwartau.

STAR COMMANDERS

Commander	Patrols	Ships Sunk
Kapitän zur See Werner Hartmann	4	26
Korvkptn Eitel-Friedrich Kentrat	9	7

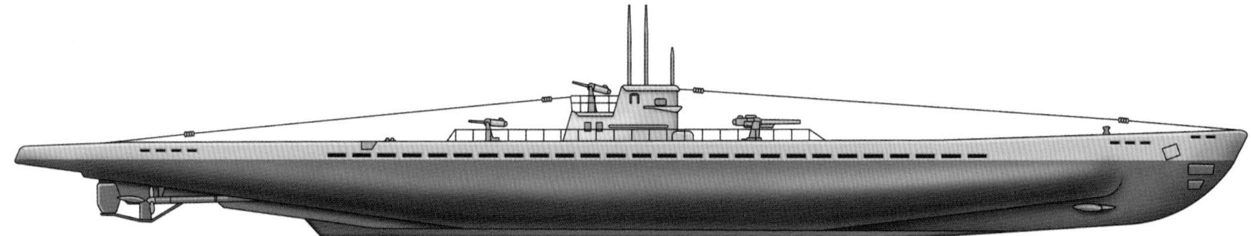

Specifications

Crew: 57
Powerplant: Diesel/electric
Max Speed: 35.6/12.8km/hr (19.2/6.9kt) s/d
Surface Range: 43,900km (23,700nm)
Displacement: 1616/1803t (1590/1775 tons) s/d
Dimensions (length/beam/draught): 87.6 x 7.5 x 5.4m (287.42 x 24.58 x 17.75ft)
Commissioned: 11 Sep 1942
Armament: 22 torpedoes (4 bow/2 stern tubes); 1 x 10.5cm (4.1in), 1 x 3.7cm (1.5in) and 1 x 2cm (0.8in) guns

▲ **U-196**

Type IXD2

The original Type IXD was a very long-range submarine transport, but production quickly changed to the armed Type IXD2. U-196 was one of these boats, and completed the longest submarine patrol of World War II.

U-118

TYPE XB

Laid down in March 1940 at Germania Werft in Kiel, U-118 was commissioned on 6 December 1941. This large Type XB boat was commanded by Werner Czygan for its entire career.

ALTHOUGH BUILT AS A MINELAYER, U-118 made only one patrol in that role. It was used as a supply boat on its other missions. On 12 June 1943, west of the Canary Islands, she was strafed by a Wildcat fighter and then sunk by depth charges from eight Avenger aircraft flying from the escort carrier USS *Bogue*. Forty-three of her crew were killed; 16 survived.

U-118 Commander

Korvkpt. Werner Czygan

(Dec 1941 – Jun 1943)

U-118 TIMETABLE

Patrol Dates	Operational Area	Boats resupplied
19 Sept 1942 – 16 Oct 1942	NW of the Azores	4
12 Nov 1942 – 13 Dec 1942	SE of the Azores	7
25 Jan 1943 – 26 Feb 1943	Minelaying W of Gibraltar (4 ships sunk)	11
25 May 1943 – 12 Jun 1943	WSW of the Canaries (sunk)	3 or 4

Specifications

Crew: 52

Powerplant: Diesel/electric

Max Speed: 30.4/13km/hr (16.4/7kt) s/d

Surface Range: 26,760km (14,450nm)

Displacement: 1763/2143t (1735/2143 tons) s/d

Dimensions (length/beam/draught): 89.8 x 9.2 x 4.7m (294.58 x 30.16 x 15.42ft)

Commissioned: 6 Dec 1941

Armament: 66 mines; 11 torpedoes (2 stern tubes); 1 x 10.5cm (4.1in), 1 x 3.7cm (1.5in) and 1 x 2cm (0.8in) guns

▲ **U-118**

Type XB

The largest submarines in service with the *Kriegsmarine* during World War II, the Type XB boats could carry 66 mines. However, the class handled poorly and its slow diving time meant that it was vulnerable to air attack.

U-461

TYPE XIV

The Third of the Type XIV submarine tankers to be built, U-461 was laid down at Deutsche Werke in Kiel early in December 1940 and was commissioned on 30 January 1942.

ON 9 DECEMBER 1942, on her third patrol, U-461 encountered two lifeboats from the merchant ship *Teesbank*, sunk four days previously by U-128. The U-boat gave the survivors some food and water, but took the captain aboard as a prisoner. On 30 July 1943, while in transit to her operational area in the Azores, U-462 was spotted in the Bay of Biscay northwest of Cape Ortegal by an RAF Liberator,

U-461 Commander

Korvkpt. Wolf-Harro Stiebler *(Apr 1942 – Jul 1943)*

which vectored an RAF Sunderland, a Catalina, an American Liberator and a Halifax on to the target. U-461 was in company with U-462 and U-504, and the three boats fought off their attackers, causing considerable damage but being damaged themselves in the process. U-461 was sunk by a newly arrived Australian Sunderland of No. 461 Sqn. Fifty-three of the boat's crew died and 15 survived. The other two boats were hunted down and destroyed soon afterwards by surface ships and aircraft.

U-461 TIMETABLE

Patrol Dates	Operational Area	Boats resupplied
21 Jun 1942 – 16 Aug 1942	W of the Azores	11
7 Sep 1942 – 17 Oct 1942	NW of the Azores	15
19 Nov 1942 – 3 Jan 1943	N of St Paul Rocks/S of the Azores	12
13 Feb 1943 – 22 Mar 1943	S/SW of Azores	10
20 Apr 1943 – 30 May 1943	Central N Atlantic	13
22 Jul 1943 – 23 Jul 1943	Patrol aborted due to leaking tank	0
27 Jul 1943 – 30 Jul 1943	En route to Cape Verde Islands	0

Specifications

Crew: 53

Powerplant: Diesel/electric

Max Speed: 26.7/11.7km/hr (14.4/6.3kt) s/d

Surface Range: 17,220km (9300nm)

Displacement: 1688/1932t (1661/1901 tons) s/d

Dimensions (length/beam/draught): 67.1 x 9.4 x 6.5m (220.16 x 30.83 x 21.33ft)

Commissioned: 30 Jan 1942

Armament: 2 x 3.7cm (1.5in) and 1 x 2cm (0.8in) guns

Fuel load: 439t (432 tons)

▲ **U-461**

Type XIV

In its tanker role the Type XIV could carry 439 tonnes (432 tons) of fuel oil for supply to operational boats. This was enough to provide 12 Type VIIs with an extra four weeks of endurance, or five Type IXs with an extra eight weeks.

U-852

Type IXD2

A very long-range Type IXD2 boat, U-852 was to become notorious as the command of the only U-boat commander to be guilty of a major war crime.

U-852 WAS HEADING FOR the Indian Ocean to join the *Monsun* (*Monsoon*) wolfpack operating there. On its way south, the boat torpedoed and sank the Greek steamer *Peleus* off West Africa on the night of 13/14 March 1944. Since several *Monsoon* boats had been detected and sunk on their way to the Indian Ocean, Eck decided to erase all evidence of his actions so as not to alert Allied search forces. After leaving the scene briefly, the boat returned after midnight and called on the survivors in boats, on rafts and in the water to approach the U-boat. As they did so, the German crew opened fire with machine guns, and threw hand grenades to destroy the rafts. The boat cruised around the wreckage,

U-852 Commander

Kptlt. Heinz-Wilhelm Eck

(Jun 1943 – May 1944)

U-852 TIMETABLE		
Patrol Dates	**Operational Area**	**Ships Sunk**
18 Jan 1944 – 3 May 1944	Indian Ocean	2

firing occasional bursts before leaving the scene before dawn. However, three men survived and after a month adrift were rescued by a Portuguese steamer.

After penetrating the Arabian Sea, U-852 was located by Wellingtons of Nos. 8 and 621 Sqns RAF flying out of Aden, which damaged the boat so badly it was forced to run aground. The submarine was scuttled on 3 May 1944 in the Arabian Sea off the Somali coast. Seven crew were killed and 59 survived, who were captured ashore by the Somaliland Camel Corps and a naval landing party.

Initially, Allied investigators were most excited by the Fa330 'Bachstelze' aircraft carried by the U-boat, a rotary-winged kite that could be quickly folded and unfolded. However, the crew of U-852 had neglected to destroy the submarine's log, which proved that the U-boat had sunk a ship off Freetown on 13 March.

War crimes

Eventually it was established that the boat had been responsible for the massacre of the crew of the *Peleus* – which, contrary to the impression established by Hollywood, was the only such incident during the war. Eck, his 2nd Watch Officer, the Medical Officer, the Chief Engineer and one of the boat's petty officers were tried for war crimes in October 1945. The first three were found guilty, and were executed by firing squad on the Lüneberger Heide at the end of November 1945.

Milchkühe ('milk cows')

1942–44

The Type XIV U-boat was a modification of the Type IXD, designed to resupply other U-boats. Because of their ability to provide sustenance, the Type XIVs became known as *Milchkühe*.

The Type XIV had no offensive weaponry but had a relatively heavy anti-aircraft gun fit. During the Battle of the Atlantic, the 'milk cows' and the large Type XB minelayers pressed into service in the resupply role successfully allowed medium-range Type VIIC boats to operate along the American coast during the second 'Happy time' in the first half of 1942. They were also essential to the successful patrols of long-range Type IX boats operating in the South Atlantic, off the Cape of Good Hope and in the Indian Ocean.

The 'milk cows' acted as force multipliers, allowing operational U-boats much greater time on station. As such, they were priority targets for Allied anti-submarine forces, and the early German successes did not last long. Ultra intelligence from Allied codebreakers, High Frequency Direction Finding (HF/DF) systems that zeroed in and triangulated on U-boat radio communications, improved radar, expanded air coverage and increasingly aggressive

▸ Resupplying

Here, a 'milk cow' submarine replenishes two combat U-boats in the South Atlantic. The 'milk cow' supply boats proved vital in attacking distant sea lanes, where Allied escort levels were lighter and there was less air cover.

ASW tactics meant that the big boats were eventually hunted down and all but eliminated during the course of 1943. Many were surprised on the surface as they were refuelling combat boats, neither submarine being able to submerge quickly. 'Milk cow' duty was especially hazardous – 289 sailors were killed out of an estimated total 'milk cow' complement of around 550 men.

New types cancelled

Ten boats of this type were commissioned, but their increasing vulnerability meant that 14 planned Type XIVs were cancelled in May 1944. Also cancelled was further work on the Type XX design. This would have been an even larger transport boat, but the first would not have been ready until the summer of 1945 at the earliest.

Monsoon boats

1943–44

The idea of stationing U-boats in Malaya for operations in the Indian Ocean was first proposed by the Japanese in December 1942. However, as supplies and basing support were not available the idea was initially turned down. By 1943, however, German attitudes had changed.

Admiral Dönitz was not in favour of diverting strength from the main operational areas in the Atlantic. However, on 5 April 1943 it was decided to send U-178 to Penang to establish a naval base there. U-511 would eventually be given to the Japanese in return for rubber.

When the war in the Atlantic turned decisively in favour of the Allies in May 1943, it was decided to carry the underwater battle farther afield into less heavily protected sea lanes. The Indian Ocean was still almost on a peacetime footing, with few escorted convoys and many ships sailing individually.

Long-range boats already operating around South Africa were ordered to be replenished and sent into the Arabian Sea. More boats were also to be deployed, and were expected to arrive at the end of the monsoon season in September 1943. As a result, the group was given the name *Monsun* – German for monsoon.

Disappointing results

The *Monsun* group was expected to wreak the same kind of havoc in the Indian Ocean as the U-boats had done off the American coast in the early months of 1942. However, the boats had great difficulty in simply reaching their distant operational area – losses were incurred along the way, and the deployment was further complicated by the fact that many of the 'milk cow' resupply boats had been sunk. Of the initial 11 *Monsun* U-boats, four were destroyed in transit and two – one of which sank – were diverted on emergency refuelling duties, so effectively only five boats managed to break through.

Once in the Indian Ocean, results were less than satisfactory, due in large part to the fact that Allied signals intelligence was able to locate the German operational areas, which enabled the authorities to route shipping away from the prowling U-boats.

Most of the boats were from the 12th Flotilla, but from September 1944, with the loss of the French U-boat bases, control was passed to the 33rd Flotilla, which was set up at Penang.

12TH/33RD FLOTILLAS BASE LOCATION – FAR EAST

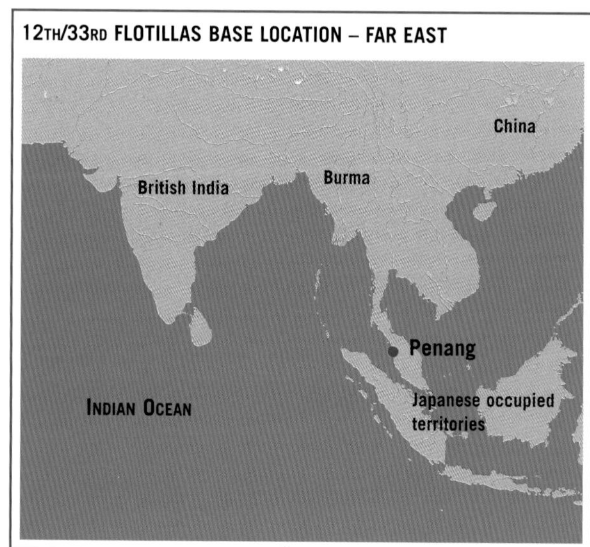

BOATS THAT SERVED WITH 12TH FLOTILLA (47 BOATS)

U-Boat	Type	Commissioned	Flotilla(s)	Patrols	Fate
U-117	XB	25-Oct-41	1 Dec 1942 – 7 Aug 1943 from 11 Flotille	5 patrols. 2 ships damaged by mines: total 14,269 GRT	Sunk with all hands in the North Atlantic while supplying U-66 on 7 Aug 1943 by depth charges and a Fido homing torpedo from five Avenger aircraft of the escort carrier USS *Card*. 62 dead
U-118	XB	6-Dec-41	1 Nov 1942 – 12 June 1943 from 10 Flotille	4 patrols. 3 ships sunk by mines: total 14,064 GRT; 1 warship sunk by mine: total 940t/925 tons; 2 ships damaged by mines: total 11,945 GRT	Sunk 12 Jun 1943 west of the Canary Islands by depth charges from eight Avenger aircraft from the escort carrier USS *Bogue*. 43 dead and 16 survivors
U-119	XB	2-Apr-42	1 Feb 1943 – 24 June 1943 from 4 Flotille	2 patrols. 1 ship sunk by mine: total 2937 GRT; 1 ship damaged by mine: total 7176 GRT	Sunk with all hands 24 Jun 1943 in the Bay of Biscay northwest of Cape Ortegal by ramming and depth charges from the sloop HMS *Starling*. 57 dead
U-177	IXD2	14-Mar-42	1 Dec 1942 – 6 Feb 1944 from 10. Flottille	3 patrols. 14 ships sunk: total 87,388 GRT; 1 ship damaged: total 2588 GRT	Sunk 6 Feb 1944 in the South Atlantic west of Ascension Island by depth charges from a US Navy Liberator of VB-107. 50 dead and 15 survivors
U-178	IXD2	14-Feb-42	1 Nov 1942 – 1 Aug 1944 from 10. Flottille	3 patrols. 13 ships sunk: total 87,030 GRT; 1 ship damaged: total 6348 GRT	Scuttled 25 Aug 1944 at Bordeaux, France, as she was not seaworthy in time to escape the advancing US Army
U-179	IXD2	7-Mar-42	1 Oct 1942 – 8 Oct 1942 from 10. Flottille	1 patrol. 1 ship sunk: total 6558 GRT	Sunk with all hands 8 Oct 1942 in the South Atlantic near Cape Town by depth charges from the destroyer HMS *Active*. 61 dead
U-180	IXD1	16-May-42	1 Apr 1944 – 23 Aug 1944 from 10. Flottille	2 patrols. 2 ships sunk: total 13,298 GRT	Missing with all hands on or after 23 Aug 1944 in the Bay of Biscay west of Bordeaux. Some sources ascribe the loss to mines. 56 dead
U-181	IXD2	9-May-42	1 Nov 1942 – 30 Sep 1944	4 patrols. 27 ships sunk: total 138,779 GRT	to 33. Flottille
U-182	IXD2	30-Jun-42	1 Dec 1942 – 16 May 1943	1 patrol. 5 ships sunk: total 30,071 GRT	Sunk with all hands 16 May 1943 northwest of Madeira, by depth charges from the destroyer USS *MacKenzie*. 61 dead
U-195	IXD1	5-Sep-42	1 May 1944 – 30 Sept 1944 from 10. Flottille	3 patrols. 2 ships sunk: total 14,391 GRT; 1 ship damaged: total 6797 GRT	to 33. Flottille
U-196	IXD2	11-Sep-42	1 Apr 1943 – 30 Sept 1944	3 patrols. 3 ships sunk: total 17,739 GRT. U-196 completed a 225-day patrol from 13 Mar to 23 Oct 1943, the longest submarine patrol of WWII	to 33. Flottille
U-197	IXD2	10-Oct-42	1 Apr 1943 – 20 Aug 1943 from 4. Flottille	1 patrol. 3 ships sunk: total 21,267 GRT; 1 ship damaged: total 7181 GRT	Sunk with all hands 20 Aug 1943 south of Madagascar by depth charges from Catalinas of Nos. 259 Sqn and 265 Sqn RAF. 67 dead
U-198	IXD2	3-Nov-42	1 Apr 1943 – 12 Aug 1944 from 4. Flottille	2 patrols. 11 ships sunk: total 59,690 GRT	Sunk with all hands 12 Aug 1944 near the Seychelles by depth charges from the frigate HMS *Findhorn* and the Indian sloop HMIS *Godavari*. 66 dead
U-199	IXD2	28-Nov-42	1 May 1943 – 31 July 1943 from 4. Flottille	1 patrol. 2 ships sunk: total 4181 GRT	Sunk 31 Jul 1943 in the South Atlantic east of Rio de Janeiro by depth charges from a US Navy Mariner and a Brazilian Catalina and Hudson. 49 dead and 12 survivors
U-200	IXD2	22-Dec-42	1 Jun 1943 – 24 Jun 1943 from 4. Flottille	1 patrol	Sunk with all hands 24 Jun 1943 southwest of Iceland by 2 depth charges from a Liberator of No. 120 Sqn RAF. 68 dead (including 7 Brandenburg commandos aboard for a special mission)
U-219	XB	12-Dec-42	1 Jul 1943 – 30 Sep 1944	2 patrols	to 33. Flottille
U-220	XB	27-Mar-43	1 Sep 1943 – 28 Oct 1943	1 patrol. 2 ships sunk: total 7199 GRT (in a field of 66 magnetic SMA mines laid off of St Johns,Canada	Sunk with all hands after supplying U-603 on 28 Oct 1943 in the North Atlantic by depth charges from Avenger and Wildcat aircraft of the escort carrier USS *Block Island*. 56 dead
U-233	XB	22-Sep-43	1 Jun 1944 – 5 Jul 1944 from 4. Flottille (training)	1 patrol	Sunk 5 Jul 1944 while on a minelaying patrol southeast of Halifax by ramming, depth charges and gunfire from the destroyer escorts USS *Baker* and USS *Thomas*. 32 dead and 29 survivors
U-459	XIV	15-Nov-41	1 Nov 1942 – 24 Jul 1943 from 10. Flottille	6 resupply patrols	Scuttled 24 Jul 1943 near Cape Ortegal, Spain, after being badly damaged by two Wellingtons from Nos. 172 and 547 Sqns. 19 dead and 41 survivors
U-460	XIV	24-Dec-41	1 Nov 1942 – 4 Oct 1943 from 10. Flottille	6 resupply patrols	Sunk 4 Oct 1943 north of the Azores by Avengers and Wildcats of the escort carrier USS *Card*. 62 dead and 2 survivors. Fate often confused with U-422, which was sunk nearby on the same day by USS *Card* aircraft.
U-461	XIV	30-Jan-42	1 Nov 1942 – 30 Jul 1943 from 10. Flottille	6 resupply patrols	Sunk 30 Jul 1943 in the Bay of Biscay northwest of Cape Ortegal by an Australian Sunderland of No. 461 Sqn. 53 dead and 15 survivors
U-462	XIV	5-Mar-42	1 Nov 1942 – 30 Jul 1943 from 10. Flottille	8 resupply patrols	Sunk 30 Jul 1943 in the Bay of Biscay by gunfire from the sloops HMS *Wren*, HMS *Kite*, HMS *Woodpecker*, HMS *Wild Goose* and HMS *Woodcock* after being forced to the surface by a Handley Page Halifax of No. 502 Sqn. 1 dead and 64 survivors
U-463	XIV	2-Apr-42	1 Nov 1942 – 16 May 1943 from 10. Flottille	5 resupply patrols	Sunk with all hands 16 May 1943 in the Bay of Biscay by depth charges from a Halifax of No. 58 Sqn RAF. 57 dead. Originally credited to another 58 Sqn Halifax the previous day, but that attack actually destroyed U-266
U-487	XIV	21-Dec-42	1 Apr 1943 – 13 Jul 1943 from 4. Flottille	2 resupply patrols	Sunk 13 Jul 1943 in the central Atlantic by Grumman Avenger and Wildcat aircraft from the escort carrier USS *Core*. 31 dead and 33 survivors
U-488	XIV	1-Feb-43	1 May 1943 – 26 Apr 1944 from 4. Flottille	3 resupply patrols	Sunk with all hands 26 Apr 1944 west of Cape Verde by depth charges from the destroyer escorts USS *Frost*, USS *Huse*, USS *Barber* and USS *Snowden*. 64 dead

BOATS THAT SERVED WITH 12TH FLOTILLA (47 BOATS)

U-Boat	Type	Commissioned	Flotilla(s)	Patrols	Fate
U-489	XIV	8-Mar-43	1 Aug 1943 – 4 Aug 1943 from 4. Flottille	1 resupply patrol	Sunk 4 Aug 1943 southeast of Iceland by a Sunderland of No. 423 Sqn RCAF. 1 dead and 53 survivors
U-490	XIV	27-Mar-43	1 Apr 1944 – 12 Jun 1944 from 4. Flottille	1 resupply patrol	Sunk 12 Jun 1944 northwest of the Azores by depth charges from aircraft of the escort carrier USS *Croatan*, and from the destroyer escorts USS *Frost*, USS *Huse* and USS *Inch*. No casualties – 60 survivors.
U-847	IXD2	23-Jan-43	1 Jul 1943 – 27 Aug 1943 from 4. Flottille	1 patrol	Sunk with all hands 27 Aug 1943 in the Sargasso Sea by Fido homing torpedoes from Avenger and Wildcat aircraft flying from the escort carrier USS *Card*. 62 dead
U-848	IXD2	20-Feb-43	1 Aug 1943 – 5 Nov 1943 from 4. Flottille	1 patrol. 1 ship sunk: total 4573 GRT	Sunk with all hands 5 Nov 1943 in the South Atlantic southwest of Ascension Island by depth charges from 3 US Navy PB4Y Liberators of VB-107 and 2 B-25 Mitchells of the USAAF 1st Composite Sqn. 63 dead
U-849	IXD2	11-Mar-43	1 Oct 1943 – 25 Nov 1943 from 4. Flottille	1 patrol	Sunk with all hands 25 Nov 1943 in the South Atlantic west of the mouth of the Congo by depth charges from a US Navy Liberator of VP-107. 63 dead
U-850	IXD2	17-Apr-43	1 Nov 1943 – 20 Dec 1943 from 4. Flottille	1 patrol	Sunk with all hands 20 Dec 1943 west of Madeira by depth charges and Fido homing torpedoes from 5 Avengers and Wildcats of the escort carrier USS *Bogue*. 66 dead
U-851	IXD2	21-May-43	1 Feb 1944 – 27 Mar 1944 from 4. Flottille	1 patrol	Missing, presumed sunk with all hands, in the North Atlantic on or after 27 Mar 1944. 70 dead
U-852	IXD2	15-Jun-43	1 Feb 1944 – 3 May 1944 from 4. Flottille	1 patrol. 2 ships sunk: total 9972 GRT	Scuttled 3 May 1944 in the Arabian Sea off the Somali coast after running aground during an attack by 6 Wellingtons of Nos. 8 and 621 Sqns RAF. 7 dead and 59 survivors
U-859	IXD2	8-Jul-43	1 Apr 1944 – 23 Sep 1944 from 4. Flottille	1 patrol. 3 ships sunk: total 20,853 GRT	Sunk 23 Sep 1944 near Penang in the Strait of Malacca, torpedoed by HM Submarine *Trenchant*. 47 dead and 20 survivors
U-860	IXD2	12-Aug-43	1 Apr 1944 – 15 Jun 1944	1 patrol	Sunk 15 Jun 1944 south of St Helena by depth charges and rockets from Avenger and Wildcat aircraft of the escort carrier USS *Solomons*. 42 dead and 20 survivors
U-861	IXD2	2-Sep-43	1 Apr 1944 – 30 Sep 1944 from 4. Flottille	2 patrols. 4 ships sunk: total 22,048 GRT; 1 ship damaged: total 8139 GRT	to 33. Flottille
U-862	IXD2	7-Oct-43	1 May 1944 – 30 Sep 1944 from 4. Flottille	2 patrols. 7 ships sunk: total 42,374 GRT	to 33. Flottille
U-863	IXD2	3-Nov-43	1 Jul 1944 – 29 Sep 1944 from 4. Flottille	1 patrol	Sunk with all hands 29 Sep 1944 in the South Atlantic southeast of Recife, Brazil, by depth charges from 2 US Navy PB4Y Liberators of VB-107. 69 dead
U-871	IXD2	15-Jan-44	1 Aug 1944 – 26 Sep 1944 from 4. Flottille	1 patrol	Sunk with all hands 26 Sep 1944 northwest of the Azores by depth charges from a B-17 Flying Fortress of No. 22 Sqn RAF. 69 dead
U-1059	VIIF	1-May-43	1 Jan 1944 – 19 Mar 1944 from 5. Flottille	1 torpedo transport patrol	Left Bordeaux with replacement torpedoes for the Monsoon boats operating in the Far East. Sunk 19 Mar 1944 southwest of the Cape Verde Islands by Avengers and Wildcats from the escort carrier USS *Block Island*. 47 dead and 8 survivors
U-1061	VIIF	25-Aug-43	1 Jan 1944 – 1 Mar 1944	5 torpedo transport patrols	Surrendered in Bergen, Norway, May 1945. Transferred to Scotland for Operation *Deadlight*. Sunk by naval gunfire 1 Dec 1945
U-1062	VIIF	19-Jun-43	1 Jan 1944 – 30 Sep 1944	3 torpedo transport patrols	Sunk with all hands 30 Sep 1944 in central Atlantic by depth charges from the destroyer escort USS *Fessenden*. 55 dead. Boat was returning from Asia: it had left Norway 3 Jan 1944 with 39 torpedoes for Monsoon boats, reaching Penang 19 Apr 1944
UIT-21	Italian Calvi class	10-Sep-43	Oct 1943 – 15 Apr 1944	No patrols	Commissioned as the *Giuseppe Finzi* in 1936. Taken over as a long-range transport boat at Bordeaux following the Italian capitulation on 9 Sep 1943. In too poor repair for operations, and decommissioned 15 Apr 1944. Scuttled 25 Aug 1944
UIT-22	Italian Liuzzi class	10-Sep-43	Oct 1943 – Mar 1944	1 patrol	Launched as the *Alpino Bagnolini* 28 Oct 1939. Taken over as a long-range transport boat at Bordeaux following the Italian capitulation on 9 Sep 1943. Sunk with all hands 11 Mar 1944 south of the Cape of Good Hope by South African Catalinas of No. 262 Sqn. 43 dead
UIT-23	Italian Liuzzi class	10-Sep-43	Dec 1943 – Feb 1944	1 patrol	Commissioned as the Italian submarine *Reginaldo Giuliani* in March 1940. Seized by Japan at Penang following the Italian capitulation. Handed over to the Germans at Singapore Sep 1943. Torpedoed 14 Feb 1944 in the Strait of Malacca by British submarine HMS *Tallyho*. 26 dead and 14 survivors
UIT-24	Italian Marcello class	10-Sep-43	Dec 1943 – Sep 1944	6 patrols	Commissioned 23 Sep 1939 as the *Comandante Capellini*. Already in use as a transport boat when taken over by the Germans, following the Italian capitulation, at Sabang in the Far East on 10 Sep 1943. Transferred to 33. Flottille in 1944
UIT-25	Italian Marconi class	12-Dec-43	Dec 1943 – Sep 1944	3 patrols	Originally commissioned as the Italian submarine *Luigi Torelli* May 1940. Seized by Japan at Singapore following the Italian Armistice in 1943. Handed over to Germany and commissioned as a long-range transport in Dec 1943. Transferred to 33. Flottille

13 Unterseebootsflottille

The first U-boats to operate in Norwegian waters were supporting the German invasion of the country in 1940. By 1942, it became clear that boats operating from Norway would be able to strike both into the Atlantic and against the increasing numbers of Arctic convoys.

Commander
Korvkpt. Rolf Rüggeberg
(Jun 1943 – May 1945)

THE 13TH FLOTILLA was established at the port of Trondheim, well to the north of the main U-boat base at Bergen, from which the boats of the 11th Flotilla sailed. The new flotilla was set up in June 1943 under the command of *Korvettenkapitän* Rolf Rüggeberg. Boats were often forward deployed even farther north at Narvik or Hammerfest. This had the advantage of taking them out of the range of easy air attack from Britain, while at the same time bringing the boats closer to the main convoy route from Iceland or the UK, around the North Cape and into the USSR.

Arctic missions

Although the primary task of the U-boats was to find and attack the convoys bringing much-needed supplies from the Western Allies to the Soviets, who were bearing the brunt of the ground war, they were also used for a variety of other missions. Boats regularly mounted weather patrols, gathering information on ice and weather conditions, and monitoring the extent of the summer and winter pack ice, which determined how far north the convoys could go. U-boats also supported *Luftwaffe* reconnaissance flights, providing fuel for Blohm und Voss Bv 138 flying boats.

13TH FLOTILLA BASE LOCATION

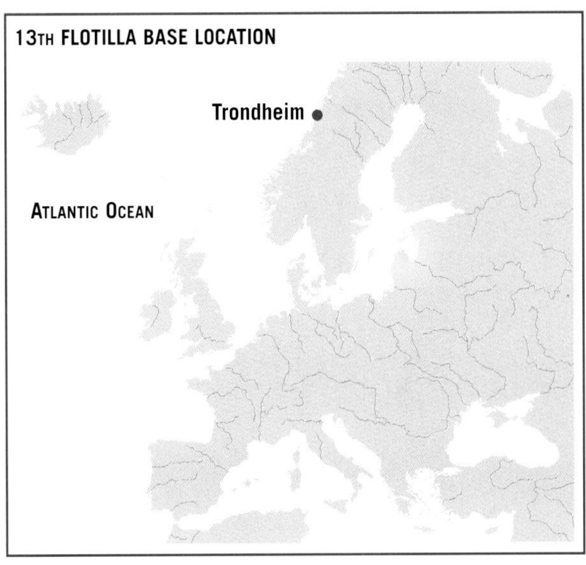

Possibly the most important mission was the setting-up and retrieval of temporary weather stations. Meteorological conditions in the polar regions have a great effect on the weather in continental Europe, and data from the region allowed for more accurate forecasting.

In September 1944, the flotilla was reorganized thanks to the influx of surviving boats forced to flee the French bases. It was finally disbanded in May 1945, when Germany surrendered.

13TH FLOTILLA INSIGNIA

The Viking ship on a white cross was an appropriate symbol for a unit based in Norway. About 10 of the flotilla's boats have been recorded as carrying the flotilla insignia.

13TH FLOTILLA (1943–45)

Type	Boats assigned
Type VIIC	47
Type VIIC/41	8

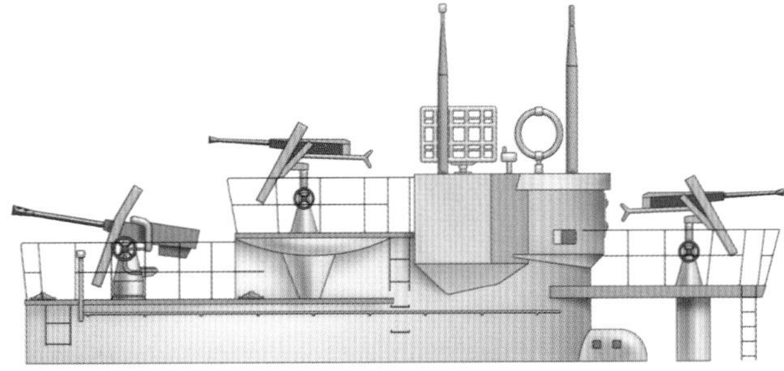

▲ **Type VIIC conversion VI with twin 2cm (0.8in) guns**

The conversion VI tower was developed to give Arctic-service boats increased forward-facing firepower in the shape of an extra twin 2cm (0.8in) mount.

U-255

TYPE VIIC

Laid down at Bremer Vulkan in Vegesack, U-255 was launched in October 1941, and went on its first operational patrol in June 1942. It was one of the most successful of all Arctic boats.

U-255 WAS ONE OF THE first German units to locate the ill-fated Convoy PQ 17, which it did on 1 July 1942, halfway through the boat's first operational patrol. U-255 sank four ships in the attack on PQ 17, and accounted for one damaged derelict a few days later. On its second patrol U-255 shelled two Soviet wireless stations, and on its third, the U-boat was damaged by an RAF Catalina south of Jan Meyen Island.

Specifications

Crew: 44
Powerplant: Diesel/electric
Max Speed: 31.4/14.1km/hr (17/7.6kt) s/d
Surface Range: 12,040km (6500nm)
Displacement: 773/879t (761/865 tons) s/d
Dimensions (length/beam/draught): 67.1 x 6.2 x 4.8m (220.1 x 20.34 x 15.75ft)
Commissioned: 29 Nov 1941
Armament: 14 torpedoes (4 bow/1 stern tubes); 1 x 8.8cm (3.5in) and 1 x 2cm (0.8in) guns

U-255 Commanders

Kptlt. Reinhart Reche *(Nov 1941 – Jun 1943)*
Oblt. Erich Harms *(Jun 1943 – Aug 1944)*
Oblt. Helmuth Heinrich *(Mar 1945 – May 1945)*

Between July and September 1943, U-255 was deployed on its first patrol with the 13th Flotilla. Moving eastwards along the northern coast of the USSR, the boat established a secret seaplane base on Novaya Zemlya and searched for convoys on the summer route to Siberia, without success.

In February 1944, U-255 began operating in the Atlantic, and was transferred to the 7th Flotilla at St Nazaire. The boat was damaged by air attack and in August 1944, it was decommissioned. Although cut

▲ **U-255**
Type VIIC
U-255's combat debut came in the Allied disaster of Convoy PQ 17. The boat was one of the first to locate the convoy, and it benefited when the Admiralty in London ordered the convoy to scatter, picking off four out of the eight vessels sunk by the U-boats in the massacre that followed.

U-255 TIMETABLE

Patrol Dates	Operational Area	Ships Sunk
15 Jun 1942 – 15 Jul 1942	Northern waters	4
4 Aug 1942 – 9 Sep 1942	Spitzbergen/Soviet Arctic	0
13 Sep 1942 – 25 Sep 1942	Greenland Sea	1
29 Sep 1942 – 3 Oct 1942	Transit to Kiel for refit	0
7 Jan 1943 – 18 Jan 1943	Transit from Kiel to Hammerfest	0
23 Jan 1943 – 9 Feb 1943	Barents Sea	3
22 Feb 1943 – 15 Mar 1943	Norwegian Sea	2
29 Mar 1943 – 29 Apr 1943	Northern waters	0
19 Jul 1943 – 19 Sep 1943	Soviet waters/Novaya Zemlya	1
26 Feb 1944 – 11 Apr 1944	North Atlantic	1
6 Jun 1944 – 15 Jun 1944	Bay of Biscay	0
17 Apr 1945 – 21 Apr 1945	Minelaying off the French Coast	0
22 Apr 1945 – 8 May 1945	Moved between La Pallice and St Nazaire several times	0
8 May 1945 – 15 May 1945	Transit to Loch Alsh and surrender	0

off, St Nazaire remained in German hands to the end of the war. U-255 was repaired and manned by personnel at the base at the end of 1944, and carried out minelaying in April 1945.

U-255 sank 10 vessels in northern waters, totalling 53,873 GRT. It also accounted for an American destroyer escort on one of its two Atlantic patrols.

Fate

The boat left St Nazaire on 8 May 1945, and was surrendered to the Royal Navy at Loch Alsh, Scotland, on the 19th. It was then moved to Loch Ryan, where it became one of 116 boats disposed of in Operation *Deadlight*. It was sunk as a target by aircraft on 13 December 1945.

U-354

TYPE VIIC

Launched at Flensburger Schiffsbau in January 1942, U-354 was commissioned in April 1942. Although initially on the strength of the 1st Flotilla, the boat spent its entire career in Norway.

U-354 REACHED BERGEN in October 1942, and over the next 18 months mounted at least 11 patrols in northern waters. However, like most boats in the region, she contributed little to the tonnage of Allied merchant shipping sunk by the U-boat arm, accounting for only two vessels sunk – although the crew claimed several Soviet vessels damaged, none of which were ever confirmed.

The boat was more successful in her final hours. On 22 August 1944, on her last patrol, U-354 unexpectedly came across a Royal Navy carrier task force off Vannoy Island. The British had just attacked the battleship *Tirpitz* at Kaafiord. The U-boat attacked the British ships, torpedoing the escort carrier HMS *Nabob* and the frigate HMS *Bickerton*. U-354 was then driven off by Fleet Air Arm aircraft. *Bickerton* was so badly damaged she had to be scuttled by a torpedo from a destroyer. The *Nabob* was towed to Scapa Flow, and saw no more wartime service.

Fate

U-354 was sunk with all hands on 24 August 1944 northeast of North Cape by depth charges from the sloops HMS *Mermaid* and HMS *Peacock*, the frigate HMS *Loch Dunvegan* and the destroyer HMS *Keppel*. Fifty-one crewmembers were killed.

U-354 Commanders

Kptlt. Karl-Heinz Herbschleb (Apr 1942 – Feb 1944)	Oblt. Hans-Jürgen Sthamer (Feb 1944 – Aug 1944)

U-354 TIMETABLE

Patrol Dates	Operational Area	Ships Sunk
10 Oct 1942 – 17 Oct 1942	Transit from Kiel to Skjomenfiord	0
29 Oct 1942 – 30 Nov 1942	Arctic Ocean	1
19 Dec 1942 – 15 Jan 1943	Arctic Ocean	1
18 Jan 1943 – 20 Jan 1943	Transit from Narvik to Trondheim	0
11 Mar 1943 – 4 Apr 1943	Northern waters	0
28 Apr 1943 – 30 Apr 1943	Transit to Hammerfest	0
9 May 1943 – 15 Jun 1943	Northern waters	0
25 Jul 1943 – 27 Jul 1943	Transit to Skjomenfiord	0
4 Aug 1943 – 22 Sep 1943	Soviet waters	0
22 Oct 1943 – 23 Oct 1943	Transit to Tromso	0
25 Oct 1943 – 6 Dec 1943	Spitzbergen/Bear Island	0
7 Dec 1943 – 5 Jan 1944	Bear Island	0
3 Jan 1944 – 4 Jan 1944	Transit to Trondheim	0
2 Mar 1944 – 5 Mar 1944	Transit to Narvik	0
8 Mar 1944 – 12 Apr 1944	Northern waters	0
18 Apr 1944 – 4 May 1944	S of Bear Island	0
6 May 1944 – 10 May 1944	Transit to Bergen	0
24 Jun 1944 – 28 Jun 1944	Transit to Bogenbucht	0
30 Jun 1944 – 28 Jul 1944	Northern waters	0
21 Aug 1944 – 24 Aug 1944	Northern waters	1

U-636

Type VIIC

Launched in June 1942 at the Blohm und Voss yard in Hamburg, U-636 spent most of its career on patrol in the Arctic, operating successively with 11th Flotilla and 13th Flotilla.

In spite of the fact that she was a very busy combat boat, carrying out no less than 15 patrols in the last two years of the war, U-636 achieved little success.

First patrol

By the time she went on her first patrol in May 1943, Allied escort techniques had been honed to an extremely fine level, and Ultra intelligence enabled the convoy planners to route ships away from known U-boat concentrations. As a result, although U-636 was assigned to at least eight wolfpacks, the boat rarely sighted Allied merchant ships or was driven off by alert escorts when she did.

U-636 TIMETABLE

Patrol Dates	Operational Area	Ships Sunk
17 Apr 1943 – 28 Apr 1943	Transit from Kiel to Trondheim	0
2 May 1943 – 8 Jun 1943	SW of Iceland/SE of Greenland	0
24 Jul 1943 – 7 Aug 1943	Minelaying in Pechora Sea	0
14 Aug 1943 – 30 Aug 1943	Minelaying in Kara Sea	1 (2?)
5 Sep 1943 – 9 Sep 1943	Transit from Narvik to Bergen	0
24 Oct 1943 – 26 Oct 1943	Transit from Bergen to Trondheim	0
27 Oct 1943 – 17 Nov 1943	Minelaying in Soviet waters	0
18 Nov 1943 – 27 Dec 1943	S of Spitzbergen	0
30 Dec 1943 – 8 Jan 1944	Northern waters	0
26 Jan 1944 – 2 Feb 1944	Northern waters	0
8 Apr 1944 – 3 May 1944	Northern waters	0
27 Jun 1944 – 24 Jul 1944	Norwegian Sea	0
25 Aug 1944 – 12 Sep 1944	Minelaying in Pechora Sea	0
25 Sep 1944 – 3 Oct 1944	SW of Bear Island	0
6 Oct 1944 – 12 Nov 1944	E of Bear Island	0
4 Dec 1944 – 30 Jan 1945	N of Kola Inlet	0
1 Apr 1945 – 21 Apr 1945	Northwest of Ireland	0

U-636 Commanders

Kptlt. Hans Hildebrandt *(Aug 1942 – Feb 1944)*

Oblt. Eberhard Schendel *(Feb 1944 – Apr 1945)*

Specifications

Crew: 44

Powerplant: Diesel/electric

Max Speed: 31.5/14.1km/hr (17/7.6kt) s/d

Surface Range: 12,040km (6500nm)

Displacement: 773/879t (761/865 tons) s/d

Dimensions (length/beam/draught): 67.1 x 6.2 x 4.8m (220.1 x 20.34 x 15.75ft)

Commissioned: 20 Aug 1942

Armament: 14 torpedoes (4 bow/1 stern tubes); 1 x 3.7cm (1.5in) and 2 x twin 2cm (0.8in) guns (1944)

▲ **U-636**

Type VIIC

U-636 was one of a number of U-boats that penetrated deep into Soviet waters, carrying out minelaying patrols as far as the Kara Sea and into the estuary of the Yenisey River.

The boat's only success came from a minelaying operation in the Kara Sea which probably sank a Soviet freighter and may have destroyed a minesweeper. In June 1944, U-636 was attacked by an RAF Liberator, but severely damaged the aircraft before it could complete its attack. In October 1944, U-636 set up a clandestine weather station on Hopen Island in the Barents Sea.

U-636 was sunk with all hands on 21 April 1945 west of Ireland by depth charges from frigates HMS *Bazely*, HMS *Drury* and HMS *Bentinck*. Forty-two crewmembers were killed.

Arctic convoys

1941–45

When Hitler invaded the Soviet Union in June 1941, Stalin's USSR and the United Kingdom became Allies in the war against Germany.

THE BRITISH AGREED to supply the Soviet Union with matériel and goods via convoys through the Arctic seas, the quantity of such assistance increasing dramatically when the United States entered the war in December 1941. The destinations were the northern ports of Murmansk and Arkhangelsk. To reach them, the convoys had to travel dangerously near the German-occupied Norwegian coastline. Convoys headed for Northern Russia were known as PQ convoys and those heading back were designated as QP convoys. Early convoys suffered few losses, but by the spring of 1942 the *Kriegsmarine* had concentrated significant U-boat and *Luftwaffe* strength in Norway, and sinkings began to increase.

▲ Depth charges

Improvements in escort protection and the widespread use of depth charges drastically reduced the losses suffered by the Allies' Arctic convoys.

Dreadful losses

The PQ/QP convoys were routed from Iceland to North Russia and back to Scotland. Eleven out of 18 convoys (eastbound PQ 7A, PQ 8, PQ 13, PQ 14, PQ 16, PQ 17 and PQ 18 and westbound QP 10, QP 11, QP 14 and QP 15) were intercepted by the Germans. In all, 29 ships of nearly 160,000 GRT were sunk by U-boats, with many more destroyed by *Luftwaffe* bombs and torpedoes.

After the losses suffered by PQ 16, PQ 17 and PQ 18, the Allies suspended Arctic convoy operations until the end of 1942, when increased numbers of escorts enabled more effective protection to be provided for the vulnerable merchant ships. The new convoys were redesignated as JW (eastbound) and RA (westbound). Thus from December 1942 the JW/RA system replaced the PQ/QP convoys. There were 21 JW convoys, comprising 552 merchant ships, and 20 RA convoys composed of 492 ships overall. The increase in escort efficiency can be measured by the fact that only nine RA ships were were sunk by U-boats and two by the *Luftwaffe*, while only five JW ships were sunk by U-boats.

The U-boat arm felt the difference, too. Four U-boats were lost while attacking PQ convoys (three in the battle for PQ 18 alone), while a further seven were destroyed in attacks on JW convoys. No U-boats were lost in attacks on QP-routed vessels, but nine were sunk in attacks on RA convoys.

Wolfpack groups *Keil* and *Donner*

April–May 1944

The *Keil* and *Donner* groups were two wolfpacks established at the end of March 1944, intended to attack eastbound Arctic convoys headed for the Soviet Union.

The two groups were given patrol areas near the edge of the ice pack to the south of Bear Island. No eastbound convoy was sighted, but late on the evening of 28 April a *Luftwaffe* reconnaissance aircraft spotted the westbound convoy RA 59.

Groups *Donner* and *Keil* were ordered to combine to mount an attack, and made contact on the afternoon of 30 April. However, by this stage in the war Allied escort tactics were very efficient, and convoys were generally protected by one or more escort carrier groups. Only U-711 managed to break through to the merchant ships, sinking the 7176-GRT American freighter SS *William S. Thayer*. Over the next two days and nights, the combined wolfpacks made repeated attacks against the escorts, but without success. Several explosions were heard, but all came from torpedoes blowing up at the ends of their runs without having hit a target.

The convoy escort was more successful: U-277 was sunk by depth charges on 1 May, as was U-959 a day later, while U-674 was also lost on 2 May, destroyed on the surface by rockets. In each case, the attack was delivered by Royal Navy Swordfish aircraft flying from the escort carrier HMS *Fencer*.

▲ Trondheim pens

The Type VII boat U-861 and the larger Type IX boat U-995 lie moored outside the 'Dora' bunker at Trondheim following their surrender in May 1945. Many of the *Donner* and *Keil* boats would have spent time here.

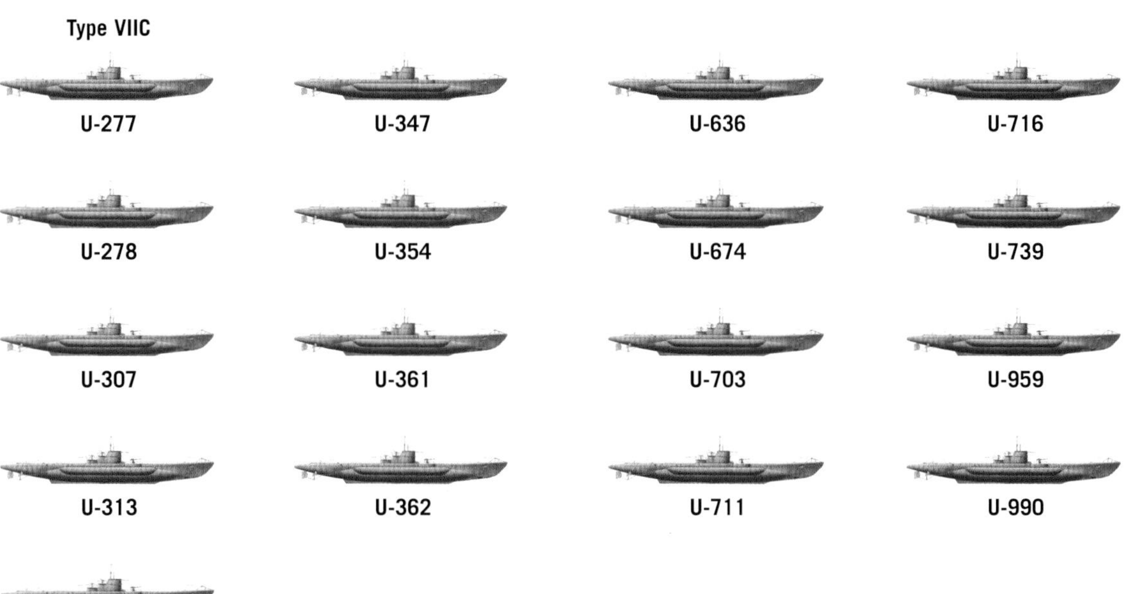

BOATS THAT SERVED WITH 13TH FLOTILLA (55 BOATS)

U-Boat	Type	Commissioned	Flotilla(s)	Patrols	Fate
U-212	VIIC	25-Apr-42	1 Jun 1943 – 31 Oct 1943 from 11. Flottille	15 patrols. 1 ship sunk: total 80 GRT	to 3. Flottille
U-251	VIIC	20-Sep-41	1 Jun 1943 – 30 Jun 1943 from 11. Flottille	9 patrols. 2 ships sunk: total 11,408 GRT	to 24. Flottille (training)
U-255	VIIC	29-Nov-41	1 Jun 1943 – 30 Nov 1943 from 11. Flottille	15 patrols. 10 ships sunk: total 47,529 GRT; 1 warship sunk: total 1219t/1200 tons; 1 ship damaged b/r: total 7191 GRT	to 7. Flottille
U-255	VIIC	29-Nov-41	1 Mar 1945 – 8 May 1945 from 7. Flottille	15 patrols. 10 ships sunk: total 47,529 GRT; 1 warship sunk: total 1219t/1200 tons; 1 ship damaged b/r: total 7191 GRT	Transferred to Scotland 14 May 1945 for Operation *Deadlight*. Sunk 13 Dec 1945
U-277	VIIC	21-Dec-42	1 Nov 1943 – 1 May 1944 from 6. Flottille	5 patrols	Sunk with all hands 1 May 1944 in the Arctic southwest of Bear Island by depth charges from a Swordfish of the escort carrier HMS *Fencer*. 50 dead
U-278	VIIC	16-Jan-43	1 Sep 1944 – 8 May 1945 from 11. Flottille	7 patrols. 1 ship sunk: total 7177 GRT; 1 warship sunk: total 1839t/1810 tons	Transferred to Scotland 19 May 1945 for Operation *Deadlight*. Sunk 31 Dec 1945
U-286	VIIC	5-Jun-43	5 Nov 1944 – 28 Feb 1945 from 11. Flottille	4 patrols. 1 warship sunk: total 1168t/1150 tons	to 11. Flottille
U-288	VIIC	26-Jun-43	1 Feb 1944 – 3 Apr 1944	2 patrols	Sunk with all hands 3 Apr 1944 in the Barents Sea southeast of Bear Island by depth charges and rockets from Swordfish, Avengers and Wildcats of the escort carriers HMS *Activity* and HMS *Tracker*. 49 dead
U-289	VIIC	10-Jul-43	1 May 1944 – 31 May 1944	2 patrols	Sunk with all hands 31 May 1944 in the Barents Sea southwest of Bear Island by depth charges from the destroyer HMS *Milne*. 51 dead
U-293	VIIC/41	8-Sep-43	5 Sep 1944 – 8 May 1945 from 13. Flottille	6 patrols. 1 warship damaged: total 1685t/1658 tons	Surrendered at Loch Alsh 11 May 1945. Sunk in Operation *Deadlight* 13 Dec 1945
U-294	VIIC/41	4-Oct-43	6 Nov 1944 – 28 Feb 1945 from 11. Flottille	5 patrols	to 14. Flottille
U-295	VIIC/41	20-Oct-43	1 Oct 1944 – 31 Mar 1945 from 11. Flottille	6 patrols. 1 warship damaged: total 1168t/1150 tons	to 14. Flottille
U-299	VIIC/41	15-Dec-43	5 Nov 1944 – 28 Feb 1945 from 11. Flottille	6 patrols	to 14. Flottille
U-302	VIIC	16-Jun-42	1 Jun 1943 – 31 Oct 1943 from 11. Flottille	10 patrols. 3 ships sunk: total 12,697 GRT	to 9. Flottille
U-307	VIIC	18-Nov-42	1 Nov 1943 – 29 Apr 1945 from 11. Flottille	19 patrols. 1 ship sunk: total 411 GRT	Sunk 29 Apr 1945 near Murmansk by depth charges from the frigate HMS *Loch Insh*. 37 dead and 14 survivors
U-310	VIIC	24-Feb-43	5 Sep 1944 – 8 May 1945 from 7. Flottille	6 patrols. 2 ships sunk: total 14,395 GRT	Surrendered 8 May 1945. Broken up at Trondheim, Norway, in Mar 1947
U-312	VIIC	21-Apr-43	1 Sep 1944 – 8 May 1945 from 11. Flottillle	12 patrols	Surrendered at Narvik, Norway, May 1945. Transferred to Scotland and sunk 29 Nov 1945 in Operation *Deadlight*
U-313	VIIC	20-May-43	15 Sep 1944 – 8 May 1945 from 11. Flottille	14 patrols	Surrendered at Narvik, Norway, 8 May 1945. Transferred to Scotland and sunk 27 Dec 1945 in Operation *Deadlight*
U-315	VIIC	10-Jul-43	15 Sep 1944 – 8 May 1945 from 11. Flottille	15 patrols. 1 ship sunk: total 6996 GRT; 1 warship damaged beyond repair: total 1392t/1370 tons	Stricken at Trondheim, Norway, 1 May 1945. Broken up in Mar 1947
U-318	VIIC/41	13-Nov-43	5 Nov 1944 – 28 Feb 1945 from 11. Flottille	8 patrols	to 14. Flottille
U-354	VIIC	22-Apr-42	1 Jun 1943 – 24 Aug 1944 from 11. Flottille	20 patrols. 2 ships sunk: total 9593 GRT; 1 warship sunk: total 1321t/1300 tons; 1 warship damaged beyond repair: total 11,603t/11,420 tons; 1 ship damaged: total 3771 GRT	Sunk with all hands 24 Aug 1944 northeast of North Cape by depth charges from the sloops HMS *Mermaid* and HMS *Peacock*, the frigate HMS *Loch Dunvegan* and the destroyer HMS *Keppel*. 51 dead. Originally credited to Swordfish of the escort carrier HMS *Vindex*, which actually destroyed U-344
U-360	VIIC	12-Nov-42	1 Jul 1943 – 2 Apr 1944 from 5. Flottille	7 patrols. 1 ship damaged: total 7153 GRT; 1 warship damaged: total 1565t/1540 tons	Sunk with all hands 2 Apr 1944 in the Norwegian Sea southwest of Bear Island by the destroyer HMS *Keppel*. 51 dead
U-362	VIIC	4-Feb-43	1 Mar 1944 – 5 Sep 1944 from 8. Flottille	7 patrols	Sunk with all hands 5 Sept 1944 in the Kara Sea near Krakovka by depth charges from the Soviet minesweeper T-116. 51 dead
U-363	VIIC	18-Mar-43	15 Sep 1944 – 8 May 1945 from 11. Flottille	10 patrols	Surrendered in Norway 8 May 1945. Transferred to Scotland for Operation *Deadlight* and was sunk 31 Dec 1945
U-365	VIIC	8-Jun-43	9 Jun 1944 – 13 Dec 1944 from 9. Flottille	11 patrols. 1 ship sunk: total 7540 GRT; 3 warships sunk: total 1377t/1355 tons, 1 warship damaged: total 1737t/1710 tons	Sunk with all hands 13 Dec 1944 in the Arctic east of Jan Mayen Island by depth charges from Royal Navy Swordfish flying from the escort carrier HMS *Campania*. 50 dead
U-366	VIIC	16-Jul-43	1 Mar 1944 – 5 Mar 1944 from 5. Flottille	2 patrols	Sunk with all hands 5 Mar 1944 in the Arctic Ocean northwest of Hammerfest by rockets from a Royal Navy Swordfish flying from the escort carrier HMS *Chaser*. 50 dead
U-387	VIIC	24-Nov-42	1 Nov 1943 – 9 Dec 1944 from 7. Flottille	15 patrols	Sunk with all hands 9 Dec 1944 in the Barents Sea near Murmansk by depth charges from the corvette HMS *Bamborough Castle*. 51 dead
U-425	VIIC	21-Apr-43	15 Sep 1944 – 17 Feb 1945 from 11. Flottille	8 patrols	Sunk 17 Feb 1945 in the Barents Sea near Murmansk by depth charges from the sloop HMS *Lark* and the corvette HMS *Alnwick Castle*. 52 dead and 1 survivor
U-427	VIIC	2-Jun-43	5 Nov 1944 – 28 Feb 1945 from 11. Flottille	5 patrols	to 14. Flottille
U-586	VIIC	4-Sep-41	1 Jun 1943 – 30 Sep 1943 from 11. Flottille	12 patrols. 2 ships sunk: total 12,716 GRT; 1 ship damaged: total 9057 GRT	to 6. Flottille
U-622	VIIC	14-May-42	1 Jun 1943 – 24 Jul 1943 from 11. Flottille	4 patrols	Sunk 24 Jul 1943 at Trondheim during a raid by heavy bombers of the 8th USAAF

BOATS THAT SERVED WITH 13TH FLOTILLA (55 BOATS)

U-Boat	Type	Commissioned	Flotilla(s)	Patrols	Fate
U-625	VIIC	4-Jun-42	1 Jun 1943 – 31 Oct 1943 from 11. Flottille	9 patrols. 3 ships sunk: total 18,751 GRT; 2 auxiliary warships sunk: total 939 GRT	to 1. Flottille
U-636	VIIC	20-Aug-42	1 Nov 1943 – 21 Apr 1945 from 11. Flottille	14 patrols. 1 ship sunk: total 7169 GRT	Sunk with all hands 21 Apr 1945 west of Ireland by depth charges from the frigates HMS *Bazely*, HMS *Drury* and HMS *Bentinck*. 42 dead
U-639	VIIC	10-Sep-42	1 Jun 1943 – 28 Aug 1943 from 11. Flottille	4 patrols	Sunk with all hands 28 Aug 1943 in the Kara Sea north of Mys Zhelaniya, torpedoed by the Soviet submarine S-101. 47 dead
U-668	VIIC	16-Nov-42	1 Jun 1944 – 8 May 1945 from 6. Flottille	6 patrols	Surrendered at Narvik, Norway, 8 May 1945. Transferred to Scotland for Operation *Deadlight*. Sunk 31 Dec 1945
U-673	VIIC	8-May-43	21 Jun 1944 – 31 Jul 1944 from 6. Flottille	5 patrols	to 6. Flottille
U-703	VIIC	16-Oct-41	1 Jun 1943 – 16 Sep 1944 from 11. Flottille	13 patrols. 5 ships sunk: total 29,523 GRT; 1 auxiliary warship sunk: total 559 GRT; 1 warship sunk: total 1900t/1870 tons	Missing with all hands on or after 16 Sep 1944 east of Iceland. 54 dead
U-711	VIIC	26-Sep-42	1 Jun 1943 – 4 May 1945 from 11. Flottille	12 patrols. 1 ship sunk: total 7176 GRT; 1 warship sunk: total 940t/925 tons; 1 ship damaged: total 20 GRT	Sunk 4 May 1945 near Harstad, Norway, by Avengers and Wildcats of the escort carriers HMS *Searcher*, HMS *Trumpeter* and HMS *Queen*. U-711 was damaged while alongside the depot ship *Black Watch*. The in-port watch of 12 men cut her loose from the sinking depot ship, but they had to abandon the boat and it sank nearby. 40 dead (killed aboard the *Black Watch* when it blew up) and 12 survivors. U-711 was the last U-boat sunk by the Royal Navy Fleet Air Arm
U-713	VIIC	29-Dec-42	1 Nov 1943 – 24 Feb 1944 from 11. Flottille	5 patrols	Sunk with all hands 24 Feb 1944 in the Arctic northwest of Narvik by depth charges from the destroyer HMS *Keppel*. 50 dead
U-716	VIIC	15-Apr-43	1 Oct 1944 – 31 Mar 1945 from 11. Flottille	10 patrols. 1 ship sunk: total 7200 GRT	to 14. Flottille
U-737	VIIC	30-Jan-43	1 Jul 1943 – 19 Dec 1944 from 8. Flottille	8 patrols	Sank 19 Dec 1944 in the Vestfjorden after a collision with minesweeper MRS 25. 31 dead and 20 survivors
U-739	VIIC	6-Mar-43	1 Jan 1944 – 8 May 1945 from 9. Flottille	8 patrols. 1 warship sunk: total 635t/625 tons	Surrendered at Wilhelmshaven 8 May 1945. Transferred to Scotland for Operation *Deadlight*. Sunk as a target by aircraft 16 Dec 1945
U-742	VIIC	1-May-43	1 Jun 1944 – 18 Jul 1944 from 6. Flottille	2 patrols	Sunk with all hands 18 Jul 1944 west of Narvik by depth charges from a Catalina of No. 210 Sqn RAF. 52 dead. The pilot, Flying Officer Cruickshank, was awarded the Victoria Cross for pressing home the attack even though his aircraft was badly damaged, one of his crew had been killed and he and another crewman were wounded
U-771	VIIC	18-Nov-43	1 Oct 1944 – 11 Nov 1944 from 11. Flottille	2 patrols	Sunk with all hands 11 Nov 1944 in the Andfjord near Harstad, Norway, by torpedoes from HM Submarine *Venturer*. 51 dead
U-921	VIIC	30-May-43	1 Jun 1944 – 2 Oct 1944	3 patrols	Missing with all hands northwest of Narvik after 2 Oct 1944. 51 dead. Previously credited to depth charges from aircraft of the escort carrier HMS *Campania* 30 Sep 1944 northwest of Hammerfest. That was against U-636 and U-968 and caused no damage
U-956	VIIC	6-Jan-43	1 Oct 1944 – 8 May 1945 from 11. Flottille	13 patrols. 1 warship sunk: total 1209t/1190 tons; 1 ship damaged beyond repair: total 7176 GRT	Surrendered 13 May 1945 at Loch Eriboll, Scotland. Sunk by naval gunfire in Operation *Deadlight* 17 Dec 1945
U-957	VIIC	7-Jan-43	1 Oct 1944 – 21 Oct 1944 from 11. Flottille	6 patrols. 2 ships sunk: total 7353 GRT; 2 warships sunk: total 614t/604 tons	Collided with a German supply vessel in the Lofoten Islands 19 Oct 1944. Decommissioned at Trondheim 21 Oct 1944. Transferred to England 29 May 1945. Broken up
U-959	VIIC	21-Jan-43	1 Mar 1944 – 2 May 1944 from 5. Flottille	2 patrols	Sunk with all hands in the Arctic southeast of Jan Mayen Island 2 May 1944 by depth charges from a Swordfish of the escort carrier HMS *Fencer*. 53 dead
U-965	VIIC	25-Feb-43	1 Oct 1944 – 30 Mar 1945 from 11. Flottille	7 patrols	Sunk with all hands 30 Mar 1945 north of Scotland by depth charges from frigates HMS *Rupert* and HMS *Conn*. 51 dead. Formerly credited to the *Conn* on 27 Mar, but that attack probably sank U-905
U-968	VIIC	18-Mar-43	1 Mar 1944 – 8 May 1945 from 5. Flottille	7 patrols. 2 ships sunk: total 14,386 GRT; 1 warship sunk: total 1372t/1350 tons; 1 ship damaged beyond repair: total 7200 GRT; 1 warship damaged beyond repair: total 1372t/1350 tons; 1 ship damaged: total 8129 GRT	Surrendered 16 May 1945 at Loch Eriboll, Scotland. Sunk 29 Nov 1945 in Operation *Deadlight*
U-992	VIIC	2-Aug-43	1 Oct 1944 – 8 May 1945 from 11. Flottille	8 patrols. 1 warship damaged beyond repair: total 1077t/1060 tons	Transferred from Narvik to Scotland 19 May 1945 for Operation *Deadlight*. Sunk by gunfire 16 Dec 1945
U-994	VIIC	2-Sep-43	5 Nov 1944 – 8 May 1945 from 11. Flottille	1 patrol	Transferred from Trondheim to Scotland 19 May 1945 for Operation *Deadlight*. Sank while on tow to the scuttling grounds 5 Dec 1945
U-995	VIIC/41	16-Sep-43	1 Jun 1944 – 28 Feb 1945 from 5. Flottille	9 patrols. 3 ships sunk: total 1560 GRT; 1 auxiliary warship sunk: total 633 GRT; 1 warship sunk: total 107t/105 tons; 1 ship damaged beyond repair: total 7176 GRT	to 14. Flottille
U-997	VIIC/41	23-Sep-43	1 Jun 1944 – 1 Mar 1945 from 9. Flottille	7 patrols. 1 ship sunk: total 1603 GRT; 1 warship sunk: total 107t/105 tons; 1 ship damaged: total 4287 GRT	to 14. Flottille
U-1163	VIIC/41	6-Oct-43	1 Oct 1944 – 8 May 1945 from 11. Flottille	4 patrols. 1 ship sunk: total 433 GRT	Transferred from Kristiansand to Scotland 29 May 1945 for Operation *Deadlight*. Sunk by aircraft 11 Dec 1945

14 Unterseebootsflottille

Formed late in the war after the U-boat force had been forced to flee its French bases, the 14th Flotilla was based at Narvik under the command of *Korvettenkapitän* Helmut Möhlmann. Operating against Arctic convoys, it never had a strength of more than eight boats.

OPERATING IN THE FAR NORTH, the 14th Flotilla made the last operational patrols of the war against the Arctic convoys. The boats achieved little against the by now highly efficient Allied escorts, but all eight survived the war to be surrendered to the British in May 1945. All bar U-995 were destroyed in Operation *Deadlight*: U-995 survives to this day as a war memorial at Laboe, near Kiel.

Oberleutnant zur See Hans-Georg Hess

Born on 6 May 1923 in Berlin, Hans-Georg Hess joined the *Kriegsmarine* as a 16-year-old volunteer in 1940. After service aboard minesweepers, he transferred to the U-boat arm in April of 1942. After officer training, he served aboard U-466 in the Atlantic and Mediterranean. Promoted to *Oberleutnant* in March 1944, he took command of U-995 in September 1944.

The boat made five patrols under his command, sinking five ships and damaging one. Hess was awarded the Knight's Cross in February 1945 as one of the few late-war commanders to have had any success in the Arctic.

Commander

Korvkpt. Helmut Möhlmann *(Dec 1944 – May 1945)*

U-427

Laid down on 27 July 1942 at Danziger Werft, Danzig, the Type VIIC boat U-427 was commissioned on 2 June 1943 under the command

14TH FLOTILLA BASE LOCATION

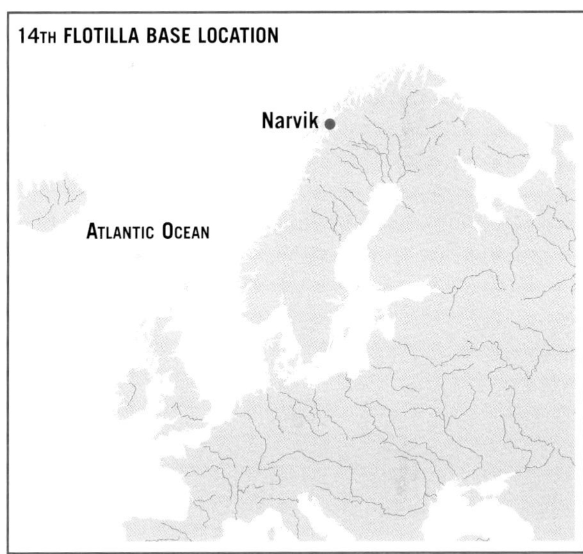

Specifications

Crew: 44

Powerplant: Diesel/electric

Max Speed: 31.5/14.1km/hr (17/7.6kt) s/d

Surface Range: 12,040km (6500nm)

Displacement: 773/879t (761/865 tons) s/d

Dimensions (length/beam/draught): 67.1 x 6.2 x 4.8m (220.1 x 20.34 x 15.75ft)

Commissioned: 2 Jun 1943

Armament: 14 torpedoes (4 bow/1 stern tubes); 1 x 3.7cm (1.5in) and 2 x twin 2cm (0.8in) guns

▲ **U-427**

Type VIIC

In her short career in northern waters, U-427 led an active life. From protecting German coastal convoys against marauding British destroyers and cruisers, the boat went on to mount attacks on the last Arctic convoys of the war.

14TH FLOTILLA	
Type	**Boats assigned**
Type VIIC	2
Type VIIC/41	6

U-427 Commander

Oblt. Graf Karl-Gabriel von Gudenus *(Jun 1943 – May 1945)*

of Oblt. Graf Karl-Gabriel von Gudenus. From August 1944, U-427 was used to escort German coastal convoys, carrying out 18 missions before February 1945. The boat also mounted five combat patrols with the 13th and 14th Flotillas.

On the night of 11/12 January, the boat attacked a British cruiser squadron that had damaged two merchantmen, but missed. On the night of 29 April 1945, U-427 attacked convoy RA 66, launching torpedoes against the destroyers HMCS *Haida* and *Iroquois*, but scoring no hits. The escorts fought back and dropped a total of 678 depth charges on U-427's estimated position during a hunt which lasted several hours. However, the boat managed to avoid damage, and worked its way clear. This was one of the last attacks made by the U-boat arm on an Arctic convoy.

Fate

U-427 was surrendered at Narvik, Norway, at the end of the war and was transferred to Loch Eriboll in Scotland for Operation *Deadlight*. The boat was sunk by naval gunfire on 21 December 1945.

U-995

U-995 was a Type VIIC/41 boat and was laid down on 25 November 1942 at Blohm und Voss in Hamburg. The submarine was commissioned on 16 September 1943 under the command of *Kapitänleutnant* Walter Köhntopp, who was succeeded on 10 October 1944 by *Oberleutnant* Hans-Georg Hess. The boat received its working up training with the 5th Flotilla before becoming operational with the 13th Flotilla in June 1944. It was transferred to the 14th Flotilla on 1 March 1945. The boat made nine patrols, sinking four ships for a total of nearly 2200 GRT. It also sank a Soviet minesweeping trawler and damaged a 7000-GRT American freighter beyond repair.

Fate

U-995 was surrendered to Britain at Trondheim in May 1945. The boat was given to Norway in October 1948, becoming the Norwegian submarine *Kaura* on 1 December 1952. Stricken in 1965, it was returned to Germany in 1970, restored to wartime standard and installed as a war memorial and museum ship at Laboe near Kiel in October 1971.

14TH FLOTILLA INSIGNIA

The flotilla's operational area in northern waters was appropriately represented by a U-boat on top of the world, backed by the midnight sun. However, there is no record that any of its boats carried the insignia.

BOATS THAT SERVED WITH 14TH FLOTILLA (8 BOATS)

U-Boat	Type	Commissioned	Flotilla(s)	Patrols	Fate
U-294	VIIC/41	4-Oct-43	1 Mar 1945 – 8 May 1945 from 13. Flottille	5 patrols	Surrendered at Narvik. Transferred to Scotland for Operation *Deadlight*. Sunk 31 Dec 1945
U-295	VIIC/41	20-Oct-43	1 Apr 1945 – 8 May 1945 from 13. Flottille	6 patrols. 1 warship damaged: total: 1168t/1150 tons	Surrendered at Narvik May 1945. Transferred to Scotland at the end of May for Operation *Deadlight*. Sunk 17 Dec 1945
U-299	VIIC/41	15-Dec-43	1 Mar 1945 – 8 May 1945 from 13. Flottille	6 patrols	Transferred from Bergen to Scotland 29 May 1945 for Operation *Deadlight*. Sunk 4 Dec 1945
U-318	VIIC/41	13-Nov-43	1 Mar 1945 – 8 May 1945 from 13. Flottille	8 patrols	Surrendered at Narvik, Norway, 8 May 1945. Transferred to Scotland for Operation *Deadlight*. Sunk 21 Dec 1945
U-427	VIIC	2-Jun-43	1 Mar 1945 – 8 May 1945 from 13. Flottille	5 patrols	Surrendered at Narvik, Norway. Transferred to Scotland for Operation *Deadlight*. Sunk 21 Dec 1945
U-716	VIIC	15-Apr-43	1 Apr 1945 – 8 May 1945 from 13. Flottille	10 patrols. 1 ship sunk: total 7200 GRT	Surrendered at Narvik 8 May 1945. Transferred to Scotland for Operation *Deadlight*. Sunk by aircraft 11 Dec 1945
U-995	VIIC/41	16-Sep-43	1 Mar 1945 – 8 May 1945 from 13. Flottille	9 patrols. 3 ships sunk: total 1560 GRT; 1 auxiliary warship sunk: total 633 GRT; 1 warship sunk: total 107t/105 tons; 1 ship damaged beyond repair: total 7176 GRT	Surrendered to Britain at Trondheim May 1945. Transferred to Norway Oct 1948, becoming the Norwegian submarine *Kaura* 1 Dec 1952. Stricken in 1965. Returned to Germany; survives as a war memorial and museum at Laboe, near Kiel
U-997	VIIC/41	23-Sep-43	1 Mar 1945 – 8 May 1945 from 13. Flottille	7 patrols. 1 ship sunk: total 1603 GRT; 1 warship sunk: total 107t/105 tons; 1 ship damaged: total 4287 GRT	Transferred from Narvik to Northern Ireland 19 May 1945 for Operation *Deadlight*. Sunk by aircraft 13 Dec 1945

23 Unterseebootsflottille

German naval planners between the wars had always considered the Mediterranean to be a potential operational zone. However, when Germany had to commit forces to the region in 1941, it was in a very different war from that which had been envisaged.

Commander

Kptlt. Fritz Frauenheim *(Sep 1941 – May 1942)*

ADOLF HITLER HAD NO intention of getting involved in southern Europe, but when his fellow fascist dictator Mussolini got into trouble in the Balkans, the Mediterranean and North Africa, Germany had to commit military forces to help its ally in the theatre.

Originally, the *Kriegsmarine* had anticipated that France would be the major enemy, but in the event it was British and Commonwealth forces in North Africa and the British Mediterranean Fleet which were encountered in battle.

Air power could provide much of the support needed by Germany's expeditionary force in Africa, the *Deutsches Afrika Korps.* However, true control would come only by denying the British command of the sea. The *Kriegsmarine* was too weak to make any difference on the surface, but the U-boat arm might be able to interfere with troop and resupply convoys that supported the British armies in North Africa, and it was decided to send a small force to the eastern Mediterranean.

A new flotilla, the 23rd, was established in Greece to control the boats. Founded on 11 September 1941 under the command of *Kapitänleutnant* Fritz Frauenheim, it was too small to be really effective and in May 1942 it was disbanded, its boats and missions being taken over by the larger 29th Flotilla. The 23rd Flotilla itself was reformed in 1943 as a training unit in the Baltic.

23RD FLOTILLA INSIGNIA

Most of the boats assigned to the 23rd Flotilla wore individual insignia. Indications are that the 'White Donkey', thought to be the flotilla's device, was carried only by Hans Heidtmann's U-559.

23RD FLOTILLA BASE LOCATION

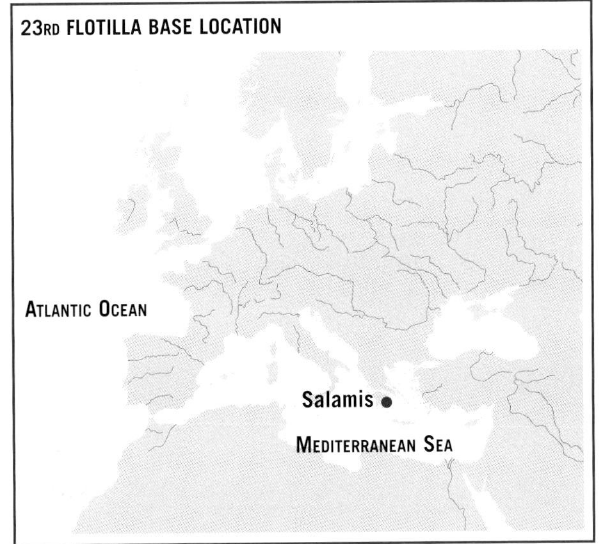

Kapitänleutnant Hans Heidtmann

Born on 8 August 1914 near Lübeck, Heidtmann joined the German Navy in Crew 34. He moved onto U-boats in January 1938, and made six non-combat patrols as acting commander of U-2 and U-14. From July 1940 he was commander of the school boat U-21 with the 21st Flotilla.

In February 1941 he commissioned the Type VIIC boat U-559. He carried out two patrols in the North Atlantic, sinking one ship before being deployed to the Mediterranean, passing safely through the Straits of Gibraltar on 26 September 1941.

Over the next 12 months U-559 carried out a further eight patrols, sinking at least three ships and an Australian sloop. U-559 was sunk in October 1942 by British destroyers, whose crews managed to capture vital codebooks before the boat went down. Heidtmann died on 5 April 1976 in Hamburg.

23RD FLOTILLA (1941–42)

Type	Boats assigned
Type VIIB	3
Type VIIC	6

U-75

Type VIIB

Built by Bremer Vulkan, Vegesack, U-75 was laid down in December 1939 and launched on 18 October 1940. It served initially with the 7th Flotilla before transferring to the Mediterranean.

U-75's first three patrols were in the Atlantic, during which the boat sank four merchant ships totalling more than 25,000 GRT. On her third patrol, U-75 made a rendezvous with the disguised commerce raider *Orion* off the Azores, escorting the vessel into the estuary of the Gironde from where it entered Bordeaux.

In September 1941, U-75 left St Nazaire with orders to pass through the Straits of Gibraltar to operate in the Mediterranean. She was one of six boats of the *Goeben* group, the first Type VII boats to enter the Mediterranean. Their orders were to operate in the eastern Mediterranean to interdict supplies being sent by the British from Alexandria to Tobruk. U-75 encountered a British convoy on 12 October and sank two troop-carrying lighters, or barges, by torpedo and gunfire. After making an unsuccessful attack on a destroyer, U-75 entered her new base at Salamis on 2 November.

U-75 Commander

Kptlt. Helmuth Ringelmann *(Dec 1940 – Dec 1941)*

Fate

U-75 left on her last patrol off the Egyptian coast on 22 December 1941. On 28 December, the boat torpedoed a British freighter off Mersa Matruh. In a radio message, the captain reported another sinking, but this has never been confirmed. Soon afterwards, British forces tracked down the boat, and it was sunk by a depth-charge attack from the fleet destroyer HMS *Kipling*. Fourteen of the crew died; 30 were taken prisoner.

U-75 TIMETABLE

Patrol Dates	Operational Area	Ships Sunk
10 Apr 1941 – 12 May 1941	S of Iceland	1
29 May 1941 – 3 Jul 1941	Central N Atlantic	1
29 Jul 1941 – 25 Aug 1941	Central N Atlantic	2
27 Sep 1941 – 2 Nov 1941	Transit from St Nazaire to Salamis	2
22 Dec 1941 – 28 Dec 1941	Off Egyptian coast	1

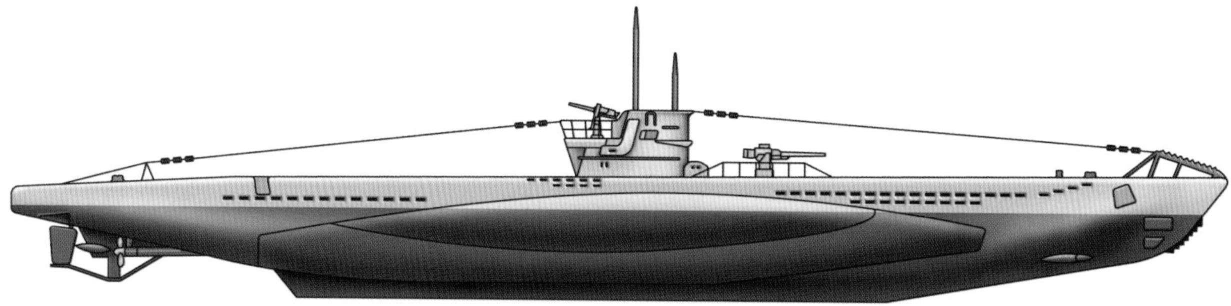

Specifications

Crew: 44

Powerplant: Diesel/electric

Max Speed: 31.9/14.8km/hr (17.2/8kt) s/d

Surface Range: 12,040km (6500nm)

Displacement: 765/871t (753/857 tons) s/d

Dimensions (length/beam/draught): 66.5 x 6.2 x 4.7m (218.1 x 20.34 x 15.4ft)

Commissioned: 19 Dec 1940

Armament: 14 torpedoes (4 bow/1 stern tubes); 1 x 8.8cm (3.5in) and 1 x 2cm (0.8in) guns

▲ **U-75**

Type VIIB

One of the first of the *Kriegsmarine*'s front-line U-boats to operate in the Meditarranean, U-75 was tasked with providing support for the *Afrika Korps* by sinking British supply convoys in the eastern Mediterranean.

U-331

Type VIIC

Launched at Nordseewerke, Emden, in December 1940, U-331 was commissioned on 31 March 1941 under the command of *Kapitänleutnant* Freiherr Hans-Diedrich von Tiesenhausen.

Assigned to the 1st U-boat Flotilla at St Nazaire, U-331 completed her combat training at Kiel. In July 1941, the boat left for her first patrol in the Atlantic, initially operating southeast of Greenland but later moving to join a patrol line stretching between Gibraltar and the Azores. Although an attempt was made to attack Convoy HG 69, the boats were driven off by the British escorts.

In September 1941, U-331 left Lorient for the eastern Mediterranean as part of the six-boat *Goeben* group. On the way the boat exchanged gunfire with a British convoy of troop-carrying barges. One crewman was killed in the firefight. One day later the boat put into her new base at Salamis.

On her third patrol in November 1941, U-331 landed commandos on the Egyptian coast near Ras Gibeisa. The soldiers' mission was to blow up the coastal railway, but they were captured.

A few days later, on 25 November 1941, U-331 encountered the British Mediterranean Fleet, which had left Alexandria the previous day. U-331 fired four torpedoes at the second battleship in line, the 31,599-tonne (31,100-ton) HMS *Barham.* The battleship blew up and sank, with the loss of 862 members of her crew; 449 survivors were picked up. After the patrol, von Tiesenhausen was flown to Berlin to be awarded the Knight's Cross.

U-331 Commander

Kptlt. Freiherr Hans-Diedrich von Tiesenhausen *(Mar 1941 – Nov 1942)*

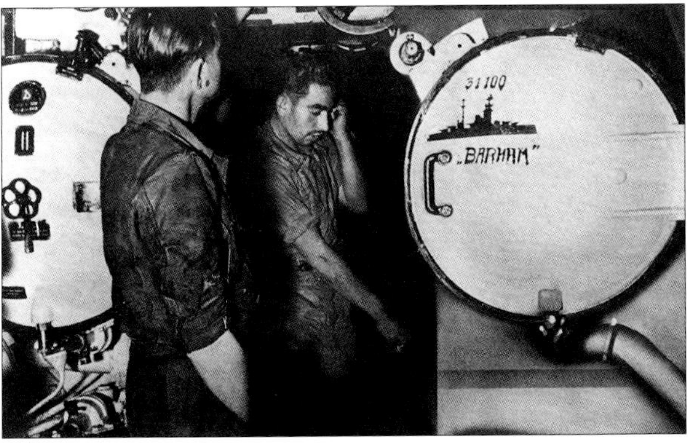

Torpedo room

Crewmembers of U-331 examine the torpedo tubes. On the back of one of the tubes is marked a kill, HMS *Barham,* which was sunk on 25 November 1941.

Specifications

Crew: 44
Powerplant: Diesel/electric
Max Speed: 31.5/14.1km/hr (17/7.6kt) s/d
Surface Range: 12,040km (6500nm)
Displacement: 773/879t (761/865 tons) s/d
Dimensions (length/beam/draught): 67.1 x 6.2 x 4.8m (220.1 x 20.34 x 15.75ft)
Commissioned: 31 Mar 1941
Armament: 14 torpedoes (4 bow/1 stern tubes); 1 x 8.8cm (3.5in) and 1 x 2cm (0.8in) guns

U-331

Type VIIC

Although U-331 had little success against Allied merchant shipping, the boat was presented with one of the greatest prizes of the war when she encountered the British Mediterranean Fleet and sank the battleship HMS *Barham.*

On her fifth patrol, off the Lebanese coast, U-331 engaged two small sailing vessels with gunfire. The U-boat had to leave the scene before the vessels were confirmed as sunk.

U-331 TIMETABLE		
Patrol Dates	**Operational Area**	**Ships Sunk**
2 Jul 1941 – 19 Aug 1941	North Atlantic/Azores	0
24 Sep 1941 – 11 Oct 1941	Transit from Lorient to Mediterranean	0
12 Nov 1941 – 3 Dec 1942	Special operations off Libya	1
14 Jan 1942 – 28 Feb 1942	Off Tobruk	0
4 Apr 1942 – 19 Apr 1942	Minelaying off Beirut	2 (possibles)
9 May 1942 – 21 May 1942	Off Tobruk	0
25 May 1942 – 15 Jun 1942	Libyan coast	0
5 Aug 1942 – 10 Aug 1942	Balearic Islands	0
12 Aug 1942 – 19 Sep 1942	Balearic Islands	0
7 Nov 1942 – 17 Nov 1942	Algerian coast	1

Fate

On 17 November 1942, after being badly damaged by a Lockheed Hudson of No. 500 Sqn RAF in the Mediterranean north of Algiers, U-331 signalled her surrender to the circling aircraft. However, the boat was attacked and destroyed by torpedo-equipped Albacores from the aircraft carrier HMS *Formidable*, which were unaware that the boat had capitulated. Thirty-two crewmembers were killed; 17 survived. The survivors were all picked up and taken into captivity.

▶ Keeping watch

The crew of a Type VIIC seek out targets in the Mediterranean in 1942. The U-boats were far less successful in the Mediterranean theatre, and Dönitz felt they would have been better deployed against convoys in the North Atlantic.

BOATS THAT SERVED WITH 23RD FLOTILLA WHEN IT WAS A COMBAT UNIT (9 BOATS)					
U-Boat	**Type**	**Commissioned**	**Flotilla(s)**	**Patrols**	**Fate**
U-75	VIIB	19-Dec-40	1 Oct 1941 – 28 Dec 1941 from 7. Flottille	5 patrols. 7 ships sunk: total 37,884 GRT; 2 warships sunk: total 756t/744 tons	Sunk 28 Dec 1941 in the Mediterranean near Mersa Matruh by depth charges from the destroyer HMS *Kipling*. 14 dead and 30 survivors
U-77	VIIC	18-Jan-41	1 Jan 1942 – 30 Apr 1942 from 7. Flottille	12 patrols. 14 ships sunk: total 31,186 GRT; 1 warship sunk: total 1067t/1050 tons; 1 ship damaged beyond repair: total 5222 GRT; 2 ships damaged: total 5384 GRT; 2 warships damaged: total 2926t/2880 tons	to 29. Flottille
U-79	VIIC	13-Mar-41	1 Oct 1941 – 23 Dec 1941 from 1. Flottille	6 patrols. 2 ships sunk: total 2983 GRT; 1 warship damaged beyond repair: total 635t/625 tons; 1 ship damaged: total 10,356 GRT	Sunk 23 Dec 1941 in the Mediterranean north of Sollum by depth charges from the destroyers HMS *Hasty* and HMS *Hotspur*. No fatalities – 44 survivors
U-83	VIIB	8-Feb-41	1 Jan 1942 – 30 Apr 1942 from 1. Flottille	12 patrols. 5 ships sunk: total 8425 GRT; 1 auxiliary warship sunk: total 91 GRT; 1 ship damaged: total 2590 GRT; 1 auxiliary warship damaged: total 6746 GRT	to 29. Flottille
U-97	VIIC	28-Sep-40	1 Nov 1941 – 30 Apr 1942 from 7. Flottille	13 patrols. 15 ships sunk: total 64,404 GRT; 1 auxiliary warship sunk: total 6833 GRT; 1 ship damaged: total 9718 GRT	to 29. Flottille
U-133	VIIB	5-Jul-41	1 Jan 1942 – 14 Mar 1942 from 7 Flottille	3 patrols. 1 warship sunk: total 1951t/1920 tons	Sunk with all hands 14 Mar 1942 near Salamis, Greece, by a German-laid mine. 45 dead
U-331	VIIC	31-Mar-41	1 Jan 1942 – 14 Mar 1942 from 7. Flottille	10 patrols. 1 auxiliary warship sunk: total 9135 GRT; 1 battleship (HMS *Barham*) sunk: total 31,599t/31,100 tons; 1 warship damaged: total 378t/372 tons	to 29. Flottille
U-371	VIIC	15-Mar-41	1 Nov 1941 – 14 Apr 1942 from 1. Flottille	19 patrols. 8 ships sunk: total 51,401 GRT; 1 auxiliary warship sunk: total 545 GRT; 2 warships sunk: total 2323t/2286 tons; 2 ships damaged b/r: total 13,341 GRT; 4 ships damaged: total 28,072 GRT; 2 warships damaged: total 2540t/2500 tons	to 29. Flottille
U-559	VIIC	27-Feb-41	1 Nov 1941 – 14 Apr 1942 from 1. Flottille	10 patrols. 4 ships sunk: total 11,811 GRT; 1 damaged: total 5917 GRT; 1 warship sunk: total 1077t/1060 tons	to 21. Flottille

29 Unterseebootsflottille

The 29th Flotilla was founded in December 1941 under the command of *Korvettenkapitän* Franz Becker. Intended for Mediterranean operations, its boats came under the operational control of the *Kriegsmarine*'s Mediterranean Command rather than the U-boat Command.

While the 23rd Flotilla in Greece operated against Allied shipping in the east, the 29th Flotilla based at La Spezia concentrated on patrols in the central and western Mediterranean. When the 23rd Flotilla was disbanded, the 29th Flotilla assumed control of its boats and mission.

Boats also used the base facilities at Salamis, Pola, and in the south of France as forward-operating locations. The flotilla's headquarters was moved to Toulon in August 1943 as Allied troops gained a foothold in Italy.

End in the Mediterranean

The last U-boat attempting to enter the Mediterranean, U-731, was sunk on 15 May 1944 by the patrol vessel HMS *Kilmarnock*, the anti-submarine trawler HMS *Blackfly* and two US Navy PBY Catalina aircraft from VP-63. On 21 May, U-boats gained their last success in the region when U-453 attacked Convoy HA 43, sinking one ship but being sunk herself soon afterwards. In September 1944, the last of 68 U-boats to serve in the Mediterranean were destroyed. U-407 was sunk south of the Greek island of Milos on the 19th. Five days later in raids on Salamis, USAAF aircraft damaged U-596 and U-565, which were scuttled. The 29th Flotilla was disbanded, as its other eight U-boats had all been destroyed or scuttled at Toulon.

29th FLOTILLA BASE LOCATIONS

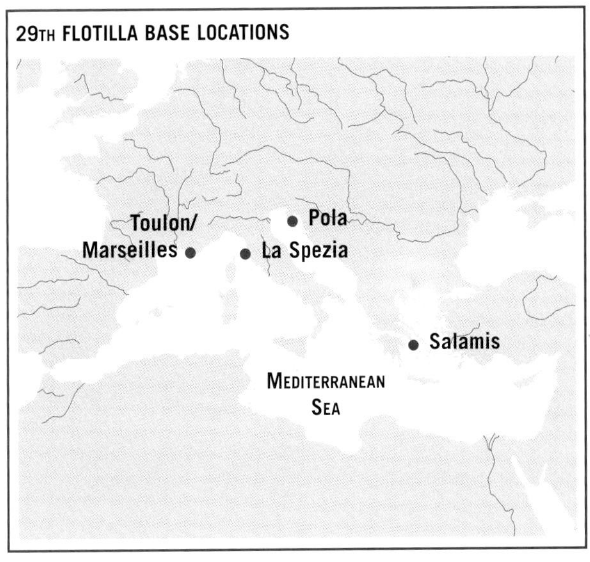

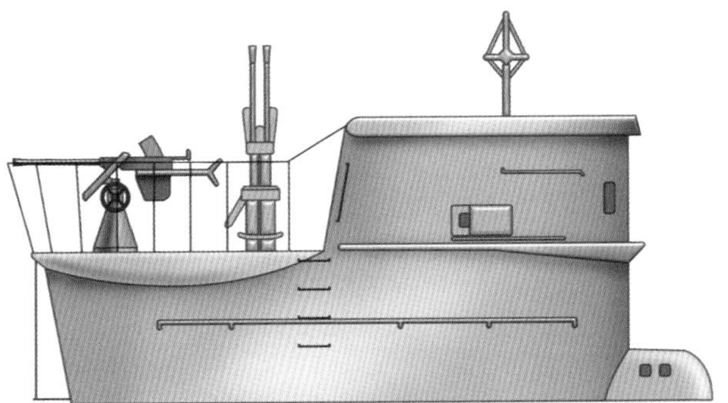

▲ Type VIIC extended bridge

The first attempt to improve the Type VIIC's defensive power came with an extension of the bridge platform to make room for two twin Breda 13.2mm (0.5in) heavy machine guns to supplement the standard single 2cm (0.8in) weapon. Even heavy machine guns were not enough, and the bridge structure was extended further to make room for extra single, and then twin, 2cm (0.8in) weapons. The diamond-shaped aerial is for the FuMB 2, the Biscay Cross, which gave warning of first-generation aircraft radars but was useless against centimetric equipment.

Commanders

Korvkpt. Franz Becker *(Dec 1941 – May 1942)*
Korvkpt. Fritz Frauenheim *(May 1942 – Jul 1943)*
Korvkpt. Gunther Jahn *(Aug 1943 – Sep 1944)*

29th FLOTILLA INSIGNIA

The flotilla's insignia was originally worn by U-338. The boat rammed a dock crane on being launched, and became known as the 'Wild Donkey'. Three or four of the flotilla's boats are known to have used this emblem.

29TH FLOTILLA (1941–44)

Type	Boats assigned
Type VIIB	3
Type VIIC	49

Star commanders
1941–44

The 29th Flotilla included in its number some of the busiest of all U-boat commanders, who made many patrols in the perilously shallow and clear waters of the Mediterranean.

Kapitänleutnant Freiherr Hans-Diedrich von Tiesenhausen

Born on 22 February 1913 in Latvia, von Tiesenhausen joined the Navy with Crew 34. He began his U-boat career on U-23 under *Kapitänleutnant* Otto Kretschmer. Together they completed three successful patrols and sank five ships for a total of 27,000 GRT, as well as one destroyer. He also served aboard U-93.

At the end of March 1941 von Tiesenhausen took command of U-331, in which he completed nine patrols with the 23rd and 29th Flotillas. On 25 November 1941, U-331 sank the battleship HMS *Barham*, for which achievement von Tiesenhausen received the Knight's Cross. U-331 was sunk in November 1942 off Algiers and von Tiesenhausen was taken prisoner. In 1947 he returned to Germany from a prison camp in Canada and worked as a joiner. In 1951 he emigrated to Canada. He died on 17 August 2000 at Vancouver in British Columbia.

STAR COMMANDERS

Commander	Patrols	Ships Sunk
Kptlt. Freiherr Hans-Diedrich von Tiesenhausen	10	2
Korvkpt. Helmut Rosenbaum	10	9
Oblt. Horst-Arno Fenski	6	8

Korvettenkapitän Helmut Rosenbaum

Born on 11 May 1913 near Leipzig, Rosenbaum joined the *Reichsmarine* with Crew 32. He commanded U-2 and U-73, sinking six ships and the aircraft carrier HMS *Eagle*. Rosenbaum died in an air crash on 10 May 1944 near Konstanza, Romania.

Oberleutnant zur See Horst-Arno Fenski

Born on 3 November 1918 in East Prussia, Fenski joined the *Kriegsmarine* with Crew 37b. He commanded U-34, U-410 and U-371, sinking six ships totalling 43,032 GRT as well as two warships totalling 7006 tonnes (6895 tons), including the cruiser HMS *Penelope* in February 1944. U-410 was destroyed by US bombs in March 1944. Oblt. Fenski then took over U-371, but on his first patrol with this boat he had to scuttle her after heavy depth-charge attacks. He spent two years as a prisoner of war. He died on 10 February 1965 at Hamburg.

Specifications

Crew: 44
Powerplant: Diesel/electric
Max Speed: 31.5/14.1km/hr (17/7.6kt) s/d
Surface Range: 12,040km (6500nm)
Displacement: 773/879t (761/865 tons) s/d
Dimensions (length/beam/draught): 67.1 x 6.2 x 4.8m (220.1 x 20.34 x 15.75ft)
Commissioned: 23 Feb 1942
Armament: 14 torpedoes (4 bow/1 stern tubes); 1 x 2cm (0.8in) quad and 2 x twin 2cm (0.8in)

▲ **U-410**

Type VIIC

Originally commanded by *Korvettenkapitän* Kurt Sturm, U-410 was taken over by *Oberleutnant* Horst-Arno Fenski in 1943. The boat was badly damaged by an American air raid on Toulon and was decommissioned in March 1944.

U-73

Type VIIB

Commissioned on 31 October 1940, U-73 made five Atlantic patrols with the 7th Flotilla before moving to the Mediterranean, where she made 10 patrols with the 29th Flotilla.

During the action against Convoy MW 10 in March 1942, U-73's stern was shattered by a bombing attack and the boat was forced to limp the 1930km (1200 miles) back to La Spezia on the surface. In August 1942 the U-boat was part of the force deployed against Operation *Pedestal*, the major British effort to support a vital supply convoy trying to reach the beleaguered island of Malta. Early in the afternoon of the 11th, U-73 closed with the convoy near Majorca and sank the 22,960-tonne (22,600-ton) aircraft carrier HMS *Eagle*. Of the warship's crew of 1160, 260 died. U-73 tried to attack the escort force on its return from Malta, but was unsuccessful, failing to hit the damaged cruiser HMS *Nigeria,* which had earlier been torpedoed by the Italian submarine *Axum.*

In August 1943, U-73 claimed two hits against the cruiser USS *Philadelphia* off the north coast of Sicily,

U-73 TIMETABLE

Patrol Dates	Operational Area	Ships Sunk
8 Feb 1941 – 2 Mar 1941	W of British Isles	1
25 Mar 1941 – 24 Apr 1941	SW of Ireland	4
20 May 1941 – 24 Jun 1941	*Bismarck* escort N Atlantic/S Iceland	0
29 Jul 1941 – 2 Aug 1941	Mission aborted due to engine trouble	0
7 Aug 1941 – 7 Sep 1941	SW of Iceland	0
11 Oct 1941 – 11 Nov 1941	SE of Greenland	0
4 Jan 1942 – 20 Jan 1942	Through Straits of Gibraltar to Messina	0
31 Jan 1942 – 26 Feb 1942	Off Cyrenaica	0
16 Mar 1942 – 26 Mar 1942	Against convoy MW 10 Alexandria/Malta	0
20 Oct 1942 – 19 Nov 1942	W Med against Operation *Torch*	0
4 Aug 1942 – 5 Sep 1942	Against Malta resupply convoy *Pedestal*	1
22 Dec 1942 – 13 Jan 1943	W Mediterranean off Algeria	1
12 Jun 1943 – 1 Jul 1943	Off Algerian coast	1
2 Aug 1943 – 29 Aug 1943	Off N coast of Sicily	0
5 Oct 1943 – 30 Oct 1943	Special operations	0
4 Dec 1943 – 16 Dec 1943	Off Algerian coast	0

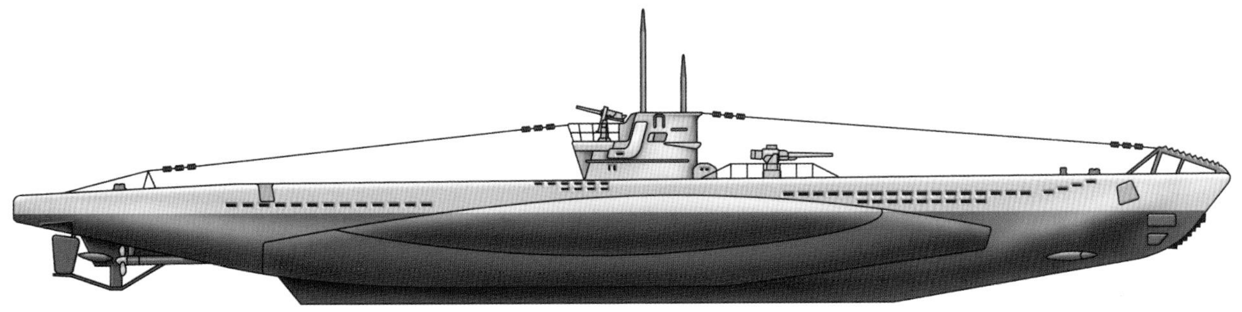

Specifications

Crew: 44
Powerplant: Diesel/electric
Max Speed: 31.9/14.8km/hr (17.2/8kt) s/d
Surface Range: 12,040km (6500nm)
Displacement: 765/871t (753/857 tons) s/d
Dimensions (length/beam/draught): 66.5 x 6.2 x 4.7m (218.1 x 20.34 x 15.4ft)
Commissioned: 31 Oct 1940
Armament: 14 torpedoes (4 bow/1 stern tubes); 1 x 8.8cm (3.5in) and 1 x 2cm (0.8in) guns

▲ **U-73**

Type VIIB

Type VIIB boats lacked the range of later variants, but in the relatively short-range war that was fought in the Mediterranean this was not a major handicap. U-73 was a particularly busy boat, making at least 16 combat patrols.

U-73 Commanders

Kptlt. Helmut Rosenbaum *(Sep 1940 – Sep 1942)*

Kptlt Horst Deckert *(Oct 1942 – Dec 1943)*

but they were never confirmed. In October 1943, U-73 landed an agent on the coast of Algeria. During the patrol she was attacked by the British submarine HMS *Ultimatum*, which claimed, wrongly, to have sunk the German boat.

U-73 was sunk on 16 December 1943 in the Mediterranean near Oran, Algeria, by depth charges and gunfire from the destroyers USS *Woolsey* and USS *Trippe*. Sixteen of the crew were killed and 34 survived.

U-371

Type VIIC

Laid down at Howaldtswerke Kiel in November 1939, U-371 commissioned in March 1941. She served with 1st Flotilla in the Atlantic and with 23rd and 29th Flotillas in the Mediterranean.

On her first patrol U-371 claimed to have torpedoed a large ship in the central Atlantic in addition to the Norwegian MV *Vigrid*, but no Allied loss has ever been confirmed.

In October 1943, U-371 claimed a ship to have 'probably been sunk' in addition to the American merchantman *James Russell Lowell*, the minesweeper HMS *Hythe* and the destroyer USS *Bristol*, but the attack has never been confirmed.

On her last patrol, U-371 fell victim to the first Allied 'Swamp' attack. During more than 24 hours of evasive manoeuvres, *Oberleutnant* Fenski took U-371 to a depth of over 200m (655ft) before eventually being forced to the surface. The crew abandoned the boat and it was destroyed.

Fate

U-371 was sunk at 04:09 on 4 May 1944 in the Mediterranean north of Constantine by depth charges from the destroyer escorts USS *Pride* and USS *Joseph E. Campbell*, the French destroyer escort *Sénégalais* and the escort destroyer HMS *Blankney*. Three crewmen were killed and 49 survivors were taken prisoner.

U-371 Commanders

Oblt. Heinrich Driver *(Mar 1941 – Apr 1942)*
Kptlt. Karl-Otto Weber *(Mar 1942 – Apr 1942)*
Kptlt. Heinz-Joachim Neumann *(Apr – May 1942)*
Kptlt. Waldemar Mehl *(May 1942 – Apr 1944)*
Oblt. Horst-Arno Fenski *(Apr 1944 – May 1944)*

U-371 TIMETABLE

Patrol Dates	Operational Area	Ships Sunk
5 Jun 1941 – 1 July 1941	W of British Isles	1
23 Jul 1941 – 19 Aug 1941	SW of Ireland	2
16 Sep 1941 – 24 Oct 1941	Transit from Brest to Mediterranean	0
4 Dec 1941 – 10 Jan 1942	E Mediterranean off Egyptian coast	0
4 Mar 1942 – 25 Mar 1942	Off Tobruk	0
21 Apr 1942 – 9 May 1942	E Mediterranean	0
1 Jul 1942 – 7 Jul 1942	Central Mediterranean	0
5 Sep 1942 – 18 Sep 1942	E Mediterranean	0
12 Oct 1942 – 16 Oct 1942	Transit from Salamis to Pola	0
1 Dec 1942 – 4 Dec 1942	Transit from Pola to Messina	0
7 Dec 1942 – 10 Jan 1943	W Mediterranean	1
14 Feb 1943 – 3 Mar 1943	Algerian coast	1
7 Apr 1943 – 11 May 1943	Algerian coast	1
3 Jul 1943 – 12 Jul 1943	W Mediterranean	0
22 Jul 1943 – 11 Aug 1943	Algerian coast	1
21 Aug 1943 – 3 Sep 1943	W Mediterranean	0
7 Oct 1943 – 28 Oct 1943	Algerian coast	3
15 Nov 1943 – 23 Nov 1943	W Mediterranean	0
22 Jan 1944 – 13 Feb 1944	Off the Anzio beachhead	0
4 Mar 1944 – 25 Mar 1944	Algerian coast	2
23 Apr 1944 – 4 May 1944	Algerian coast	0

U-559

TYPE VIIC

Laid down at Blohm und Voss, Hamburg, on 1 February 1940, U-559 was commisioned on 27 February 1941 under the command of *Kapitänleutnant* Hans Heidtmann.

ON HER SECOND PATROL in the Atlantic, U-559 sank one ship. The boat also claimed another ship sunk and a third damaged, but neither were confirmed. After transiting the Straits of Gibraltar and covering the Mediterranean from west to east on her third patrol to join the 23rd Flotilla, U-559 claimed a hit on a British destroyer off Alexandria, but it has never been confirmed. In February 1941, U-559 observed two hits on an unidentified freighter already suffering from torpedo or bomb damage, but no confirmation of this has ever been made either. The boat transferred to the 29th Flotilla in April 1942, when the 23rd Flotilla was disbanded at Salamis.

U-559 Commander

Kptlt. Hans Heidtmann

(Feb 1941 – Oct 1942)

Fate

U-559 was sunk on 30 October 1942 in the Mediterranean northeast of Port Said by depth charges from the destroyers HMS *Pakenham*, HMS *Petard* and HMS *Hero*, the escort destroyers HMS *Dulverton* and HMS *Hurworth*, and a Vickers Wellesley aircraft. Seven crewmembers died and 38 survived.

For more than 10 months, Allied codebreakers had been unable to crack the latest Enigma code used by U-boats. However, the sinking of U-559 enabled them to make a breakthrough. The wreck was boarded by three men from HMS *Petard*. They secured several secret documents and codebooks and were trying to recover the Enigma machine when the boat sank, taking two of the three men to their deaths. The items recovered greatly aided Allied codebreakers in their attempts to crack the Enigma code.

U-559 TIMETABLE

Patrol Dates	Operational Area	Ships Sunk
4 Jun 1941 – 5 Jul 1941	Denmark Strait/North Atlantic	0
26 Jul 1941 – 22 Aug 1941	Central N Atlantic	1
20 Sep 1941 – 20 Oct 1941	Transit from St Nazaire to Mediterranean	0
24 Nov 1941 – 4 Dec 1941	E Mediterranean	1
8 Dec 1941 – 31 Dec 1941	Off Tobruk	2
16 Feb 1942 – 26 Feb 1942	Off Bardia	0
4 Mar 1942 – 21 Mar 1942	E Mediterranean	0
24 Mar 1942 – 12 May 1942	Transit from Salamis to Pola and back	0
18 May 1942 – 22 Jun 1942	E Mediterranean	1
29 Aug 1942 – 21 Sep 1942	Central Mediterranean	0
29 Sep 1942 – 30 Oct 1942	E Mediterranean	0

Swamp tactics

1943–44

U-371, on its first patrol commanded by Oblt. Horst-Arno Fenski, was unlucky enough to be the first victim of a new and highly effective Allied sub-hunting tactic in the Mediterranean.

Known as the Swamp, this tactic took advantage of the fact that by 1943 the Allies had a large number of air and sea bases in the Mediterranean, from Gibraltar along the North African coast to Egypt and the Levant and on Malta. Overwhelming Allied strength meant that the area in which a U-boat was known or suspected to be operating could be packed with surface escorts and patrol aircraft in a very short time. The searchers knew where the U-boat had been if it had made an attack. They could make a fair estimate of its course after an attack – basically away from Allied bases and shipping routes. They knew how fast a U-boat could travel underwater, which meant that they could make an estimate of its position and where it would probably be over the next few hours. They would then systematically and continually search the area, forcing the submarine to remain beneath the waves until its batteries ran out of charge and it had try to escape on the surface.

U-371 was spotted recharging her batteries on the surface off Djidjelli on the Algerian coast on the night of 2/3 May 1944. The area was immediately swamped with six escorts and three aircraft squadrons. They hunted the boat until the early morning of 4 May, when Oblt. Fenski had to surface to save his crew. He managed to fight back, and torpedoed and damaged the US destroyer escort USS *Menges* and the French destroyer escort *Sénégalais* before finally being forced to abandon his boat.

Redoubled efforts

The longest Swamp operation occurred in May 1944. On 14 May, U-616 commanded by Oblt. Siegfried Koitschka attacked the convoy GUS 39 and damaged two Allied merchantmen. Immediately the Allies began to swamp the area. Two convoy escorts gained a contact, and three US Navy destroyers left Oran to join the hunt. U-616 torpedoed two more merchantmen, and four more American destroyers joined the hunt along with British and US aircraft.

The U-boat temporarily eluded the searching Allied forces, but over the next two days continuous relays of Hudsons from No. 500 Sqn RAF made sporadic contact and damaged the boat in repeated depth-charge attacks. Late on 16 May the boat was spotted by an RAF Wellington out of Gibraltar, and the destroyers closed in at high speed. Forced to the surface early on 17 May, U-616 was dispatched by gunfire in less than five minutes.

Only five hours later, U-960, commanded by Oblt. Günther Heinrich, unsuccessfully attacked the destroyer USS *Ellyson*, which was carrying survivors from U-616, off Oran. Another Swamp operation was called. U-960 was sunk two days later on 19 May, northwest of Algiers, by depth charges from the destroyers USS *Niblack* and USS *Ludlow* and from Vickers Wellingtons and Lockheed Venturas of Nos. 36 and 500 Sqns RAF. Twenty of the boat's 51 crewmembers were picked up alive.

BOATS THAT SERVED WITH 29TH FLOTILLA (52 BOATS)

U-Boat	Type	Commissioned	Flotilla(s)	Patrols	Fate
U-29	VIIA	16-Nov-36	1 Sep 1943 – 30 Nov 1943 from 24 Flottille (training)	7 patrols. 11 ships sunk: total 62,765 GRT; 1 aircraft carrier (HMS *Courageous*) sunk: total 22,861t/22,500 tons	to 21. Flottille
U-73	VIIB	31-Oct-40	1 Jan 1942 – 16 Dec 1943 from 7. Flottille	16 patrols. 8 ships sunk: total 43,945 GRT; 4 warships (including aircraft carrier HMS *Eagle*) sunk: total 23,315t/22,947 tons; 3 ships damaged: total 22,928 GRT	Sunk 16 Dec 1943 in the Mediterranean near Oran by depth charges and gunfire from the destroyers USS *Woolsey* and USS *Trippe*. 16 dead and 34 survivors
U-74	VIIB	31-Oct-40	1 Dec 1941 – 2 May 1942 from 7. Flottille	8 patrols. 4 ships sunk: total 24,694 GRT; 1 warship sunk: total 940t/925 tons; 1 ship damaged: total 97 GRT; 1 auxiliary warship damaged: total 11,402 GRT	Sunk with all hands 2 May 1942 east of Cartagena, Spain, by depth charges from the destroyers HMS *Wishart*, HMS *Wrestler* and depth charges from an RAF Catalina of No. 202 Sqn. 47 dead
U-77	VIIC	18-Jan-41	1 May 1942 – 28 Mar 1943 from 23. Flottille	12 patrols. 14 ships sunk: total 31,186 GRT; 1 warship sunk: total 1067t/1050 tons; 1 ship damaged beyond repair: total 5222 GRT; 2 ships damaged: total 5384 GRT; 2 warships damaged: total 2926t/2880 tons	Sunk 28 Mar 1943 east of Cartagena, Spain, by 4 depth charges and 1 bomb from 2 Hudson aircraft of Nos. 48 and 233 Sqns. 38 dead and 9 survivors
U-81	VIIC	26-Apr-41	1 Dec 1941 – 9 Jan 1944 from 1. Flottille	17 patrols. 23 ships sunk: total 39,711 GRT; 1 auxiliary warship sunk: total 1150 GRT; 1 aircraft carrier (HMS *Ark Royal*, 13 Nov 1941) sunk: total 22,963t/22,600 tons; 1 ship damaged beyond repair: total 5917 GRT; 2 ships damaged: total 14,143 GRT	Sunk 9 Jan 1944 at Pola by US bombs. 2 dead. Raised 22 Apr 1944 and broken up
U-83	VIIB	8-Feb-41	1 May 1942 – 4 Mar 1943 from 23. Flottille	12 patrols. 5 ships sunk: total 8425 GRT; 1 auxiliary warship sunk: total 91 GRT; 1 ship damaged: total 2590 GRT; 1 auxiliary warship damaged: total 6746 GRT	Sunk with all hands 4 Mar 1943 southeast of Cartagena by 3 depth charges from an RAF Hudson. 50 dead
U-97	VIIC	28-Sep-40	1 May 1942 – 16 Jun 1943 from 23. Flottille	13 patrols. 15 ships sunk: total 64,404 GRT; 1 auxiliary warship sunk: total 6833 GRT; 1 ship damaged: total 9718 GRT	Sunk west of Haifa 16 Jun 1943 by depth charges from an Australian Hudson aircraft of No. 459 Sqn. 27 dead and 21 survivors
U-205	VIIC	3-May-41	1 Nov 1941 – 17 Feb 1943 from 3. Flottille	11 patrols. 1 ship sunk: total 2623 GRT; 1 warship sunk: total 5537t/5450 tons	Sunk 17 Feb 1943 north of Cyrene in the Mediterranean by depth charges from the destroyer HMS *Paladin* and a South African Bisley (Blenheim) aircraft. 8 dead and 42 survivors
U-223	VIIC	6-Jun-42	1 Nov 1943 – 30 Mar 1944 from 6. Flottille	6 patrols. 2 ships sunk: total 12,556 GRT; 1 warship sunk: total 1966t/1935 tons; 1 ship damaged beyond repair: total 4970 GRT; 1 warship damaged beyond repair: total 1321t/1300 tons	Sunk 30 Mar 1944 in the Mediterranean north of Palermo by depth charges from destroyers HMS *Laforey* and HMS *Tumult* and escort destroyers HMS *Hambledon* and HMS *Blencathra*. 23 dead and 27 survivors

BOATS THAT SERVED WITH 29TH FLOTILLA (52 BOATS)

U-Boat	Type	Commissioned	Flotilla(s)	Patrols	Fate
U-230	VIIC	24-Oct-42	1 Dec 1943 – 21 Aug 1944	8 patrols. 1 ship sunk: total 2868 GRT; 3 warships sunk: total 3643t/3585 tons	Ran aground 21 Aug 1944 in the Toulon roads during the Allied invasion of southern France. Scuttled. No casualties – 50 survivors
U-301	VIIC	9-May-42	1 Jan 1943 – 21 Jan 1943 from 1. Flottille	3 patrols	Sunk 21 Jan 1943 in the Mediterranean west of Bonifacio, torpedoed by the submarine HMS *Sahib*. 45 dead and 1 survivor
U-303	VIIC	7-Jul-42	1 Apr 1943 – 21 May 1943 from 7. Flottille	2 patrols. 1 ship sunk: total 4959 GRT	Sunk 21 May 1943 in the Mediterranean south of Toulon by torpedoes from the submarine HMS *Sickle*. 20 dead and 28 survivors
U-331	VIIC	31-Mar-41	15 Apr 1942 – 17 Nov 1942 from 23. Flottille	10 patrols. 1 auxiliary warship sunk: total 9135 GRT; 1 battleship (HMS *Barham*) sunk: total 31,599t/31,100 tons; 1 warship damaged: total 378t/372 tons	Badly damaged 17 Nov 1942 in the Mediterranean north of Algiers by an RAF Hudson. U-331 signalled surrender, but was sunk by a torpedo from an Albacore of HMS *Formidable*. 32 dead and 17 survivors
U-343	VIIC	18-Feb-43	1 Feb 1944 – 10 Mar 1944 from 3. Flottille	4 patrols	Sunk with all hands 10 Mar 1944 in the Mediterranean south of Sardinia by depth charges from the minesweeper/trawler HMS *Mull*. 51 dead
U-371	VIIC	15-Mar-41	15 Apr 1942 – 4 May 1944 from 23. Flottille	19 patrols. 9 ships sunk: total 57,235 GRT; 1 auxiliary warship sunk: total 545 GRT; 2 warships sunk: total 2322t/2286 tons; 2 ships damaged beyond repair: total 13,341 GRT; 4 ships damaged: total 28,072 GRT; 2 warships damaged: total 2540t/2500 tons	Scuttled on 4 May 1944 in the Mediterranean north of Constantine after attack by depth charges from destroyer escorts USS *Pride* and USS *Joseph E. Campbell*, French destroyer escort *Sénégalais* and escort destroyer HMS *Blankney*. 3 dead and 49 survivors
U-372	VIIC	19-Apr-41	14 Dec 1941 – 4 Aug 1942 from 1. Flottille	8 patrols. 3 ships sunk: total 11,751 GRT; 1 auxiliary warship sunk: total 14,650 GRT	Sunk 4 Aug 1942 southwest of Haifa by depth charges from destroyers HMS *Sikh* and HMS *Zulu*, escort destroyers HMS *Croome* and HMS *Tetcott*, and a Wellington of No. 221 Sqn RAF. All 48 crew survived
U-374	VIIC	21-Jun-41	14 Dec 1941 – 12 Jan 1942 from 1. Flottille	3 patrols. 1 ship sunk: total 3349 GRT; 2 auxiliary warships sunk: total 992 GRT	Sunk 12 Jan 1942 in the western Mediterranean east of Cape Spartivento, torpedoed by submarine HMS *Unbeaten*. 42 dead and 1 survivor
U-375	VIIC	19-Jul-41	1 Jan 1942 – 30 Jul 1943 from 3. Flottille	11 patrols. 9 ships sunk: total 16,847 GRT; 1 ship damaged beyond repair: total 6288 GRT; 1 warship damaged: total 2693t/2650 tons	Sunk with all hands 30 Jul 1943 northwest of Malta by depth charges from the submarine chaser USS *PC-624*. 46 dead
U-380	VIIC	22-Dec-41	1 Dec 1942 – 11 Mar 1944 from 6. Flottille	12 patrols. 2 ships sunk: total 14,063 GRT; 1 ship damaged beyond repair: total 7178 GRT; 1 ship damaged: total 7191 GRT	Sunk 11 Mar 1944 in the Mediterranean near Toulon by US bombs. 1 dead
U-407	VIIC	18-Dec-41	1 Dec 1942 – 19 Sep 1944 from 9. Flottille	12 patrols. 3 ships sunk: total 26,892 GRT; 1 ship damaged beyond repair: total 7176 GRT; 1 ship damaged: total 6207 GRT; 2 warships damaged: total 18,187t/17,900 tons	Sunk 19 Sep 1944 south of the Greek island of Milos by depth charges from the destroyers HMS *Troubridge*, HMS *Terpsichore* and the Polish destroyer *Garland*. 5 dead and 48 survivors
U-409	VIIC	21-Jan-42	1 Jul 1943 – 12 Jul 1943 from 9. Flottille	6 patrols. 3 ships sunk: total 16,199 GRT; 1 ship damaged: total 7519 GRT	Sunk 12 Jul 1943 northeast of Algiers by depth charges from the destroyer HMS *Inconstant*. 11 dead and 37 survivors
U-410	VIIC	23-Feb-42	1 Jun 1943 – 11 Mar 1944 from 7. Flottille	7 patrols. 7 ships sunk: total 47,244 GRT; 2 warships sunk: total 7006t/6895 tons; 1 ship damaged beyond repair: total 3722 GRT; 1 ship damaged: total 7134 GRT	Damaged beyond repair 11 Mar 1944 at Toulon in the south of France by USAAF bombs
U-414	VIIC	1-Jul-42	1 May 1943 – 25 May 1943 from 6. Flottille	3 patrols. 1 ship sunk: total 5979 GRT; 1 ship damaged: total 7134 GRT	Sunk with all hands 25 May 1943 in the western Mediterranean by depth charges from the corvette HMS *Vetch*. 47 dead
U-421	VIIC	13-Jan-43	1 Apr 1944 – 29 Apr 1944 from 9. Flottille	2 patrols	Sunk 29 Apr 1944 in Toulon by US bombs
U-431	VIIC	5-Apr-41	1 Jan 1942 – 21 Oct 1943 from 3. Flottille	16 patrols. 7 ships sunk: total 9752 GRT; 1 auxiliary warship sunk: total 313 GRT; 2 warships sunk: total 3605t/3548 tons; 1 ship damaged beyond repair: total 6415 GRT; 1 ship damaged: total 3560 GRT; 1 warship damaged: total 457t/450 tons	Sunk with all hands 21 Oct 1943 near Algiers by depth charges from a Vickers Wellington of No. 179 Sqn RAF. 52 dead
U-443	VIIC	18-Apr-42	1 Jan 1943 – 23 Feb 1943 from 9. Flottille	3 patrols. 3 ships sunk: total 19,435 GRT; 1 warship sunk: total 1104t/1087 tons	Sunk with all hands 23 Feb 1943 in the Mediterranean near Algiers by depth charges from escort destroyers HMS *Bicester*, HMS *Lamerton* and HMS *Wheatland*. 48 dead
U-450	VIIC	12-Sep-42	1 Dec 1943 – 10 Mar 1944 from 9. Flottille	4 patrols	Sunk 10 Mar 1944 off the Italian coast south of Ostia by depth charges from escort destroyers HMS *Blankney*, HMS *Blencathra*, HMS *Brecon* and HMS *Exmoor* and destroyer USS *Madison*. No casualties – 42 survivors
U-453	VIIC	26-Jun-41	1 Jan 1942 – 21 May 1944 from 7. Flottille	17 patrols. 9 ships sunk: total 23,289 GRT; 1 warship sunk: total 848t/835 tons; 1 warship damaged beyond repair: total 1732t/1705 tons; 2 ships damaged: total 16,610 GRT	Sunk 21 May 1944 in the Ionian Sea northeast of Cape Spartivento by depth charges from destroyers HMS *Termagant* and HMS *Tenacious* and escort destroyer HMS *Liddesdale*. 1 dead and 51 survivors
U-455	VIIC	21-Aug-41	1 Mar 1944 – 6 Apr 1944 from 7. Flottille	10 patrols. 3 ships sunk: total 17,685 GRT	Missing with all hands in the Mediterranean on or after 2 Apr 1944, while returning from a patrol off Algiers. 51 dead. May have been sunk 6 Apr 1944 near La Spezia by a German mine
U-458	VIIC	12-Dec-41	1 Nov 1942 – 22 Aug 1943 from 3. Flottille	7 patrols. 2 ships sunk: total 7584 GRT	Sunk 22 Aug 1943 in the Mediterranean southeast of Pantelleria by depth charges from escort destroyer HMS *Easton* and Greek escort destroyer *Pindos*. 8 dead and 39 survivors
U-466	VIIC	17-Jun-42	1 Apr 1944 – 19 Aug 1944 from 3. Flottille	5 patrols	Damaged at Toulon 5 Jul 1944 by bombs from USAAF B-24s. Scuttled 19 Aug 1944 during the Allied invasion of southern France
U-471	VIIC	5-May-43	1 May 1944 – 6 Aug 1944 from 1. Flottille	3 patrols	Bombed in dry dock 6 Aug 1944 in Toulon by USAAF B-24 Liberator. Raised in 1945 and entered French service as the *Millé*. Redesignated Q339, and stricken 9 Jul 1963

BOATS THAT SERVED WITH 29TH FLOTILLA (52 BOATS)

U-Boat	Type	Commissioned	Flotilla(s)	Patrols	Fate
U-557	VIIC	13-Feb-41	5 Dec 1941 – 16 Dec 1941 from 1. Flottille	4 patrols. 6 ships sunk: total 31,729 GRT; 1 warship (HMS *Galatea*) sunk: total 5304t/5220 tons	Sank with all hands 16 Dec 1941 in the Mediterranean west of Crete, after being rammed by the Italian torpedo boat *Orione*, which had mistaken the U-boat for a British submarine. 43 dead
U-559	VIIC	27-Feb-41	15 Apr 1942 – 30 Oct 1942 from 23. Flottille	11 patrols. 4 ships sunk: total 11,811 GRT; 1 warship sunk: total 1077t/1060 tons	Sunk 30 Oct 1942 northeast of Port Said by depth charges from destroyers HMS *Pakenham*, HMS *Petard* and HMS *Hero*, escort destroyers HMS *Dulverton* and HMS *Hurworth*, and an RAF Wellesley. 7 dead and 38 survivors. Boarded by three British sailors, who recovered vital Enigma material before the boat sank, taking two of the boarders to their deaths
U-562	VIIC	20-Mar-41	1 Jan 1942 – 19 Feb 1943 from 1. Flottille	9 patrols. 6 ships sunk: total 37,287 GRT; 1 ship damaged: total 3359 GRT	Sunk with all hands 19 Feb 1943 in the Mediterranean northeast of Benghazi by depth charges from destroyer HMS *Isis*, escort destroyer HMS *Hursley* and a Wellington of No. 38 Sqn RAF. 49 dead
U-565	VIIC	10-Apr-41	1 Jan 1942 – 24 Sep 1944 from 1. Flottille	21 patrols. 3 ships sunk: total 11,347 GRT; 3 warships sunk (including cruiser HMS *Naiad* and HM Submarine *Simoom*): total 7829t/7705 tons; 3 ships damaged: total 33,862 GRT	Badly damaged by US bombs 19 Sep 1944 at Piraeus (Athens). 5 crewmen killed. Scuttled five days later
U-568	VIIC	1-May-41	1 Jan 1942 – 29 May 1942 from 3. Flottille	5 patrols. 1 ship sunk: total 6023 GRT; 2 warships sunk: total 1880t/1850 tons; 1 warship damaged: total 1656t/1630 tons	Sunk 29 May 1942 northeast of Tobruk by depth charges from destroyer HMS *Hero* and escort destroyers HMS *Eridge* and HMS *Hurworth*. No casualties – 47 survivors
U-573	VIIC	5-Jun-41	1 Jan 1942 – 2 May 1942	4 patrols. 1 ship sunk: total 5289 GRT	Damaged northwest of Algiers by depth charges from a Hudson of No. 233 Sqn RAF. 1 dead and 43 survivors. Interned at Cartagena 2 May 1942. Sold to Spain 2 Aug 1942. Became the Spanish submarine G 7 (later S-01). In commission until 1971 – the last WWII U-boat in service
U-577	VIIC	3-Jul-41	1 Jan 1942 – 15 Jan 1942 from 7. Flottille	3 patrols	Sunk with all hands 15 Jan 1942 northwest of Mersa Matruh by depth charges from a Royal Navy Swordfish of No. 815 Sqn. 43 dead. Previously credited to an RAF Sunderland on 9 Jan, which actually attacked U-568, causing minor damage
U-586	VIIC	4-Sep-41	1 Mar 1944 – 5 Jul 1944 from 6. Flottille	12 patrols. 2 ships sunk: total 12,716 GRT; 1 ship damaged: total 9057 GRT	Sunk 5 Jul 1944 at Toulon by bombs from USAAF B-24s of the 233rd BS
U-593	VIIC	23-Oct-41	1 Nov 1942 – 13 Dec 1943 from 7. Flottille	16 patrols. 9 ships sunk: total 38,290 GRT; 3 warships sunk: total 2949t/2902 tons; 1 ship damaged b/r: total 8426 GRT; 1 warship damaged b/r: total 1651t/1625 tons; 1 ship damaged: total 4853 GRT; 1 warship damaged: total 1651t/1625 tons	Sunk 13 Dec 1943 after a 32-hour chase in the western Mediterranean, by depth charges from the destroyer USS *Wainwright* and the escort destroyer HMS *Calpe*. No casualties – 51 survivors
U-596	VIIC	13-Nov-41	19 Nov 1942 – 24 Sep 1944 from 3. Flottille	12 patrols. 12 ships sunk: total 41,411 GRT; 1 warship sunk: total 250t/246 tons; 2 ships damaged: total 14,180 GRT	Scuttled 24 Sep 1944 Skaramanga Bay, Greece, after damage by US bombs. 1 crewman killed
U-602	VIIC	29-Dec-41	1 Jan 1943 – 19 Apr 1943 from 7. Flottille	4 patrols. 1 warship damaged beyond repair: total 1565t/1540 tons	Missing with all hands on or after 19 Apr 1943, when last message was sent from north of Oran. 48 dead. Wreck found in 2005 off the coast of Ibiza. Loss previously credited to an RAF Hudson, but that attack was against U-453 and caused no damage
U-605	VIIC	15-Jan-42	1 Nov 1942 – 14 Nov 1942 from 9. Flottille	3 patrols. 3 ships sunk: total 8409 GRT	Sunk with all hands 14 Nov 1942 near Algiers by depth charges from an RAF Hudson of No. 233 Sqn. 46 dead. Loss previously credited to corvettes HMS *Lotus* and HMS *Poppy* 13 Nov 1942, but in fact they attacked U-77, causing minor damage
U-616	VIIC	2-Apr-42	1 Jun 1943 – 17 May 1944 from 6. Flottille	9 patrols. 2 warships sunk: total 2216t/2181 tons; 2 ships damaged: total 17,754 GRT	Sunk 17 May 1944 east of Cartagena after a three-day battle with the destroyers USS *Nields*, USS *Gleaves*, USS *Ellyson*, USS *Macomb*, USS *Hambleton*, USS *Rodman* and USS *Emmons*, and an RAF Wellington. No casualties – 53 survivors
U-617	VIIC	9-Apr-42	1 Dec 1942 – 12 Sep 1943 from 7. Flottille	7 patrols. 8 ships sunk: total 25,879 GRT; 1 auxiliary warship sunk: total 810 GRT; 2 warships sunk: total 3759t/3700 tons	Ran aground in the Mediterranean near Melilla 12 Sep 1943, attacked by RAF Hudsons and Royal Navy Swordfish. Destroyed by gunfire from corvette HMS *Hyacinth* and minesweeper HMAS *Wollongong*. No casualties – 49 survivors
U-642	VIIC	1-Oct-42	1 Dec 1943 – 5 Jul 1944 from 6. Flottille	4 patrols. 1 ship sunk: total 2125 GRT	Sunk in port 5 July 1944 at Toulon by US bombs
U-652	VIIC	3-Apr-41	1 Jan 1942 – 2 Jun 1942 from 3. Flottille	8 patrols. 2 ships sunk: total 8152 GRT; 1 auxiliary warship sunk: total 558 GRT; 2 warships sunk: total 2784t/2740 tons; 2 ships damaged: total 9918 GRT; 1 auxiliary warship damaged: total 10,917 GRT	Badly damaged in the Mediterranean in the Gulf of Sollum by depth charges from a Royal Navy Swordfish. Scuttled 2 Jun 1942 by torpedoes from U-81. No casualties – 46 survivors
U-660	VIIC	8-Jan-42	1 Nov 1942 – 12 Nov 1942 from 9. Flottille	3 patrols. 2 ships sunk: total 10,066 GRT; 2 ships damaged: total 10,447 GRT	Scuttled 12 Nov 1942 in the Mediterranean off Oran, after depth-charge attack by corvettes HMS *Lotus* and HMS *Starwort*. 2 dead and 45 survivors
U-755	VIIC	3-Nov-41	1 Dec 1942 – 28 May 1943 from 9. Flottille	5 patrols. 1 ship sunk: total 928 GRT; 2 auxiliary warships sunk: total 2974 GRT	Sunk 28 May 1943 northwest of Majorca by rockets from a Hudson of No. 608 Sqn RAF. 40 dead and 9 survivors (picked up by the neutral Spanish destroyer *Velasco*)
U-952	VIIC	10-Dec-42	1 Feb 1944 – 6 Aug 1944 from 3. Flottille	5 patrols. 2 ships sunk: total 13,374 GRT; 1 warship sunk: total 940t/925 tons; 1 ship damaged: total 7176 GRT	Sunk 6 Aug 1944 in Toulon by US bombs
U-967	VIIC	11-Mar-43	1 Mar 1944 – 11 Aug 1944 from 29 Flottille	3 patrols. 1 warship sunk: total 1321t/1300 tons	Scuttled 11 Aug 1944 in Toulon. 2 crewmen killed
U-969	VIIC	24-Mar-43	1 Mar 1944 – 6 Aug 1944 from 7. Flottille	3 patrols. 2 ships damaged beyond repair: total 14,352 GRT	Destroyed 6 Aug 1944 in Toulon by USAAF bombs

30 Unterseebootsflottille

The 30th Flotilla was founded in October 1942 under the command of Kptlt. Helmut Rosenbaum. The operational area was the Black Sea, where a handful of Type II boats were sent to prevent Soviet reinforcements reaching areas being attacked by the *Wehrmacht* in the summer of 1942.

GETTING THE BOATS TO the Black Sea presented a major challenge. Type IIs lacked the range to reach the area, and in any case would not have been allowed to pass through the Bosphorous.

In order to get the boats to the operational area, they had to be broken down into manageable portions. Engines, keels, conning towers, deck sections, hydroplanes, batteries and propellers were removed. The hulls were barged up the Elbe towards Dresden, where each was moved onto two 70-tonne (69-ton) vehicles for transport at less than walking pace along the autobahn to Ingolstadt.

Again mounted on the pontoons that had been transported by rail from Dresden, the stripped boats were moved by water to Linz, where they were reassembled. From there, they went under their own power downriver to Konstanza.

30TH FLOTILLA BASE LOCATION

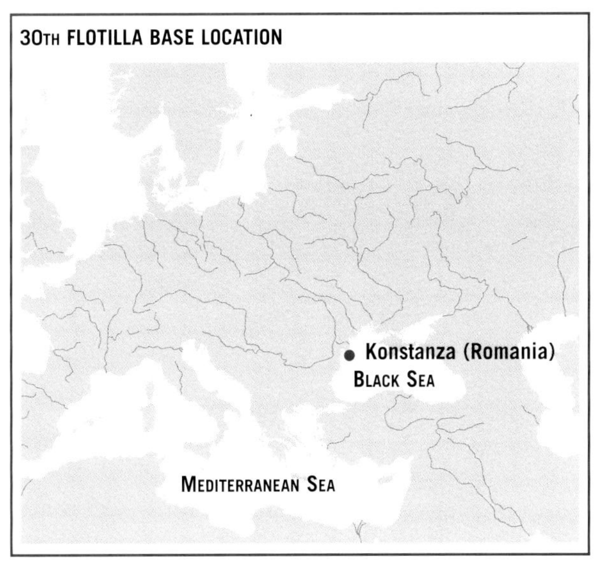

▲ **Showing the strain**

The engine room was the hottest place to work in a U-boat, and was especially cramped on the smaller Type II submarines.

Commanders

Kptlt. Helmut Rosenbaum *(Oct 1942 – May 1944)*
Kptlt. Clemens Schöler *(May 1944 – Jul 1944)*
Kptlt. Klaus Petersen *(Jul 1944 – Oct 1944)*

U-9

From 28 October 1942 to 11 August 1944, U-9 (formerly of 1st Flotilla) mounted 12 patrols in the Black Sea, operating out of Konstanza against Soviet coastal convoys off the Caucasus. In May 1943 she damaged a Soviet tanker beyond repair, and claimed another probably sunk in October. In March 1944 her crew claimed to have shot down two Soviet aircraft, and in March damaged a Soviet patrol vessel. U-9 claimed to have damaged another tanker in May 1944. U-9 was sunk in port on 20 August 1944 at Konstanza by bombs from Soviet aircraft.

U-19

From 21 January 1943 to 10 September 1944, U-19 mounted 11 patrols in the Black Sea, operating out of Konstanza against Soviet coastal convoys off the Caucasus. On 14 February 1943 she sank a Soviet freighter, and claimed damage to a passenger/troop ship on 23 March.

On 27 June 1944 U-19 sank a cargo barge, and on 29 August 1944 she sank a Soviet minesweeper after she had evacuated Konstanza following Romania's surrender. This was the last sinking by a U-boat in the Black Sea.

U-19 was scuttled on 10 September 1944 off the coast of Turkey in the Black Sea, in position 41.16N, 31.26E.

U-19 TIMETABLE (PRE-BLACK SEA DEPLOYMENT)

Patrol Dates	Operational Area	Ships Sunk
25 Aug 1939 – 15 Sep 1939	Reconnaissance of North Sea	0
14 Oct 1939 – 18 Oct 1939	Minelaying off English E Coast	3
15 Nov 1939 – 20 Nov 1939	Minelaying off Orford Ness	1
4 Jan 1940 – 12 Jan 1940	NE Scotland	1
18 Jan 1940 – 28 Jan 1940	NE coast of England	4
12 Feb 1940 – 26 Feb 1940	E of the Shetlands	0
14 Mar 1940 – 23 Mar 1940	Pentland Firth/NE Scotland	4
3 Apr 1940 – 23 Apr 1940	Norwegian waters	0
May 1940 – Apr 1942	Training	0

Soviet advances

Two other flotilla boats – U-20 and U-23 – were also scuttled on 10 September 1944 near the Turkish coast, as Soviet troops advanced from the Ukraine towards the German base at Konstanza.

U-19 Commanders

Kptlt. Viktor Schütze *(Jan 1936 – Sep 1937)*
Kptlt. Hans Meckel *(Sep 1937 – Nov 1939)*
KrvKpt. Wilhelm Müller-Arnecke *(Nov 1939 – Jan 1940)*
Kptlt. Joachim Schepke *(Jan 1940 – Apr 1940)*
Kptlt. Wilfried Prellberg *(May 1940 – Jun 1940)*
Kptlt. Peter Lohmeyer *(Jun 1940 – Oct 1940)*
Wolfgang Kaufmann *(Oct 1940 – Nov 1940)*
KrvKpt. Rudolf Schendel *(Nov 1940 – May 1941)*
Oblt. Gerhard Litterscheid *(Jun 1941 – Feb 1942)*
Kptlt. Hans-Ludwig Gaude *(Dec 1941 – Dec 1943)*
Oblt. Willy Ohlenburg *(Dec 1943 – Sep 1944)*
Oblt. Hubert Verpoorten *(Sep 1944 – Sep 1944)*

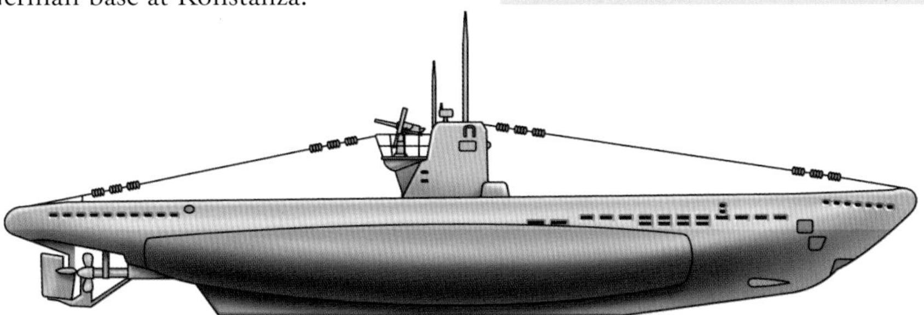

Specifications

Crew: 25
Powerplant: Diesel/electric
Max Speed: 33/15.4km/hr (17.8/8.3kt) s/d
Surface Range: 3334km (1800nm)
Displacement: 283/334t (279/329 tons) s/d
Dimensions (length/beam/draught): 42.7 x 4.1 x 3.8m (140.1 x 13.5 x 12.5ft)
Commissioned: 16 Jan 1936
Armament: 6 torpedoes (3 bow tubes); 1 x 2cm (0.8in) gun

▲ **U-19**

Type IIB

Until the arrival of the six Type II boats operated by the 30th Flotilla, supported by torpedo boats, minesweepers and other small craft, the Soviet Navy had been the dominant force in the Black Sea.

BOATS THAT SERVED WITH 30TH FLOTILLA (6 BOATS)

U-Boat	Type	Commissioned	Flotilla(s)	Patrols	Fate
U-9	IIB	21-Aug-35	1 Oct 1942 – 20 Aug 1944 from 24. Flottille	19 patrols. 7 ships sunk: total 16,669 GRT; 1 warship sunk: total 561t/552 tons; 1 warship damaged: total 419t/412 tons	Sunk by Soviet aircraft 20 Aug 1944 at Konstanza, Black Sea
U-18	IIB	4-Jan-36	6 May 1943 – 25 Aug 1944 from 24. Flottille	14 patrols. 3 ships sunk: total 1985 GRT; 1 ship damaged: total 7745 GRT; 1 warship damaged: total 57t/56 tons	Scuttled 25 Aug 1944 at Konstanza, Black Sea
U-19	IIB	16-Jan-36	1 Oct 1942 – 10 Sep 1944 from 22. Flottille	20 patrols. 14 ships sunk: total 35,430 GRT; 1 warship sunk: total 448t/441 tons	Scuttled in the Black Sea 10 Sept 1944 off the coast of Turkey
U-20	IIB	1-Feb-36	1 Oct 1942 – 10 Sep 1944 from 21. Flottille	17 patrols. 14 ships sunk: total 37,669 GRT; 1 ship damaged beyond repair: total 844 GRT; 1 ship damaged: total 1846 GRT	Scuttled in the Black Sea 10 Sept 1944 off the coast of Turkey
U-23	IIB	24-Sep-36	1 Oct 1942 – 10 Sep 1944 from 21. Flottille	16 patrols. 7 ships sunk: total 11,094 GRT; 2 warships sunk: total 1433t/1410 tons; 3 ships damaged beyond repair: total 18,199 GRT; 1 ship damaged: total 1005 GRT; 1 warship damaged: total 57t/56 tons	Scuttled in the Black Sea 10 Sept 1944 off the coast of Turkey
U-24	IIB	10-Oct-36	1 Oct 1942 – 25 Aug 1944 from 21. Flottille	20 patrols. 1 ship sunk: total 961 GRT; 5 warships sunk: total 580t/571 tons; 1 ship a total loss: total 7886 GRT; 1 ship damaged: total 7661 GRT	Scuttled 25 Aug 1944 at Konstanza, Black Sea

33 Unterseebootsflottille

The 33rd Flotilla was founded in September 1944 under the command of *Korvettenkapitän* Georg Schewe. Nominally based at Flensburg, to the north of Kiel, the flotilla's boats were in fact scattered in operating bases from France to the Far East.

THE LOSS OR ISOLATION of the main U-boat operating bases in France in 1944 saw boats being transferred, where possible, to Germany or Norway. The long-range boats that had been controlled by 12th Flotilla at Bordeaux were now operating under the auspices of the 33rd Flotilla, though a number of its boats that had been undergoing repair were trapped in encircled bases like St Nazaire. However, a good proportion of the long-range boats had been at sea during the Allied invasion of Europe – operating in such diverse locations as off the South American coast, off South Africa, in the Indian Ocean and the Arabian Sea – or were alongside in the Japanese-held ports of Penang, Singapore and Batavia or at Kobe in the Home Islands.

33RD FLOTILLA BASE LOCATION – EUROPE

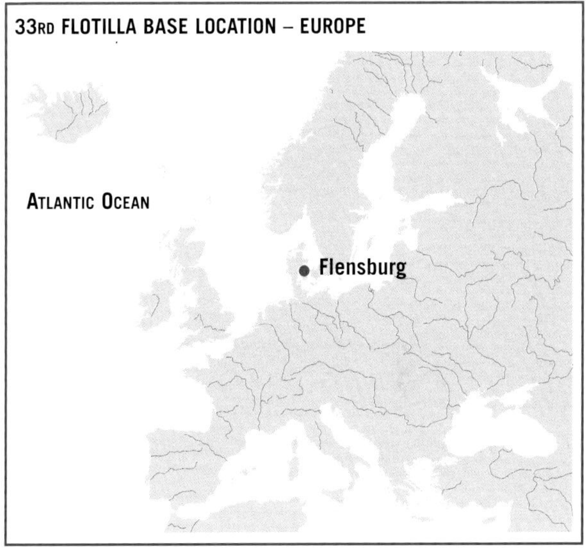

33RD FLOTILLA (1944–45)

Type	Boats assigned
Type VIIC (incl 4 x Type VIIC/41)	18
Type IXC	3
Type IXC/40	41
Type IXD2 (incl 1 x Type IXD1)	9
Type XB	2
Italian UIT	2

U-boats still mounted offensive patrols from these bases, but at least as important was their transport function. A submarine will never make a good freighter, but the large Type IXD and Type XB boats could bring 200 tonnes (197 tons) or so of strategic materials, which would otherwise be unobtainable. Most of the boats still in the Far East when Germany surrendered in May 1945 were given to the Imperial Japanese Navy.

Commanders

Korvkpt. Georg Schewe *(Sep 1944 – Oct 1944)*

Korvkpt. Günther Kuhnke *(Oct 1944 – May 1945)*

U-857 INSIGNIA

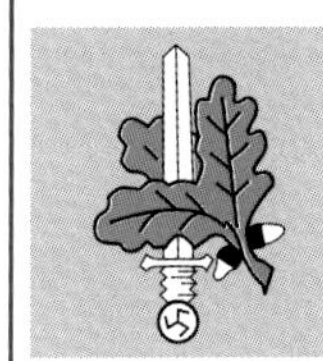

There is no photographic evidence that the 33rd Flotilla had a unit insignia. However, many of the boats used their own symbols, like the sword and oak leaves carried by the Type IXC/40 boat U-857.

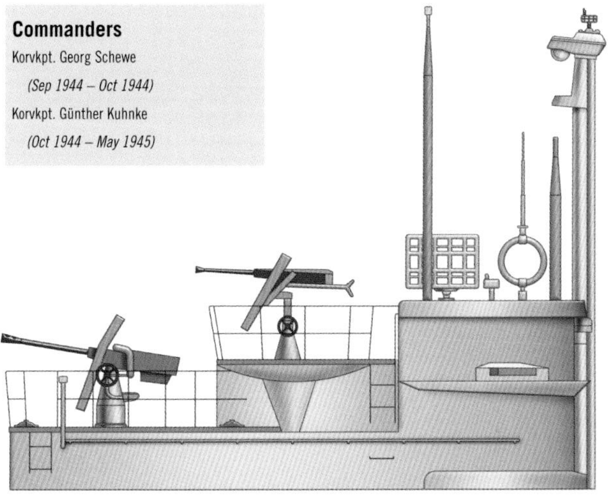

◀ Type VIIC 1945 conversion bridge

The standard weapons fit on late-war conning towers included a single or twin 3.7cm (1.5in) mount aft with two twin 2cm (0.8in) C38 mounts side by side immediately aft of the armoured bridge. The increasingly cluttered towers were also fitted with *Schnorchels*, direction-finding loops and radar-warning aerials, in addition to the two periscopes standard since the beginning of the war.

Star commanders
1944–45

Operating in the distant and challenging waters of the Indian Ocean and Southeast Asia called for great seamanship skills from the captains and crews of the 33rd Flotilla's boats.

Fregattenkapitän Ottoheinrich Junker

Born on 12 July 1905 at Freiburg, Junker joined the *Reichsmarine* with Crew 24. One of the earliest members of the U-boat arm, he commanded the early Type VII boat U-33 before the war, going on to serve with the TEK (Torpedo Testing Command) before he commissioned U-532 in November 1942. After one Atlantic mission, Junker took the submarine to the Far East as one of the *Monsun* boats. In four patrols he sank eight ships for a total of 46,895 GRT. The boat returned from Jakarta in January 1945, and surrendered in England in May of that year. Junker died on 28 July 2000, aged 95.

STAR COMMANDERS

Commander	Patrols	Ships Sunk
Fregattenkapitän Ottoheinrich Junker	4	8
Kapitänleutnant Alfred Eick	3	8

Kapitänleutnant Alfred Eick

Born on 9 March 1916 in Essen, Eick joined the *Kriegsmarine* with Crew 37. He commanded U-510 on three patrols, sinking eight ships totalling 56,972 GRT and damaging two more, as well as sinking one small auxiliary warship. He surrendered his boat at St Nazaire in May 1945.

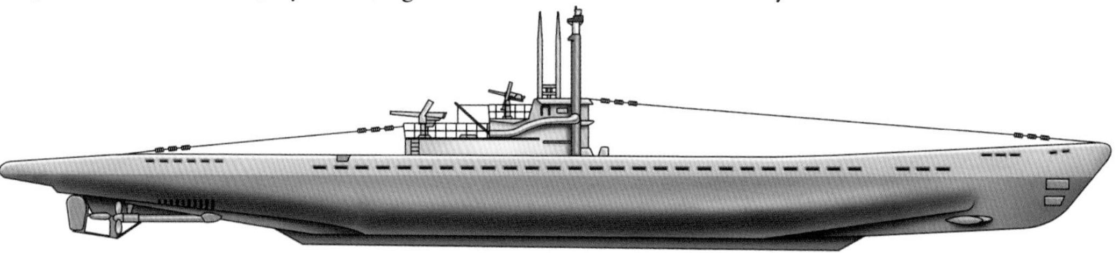

Specifications

Crew: 48–50
Powerplant: Diesel/electric
Max Speed: 33.9/13.5km/hr (18.3/7.3kt) s/d
Surface Range: 20,370km (11,000nm)
Displacement: 1138/1252t (1120/1232 tons) s/d
Dimensions (length/beam/draught): 76.8 x 6.9 x 4.7m (252 x 22.6 x 15.42ft)
Commissioned: 11 Nov 1942
Armament: 22 torpedoes (4 bow/2 stern tubes); 1 x 10.5cm (4.1in), 1 x 3.7cm (1.5in) and 1 x 2cm (0.8in) guns

▲ **U-532**
Type IXC/40
Commanded by torpedo expert Ottoheinrich Junker, U-532 surrendered at Liverpool on 10 May 1945. She was carrying a cargo of tin, rubber, wolfram and molybdenum.

U-195
Type IXD1

One of only two Type IXD1 boats, U-195 was commissioned in September 1942. The boat was fitted with experimental high-speed diesels, which proved unsatisfactory in service.

On her first patrol in South African waters, U-195 sank two ships. However, her six S-boat diesels, fitted to provide a higher surface speed, caused continual problems, and they also belched clouds of black smoke when in operation on the surface. They were replaced by standard Type IX engines, and both U-195 and her sister, U-180, were converted to transport boats. They lost their torpedo armament, and carried up to 256 tonnes (252 tons) of cargo. In May 1945, U-195 passed to Japan, becoming the I-506 on 15 July. The boat was surrendered to the Allies at Jakarta in August 1945.

U-195 Commanders

Korvkpt. Heinz Buchholz *(Sep 1942 – Oct 1943)*
Oblt. Friedrich Steinfeldt *(Apr 1944 – May 1945)*

U-195 TIMETABLE

Patrol Dates	Operational Area	Ships Sunk
20 Mar 1943 – 23 Jul 1943	South Atlantic off South Africa	3
24 Aug 1944 – 28 Dec 1944	Transit from Bordeaux to Asia	0
19 Jan 1945 – 4 March 1945	Transit to France but returned to Batavia	0

Specifications

Crew: 55
Powerplant: Diesel/electric
Max Speed: 38.5/12.8km/hr (20.8/6.9kt) s/d
Surface Range: 18,335km (9900nm)
Displacement: 1636/1828t (1610/1799 tons) s/d
Dimensions (length/beam/draught): 87.6 x 7.5 x 5.4m (287.42 x 24.58 x 17.75ft)
Commissioned: 11 Sep 1942
Armament: 24 torpedoes; 1 x 10.5cm (4.1in), 1 x 3.7cm (1.5in) and 1 x 2cm (0.8in) guns

▲ **U-195**

Type IXD1

U-195's last patrol was to be a cargo run back to France from the Dutch East Indies, but after about three weeks the boat developed a mechanical fault and was forced to return to Batavia, where she was given to the Japanese.

U-196

TYPE IXD2

Built by AG Weser at Bremen, U-196 was commissioned in September 1942 under the command of the experienced *Korvettenkapitän* Eitel-Friedrich Kentrat.

On its first patrol to the Indian Ocean, U-196 was at sea for 225 days before returning to Bordeaux, the longest submarine patrol of the war. In all that time she destroyed just two ships and damaged another.

The boat's second patrol, which ended at Penang, lasted some five months, and accounted for only one victim.

On its third patrol, under a new commander, U-196 put into Batavia before setting off into the Indian Ocean. The boat was declared missing with all hands on 1 December 1944 south of Java, just one day after setting off, and may have been lost on the day of her departure as she traversed the Sunda Strait. All 65 crew were killed.

U-196 TIMETABLE

Patrol Dates	Operational Area	Ships Sunk
13 Mar 1943 – 23 Oct 1943	Indian Ocean	2
16 Mar 1944 – 10 Aug 1944	Indian Ocean	1
30 Nov 1944 – 1 Dec 1944	East Indies	0

U-196 Commanders

Korvkpt. Eitel-Friedrich Kentrat *(Sep 1942 – Sep 1944)*
Korvkpt. Werner Striegler *(Oct 1944 – Dec 1944)*

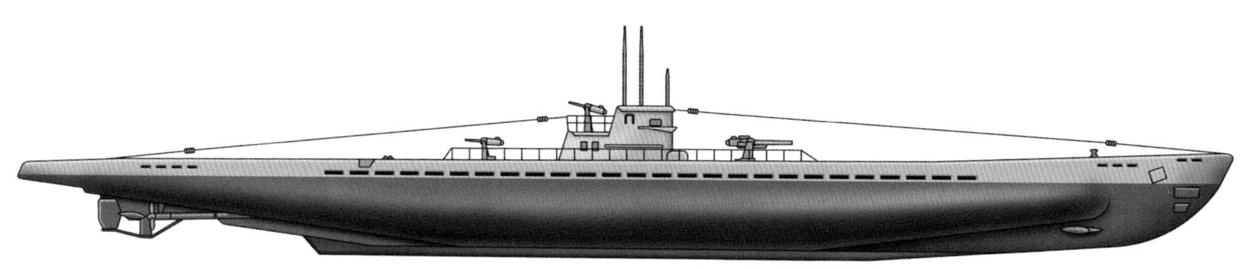

Specifications

Crew: 57

Powerplant: Diesel/electric

Max Speed: 35.6/12.8km/hr (19.2/6.9kt) s/d

Surface Range: 43,900km (23,700nm)

Displacement: 1616/1803t (1590/1775 tons) s/d

Dimensions (length/beam/draught): 87.6 x 7.5 x 5.4m (287.42 x 24.58 x 17.75ft)

Commissioned: 11 Sep 1942

Armament: 22 torpedoes; 1 x 10.5cm (4.1in), 1 x 3.7cm (1.5in) and 1 x 2cm (0.8in) guns

▲ **U-196**

Type IXD2

Although not particularly successful in terms of sinking enemy ships, U-196, under the command of Eitel-Friedrich Kentrat, mounted two of the longest U-boat patrols undertaken during World War II.

U-510

Type IXC

Laid down at Deutsche Werft, Hamburg, at the beginning of November 1940, U-510 was commissioned there just over a year later, on 25 November 1941.

After its initial training with the 4th Flotilla, U-510 was assigned to the 10th Flotilla at Lorient. After four patrols in the central and western Atlantic, the boat was sent to the Indian

U-510 TIMETABLE

Patrol Dates	Operational Area	Ships Sunk
7 Jul 1942 – 13 Sep 1942	Western Atlantic	2
14 Oct 1942 – 12 Dec 1942	Central Atlantic	0
16 Jan 1943 – 16 Apr 1943	Central Atlantic	2
3 Jun 1943 – 29 Aug 1943	Central Atlantic	3
3 Nov 1943 – 5 Apr 1944	Indian Ocean	6
12 Apr 1944 – 3 Dec 1944	Various ports in SE Asia and Japan	0
11 Jan 1945 – 23 Apr 1945	Transit from Batavia to St Nazaire	1

U-510 Commanders

Fregkpt. Karl Neitzel *(Nov 1941 – May 1943)*

Kptlt. Alfred Eick *(May 1943 – May 1945)*

Specifications

Crew: 48–50

Powerplant: Diesel/electric

Max Speed: 33.9/13.5km/hr (18.3/7.3kt) s/d

Surface Range: 20,370km (11,000nm)

Displacement: 1138/1252t (1120/1232 tons) s/d

Dimensions (length/beam/draught): 76.8 x 6.8 x 4.7m (252 x 22.31 x 15.42ft)

Commissioned: 25 Nov 1941

Armament: 22 torpedoes; 1 x 10.5cm (4.1in), 1 x 3.7cm (1.5in) and 1 x 2cm (0.8in) guns

▲ **U-510**

Type IXC

On its third patrol, U-510 attacked the Trinidad-bound convoy BT 6 to the north of Cayenne. In addition to sinking two ships totalling over 10,000 GRT, the boat torpedoed and damaged a further six vessels totalling nearly 45,000 GRT.

Ocean. Late in 1944 as part of the 33rd Flotilla the boat shuttled between Penang, Singapore, Kobe in Japan and Batavia before returning to Europe. Surrendered to French forces at St Nazaire on 12 May 1945, she was taken into French Navy use and renamed the *Bouan* in French service. U-510 was decommissioned on 1 May 1959 as the Q176, and was broken up a year later.

The surrender of U-234

Type XB

After the loss of U-233 in July 1944, it was decided not to use U-234 as a minelaying boat. She was rebuilt as a long-range transport intended to ship vital cargoes to Japanese ports.

On 25 March 1945 U-234 left Kiel and a few days later reached Kristiansand, Norway. On board was a high-value cargo, which included technical drawings of advanced weapons, an Me-262 jet fighter in crates, several high-ranking German experts on various technologies, including rocketry and jets, two Japanese naval officers – Hideo Tomonaga and Genzo Shoji – and 560kg (1230lb) of uranium oxide intended for Japanese nuclear research laboratories in Osaka and Tokyo.

On 16 April 1945, U-234 left Norway en route to Japan. With such an important cargo the submarine's commander, *Kapitänleutnant* Fehler, had to avoid any possible contact with the enemy. U-234 ran deep and submerged for two weeks after leaving Kristiansand. Only after making it into the Atlantic did Kptlt. Fehler feel sufficiently confident to surface for two hours each night.

On 10 May, U-234 picked up a shortwave transmission carrying Karl Dönitz's announcement of Germany's surrender: 'My U-boat men … you have fought like lions … lay down your arms.' Instructions were given to proceed to the nearest Allied port, but U-234 was so positioned that several possible destinations existed. Fehler decided to head to the United States. Unwilling to be captured, Hideo Tomonaga and Genzo Shoji committed suicide by taking sleeping pills.

Nuclear surprise

On 14 May an American boarding party took over and directed U-234 to Portsmouth, New Hampshire. Despite tight security, the arrival of U-234 at the docks became a major news event. Much of U-234's top secret cargo, 245 tonnes (240 tons) of documents and war materials, was shipped to Washington and opened out of sight of the press's cameras. The presence of so much uranium oxide was perhaps the biggest shock, indicating that both Germany and Japan had ongoing nuclear programmes.

▲ **U-234**

Type XB

Built as minelayers, the large Type XB boats were used more often as milchcow supply boats or as submarine transports, bringing scarce strategic materials through the tight Allied blockade of the coast of occupied Europe.

Specifications

Crew: 52

Powerplant: Diesel/electric

Max Speed: 30.4/13km/hr (16.4/7kt) s/d

Surface Range: 26,760km (14,450nm)

Displacement: 1763/2177t (1735/2143 tons) s/d

Dimensions (length/beam/draught): 89.8 x 9.2 x 4.7m (294.58 x 30.16 x 15.42ft)

Commissioned: 2 Mar 1944

Armament: 66 mines; 11 torpedoes; 1 x 10.5cm (4.1in), 1 x 3.7cm (1.5in) and 1 x 2cm (0.8in) guns

Schnorchel patrols
1944–45

The submarine *schnorchel* was invented by the Dutch just before World War II and perfected by the Germans during the war for use by U-boats.

UNTIL THE ADVENT of nuclear power, submarines were more properly described as submersibles: their limited underwater endurance meant that they were designed to operate on the surface most of the time. In the early years of the war, U-boats were safer on the surface than submerged because ASDIC and Sonar could detect boats underwater but were useless against a surface vessel. However, as the war progressed, the introduction of maritime patrol aircraft carrying ever more capable radar systems meant that a surfaced submarine became vulnerable on even the darkest of nights. As a result, U-boats were forced to spend more and more time submerged, and every time they surfaced to recharge their batteries they became targets.

Dutch invention

In 1940 the German conquest of the Netherlands gave the *Kriegsmarine* access to Dutch snorkel technology. The snorkel (*Schnorchel* in German) was a simple air tube that enabled submarines to travel at periscope depth while using diesels. In 1943, as more U-boats were lost, it was retrofitted to the VIIC and IXC classes and designed into the new XXI and XXIII types. The first boats to be fitted were U-57 and U-58, which ran trials in the Baltic in the summer of 1943. Boats began to use them operationally in early 1944, and by June 1944 about half of the boats stationed in France had them fitted. The Type VIICs U-211 and U-264 were the first operational boats to carry the equipment, but the first *Schnorchel* U-boat to leave for combat patrol was the U-539, which left France on 2 January 1944.

On Type VII boats the *Schnorchel* folded forward and was stored in a recess on the port side of the hull while on the Type IXs the recess was on the starboard side. The XXI and XXIII types both had telescopic masts that rose vertically through the conning tower close to the periscope.

Schnorchels were not perfect, however. A U-boat travelling at more than 11km/hr (6kt) risked damaging the tube, and hydrophones were made ineffective by the roaring of air being sucked down it. *Schnorchels* were fitted with automatic valves to prevent seawater from being sucked into the diesels, but when these valves slammed shut the engines would draw air from the boat before shutting down, causing a partial vacuum which was very painful and in extreme cases caused ruptured eardrums.

One further problem arose out of extended submerged operations: a boat which remained underwater for long periods could not easily dispose of garbage and human waste, adding further to the already foul conditions aboard.

▲ **U-3008 *Schnorchel***

This photograph shows the *Schnorchel* of U-3008, a Type XXI U-boat. Unlike earlier submarines, the Type XXI had a telescopic *Schnorchel*, which was raised from a special housing by electric motors.

BOATS THAT SERVED WITH 33RD FLOTILLA (76 BOATS)

U-Boat	Type	Commissioned	Flotilla(s)	Patrols	Fate
U-155	IXC/40	10-Sep-42	1 Oct 1944 – 6 Oct 1944 from 2. Flottille	10 patrols. 25 ships sunk: total 126,664 GRT; 1 warship sunk: total 14,006t/13,785 tons; 1 aux warship damaged: total 6736 GRT	Transferred from Wilhelmshaven to Scotland 30 Jun 1945 for Operation *Deadlight*. Sunk 21 Dec 1945
U-168	IXC/40	19-Jan-43	1 Nov 1944 – 8 May 1945 from 10. Flottille	4 patrols. 2 ships sunk: total 6568 GRT; 1 auxiliary warship sunk: total 1440 GRT; 1 ship damaged: total 9804 GRT	Sunk 6 Oct 1944 in the Java Sea by a torpedo from the Dutch submarine HrMs *Zwaardvisch*. 23 dead and 27 survivors
U-170	IXD2	9-May-42	1 Oct 1944 – 8 May 1945	4 patrols. 1 ship sunk: total 4663 GRT	Surrendered May 1945. Transferred from Norway to Scotland 29 May for Operation *Deadlight*. Sunk 30 Nov 1945
U-181	IXC/40	1-Apr-42	1 Oct 1944 – 23 Apr 1945 from 2. Flottille	6 patrols. 4 ships sunk: total 19,260 GRT; 1 ship damaged beyond repair: total 6993 GRT	In the Far East at the end of the war. Taken over by Japan in May 1945 and became the Japanese submarine I-501 on 15 Jul 1945. Surrendered in Singapore Aug 1945
U-183	IXC/40	24-Sep-42	1 Oct 1944 – 1 May 1945 from 2. Flottille	6 patrols. 1 ship sunk: total 7015 GRT; 1 warship sunk: total 599t/590 tons	Sunk 23 Apr 1945 in the Java Sea by a torpedo from the submarine USS *Besugo*. 54 dead and 1 survivor
U-190	IXD1	5-Sep-42	1 Oct 1944 – 8 May 1945 from 12. Flottille	3 patrols. 2 ships sunk: total 14,391 GRT; 1 ship damaged: total 6797 GRT	Surrendered at Bulls Bay, Newfoundland, 12 May 1945. Used for tests, and was sunk 21 Oct 1947 southwest of Newfoundland by naval gunfire and aircraft bombs
U-195	IXD1	11-Sep-42	1 Oct 1944 – 1 Dec 1944	3 patrols. 3 ships sunk: total 17,739 GRT	Taken over by Japan in May 1945 and became the Japanese submarine I-506 15 Jul 1945. Surrendered at Jakarta Aug 1945
U-196	IXC	23-Aug-41	15 Aug 1944 – 8 May 1945 from 10. Flottille	3 patrols. 3 ships sunk: total 17,739 GRT. U-196 completed a 225-day patrol from 13 Mar to 23 Oct 1943, the longest submarine patrol of WWII	Declared missing with all hands 1 Dec 1944 south of Java. 65 dead
U-219	XB	12-Dec-42	1 Oct 1944 – 8 May 1945	2 patrols	Taken over by Japan 8 May 1945 in Batavia and became the Japanese submarine I-505 on 15 Jul 1945. Surrendered at Djakarta Aug 1945; broken up in 1948
U-234	XB	2-Mar-44	1 Mar 1945 – 8 May 1945 from 5. Flottille (training)	1 patrol	Surrendered at Portsmouth, New Hampshire, 16 May 1945. No casualties, though two Japanese passengers committed suicide. U-234 carried technical drawings, a crated Me-262 jet fighter, 560kg (1230lb) of uranium oxide, German experts on various technologies and 2 Japanese officers. Sunk as a target by a torpedo from USS *Greenfish* off Cape Cod 20 Nov 1947
U-245	VIIC	18-Dec-43	1 Oct 1944 – 8 May 1945 from 3. Flottille	3 patrols. 3 ships sunk: total 17,087 GRT	Surrendered and transferred from Norway to Scotland 30 May 1945 for Operation *Deadlight*. Sunk 7 Dec 1945
U-260	VIIC	14-Mar-42	1 Nov 1944 – 12 Mar 1945 from 6. Flottille	9 patrols. 1 ship sunk: total 4893 GRT	Scuttled 12 Mar 1945 south of Ireland after being mined at 80m (260ft) depth. No casualties – 48 survivors. Whole crew interned in Ireland
U-262	VIIC	15-Apr-42	10 Nov 1944 – 2 Apr 1945 from 3. Flottille	10 patrols. 3 ships sunk: total 13,010 GRT; 1 warship sunk: total 940t/925 tons	Bombed at Gotenhafen in Dec 1944. Stricken at Kiel 2 Apr 1945. Broken up in 1947
U-267	VIIC	11-Jul-42	1 Oct 1944 – 4 May 1945 from 7. Flottille	7 patrols	Scuttled 4 May 1945 in Gelting Bay
U-281	VIIC	27-Feb-1943	10 Nov 1944 – 8 May 1945 from 7. Flottille	4 patrols	Surrendered at Kristiansand 8 May 1945. Transferred to Scotland for Operation *Deadlight*. Sunk 30 Nov 1945
U-309	VIIC	27-Jan-43	1 Oct 1944 – 16 Feb 1945	11 patrols. 1 ship damaged beyond repair: total 7219 GRT	Sunk with all hands 16 Feb 1945 in the North Sea off the northeast coast of Scotland by depth charges from the frigate HMCS *St. John*. 47 dead
U-382	VIIC	25-Apr-42	1 Nov 1944 – 23 Jan 1945 from 7. Flottille	6 patrols. 1 ship damaged: total 9811 GRT	Sunk in Jan 1945 at Wilhelmshaven by British bombs. Raised 20 Mar 1945 and scuttled 8 May 1945
U-398	VIIC	18-Dec-43	1 Nov 1944 – 17 Apr 1945 from 3. Flottille	2 patrols	Missing with all hands after 17 Apr 1945 in the North Sea or in the Arctic. 43 dead. May have been sunk by a Liberator of No. 120 Sqn RAF 29 Apr 1945. That attack is usually considered to have been against U-1017, but both boats disappeared at about the same time and in the same waters
U-510	IXC	25-Nov-41	1 Oct 1944 – 8 May 1945 from 10. Flottille	7 patrols. 14 ships sunk: total 78,526 GRT; 1 auxiliary warship sunk: total 249 GRT; 3 ships damaged beyond repair: total 24,338 GRT; 8 ships damaged: total 53,289 GRT	Surrendered at St Nazaire and ceded to France 12 May 1945. Renamed the *Bouan* in French service. Stricken 1 May 1959 as Q176. Broken up in 1960
U-516	IXC	21-Feb-42	1 Oct 1944 – 8 May 1945 from 10. Flottille	6 patrols. 16 ships sunk: total 89,385 GRT; 1 ship damaged: total 9687 GRT	Surrendered at Lough Foyle, Northern Ireland. Sunk 2 Jan 1946 in Operation *Deadlight*
U-518	IXC	25-Apr-42	1 Nov 1944 – 22 Apr 1945 from 10. Flottille	7 patrols. 9 ships sunk: total 55,747 GRT; 3 ships damaged: total 22,616 GRT	Sunk with all hands 22 Apr 1945 northwest of the Azores by depth charges from the destroyer escorts USS *Carter* and USS *Neal A. Scott*. 56 dead
U-530	IXC/40	14-Oct-42	1 Oct 1944 – 8 May 1945 from 10. Flottille	7 patrols. 2 ships sunk: total 12,063 GRT; 1 ship damaged: total 10,195 GRT	Surrendered in the Mar del Plata, Argentina, 10 Jul 1945. Transferred to the US and used for trials. Sunk as a target 28 Nov 1947 by a torpedo
U-532	IXC/40	11-Nov-42	1 Oct 1944 – 8 May 1945 from 2. Flottille	4 patrols. 8 ships sunk: total 46,895 GRT; 2 ships damaged: total 13,128 GRT	Surrendered at Liverpool 10 May 1945. Sunk by sub-launched torpedo as part of Operation *Deadlight* 9 Dec 1945
U-534	IXC/40	23-Dec-42	1 Nov 1944 – 5 May 1945 from 2. Flottille	3 patrols	Sunk 5 May 1945 in the Kattegat by depth charges from a British Liberator of No. 86 Sqn RAF after shooting down another Liberator. 3 dead and 49 survivors. Raised in 1993, the wreck has been on display at Birkenhead, near Liverpool, in England
U-537	IXC/40	27-Jan-43	1 Oct 1944 – 9 Nov 1944 from 10. Flottille	3 patrols	Sunk with all hands 9 Nov 1944 in the Java Sea east of Surabaya, torpedoed by the US submarine *Flounder*. 58 dead
U-539	IXC/40	24-Feb-43	1 Oct 1944 – 8 May 1945 from 10. Flottille	3 patrols. 1 ship sunk: total 1517 GRT; 2 ships damaged: total 12,896 GRT. U-539 was the first *Schnorchel*-equipped U-boat to go on a combat patrol on 2 Jan 1944	Surrendered at Bergen, Norway. Transferred to Scotland for Operation *Deadlight*. Foundered while on tow to the scuttling grounds 4 Dec 1945

BOATS THAT SERVED WITH 33RD FLOTILLA (76 BOATS)

U-Boat	Type	Commissioned	Flotilla(s)	Patrols	Fate
U-541	IXC/40	24-Mar-43	1 Nov 1944 – 8 May 1945 from 10. Flottille	4 patrols. 1 ship sunk: total 2140 GRT	Surrendered at Gibraltar 14 May 1945. Transferred to Northern Ireland for Operation *Deadlight*. Sunk 5 Jan 1946
U-546	IXC/40	2-Jun-43	10 Nov 1944 – 24 Apr 1945 from 10. Flottille	3 patrols. 1 warship sunk: total 1219t/1200 tons	Sunk 24 Apr 1945 northwest of the Azores by depth charges from 8 destroyer escorts (USS *Flaherty*, USS *Neunzer*, USS *Chatelain*, USS *Varian*, USS *Hubbard*, USS *Janssen*, USS *Pillsbury* and USS *Keith*). 26 dead and 33 survivors
U-547	IXC/40	16-Jun-43	1 Oct 1944 – 1 Nov 1944 from 2. Flottille	3 patrols. 2 ships sunk: total 8371 GRT; 1 auxiliary warship sunk: total 750 GRT	Damaged by mines in the Gironde near Pauillac 13 Aug 1944. Decommissioned at Stettin 31 Dec 1944
U-548	IXC/40	30-Jun-43	1 Oct 1944 – 19 Apr 1945 from 2. Flottille	4 patrols. 1 warship sunk: total 1468t/1445 tons	Sunk with all hands 19 Apr 1945 southeast of Nova Scotia by depth charges from destroyer escorts USS *Reuben James* and USS *Buckley*. 58 dead. Previously credited 30 Apr 1945 to the patrol frigate USS *Natchez* and the destroyer escorts USS *Coffman*, USS *Bostwick* and USS *Thomas*. That attack is more likely to have sunk U-879
U-714	VIIC	10-Feb-43	11 Nov 1944 – 14 Mar 1945 from 7. Flottille	6 patrols. 1 ship sunk: total 1226 GRT; 1 auxiliary warship sunk: total 425 GRT	Sunk with all hands 14 Mar 1945 in the North Sea off the Firth of Forth by depth charges from the South African frigate *Natal*. 50 dead
U-758	VIIC	5-May-42	15 Oct 1944 – 1 Mar 1945 from 6. Flottille	7 patrols. 2 ships sunk: total 13,989 GRT	Damaged at Kiel by British bombs and stricken 16 Mar 1945. Broken up postwar
U-763	VIIC	13-Mar-43	1 Oct 1944 – 31 Oct 1944 from 3. Flottille	4 patrols. 1 ship sunk: total 1499 GRT	to 24. Flottille
U-802	IXC/40	12-Jun-43	1 Dec 1944 – 8 May 1945 from 2. Flottille	4 patrols. 1 ship sunk: total 1621 GRT	Surrendered at Loch Eriboll, Scotland, 11 May 1945. Sunk 31 Dec 1945 as part of Operation *Deadlight*
U-804	IXC/40	4-Dec-43	1 Oct 1944 – 9 Apr 1945 from 10. Flottille	2 patrols. 1 warship sunk: total 1321t/1300 tons	Blown up with all hands 9 Apr 1945 in the Kattegat after massed rocket attack by 13 de Havilland Mosquitoes of the Banff Strike Wing (Nos. 143, 235 and 248 Sqns RAF). 55 dead. U-1065 was destroyed in the same action
U-805	IXC/40	12-Feb-44	1 Mar 1945 – 8 May 1945 from 4. Flottille	1 patrol	Surrendered to the US Navy 14 May 1945 near Portsmouth, New Hampshire.
U-806	IXC/40	29-Apr-44	1 Nov 1944 – 8 May 1945 from 4. Flottille	1 patrol. 1 warship sunk: total 683t/672 tons; 1 ship damaged: total 7219 GRT	Surrendered May 1945. Transferred from Wilhelmshaven to Scotland 22 Jun 1945 for Operation *Deadlight*. Sunk 21 Dec 1945
U-843	IXC/40	24-Mar-43	1 Oct 1944 – 9 Apr 1945 from 2. Flottille	4 patrols. 1 ship sunk: total 8261 GRT	Sunk 9 Apr 1945 in the Kattegat, west of Gothenburg, by rockets from Mosquitoes of the Banff Strike Wing (Nos. 143, 235 and 248 Sqns RAF). 44 dead and 12 survivors
U-853	IXC/40	25-Jun-43	1 Oct 1944 – 6 May 1945 from 10. Flottille	3 patrols. 1 ship sunk: total 5353 GRT; 1 warship sunk: total 437t/430 tons	Sunk with all hands 6 May 1945 off the American coast southeast of New London by depth charges from the destroyer USS *John D. Ericsson*, the destroyer escort USS *Atherton* and the patrol frigate USS *Moberly*. 55 dead
U-857	IXC/40	16-Sep-43	1 Oct 1944 – 7 Apr 1945 from 10. Flottille	3 patrols. 2 ships sunk: total 15,259 GRT; 1 ship damaged: total 6825 GRT	Missing with all hands Apr 1945 off the US east coast. 59 dead. May have been sunk by US escort vessels at the same time as U-879, or by a US Navy blimp (airship) which dropped a homing torpedo on a possible submarine 18 Apr 1945
U-858	IXC/40	30-Sep-43	1 Oct 1944 – 8 May 1945 from 2. Flottille	2 patrols	Surrendered at Delaware, US, 14 May 1945 – the first German warship to surrender to US forces. Scuttled at the end of 1947 after being used for torpedo trials by the US Navy
U-861	IXD2	2-Sep-43	1 Oct 1944 – 6 May 1945 from 12. Flottille	2 patrols. 4 ships sunk: total 22,048 GRT; 1 ship damaged: total 8139 GRT	Surrendered at Trondheim, Norway, 6 May 1945. Transferred to Northern Ireland 29 May 1945 for Operation *Deadlight*. Sunk 31 Dec 1945
U-862	IXD2	7-Oct-43	1 Oct 1944 – 6 May 1945 from 12. Flottille	2 patrols. 7 ships sunk: total 42,374 GRT	Taken over by Japan at Singapore 6 May 1945, and became the Japanese submarine I-502. Surrendered at Singapore in Aug 1945 and was scuttled 13 Feb 1946
U-864	IXD2	9-Dec-43	1 Nov 1944 – 9 Feb 1945 from 4. Flottille	1 patrol	Sunk with all hands 9 Feb 1945 west of Bergen by torpedoes from HM Submarine *Venturer*. 73 dead. Both boats were submerged – the only such event in naval history
U-866	IXC/40	17-Nov-43	1 Oct 1944 – 18 Mar 1945 from 10. Flottille	1 patrol	Sunk with all hands 18 Mar 1945 northeast of Boston by depth charges from destroyer escorts USS *Lowe*, USS *Menges*, USS *Pride* and USS *Mosley*. 55 dead
U-868	IXC/40	23-Dec-43	1 Oct 1944 – 5 May 1945 from 2. Flottille	2 patrols. 1 warship sunk: total 683t/672 tons	Surrendered at Bergen May 1945. Transferred to Scotland 30 May 1945 for Operation *Deadlight*. Sunk 30 Nov 1945
U-869	IXC/40	26-Jan-44	1 Dec 1944 – 11 Feb 1945 from 4. Flottille	1 patrol	Sunk with all hands 11 Feb 1945 off New Jersey by Hedgehogs and depth charges from the destroyer escorts USS *Howard D. Crow* and USS *Koiner*. 56 dead. Previously credited to destroyer escort USS *Fowler* and French submarine chaser *L'Indiscret* 28 Feb off the Moroccan coast near Rabat
U-870	IXC/40	3-Feb-44	1 Oct 1944 – 30 Mar 1945 from 4. Flottille	1 patrol. 2 warships sunk: total 1991t/1960 tons; 2 ships damaged beyond repair: total 11,844 GRT; 1 warship damaged: total 1422t/1400 tons	Sunk in port 30 Mar 1945 at Bremen by US bombs
U-873	IXD2	1-Mar-44	1 Feb 1945 – 8 May 1945 from 4. Flottille	1 patrol	Surrendered at Portsmouth, New Hampshire, 16 May 1945. Used for trials. Broken up 1948
U-874	IXD2	8-Apr-44	1 Mar 1945 – 8 May 1945 from 4. Flottille	No patrols	Transferred from Horten, Norway, to Northern Ireland 29 May 1945 for Operation *Deadlight*. Sunk 31 Dec 1945
U-875	IXD2	21-Apr-44	1 Mar 1945 – 8 May 1945 from 4. Flottille	No patrols	Transferred from Bergen, Norway, to Northern Ireland 30 May 1945 for Operation *Deadlight*. Sunk 31 Dec 1945

BOATS THAT SERVED WITH 33RD FLOTILLA (76 BOATS)

U-Boat	Type	Commissioned	Flotilla(s)	Patrols	Fate
U-877	IXC/40	24-Mar-44	1 Dec 1944 – 27 Dec 1944 from 4. Flottille	1 patrol	Sunk 27 Dec 1944 northwest of the Azores by Squid anti-submarine launcher of the corvette HMCS *St. Thomas*. No casualties – 56 survivors
U-878	IXC/40	14-Apr-44	1 Feb 1945 – 10 Apr 1945 from 4. Flottille	2 patrols	Sunk with all hands 10 Apr 1945 west of St Nazaire by depth charges from the destroyer HMS *Vanquisher* and the corvette HMS *Tintagel Castle*. 51 dead
U-879	IXC/40	19-Apr-44	1 Feb 1945 – 30 Apr 1945 from 4. Flottille	1 patrol. 1 ship damaged: total 8537 GRT	Sunk with all hands 30 Apr 1945 east of Cape Hatteras by depth charges from frigate USS *Natchez* and destroyer escorts USS *Coffmann*, USS *Bostwick* and USS *Thomas*. 52 dead. Previously credited to USS *Buckley* and USS *Reuben James* east of Boston 19 Apr 1945. They probably destroyed U-548
U-880	IXC/40	11-May-44	1 Dec 1944 – 16 Apr 1945 from 4. Flottille	1 patrol	Sunk with all hands 16 Apr 1945 in the North Atlantic by depth charges from the destroyer escorts USS *Stanton* and USS *Frost*. 49 dead
U-881	IXC/40	27-May-44	1 Mar 1945 – 6 May 1945 from 4. Flottille	1 patrol	Sunk with all hands 6 May 1945 southeast of Newfoundland by depth charges from the destroyer escort USS *Farquhar*. 53 dead
U-889	IXC/40	4-Aug-44	15 Mar 1945 – 8 May 1945 from 4. Flottille	1 patrol	Surrendered 15 May 1945 at Shelburne, Nova Scotia. Transferred to the US Navy 10 Jan 1946. Used for torpedo trials before being scuttled at the end of 1947
U-953	VIIC	17-Dec-42	15 Oct 1944 – 8 May 1945 from 3. Flottille	10 patrols. 1 ship sunk: total 1927 GRT	Transferred 29 May 1945 from Norway to England. Used by the Royal Navy as a trials boat. Broken up in 1950
U-989	VIIC	22-Jul-43	1 Oct 1944 – 14 Feb 1945 from 9. Flottille	5 patrols. 1 ship sunk: total 1791 GRT; 1 ship damaged: total 7176 GRT	Sunk with all hands 14 Feb 1945 in the Faroe Islands by depth charges from frigates HMS *Bayntun*, HMS *Braithwaite*, HMS *Loch Eck* and HMS *Loch Dunvegan*. 47 dead
U-1106	VIIC/41	5-Jul-44	16 Feb 1945 – 29 Mar 1945 from 8. Flottille	1 patrol	Sunk with all hands 29 Mar 1945 northeast of the Faroes by depth charges from a Liberator of No. 224 Sqn RAF. 46 dead
U-1170	VIIC/41	1-Mar-44	1 Oct 1944 – 3 May 1945 from 8. Flottille (training)	Training	Scuttled 3 May 1945 at Travemünde
U-1205	VIIC	2-Mar-44	1 Oct 1944 – 3 May 1945 from 8. Flottille (training)	Training	Scuttled 3 May 1945 at Kiel
U-1221	IXC/40	11-Aug-43	1 Dec 1944 – 3 Apr 1945 from 10. Flottille	1 patrol	Sunk 3 Apr 1945 at Kiel by US bombs. 7 dead and 11 survivors
U-1223	IXC/40	6-Oct-43	30 Dec 1944 – 15 Apr 1945 from 2. Flottille	1 patrol. 1 ship damaged: total 7134 GRT; 1 warship damaged beyond repair: total 1392t/1370 tons	Stricken 14 Apr 1945 and scuttled 5 May 1945 west of Wesermünde
U-1226	IXC/40	24-Nov-43	1 Oct 1944 – 28 Oct 1944 from 2. Flottille	1 patrol	Missing with all hands on or after 23 Oct 1944 in the Atlantic. 56 dead. In its last message on that date, the boat reported a *Schnorchel* defect, which may have contributed to its loss
U-1227	IXC/40	8-Dec-43	1 Jan 1945 – 10 Apr 1945 from 2. Flottille	1 patrol. 1 warship damaged beyond repair: total 1392t/1370 tons	Damaged at Kiel by British night bombing 9 Apr 1945 and stricken the next day. Scuttled 3 May 1945
U-1228	IXC/40	22-Dec-43	1 Nov 1944 – 8 May 1945 from 31. Flottille	2 patrols. 1 warship sunk: total 914t/900 tons	Surrendered at Portsmouth, New Hampshire, 17 May 1945. Scuttled by the US Navy 5 Feb 1946
U-1230	IXC/40	26-Jan-44	1 Oct 1944 – 8 May 1945 from 10. Flottille	1 patrol. 1 ship sunk: total 5458 GRT. The patrol included the landing of 2 agents on the US coast at Hancock Point in Maine	Transferred from Wilhelmshaven to Scotland 24 Jun 1945 for Operation *Deadlight*. Sunk by naval gunfire 17 Dec 1945
U-1231	IXC/40	9-Feb-44	1 Oct 1944 – 8 May 1945 from 11. Flottille	2 patrols	Surrendered at Lough Foyle, Northern Ireland, 14 May 1945. Ceded to the USSR and became the Soviet submarine N-25. Broken up in 1960
U-1232	IXC/40	8-Mar-44	1 Nov 1944 – 8 May 1945 from 31. Flottille	1 patrol. 3 ships sunk: total 17,355 GRT; 1 ship damaged beyond repair: total 7176 GRT; 1 ship damaged: total 2373 GRT	Stricken at Wesermünde Apr 1945. Captured by the British. Foundered and sank 4 Mar 1946 while under tow to the Operation *Deadlight* scuttling grounds
U-1233	IXC/40	22-Mar-44	1 Nov 1944 – 8 May 1945 from 31. Flottille	1 patrol	Transferred from Wilhelmshaven to Scotland 24 Jun 1945 for Operation *Deadlight*. Sunk by naval gunfire 29 Dec 1945
U-1235	IXC/40	17-May-44	1 Dec 1944 – 15 Apr 1945 from 31. Flottille	1 patrol	Sunk with all hands 15 Apr 1945 in North Atlantic by depth charges from destroyer escorts USS *Stanton* and USS *Frost*. 57 dead
U-1271	VIIC/41	12-Jan-44	1 Oct 1944 – 8 May 1945 from 8. Flottille	Training	Transferred from Bergen to Scotland 30 May 1945 for Operation *Deadlight*. Sunk 8 Dec 1945
U-1305	VIIC/41	13-Sep-44	16 Mar 1945 – 8 May 1945 from 4. Flottille	1 patrol. 1 ship sunk: total 878 GRT	Surrendered at Loch Eriboll, Scotland, 10 May 1945. Ceded to the USSR and became Soviet submarine S-84 Nov 1945
UIT-24	Italian Marcello class	10-Sep-43	Oct 1944 – May 1945 from 12. Flottille	6 patrols	Taken over by Japan at Kobe following the German surrender; recommissioned as I-503 10 May 1945. Scuttled at Kii Suido 16 April 1946 by the US Navy
UIT-25	Italian Marconi class	12-Dec-43	Oct 1944 – May 1945	3 patrols	Taken over by Japan at Kobe 10 May 1945 and commissioned as I-504. After the Japanese surrender the boat was scuttled by the Americans

Training Flotillas

At the outbreak of war, the *Kriegsmarine*'s U-boat arm was dedicated to turning out some of the best-trained submariners in the world. Basic training, or school, units gave new U-boat men their first experience of manning a U-boat at sea. Operational training was carried out under the aegis of the Front flotillas. However, the expansion of the U-boat arm through the war years saw an equally large expansion in the training establishment, with specialist flotillas being set up to provide weapons and tactical training. Final operational, or 'working up', training was now provided by the 4th, 5th and 8th Flotillas, through which all boats passed before being assigned to a combat flotilla based in Norway or France.

◀ Ready for inspection

A flotilla commander inspects the crew of a newly commissioned U-boat with the boat's commander. Ahead lay up to six months of tactical training before the boat could join a combat flotilla for operations.

4 Unterseebootsflottille

Before the war and in the first two years of the conflict, U-boats were assigned to one of the front flotillas, undergoing working-up training at the flotilla's German base before being declared operational. However, in 1941 the system changed.

FRONT FLOTILLAS WERE NOW BASED in France or Norway, and responsibility for working up U-boats to operational standard was passed to three new training flotillas, the 4th, 5th and 8th, which were based at Stettin, Kiel and Königsberg. Boats were assigned to one of the flotillas on commissioning, and went through a process that could last from three to seven months before being declared ready for operations.

Officers and senior crew members were assigned to a boat in the last stages of construction, up to three months before commissioning, in a process known as *Baubelehrung*, or familiarization training. The idea was to make them totally familiar with every aspect of the boat. A week or two before commissioning, they would be joined by the rest of the crew.

Although the boat was assigned to a training flotilla after the commissioning ceremony, the next stage in its working up was to pass through the U-boat Acceptance Command – the *Unterseeboots-abnehmenkommando*, or UAK. This was a two-week process in which all of the boat's systems were tested, diving trials were carried out and any faults were identified. From there, the boat passed on to the much-feared *Agru Front* for final tactical training.

4TH FLOTILLA BASE LOCATION

U-3030 INSIGNIA

The 4th Flotilla had no recorded flotilla insignia other than standard training markings. Some boats acquired individual insignia: that carried by U-3030 was designed by the I WO (first officer) Oblt. Dr Hansmann.

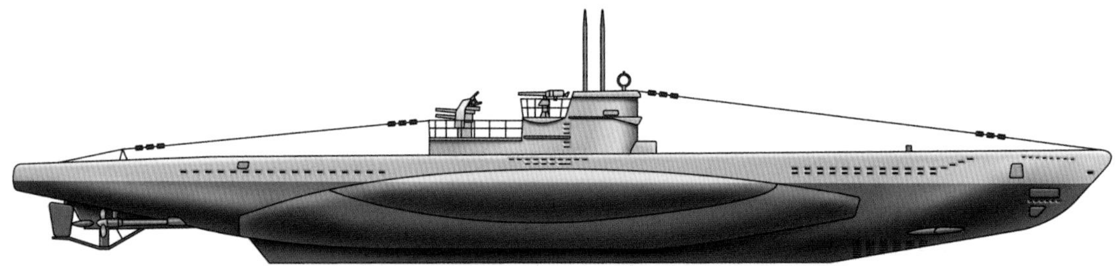

Specifications

Crew: 44
Powerplant: Diesel/electric
Max Speed: 31.5/14.1km/hr (17/7.6kt) s/d
Surface Range: 12,040km (6500nm)
Displacement: 771/874t (759/860 tons) s/d
Dimensions (length/beam/draught): 67.2 x 6.2 x 4.8m (220.5 x 20.34 x 15.75ft)
Commissioned: 12 Apr 1945
Armament: 14 torpedoes (4 bow/1 stern tubes); 1 x 2cm (0.8in) quad and 2 x twin 2cm (0.8in) guns (1944–45)

▲ **U-1025**

Type VIIC/41

One of the last Type VIIs to be commissioned, the Type VIIC/41 boat U-1025 was the same size as a standard Type VIIC, but was made from thicker steel and could dive more deeply. It was withdrawn from service after only two weeks due to defective batteries.

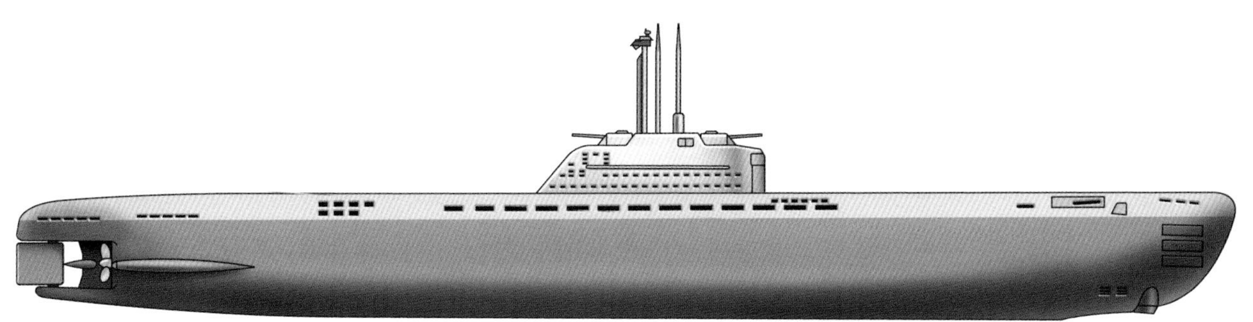

Specifications

Crew: 57

Powerplant: Diesel/electric

Max Speed: 28.9/31.9km/hr (15.6/17.2kt) s/d

Surface Range: 20,650km (11,150nm)

Displacement: 1647/1848t (1621/1819 tons) s/d

Dimensions (length/beam/draught): 76.7 x 6.6 x 6.3m (251.7 x 21.7 x 20.7ft)

Commissioned: 20 Jul 1944

Armament: 23 torpedoes (6 bow tubes); 2 x twin 2cm (0.8in) gun turrets

▲ U-3001

Type XXI

U-3001 was one of the first Type XXI boats to be commissioned.

Commanders

Kptlt. Werner Jacobsen *(May 1941 – Aug 1941)*

Kptlt. Fritz Frauenheim *(Jul 1941)*

Fregkpt. Heinz Fischer *(Aug 1941)*

BOATS THAT TRAINED WITH THE 4TH FLOTILLA

Type	Boats ordered
Type IX, IXC	U-37, U-38, U-129, U-130, U-153, U-154, U-155, U-156, U-157, U-158, U-159, U-160, U-161, U-162, U-163, U-164, U-165, U-166, U-171, U-172, U-173, U-174, U-175, U-176, U-504, U-505, U-506, U-507, U-508, U-509, U-510, U-511, U-512, U-513, U-514, U-515, U-516, U-517, U-518, U-519, U-520, U-521, U-522, U-523, U-524
Type IXC/40	U-167, U-168, U-169, U-170, U-183, U-184, U-185, U-186, U-187, U-188, U-189, U-190, U-191, U-192, U-193, U-194, U-525, U-526, U-527, U-528, U-529, U-530, U-531, U-532, U-533, U-534, U-535, U-536, U-537, U-538, U-539, U-540, U-541, U-542, U-543, U-544, U-545, U-546, U-547, U-548, U-549, U-550, U-801, U-802, U-803, U-804, U-805, U-806, U-841, U-842, U-843, U-844, U-845, U-846, U-853, U-854, U-855, U-856, U-857, U-858, U-865, U-866, U-867, U-868, U-869, U-870, U-877, U-878, U-879, U-880, U-881, U-883, U-889, U-1221, U-1222, U-1223, U-1234
Type IXD1, 2	U-177, U-178, U-179, U-180, U-181, U-182, U-195, U-196, U-197, U-198, U-199, U-200, U-847, U-848, U-849, U-850, U-851, U-852, U-859, U-860, U-861, U-862, U-863, U-864, U-871, U-872, U-873, U-874, U-875, U-876
Type VIIC	U-78, U-131, U-290, U-351, U-370, U-475, U-579, U-676, U-821, U-822, U-901, U-906, U-925, U-926, U-927, U-928
Type VIIC/41	U-317, U-318, U-319, U-320, U-321, U-322, U-323, U-324, U-325, U-326, U-327, U-328, U-929, U-930, U-1025, U-1301, U-1302, U-1303, U-1304, U-1305, U-1306, U-1307, U-1308
UA	UA (ex-Turkish)
Type XB	U-118, U-119, U-219, U-220, U-233
Type XIV	U-459, U-460, U-461, U-462, U-463, U-464, U-487, U-488, U-489, U-490
Type XXI	U-3001, U-3002, U-3003, U-3004, U-3005, U-3006, U-3007, U-3008, U-3009, U-3010, U-3011, U-3012, U-3013, U-3014, U-3015, U-3016, U-3017, U-3018, U-3019, U-3020, U-3021, U-3022, U-3023, U-3024, U-3025, U-3026, U-3027, U-3028, U-3029, U-3030, U-3031, U-3032, U-3033, U-3034, U-3035, U-3037, U-3038, U-3039, U-3040, U-3041, U-3044
Type XXIII	U-2321, U-2322, U-2323, U-2324, U-2325, U-2326, U-2336, U-2339, U-2343, U-2346, U-2347, U-2348, U-2349, U-2350, U-2351, U-2352, U-2353, U-2354, U-2355, U-2356, U-2357, U-2358, U-2359, U-2360, U-2361, U-2362, U-2363, U-2364, U-2365, U-2366, U-2367, U-2368, U-2369, U-2370, U-2371

4TH FLOTILLA BOATS LOST WHILE TRAINING/BOATS THAT MADE OPERATIONAL PATROLS WHILE TRAINING

U-Boat	Type	Commissioned	Flotilla(s)	Patrols	Fate
U-78	VIIC	15-Feb-41	1 Mar 1945 – 16 Apr 1945 from 22. Flottille	No patrols – used as an electricity generator	Sunk 16 Apr 1945 at the electricity supply station at Pillau pier by Soviet artillery fire
U-319	VIIC/41	4-Dec-43	4 Dec 1943 – 15 Jul 1944 (operational from 1 Jun)	1 patrol	Sunk with all hands 15 Jul 1944 southwest of the Lindesnes, Norway, by depth charges from a Liberator of No. 206 Sqn RAF. 51 dead
U-579	VIIC	17-Jul-41	1 Mar 1945 – 5 May 1945 from 23. Flottille	Training	Sunk for a second time 5 May 1945 in the Kattegat by depth charges from a Liberator of No. 547 Sqn RAF. 24 dead
U-676	VIIC	4-Aug-43	16 Feb 1945 – 19 Feb 1945 from 8. Flottille	2 patrols	Sunk with all hands on or after 12 Feb 1945 in the Gulf of Finland, probably by a Soviet mine. 57 dead
U-803	IXC/40	7-Sep-43	7 Sep 1943 – 27 Apr 1944	Training	Sunk 27 Apr 1944 in the Baltic near Swinemünde by a mine. 9 dead and 35 survivors
U-854	IXC/40	19-Jul-43	19 Jul 1943 – 4 Feb 1944	Training	Sunk 4 Feb 1944 in the Baltic north of Swinemünde by mines. 51 dead and 7 survivors
U-872	IXD2	10-Feb-44	10 Feb 1944 – 29 Jul 1944	Training	Damaged 29 Jul 1944 at Bremen by US bombs. 1 crewman killed. Stricken 10 Aug 1944 and broken up
U-876	IXD2	24-May-44	24 May 1944 – 3 May 1945	Training	Damaged by British bombs 9 Apr 1945. Scuttled at Eckernförde 3 May 1945
U-906	VIIC	15-Jul-44	15 Jul 1944 – 31 Dec 1944	Training	Sunk in harbour at Hamburg 29 Dec 1944 by US bombs. Wreck further damaged in Apr 1945
U-2323	XXIII	18-Jul-44	18 Jul 1944 – 26 Jul 1944	Training	Sunk 26 July 1944 west of Möltenort by a mine. 2 dead and 12 survivors
U-2336	XXIII	30-Sep-44	16 Feb 1945 – 8 May 1945	1 patrol. 2 ships sunk: total 4669 GRT	Surrendered at Wilhelmshaven, Germany. Taken to Lisahally 21 Jun 1945 for Operation *Deadlight*. Sunk 3 Jan 1946 by naval gunfire
U-2351	XXIII	30-Dec-44	16 Feb 1945 – 1 Apr 1945 from 32. Flottille	Training	Taken out of service at Kiel in Apr 1945, after being bombed. Surrendered in May 1945. Transferred to Lisahally for Operation *Deadlight*. Sunk 3 Jan 1946 by naval gunfire
U-2359	XXIII	16-Jan-45	16 Feb 1945 – 2 May 1945 from 32. Flottille	Training	Sunk with all hands 2 May 1945 in the Kattegat by rockets from Mosquitoes of Nos. 143, 235 and 248 Sqns RAF, No. 333 Sqn RNoAF, and No. 404 Sqn RCAF. 12 dead
U-2365	XXIII	2-Mar-45	2 Mar 1945 – 8 May 1945	Training	Scuttled 8 May 1945 in the Kattegat. Raised in Jun 1956 and commissioned as *U-Hai* (S-170) in the German Federal Navy 15 Aug 1957. Sank 14 Sep 1966 in the North Sea after taking in water. Raised in 1966 and broken up
U-2367	XXIII	17-Mar-45	17 Mar 1945 – 5 May 1945	Training	Sank 5 May 1945 near Schleimünde after a collision with another U-boat. Raised in Aug 1956. Renamed *U-Hecht* (Pike) and commissioned in the Federal Navy 1 Oct 1957. Stricken 30 Sep 1968 and broken up at Kiel in 1969
U-3003	XXI	22-Aug-44	22 Aug 1944 – 4 Apr 1945	Trials boat	Sunk by bombs 4 Apr 1945 at Kiel
U-3004	XXI	30-Aug-44	30 Aug 1944 – 2 May 1945	Training	One of 3 type XXI boats buried in the wreckage of the Elbe II bunker in Hamburg
U-3007	XXI	22-Oct-44	22 Oct 1944 – 24 Feb 1945	Training	Sunk 24 Feb 1945 at Bremen, by bombs. 1 crewman killed
U-3032	XXI	12-Feb-45	12 Feb 1945 – 3 May 1945	Training	Sunk 3 May 1945 east of Fredericia by rockets from Typhoons of No. 184 Sqn RAF. 36 dead and 24 survivors

5 Unterseebootsflottille

The 5th Flotilla was originally an operational unit but was disbanded in January 1940. It was re-established in June 1941 as a training flotilla, dedicated to working up new boats to operational readiness.

Boats which passed their acceptance trials at the UAK would then go through one of the technical training flotillas where crews would be put through a variety of simulated combat situations, learn how to fire live torpedoes, and undergo their first deep dives. These were carried out in a deep trench in the Baltic near the Danish island of Bornholm. Not all boats progressed, however. Those with serious faults often had to go back to the dockyard for repair, their crews being sent on an unexpected but not unwelcome leave until their boats were fixed.

Before the war, U-boat commanders were forbidden to take their vessels below 50m (165ft),

Commanders

Kptlt. Karl-Heinz Moehle *(June 1941 – Aug 1942)*

Korvkpt. Hans Pauckstadt *(Sep 1942 – Nov 1942)*

Korvkpt. Karl-Heinz Moehle *(Nov 1942 – May 1945)*

U-3501 INSIGNIA

At least three different insignia designs have been claimed for the 5th Flotilla. The Type XXI boat U-3501 carried the insignia of Crew 37b, since that had been the intake with which the commander, Oblt. Helmut Münster, had joined the *Kriegsmarine*.

even though most U-boats had been designed for diving depths of 200m (655ft) or more.

Combat experience showed that boats and their crews had to be able to make deep dives to survive attacks by enemy escort vessels, but although training was changed to reflect the new reality, it was discovered that many boats had a faulty engine-room vent. Designed to close underwater, the vent often failed under pressure of a deep dive or from the blast of a nearby depth charge, and expensive modifications had to be made to all boats.

Torpedo crisis

Live torpedo firing also highlighted some serious problems with the main weapons used by the U-boats. New torpedoes had been designed in the 1920s, but they had been tested only twice, and on both occasions they had failed. Even so, they were declared operational. As a result, in the first two years of the war the U-boat arm underwent a torpedo crisis, in which commanders could not be sure if the weapons they fired would detonate early or would even explode at all. By the time the 5th Flotilla had

BOATS THAT TRAINED WITH THE 5TH FLOTILLA

Type	Boats ordered
Type IIB	U-11
Type VIIB	U-86
Type VIIC	U-91, U-92, U-134, U-135, U-208, U-210, U-211, U-221, U-224, U-225, U-226, U-227, U-228, U-229, U-230, U-231, U-232, U-235, U-236, U-237, U-238, U-239, U-240, U-241, U-242, U-243, U-244, U-245, U-246, U-247, U-248, U-249, U-250, U-257, U-258, U-259, U-262, U-301, U-333, U-336, U-337, U-348, U-353, U-354, U-355, U-360, U-364, U-365, U-366, U-374, U-375, U-380, U-381, U-382, U-384, U-385, U-386, U-387, U-388, U-389, U-390, U-391, U-392, U-393, U-394, U-396, U-397, U-398, U-399, U-400, U-403, U-407, U-408, U-409, U-410, U-435, U-436 , U-439, U-440, U-441, U-442, U-454, U-455, U-466, U-467, U-468, U-469, U-470, U-471, U-472, U-473, U-475, U-476, U-477, U-478, U-479, U-480, U-481, U-482, U-483, U-484, U-485, U-486, U-578, U-579, U-580, U-581, U-582, U-583, U-584, U-600, U-601, U-602, U-603, U-604, U-605, U-606, U-607, U-608, U-609, U-610, U-611, U-612, U-617, U-618, U-619, U-626, U-627, U-628, U-629, U-630, U-631, U-632, U-633, U-634, U-635, U-636, U-637, U-638, U-639, U-640, U-641, U-642, U-643, U-644, U-645, U-646, U-647, U-648, U-649, U-650, U-654, U-656, U-659, U-660, U-661, U-662, U-663, U-665, U-666, U-667, U-668, U-669, U-670, U-671, U-672, U-673, U-674, U-675, U-676, U-677, U-678, U-702, U-705, U-706, U-708, U-709, U-710, U-711, U-714, U-715, U-716, U-717, U-718, U-719, U-749, U-750, U-754, U-755, U-759, U-904, U-951, U-952, U-953, U-954, U-955, U-956, U-957, U-958, U-959, U-960, U-961, U-962, U-963, U-964, U-965, U-966, U-967, U-968, U-969, U-970, U-971, U-972, U-973, U-974, U-975, U-976, U-977, U-978, U-979, U-980, U-981, U-982, U-983, U-984, U-985, U-986, U-987, U-988, U-989, U-990, U-991, U-992, U-993, U-994, U-1051, U-1052, U-1053, U-1054, U-1055, U-1056, U-1057, U-1058, U-1131, U-1132, U-1161, U-1162, U-1195, U-1207, U-1210
Type VIIC/41	U-320, U-828, U-995, U-997, U-998, U-999, U-1001, U-1008, U-1063, U-1064, U-1065, U-1105, U-1108, U-1110, U-1168, U-1274, U-1275
Type VIID	U-213, U-214, U-215, U-216, U-217, U-218
Type VIIF	U-1059, U-1060, U-1061, U-1062
Type IXA	U-38
Type XB	U-234
Type XVIIA, B	U-792, U-793, U-794, U-795, U-1405, U-1406, U-1407
Type XXI	U-3501, U-3502, U-3503, U-3504, U-3505, U-3506, U-3507, U-3508, U-3509, U-3510, U-3511, U-3512, U-3513, U-3514, U-3515, U-3516, U-3517, U-3518, U-3519, U-3521, U-3522, U-3523, U-3524, U-3525, U-3526, U-3527, U-3528, U-3529, U-3530
Type XXIII	U-2332, U-2333, U-4701, U-4702, U-4703, U-4704, U-4705, U-4706, U-4707, U-4709, U-4710, U-4711, U-4712
British H class	UD-1 (ex-Dutch)
O 21 class	UD-3, UD-4 (ex-Dutch)
Aurore class	UF-2 (ex-French)

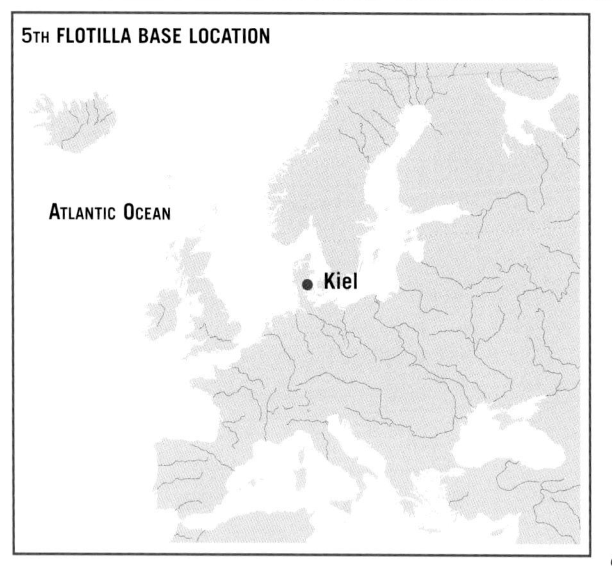

been set up as a training unit, things had improved, but they were still far from satisfactory.

The next stage in the training process was the much-feared *Agru Front*, the series of anti-convoy exercises in the Baltic which served as a boat's graduation from training.

The 5th Flotilla was founded as a training establishment in June of 1941. More than 330 boats passed through the flotilla while working up for operations, with at least eight boats being sunk in training accidents. Many more were destroyed by Allied air attack, and a number of boats that made operational patrols at the end of the war were destroyed by Allied warships. The flotilla was disbanded in May 1945.

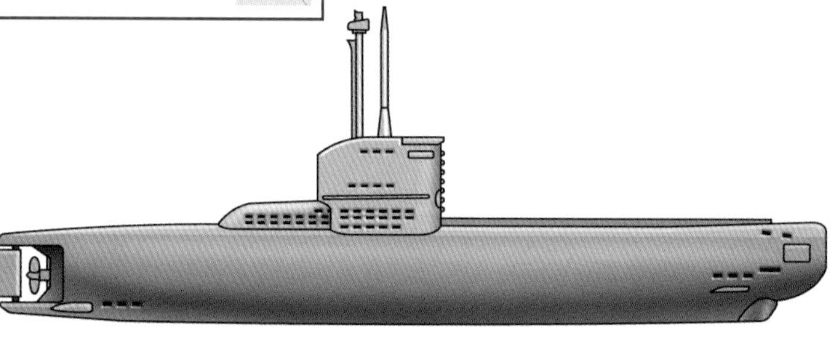

Specifications

Crew: 14

Powerplant: Diesel/electric

Max Speed: 18/23.2km/hr (9.7/12.5kt) s/d

Surface Range: 4815km (2600nm)

Displacement: 238/262t (234/258 tons) s/d

Dimensions (length/beam/draught): 34.7 x 3 x 3.7m (113.9 x 9.9 x 12.1ft)

Commissioned: 18 Dec 1944

Armament: 2 torpedoes (2 bow tubes)

▲ **U-2332**

Type XXIII

U-2332 was one of a small number of Type XXIII boats that served with the 5th Flotilla. Most boats of this type trained with the 32nd Flotilla. The boat was scuttled on 5 May 1945.

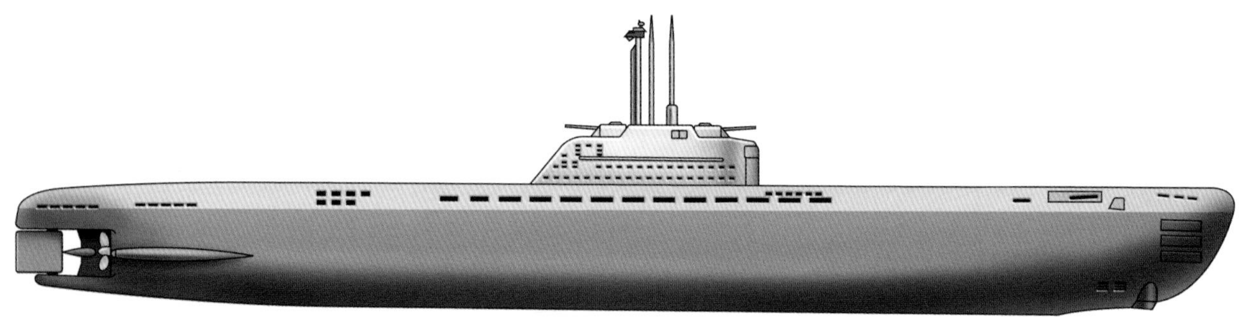

Specifications

Crew: 57

Powerplant: Diesel/electric

Max Speed: 28.9/31.9km/hr (15.6/17.2kt) s/d

Surface Range: 20,650km (11,150nm)

Displacement: 1647/1848t (1621/1819 tons) s/d

Dimensions (length/beam/draught): 76.7 x 6.6 x 6.3m (251.7 x 21.7 x 20.7ft)

Commissioned: 23 Jan 1945

Armament: 23 torpedoes (6 bow tubes); 2 x twin 2cm (0.8in) gun turrets

▲ **U-3523**

Type XXI

U-3523 was outward bound from Kiel in the last days of the war. She was sunk with all 58 hands on 6 May 1945 in the Skagerrak east of Arhus, Denmark, by depth charges from a Liberator of No. 86 Sqn RAF.

5TH FLOTILLA BOATS LOST WHILE TRAINING/BOATS THAT MADE OPERATIONAL PATROLS WHILE TRAINING

U-Boat	Type	Commissioned	Flotilla(s)	Patrols	Fate
U-235	VIIC	19-Dec-42	19 Dec 1942 – 20 May 1943	Training	Sunk 14 May 1943 at the Germaniawerft dockyard, Kiel, by US bombs. Raised, repaired, and returned to service in Oct 1943. To 22. Flottille
U-237	VIIC	30-Jan-43	30 Jan 1943 – 20 May 1943	Training	Sunk 14 May 1943 at Kiel, by US bombs. Raised, repaired, and returned to service in Oct 1943. To 23. Flottille
U-239	VIIC	13-Mar-43	25 Jul 1944 – 5 Aug 1944	Training	Damaged 24 Jul 1944 at Kiel, by British bombs. 1 crewman killed. Stricken 5 Aug 1944 and broken up
U-242	VIIC	14-Aug-43	16 Feb 1945 – 5 Apr 1945 from 8. Flottille	7 patrols. 3 ships sunk: total 2595 GRT	Sunk with all hands 5 Apr 1945 by a mine in St Georges Channel. Originally thought to have been sunk 30 Apr 1945 in the Irish Sea west of Blackpool by depth charges from the destroyers HMS *Hesperus* and HMS *Havelock* but they were attacking the wreck of U-246
U-320	VIIC/41	30-Dec-43	1 Apr 1945 – 8 May 1945 from 4. Flottille	2 patrols	Damaged 8 May 1945 west of Bergen by depth charges from a Catalina of No. 210 Sqn RAF. Thought to have been sunk, but managed to get to Sotre near Bergen; beached and scuttled
U-348	VIIC	10-Aug-43	16 Feb 1945 – 30 Mar 1945 from 8. Flottille	Training	Sunk 30 Mar 1945 in Hamburg by US bombs during a daylight air raid. 2 crewmen killed
U-393	VIIC	3-Jul-43	1 Apr 1945 – 5 May 1945	Training	Attacked 4 May 1945 in Gelting Bay by USAAF tactical aircraft. 2 crewmen killed. Scuttled the next day in Flensburger Fjord. Previously credited to 6 Beaufighters, but that attack was against U-2351 and only caused minor damage
U-579	VIIC	17-Jul-41	17 Jul 1941 – 22 Oct 1941	Training	Sank in an Oct 1941 collision in the Baltic. Raised, returned to service Apr/May 1942 with 24. Flottille
U-580	VIIC	24-Jul-41	24 Jul 1941 – 11 Nov 1941	Training	Sank 11 Nov 1941 in the Baltic near Memel after a collision with the target ship *Angelburg*. 12 dead and 32 survivors
U-583	VIIC	14-Aug-41	14 Aug 1941 – 15 Nov 1941	Training	Sank with all hands 15 Nov 1941 near Danzig after colliding with U-153. 45 dead
U-649	VIIC	19-Nov-42	19 Nov 1942 – 24 Feb 1943	Training	Collided with U-232 24 Feb 1943 in the Baltic and sank. 35 dead and 11 survivors
U-670	VIIC	26-Jan-43	26 Jan 1943 – 20 Aug 1943	Training	Sank off Danzig after a collision with the target ship *Bolkoburg* 20 Aug 1943. 21 dead and 22 survivors
U-717	VIIC	19-May-43	16 Feb 1945 – 2 May 1945 from 8. Flottille	Training	Scuttled 2 May 1945 in the Wasserlebenbucht after being damaged by British bombs
U-718	VIIC	25-Jun-43	25 Jun 1943 – 18 Nov 1943	Training	Collided with U-476 18 Nov 1943 in the Baltic northeast of Bornholm and sank. 43 dead and 7 survivors
U-749	VIIC	14-Aug-43	1 Apr 1945 – 4 Apr 1945 from 24. Flottille	Training	Sunk 4 Apr 1945 at Germaniawerft in Kiel by US bombs. 2 crewmen killed
U-958	VIIC	14-Jan-43	16 Feb 1945 – 3 May 1945 from 8. Flottille	3 patrols. 1 ship sunk: total 40 GRT; 1 ship damaged: total 40 GRT	Decommissioned at Kiel Aug 1944. Scuttled 3 May 1945. Broken up in 1947
U-961	VIIC	4-Feb-43	4 Feb 1943 – 29 Mar 1944	1 patrol	Sunk with all hands 29 Mar 1944 east of Iceland by depth charges from the sloop HMS *Starling*. 49 dead
U-973	VIIC	15-Apr-43	15 Apr 1943 – 6 Mar 1944	2 patrols	Sunk 6 Mar 1944 northwest of Narvik by rockets from a Swordfish from the escort carrier HMS *Chaser*. 51 dead and 2 survivors
U-983	VIIC	16-Jun-43	16 Jun 1943 – 8 Sep 1943	Training	Sank 8 Sep 1943 after collision with U-988 in the Baltic. 5 dead and 38 survivors
U-998	VIIC/41	7-Oct-43	7 Oct 1943 – 27 Jun 1944	1 patrol	Damaged 16 Jun 1944 in Bergen by depth charges from a Norwegian Mosquito. Stricken 27 June 1944. Scrapped
U-1001	VIIC/41	18-Nov-43	16 Feb 1945 – 8 Apr 1945 from 8. Flottille	6 patrols	Sunk with all hands 8 Apr 1945 southwest of Land's End by depth charges from frigates HMS *Fitzroy* and HMS *Byron*. 45 dead
U-1008	VIIC/41	1-Feb-44	1 Mar 1945 – 6 May 1945 from 18. Flottille	No patrols	Sunk 6 May 1945 in the Kattegat north of Hjelm by depth charges from a Liberator of No. 86 Sqn RAF. All 44 crew survived
U-1054	VIIC	25-Mar-44	25 Mar 1944 – 16 Sep 1944	Training	Collided with ferry *Peter Wessel* at Kiel. Stricken 16 Sep 1944. Surrendered to Britain in 1945 and broken up
U-1060	VIIF	15-May-43	15 May 1943 – 27 Oct 1944	6 torpedo transport patrols	Ran aground and wrecked 27 Oct 1944 south of Bronnoysund after being damaged by rockets and depth charges from Fireflies and Barracudas of the fleet carrier HMS *Implacable*, and depth charges from Handley Page Halifaxes of No. 502 Sqn RAF and Czech Liberators of No. 311 Sqn. 12 dead and 43 survivors
U-1065	VIIC/41	23-Sep-44	23 Sep 1944 – 9 Apr 1945	1 patrol	Sunk with all hands 9 Apr 1945 northwest of Göteborg by 10 rocket-firing Mosquitoes of Nos. 143 and 235 Sqns RAF. 45 dead
U-1131	VIIC	20-May-44	20 May 1944 – 30 Mar 1945	Training	Scuttled 29 Mar 1945 at Hamburg-Finkenwärder; further damaged afterwards by British bombs
U-1210	VIIC	22-Apr-44	16 Feb 1945 – 3 May 1945 from 8. Flottille	Training	Sunk 3 May 1945 near Eckernförde by US bombs. 1 crewman killed
U-1274	VIIC/41	1-Mar-44	1 Mar 1945 – 16 Apr 1945 from 8. Flottille	1 patrol. 1 ship sunk: total 8966 GRT	Sunk with all hands 16 Apr 1945 off the Northumberland coast by depth charges from the destroyer HMS *Viceroy*. 44 dead
U-3503	XXI	9-Sep-44	16 Feb 1945 – 8 May 1945 from 8. Flottille	School boat	Scuttled 8 May 1945 in the Kattegat west of Göteborg, Sweden. Raised in 1946 and broken up. Previously credited to a Liberator of No. 86 Sqn RAF in the Kattegat 5 May 1945. The attack actually destroyed U-534
U-3505	XXI	7-Oct-44	16 Feb 1945 – 3 May 1945 from 8. Flottille	Training	Sunk by bombs 3 May 1945 in port at Kiel. 1 crewman killed
U-3506	XXI	16-Oct-44	16 Feb 1945 – 2 May 1945 from 8. Flottille	Training	One of 3 type XXI boats remaining buried in the wreckage of the Elbe II bunker in Hamburg
U-3508	XXI	2-Nov-44	16 Feb 1945 – 4 Mar 1945 from 8. Flottille	Training	Sunk 4 Mar 1945 at Wilhelmshaven by bombs
U-3509	XXI	29-Jan-45	29 Jan 1945 – 3 May 1945 from 8. Flottille	Training	Damaged by bombs in September 1944 in an air raid on the building slips. Repaired and completed. Scuttled 3 May 1945 in the Weser estuary
U-3512	XXI	27-Nov-44	16 Feb 1945 – 8 Apr 1945 from 8. Flottille	Training	Sunk 8 Apr 1945 at Kiel, by bombs
U-3519	XXI	6-Jan-45	16 Feb 1945 – 2 Mar 1945 from 8. Flottille	Training	Sunk 2 Mar 1945 north of Warnemünde by mines. 75 dead and 3 survivors
U-3523	XXI	23-Jan-45	23 Jan 1945 – 6 May 1945	Training	Sunk with all hands 6 May 1945 in the Skagerrak east of Arhus, Denmark, by depth charges from a Liberator of No. 86 Sqn RAF. 58 dead. Previously credited to a 224 Sqn Liberator the day before, but that attack caused only slight damage to U-1008
U-3525	XXI	31-Jan-45	31 Jan 1945 – 30 Apr 1945	Training	Damaged by bombs 30 Apr 1945 in the western Baltic. Scuttled at Kiel 3 May 1945

8 Unterseebootsflottille

Like the 4th Flotilla, the 8th Flotilla was a training unit dedicated to working up newly commissioned U-boats to combat readiness before they departed to join a front flotilla. It was established at Königsberg in 1941, moving to Danzig in 1942.

THE BOATS ASSIGNED TO the 8th Flotilla typically went through a similar training process to those passing through the 4th or 5th Flotillas. After acceptance trials with the UAK and passing through the various technical flotillas, boats were assigned to the final graduating exercise at the *Technische Ausbildungsgruppe für Frontunterseeboote* – the Technical Training Group for Combat U-boats, otherwise known as the *Agru Front.* This final graduating exercise was a dreaded ordeal for new crews. Boats which had a fair proportion of experienced men aboard had fewer problems, but late in the war experienced men were in short supply. The aim was to put the boat through a series of exercises intended to simulate as closely as possible true combat conditions.

Boats went out to sea with an experienced combat commander as training officer and assessor. During the exercises, he would arbitrarily decide that a piece of equipment was inoperative through combat damage or mechanical failure. He would then see how the captain dealt with the loss of a diesel while being chased by an escort, or how the crew would cope with a failure of the main lighting circuit in the middle of an attack, or what a command team might do if the main attack periscope failed during a night

Commanders

Kptlt. Wilhelm Schulz *(Oct 1941 – Jan 1942)*
Korvkpt. Hans Eckermann *(Jan 1942 – Jan 1943)*
Kpt. z. S. Bruno Mahn *(Jan 1943 – May 1943)*
Korvkpt. Werner von Schmidt *(June 1943 – Apr 1944)*
Fregkpt. Hans Pauckstadt *(May 1944 – Jan 1945)*

BOATS THAT TRAINED WITH THE 8TH FLOTILLA

Type	Boats ordered
Type VIIC	U-88, U-89, U-90, U-212, U-222, U-223, U-242, U-250, U-253, U-254, U-255, U-256, U-260, U-261, U-263, U-264, U-265, U-266, U-267, U-268, U-269, U-270, U-271, U-272, U-273, U-274, U-275, U-276, U-277, U-278, U-279, U-280, U-281, U-282, U-283, U-284, U-285, U-286, U-288, U-289, U-290, U-291, U-302, U-303, U-304, U-305, U-306, U-307, U-308, U-309, U-310, U-311, U-312, U-313, U-314, U-315, U-334, U-335, U-338, U-339, U-340, U-341, U-342, U-343, U-345, U-346, U-347, U-348, U-349, U-357, U-358, U-359, U-361, U-362, U-363, U-370, U-378, U-379, U-383, U-405, U-406, U-411, U-412, U-413, U-414, U-415, U-416, U-417, U-418, U-419, U-420, U-421, U-422, U-423, U-424, U-425, U-426, U-427, U-428, U-429, U-430, U-438, U-443, U-444, U-445, U-446, U-447, U-448, U-449, U-450, U-458, U-465, U-475, U-479, U-481, U-593, U-594, U-595, U-596, U-597, U-598, U-599, U-613, U-614, U-615, U-616, U-620, U-621, U-622, U-623, U-624, U-625, U-637, U-657, U-658, U-664, U-676, U-679, U-704, U-707, U-708, U-712, U-713, U-717, U-731, U-732, U-733, U-734, U-735, U-736, U-737, U-738, U-739, U-740, U-741, U-742, U-743, U-744, U-745, U-760, U-761, U-762, U-763, U-764, U-765, U-766, U-767, U-825, U-826, U-921, U-958, U-1102, U-1191, U-1192, U-1193, U-1199, U-1200, U-1201, U-1202, U-1203, U-1204, U-1205, U-1206, U-1207, U-1208, U-1209, U-1210
Type VIIC/41	U-292, U-293, U-294, U-295, U-296, U-297, U-298, U-299, U-300, U-827, U-828, U-1000, U-1001, U-1103, U-1104, U-1105, U-1106, U-1107, U-1108, U-1109, U-1110, U-1163, U-1164, U-1165, U-1166, U-1167, U-1168, U-1169, U-1170, U-1171, U-1172, U-1271, U-1272, U-1273, U-1274, U-1275, U-1276, U-1277, U-1278, U-1279
Type VIID	U-218
Type IXB	U-108
Type XVIIA, B	U-792, U-793, U-794, U-795, U-1405, U-1406
Type XXI	U-2501, U-2504, U-3501, U-3502, U-3503, U-3504, U-3505, U-3506, U-3507, U-3508, U-3510, U-3511, U-3512, U-3513, U-3514, U-3515, U-3516, U-3517, U-3518, U-3519, U-3520, U-3521, U-3522
Type XXIII	U-2339

8TH FLOTILLA INSIGNIA

U-boat insignia derived from a number of different sources. The 8th Flotilla was founded at Königsberg, but moved to Danzig in 1942, and the flotilla symbol incorporated the latter city's coat of arms.

8TH FLOTILLA BASE LOCATIONS

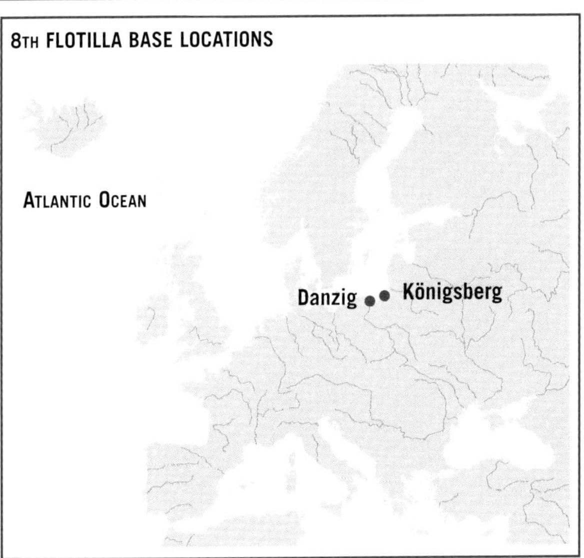

attack. The stresses were real: more than 30 boats were lost in training accidents that killed over 850 U-boat men. Later in the war, these losses would be outstripped by the number of boats destroyed in port by Allied bombers or lost at sea when surprised on the surface by fighter-bombers.

Once a boat had passed the final exercise – no sure thing, as crews whose performance was unsatisfactory could be ordered to go through the whole process

Specifications

Crew: 19
Powerplant: Diesel/Walter turbine/electric
Max Speed: 16.7/44.4km/hr (9/24kt) s/d
Surface Range: 3408km (1840nm)
Displacement: 240/263t (236/259 tons) s/d
Dimensions (length/beam/draught): 41.5 x 3.3 x 4.3m (136.2 x 10.8 x 14.1ft)
Commissioned: 21 Dec 1944
Armament: 4 shortened 533mm (21in) torpedoes (2 bow tubes)

▲ U-1405

Type XVIIB

An experimental high-speed coastal boat powered by a Walter air-independent turbine, U-1405 was used as a training and trials vessel with the 8th Flotilla between December 1944 and January 1945.

Specifications

Crew: 57
Powerplant: Diesel/electric
Max Speed: 28.9/31.9km/hr (15.6/17.2kt) s/d
Surface Range: 20,650km (11,150nm)
Displacement: 1647/1848t (1621/1819 tons) s/d
Dimensions (length/beam/draught): 76.7 x 6.6 x 6.3m (251.7 x 21.7 x 20.7ft)
Commissioned: 28 Jun 1944
Armament: 23 torpedoes (6 bow tubes); 2 x twin 2cm (0.8in) gun turrets

▲ U-2501

Type XXI

This U-boat served with the 8th Flotilla from 21 November 1944 until the end of the war. It was commanded by Oblt. Otto Hübschen, but did not take part in any combat actions. U-2501 was scuttled on 3 May 1945 at Hamburg and eventually broken up.

again – it was returned to the dockyard for an overhaul while the crew went on their final leave.

After a boat had been declared *frontreif*, or combat ready, it was moved to the training flotilla's home base for final fitting-out, during which it would take on a full load of torpedoes, ammunition and supplies. It was then transferred to a front flotilla, and its first operational patrol was made while in transit to its new home base.

In the last months of the war some 8th Flotilla boats were in combat against the Soviet Navy in the Baltic. The flotilla was disbanded in January 1945.

8TH FLOTILLA BOATS LOST WHILE TRAINING/BOATS THAT MADE OPERATIONAL PATROLS WHILE TRAINING

U-Boat	Type	Commissioned	Flotilla(s)	Patrols	Fate
U-108	IXB	22-Oct-40	1 Sep 1943 – 11 Apr 1944 from 2. Flottille	Training	Sunk 11 Apr 1944 at Stettin, by bombs; raised and decommissioned 17 Jul 1944. Scuttled 24 Apr 1945
U-222	VIIC	23-May-42	23 May 1942 – 2 Sep 1942	Training	Sank 2 Sep 1942 in the Baltic west of Pillau after colliding with U-626. 42 dead and 3 survivors
U-250	VIIC	12-Dec-43	1 Jul 1944 – 30 Jul 1944 from 5. Flottille (training)	1 patrol. 1 warship sunk: total 57t/ 56 tons	Sunk 30 Jul 1944 in the Gulf of Finland by depth charges from the Russian submarine chaser MO-103. 46 dead and 6 survivors. Raised in Sept 1944 and commissioned into Soviet Navy from 12 Apr 1945
U-272	VIIC	7-Oct-42	7 Oct 1942 – 12 Nov 1942	Training	Collided with U-634 and sank 12 Nov 1942 near Hela. 29 dead and 19 survivors
U-290	VIIC	24-Jul-43	28 Aug 1944 – 15 Feb 1945 from 11. Flottille	3 patrols	to 4. Flottille
U-346	VIIC	7-Jun-43	7 Jun 1943 – 20 Sep 1943	Training	Sunk in a diving accident 20 Sep 1943 in the Baltic near Hela. 37 dead and 6 survivors
U-348	VIIC	10-Aug-43	12 Jul 1944 – 15 Feb 1945 from 9. Flottille	9 (possibly as many as 15) patrols	to 5. Flottille
U-370	VIIC	19-Nov-43	1 Aug 1944 – 15 Feb 1945 from 4. Flottille	12 patrols. 2 warships sunk: total 845t/832 tons	to 4. Flottille
U-423	VIIC	3-Mar-43	3 Mar 1943 – 17 June 1944	1 patrol	Sunk with all hands 17 Jun 1944 northeast of the Faroes on its way to join 3. Flottille by depth charges from a Norwegian-crewed Catalina of No. 333 Sqn RAF. 53 dead
U-446	VIIC	20-Jun-42	20 Jun 1942 – 21 Sep 1942	Training	Sunk 21 Sep 1942 near Kahlberg in the Gulf of Danzig by a British air-laid mine. 23 dead and 18 survivors. Raised 8 Nov 1942 and decommissioned. Scuttled 3 May 1945 near Kiel
U-475	VIIC	7-Jul-43	1 Aug 1944 – 15 Feb 1945 from 5. Flottille	4 patrols. 1 warship sunk: total 732t/720 tons; 1 warship damaged: total 57t/56 tons	to 4. Flottille
U-479	VIIC	27-Oct-43	1 Aug 1944 – 15 Nov 1944 from 5. Flottille	6 patrols. 1 warship damaged: total 57t/56 tons	Missing with all hands in the Gulf of Finland on or after 15 Nov 1944. 51 dead. Loss was attributed to ramming by Soviet submarine *Lembit*, but research indicates that most of *Lembit*'s official history was fabricated
U-481	VIIC	10-Nov-43	1 Aug 1944 – 8 May 1945 from 5. Flottille	3 patrols. 6 ships sunk: total 1217 GRT; 1 warship sunk: total 110t/108 tons; 1 ship damaged: total 26 GRT	Surrendered at Narvik, Norway. Transferred to Scotland for Operation *Deadlight*. Sunk 30 Nov 1945
U-637	VIIC	27-Aug-42	6 Jul 1944 – 1 Jan 1945 from 1. Flottille	3 patrols. 1 warship sunk: total 57t/ 56 tons	to 5. Flottille
U-676	VIIC	4-Aug-43	1 Sep 1944 – 15 Feb 1945 from 5. Flottille	2 patrols	to 4. Flottille
U-679	VIIC	29-Nov-43	1 Aug 1944 – 9 Jan 1945 from 31. Flottille	3 patrols. 1 warship sunk: total 40t/ 39 tons; 1 ship damaged: total 36 GRT	Sunk with all hands 9 Jan 1945 in the Baltic by depth charges from the Soviet patrol boat MO-124. 51 dead
U-717	VIIC	19-May-43	1 Aug 1944 – 15 Feb 1945 (operational 1 Aug 1944 – 1 Oct 1944) from 22. Flottille	5 patrols	to 5. Flottille
U-738	VIIC	25-Feb-42	20 Feb 1943 – 14 Feb 1944	Training	Sank 14 Feb 1944 in the Baltic near Gotenhafen after being hit in a collision by the steamship *Erna*. 22 dead and 24 survivors. Raised 3 Mar 1944 and broken up
U-745	VIIC	19-Jun-43	19 Jun 1943 – 4 Feb 1945 (operational from 1 May 1944)	4 patrols. 1 auxiliary warship sunk: total 140 GRT; 1 warship sunk: total 610t/ 600 tons	Built for Italy as submarine S-11; taken over after the armistice in 1943. Missing with all hands 30 Jan 1945 in the Gulf of Finland; probably hit a mine. 48 dead
U-958	VIIC	14-Jan-43	1 Aug 1944 – 15 Feb 1945 from 5. Flottille	3 patrols. 1 ship sunk: total 40 GRT; 1 ship damaged: total 40 GRT	to 5. Flottille
U-1000	VIIC/41	4-Nov-43	1 Aug 1944 – 29 Sep 1944	Training	Badly damaged by a mine 15 Aug 1944 in the Baltic. Stricken 29 September and scrapped
U-1164	VIIC/41	27-Oct-43	27 Oct 1943 – 24 Jul 1944 (operational from 1 Jul 1944)	Training	Stricken at Kiel 24 Jul 1944 after being damaged by British bombs
U-1166	VIIC/41	8-Dec-43	8 Dec 1943 – 22 Jul 1944	Training	Damaged by a torpedo accident 28 Jul 1944 at Eckernförde. Stricken at Kiel 28 Aug 1944. Scuttled in May 1945 at Kiel
U-1193	VIIC	7-Oct-43	1 Jun 1944 – 1 Aug 1944 from 24. Flottille	1 patrol	to 24. Flottille
U-2504	XXI	12-Aug-44	20 Nov 1944 – 3 May 1945 from 31. Flottille	Numerous construction faults limited the boat to training and experimental tasks only	Scuttled 3 May 1945 near Hamburg
U-3520	XXI	12-Jan-45	12 Jan 1945 – 31 Jan 1945	Training	Sunk with all hands by mines 31 Jan 1945 in the Baltic northeast of Bülk. 85 dead
U-3521	XXI	14-Jan-45	14 Jan 1945 – 15 Feb 1945	Training	to 5. Flottille
U-3522	XXI	21-Jan-45	21 Jan 1945 – 15 Feb 1945	Training	to 5. Flottille

18 Unterseebootsflottille

The 18th Flotilla, officially a training flotilla, existed for only two months early in 1945 and spent that time as a nominal combat formation in the Baltic Sea. However, none of its boats made any recorded operational patrols.

THE FLOTILLA WAS BASED AT HELA (now the Polish port of Hel) in the Baltic. Late in February 1945, as the the Red Army approached the town, the unit was evacuated. By using every inch of available space on board, some of the boats managed to cram in up to 100 civilian refugees and wounded soldiers. The flotilla was disbanded and surviving boats were transferred to the 5th Flotilla.

Commander

Korvkpt. Rudolf Franzius *(Jan 1945 – Mar 1945)*

18TH FLOTILLA BASE LOCATION

18TH FLOTILLA (5 BOATS)	
Type	**Boats ordered**
Type VIIC	U-1008, U-1161, U-1162
Type UA	UA
Type UD-4	UD-4

Specifications

Crew: 44

Powerplant: Diesel/electric

Max Speed: 31.5/14.1km/hr (17/7.6kt) s/d

Surface Range: 12,040km (6500nm)

Displacement: 771/874t (759/860 tons) s/d

Dimensions (length/beam/draught): 67.2 x 6.2 x 4.8m (220.5 x 20.34 x 15.75ft)

Commissioned: 1 Feb 1945

Armament: 14 torpedoes (4 bow/1 stern tubes); 1 x 2cm (0.8in) quad and 2 x twin 2cm (0.8in) guns

▲ **U-1008**

Type VIIC/41

Serving briefly with the 18th Flotilla as a trials boat before being transferred to the 5th Flotilla, U-1008 was sunk on 6 May 1945 in the Kattegat by depth charges from a Liberator of No. 86 Sqn RAF. All 44 crewmembers survived.

BOATS THAT SERVED WITH 18TH FLOTILLA

U-Boat	Type	Commissioned	Flotilla(s)	Patrols	Fate
U-1008	VIIC/41	1-Feb-45	1 Feb 1945 – 28 Feb 1945 from 24. Flottille	Trials boat; nominally operational	to 5. Flottille
U-1161	VIIC	25-Aug-43	1 Feb 1945 – 28 Feb 1945 from 24. Flottille	Combat training/operational	Originally commissioned as Italian submarine S-8. Taken over by *Kriegsmarine* after the Italian Armistice. Transferred to 5. Flottille 1 Mar 1945
U-1162	VIIC	15-Sep-43	1 Feb 1945 – 28 Feb 1945 from 24. Flottille	Combat training/operational	Originally built as Italian submarine S-10. Taken over and completed by Germany after the Italian Armistice. Transferred to 5. Flottille 1 Mar 1945
UA	Turkish	20-Sep-39	Jan 1945 – Mar 1945 from 24. Flottille	School boat	Back to 24. Flottille. Scuttled 3 May 1945 at the Kiel Arsenal
UD-4	Dutch 0 21 class	28-Jan-41	Jan 1945 – Mar 1945 from 24. Flottille	School boat	Taken out of service 19 Mar 1945. Scuttled 3 May 1945 at the Kiel Arsenal

19 Unterseebootsflottille

The 19th Flotilla was founded in October 1943 for training future U-boat commanders. After completing basic naval officer training, the prospective commander was sent on a 12-week training course, which included theory work and exercises at sea.

THE 19TH FLOTILLA specialized in teaching future officers the techniques of boat handling, before they were sent on to tactical and weapons courses with other flotillas. The submarines used were Type IIC coastal boats, all of which had been used for combat operations with the 1st Flotilla in the early months of the war. The commander training school was disbanded in May 1945, when Germany surrendered.

19TH FLOTILLA BASE LOCATIONS

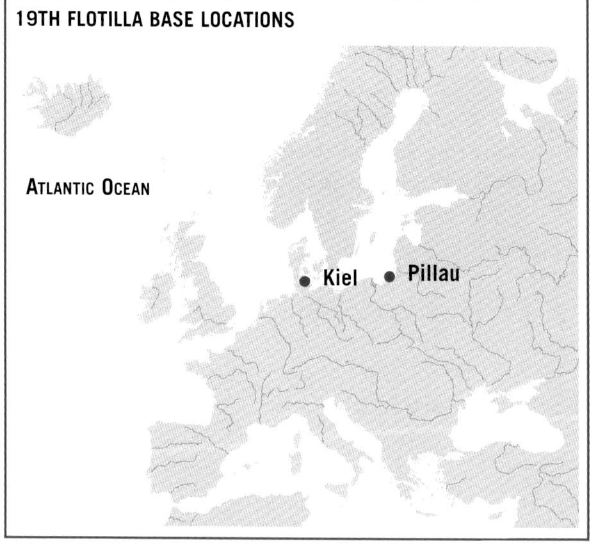

19TH FLOTILLA (4 BOATS)	
Type	**Boats ordered**
Type IIC	U-56, U-57, U-58, U-59

19TH FLOTILLA INSIGNIA

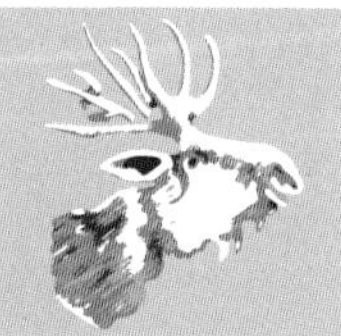

Although the 19th Flotilla had its own insignia of a stag's head, the four Type IIC boats assigned to the unit carried their own symbols, originally applied while they had been front boats with the 1st Flotilla.

Commander

Korvkpt. Jost Metzler *(Oct 1943 – May 1945)*

BOATS THAT SERVED WITH 19TH FLOTILLA (4 BOATS)

U-Boat	Type	Commissioned	Flotilla(s)	Patrols	Fate
U-56	IIC	26-Nov-38	1 Jul 1944 – 28 Apr 1945 from 22. Flottille	Initial commander training	Sunk 28 Apr 1945 at Kiel by British aircraft bombs. 6 dead and 19 survivors
U-57	IIC	29-Dec-38	1 Jul 1944 – 3 May 1945 from 22. Flottille	Initial commander training	Sank 3 Sep 1940 at Brunsbüttel after an accidental collision with the Norwegian steamship *Rona*. 6 dead and 19 survivors. Raised in the same month, repaired and returned to service 11 Jan 1941. Scuttled 3 May 1945 at Kiel
U-58	IIC	4-Feb-39	1 Jul 1944 – 3 May 1945 from 22 Flottille	Initial commander training	Scuttled 3 May 1945 at Kiel
U-59	IIC	4-Mar-39	1 Jul 1944 – 1 Apr 1945 from 22. Flottille	Initial commander training	Scuttled in the Kiel Arsenal in May 1945

20 Unterseebootsflottille

During their initial officer training, prospective U-boat officers underwent the standard training experienced by all naval officers. They would have taken courses on weapons and weapons handling as well as ship handling and navigation.

ON COMPLETION THE CADET was promoted to the rank of *Fähnrich zur See*, or midshipman, before being attached to a surface warship, where he was expected to develop practical experience of ship handling. On finally passing out of the academy, a successful cadet was promoted to the rank of

Oberfähnrich sur See, or senior midshipman. Line officers destined for the *U-Bootwaffe* then went on to the U-boat training schools. In the second half of the war, these were located at Pillau, on the Baltic in the Bay of Danzig, and were supported by the 19th and 20th Flotillas. The Baltic was firmly under German control until near the end of the war, and the waters around Pillau offered reasonably safe training grounds for inexperienced crews.

U-boat training schools

The 20th Flotilla was founded in June 1943 as a training flotilla. Here, prospective submarine officers were given introductory courses in tactical training – *Vortaktische Ausbildung*. Classroom exercises were carried out in fully equipped U-boat simulators, during which trainees learned the trade of submarine warfare.

Eventually, the trainees would carry out numerous simulated attack runs on scale models of convoys. The passing grade was to make a total of 15 successful simulated attacks. Candidates also underwent practical submarine boat-handling training with the 19th Flotilla.

On completion of their training, the more promising candidates were posted directly to operational boats, where they served as 'apprentices' to experienced U-boat commanders. If they survived – which was no certainty after 1943 – they would be assigned to a new U-boat under construction, in the rank of *Leutnant zur See*, or junior lieutenant. Other candidates were sent on to operational training flotillas, where they went through courses on underwater tactics and torpedo shooting.

The 20th Flotilla was in existence for less than two years, being formed at the height of the massive expansion of the U-boat arm in 1943, and being disbanded in February 1945.

20TH FLOTILLA BASE LOCATION

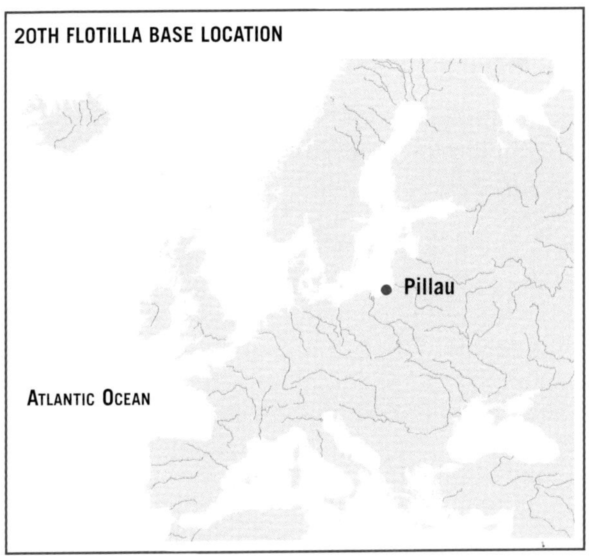

Commander

Korvkpt. Ernst Mengersen *(Jun 1943 – Feb 1945)*

21 Unterseebootsflottille

In the first years of the Third Reich, U-boat training was necessarily theoretical: until the shackles of the Treaty of Versailles had been thrown off, Germany was forbidden to build or operate submarines of any sort.

PROSPECTIVE U-BOAT OFFICERS attended the *Unterseebootsabwehrschule* at Kiel, which as its name suggests had been given the cover identity of an anti-submarine warfare school. In fact, it was purely intended to train U-boat crews.

The announcement of German rearmament in 1935 saw the establishment of the 1st U-boat Flotilla and the setting up of a new training establishment at Neustadt, which was commonly known as the *Unterseebootsschule*.

Commanders

Kpt. z. S. Kurt Slevogt *(1935 – Oct 1937)*
Kptlt. Heinz Beduhn *(Nov 1937 – Mar 1940)*
Korvkpt. Paul Büchel *(Mar 1940 – June 1943)*
Korvkpt. Otto Schuhart *(June 1943 – Sep 1944)*
Kptlt. Herwig Collmann *(Sep 1944 – Mar 1945)*

U-1 to U-6 were from the beginning designated as training boats, and formed the *Schulverband der U-Bootschule*. The *U-Bootwaffe* grew rapidly, and by the late 1930s the *Schulverband* had doubled in size. It was now known as the *Unterseebootsschulflottille*.

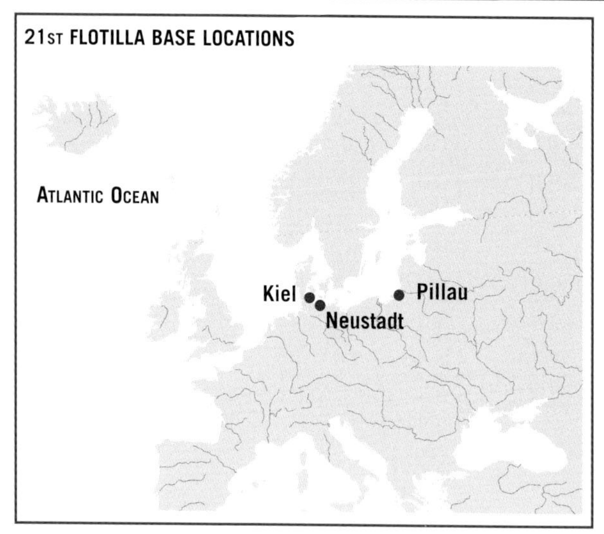

In April of 1940, the school was renamed the 1. *Unterseebootslehrdivision*, or 1.ULD, and was moved to Pillau on the Bay of Danzig in the Baltic, where it was less vulnerable to British bomber attacks. A second *Lehrdivision*, 2.ULD, was set up at Gotenhafen later in 1940. Each of the ULDs was training up to 4000 U-boat men at any one time. Practical instruction was carried out aboard the flotillas attached to each *Lehrdivision* – the 21st Flotilla at Pillau and the 22nd Flotilla at Gotenhafen.

Specialists joined the U-boat arm already having learned a trade, which included diesel or electrical mechanic, wireless operator, torpedo mechanic, and cook. Members of the seaman branch performed the other functions, which included steering, working the hydroplanes, lookout, and gunners.

Specifications

Crew: 25

Powerplant: Diesel/electric

Max Speed: 33/15.4km/hr (17.8/8.3kt) s/d

Surface Range: 1945km (1050nm)

Displacement: 258/308t (254/303 tons) s/d

Dimensions (length/beam/draught): 40.9 x 4.1 x 3.8m (1134.2 x 13.5 x 12.5ft)

Commissioned: 6 Aug 1935

Armament: 6 torpedoes (3 bow tubes); 1 x 2cm (0.8in) gun

▲ **U-3**

Type IIA

First commissioned in August 1935, U-3 was one of the first training U-boats of the newly created *U-Bootschulflottille* (U-boat School Flotilla). From 1 July 1940 to 31 July 1944, it served as a training boat with the 21st Flotilla. It was then decommissioned and scrapped.

◀ ***U-Bootschulflottille* – U-4 and U-6**

Type IIA training boats U-6 (centre) and U-4 (right) are shown in the docks at Kiel, 1937. Both submarines served with the *U-Bootschulflottille* until being transfered to the 21st Training Flotilla in July 1940. Although too lacking in range to be truly combat effective, the Type IIA boats briefly became operational at the outbreak of war in 1939. U-4 made four patrols, sinking three ships and the British submarine HMS *Thistle*. U-6 made two patrols, but had no success. Both were back in their training role when the 21st Flotilla was established in July 1940.

21ST FLOTILLA INSIGNIA

Although the 21st Flotilla had its own insignia, there is no record of any of the boats assigned to the unit ever having carried it. Most former front boats in the flotilla had their own individual symbols.

Non-commissioned officers (NCOs) were promoted after a period of service in the ranks. During the war, they attended a purpose-built NCO training school at Plon. War pressures saw courses reduced to as little as two months, and by the end of the war some seamen were being drafted into U-boats without any training at all.

The 21st Flotilla's history ended in March 1945, when the unit was disbanded.

21ST FLOTILLA (54 BOATS)

Type	Boats ordered
Type IA	U-25
Type IIA	U-2, U-3, U-4, U-5, U-6
Type IIB	U-7, U-9, U-10, U-11, U-20, U-21, U-23, U-24, U-120, U-121
Type IIC	U-60, U-61, U-62
Type IID	U-139, U-141, U-148, U-151, U-152
Type VIIA	U-29, U-34
Type VIIB	U-48, U-101
Type VIIC	U-72, U-80, U-236, U-251, U-291, U-368, U-416, U-430, U-555, U-704, U-708, U-712, U-720, U-733, U-746, U-922, U-977, U-1101, U-1194, U-1195, U-1196, U-1197, U-1198, U-1201, U-1204
Type IX	U-38

21ST FLOTILLA BOATS LOST WHILE TRAINING/BOATS THAT MADE OPERATIONAL PATROLS WHILE TRAINING

U-Boat	Type	Commissioned	Flotilla(s)	Patrols	Fate
U-2	IIA	25-Jul-35	1 Jul 1940 – 8 Apr 1944 from *U-Bootschulflottille*	School boat. 2 patrols	Sank 8 Apr 1944 west of Pillau, in position 54.48N, 19.55E, after a collision with the German steam trawler *Helmi Söhle*. 17 dead and 18 survivors
U-5	IIA	31-Aug-35	1 Jul 1940 – 19 March 1943 from *U-Bootschulflottille*	School boat. 2 patrols	Sank 19 Mar 1943 west of Pillau in a diving accident. 21 dead and 16 survivors
U-7	IIB	18-Jul-35	1 Jul 1940 – 31 Jul 1944 from *U-Bootschulflottille*	School boat. 6 patrols. 2 ships sunk: total 4524 GRT	Sank with all hands 18 Feb 1944 west of Pillau in a diving accident. 29 dead
U-21	IIB	3-Aug-36	1 Jul 1940 – 5 Aug 1944 from 1. Flottille	School boat	Stranded 27 Mar 1940 after running aground off Oldknuppen Island following a navigational error. Interned in Norway at Kristiansand-Süd. Released to Germany 9 Apr 1940. Stricken 5 Aug 1944 at Pillau. Scrapped in Feb 1945.
U-72	VIIC	4-Jan-41	2 Jul 1941 – 30 Mar 1945 from 24. Flottille	School boat	Damaged 30 Mar 1945 in Bremen by American daylight bombers. Scuttled 2 May 1945
U-80	VIIC	8-Apr-41	1 Dec 1943 – 28 Nov 1944 from 23. Flottille	School boat	Sunk with all hands 28 Nov 1944 west of Pillau in a diving accident. 50 dead
U-139	IID	24-Jul-40	4 Oct 1940 – 30 Apr 1941	School boat; 2 patrols	to 22. Flottille
U-416	VIIC	4-Nov-42	1 Jul 1944 – 12 Dec 1944 from 23. Flottille	School boat	Sunk 30 Mar 1943 in the Baltic near Bornholm by a mine laid by the Soviet submarine L-3. Number of fatalities unknown. Raised in Apr 1943, and refurbished. Used for training from Oct 1943. Sank again 12 Dec 1944 northwest of Pillau after a collision with the German minesweeper M-203. 36 dead and 5 survivors

22 Unterseebootsflottille

As with the 21st Flotilla, the 22nd Flotilla was created to support one of the main U-boat training schools, where personnel assigned to the *U-Bootwaffe* were sent to gain their basic submarine training.

THE FLOTILLA WAS FOUNDED at Gotenhafen in January 1941, where it provided the training boats for 2. *Unterseebootslehrdivision*, or 2.ULD.

Before arriving at the ULD, a recruit had to go through basic naval training. In the prewar years, applicants registered at the local *Wehrkreis*, or military district registration office, where they were given a medical. Initially, high educational standards were demanded of recruits destined for U-boats, but these were being relaxed by the time the 22nd Flotilla came into existence, and unskilled manual workers were now allowed to serve in the *U-Bootwaffe*.

Recruiting grounds

Curiously, the majority of lower-ranking volunteers for the *U-Bootwaffe* came from central Germany, far from the sea. Most were Protestant, and came from skilled blue-collar backgrounds. The standard period of enlistment both for seamen and for those who indicated that they would like to become NCOs was 12 years. Recruits were assessed and assigned to a specific trade by the *Kriegsmarine.*

One of the most important parts of a U-boat crewman's training at the U-boat school was in underwater escape techniques. Little did the recruits know, as they practised using breathing apparatus in the deep tanks at the U-boat schools, that the chances of escape from a submerged boat were almost nil. Only if a boat was destroyed on the surface did any of the crew have a real chance of escaping.

Commanders

Korvkpt. Wilhelm Ambrosius *(Jan 1941 – Jan 1944)*

Korvkpt. Wolfgang Lüth *(Jan 1944 – Jul 1944)*

Korvkpt. Heinrich Bleichrodt *(Jul 1944 – May 1945)*

The six Type II boats from the flotilla which were briefly operational during Operation *Barbarossa* achieved some success, sinking three Soviet submarines. However, in August 1941, U-144 suffered the same fate, when it was sunk by the Soviet submarine SC-307. The flotilla moved in early 1945 to Wilhelmshaven, where it was finally disbanded in May 1945 with Nazi Germany's surrender.

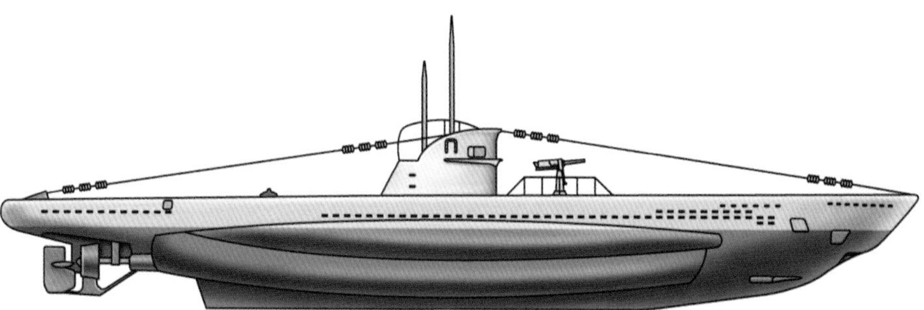

▲ **U137**

Type IID

This was the last of the Type IIs to enter service. Many Type IID boats made operational patrols with the 1st and 3rd Flotillas before becoming training boats.

Specifications

Crew: 25

Powerplant: Diesel/electric

Max Speed: 23.5/13.7km/hr (12.7/7.4kt) s/d

Surface Range: 6389km (3450nm)

Displacement: 319/370t (314/364 tons) s/d

Dimensions (length/beam/draught): 44 x 4.9 x 3.9m (144.4 x 16.8 x 12.8ft)

Commissioned: 15 Jun 1940

Armament: 6 torpedoes (3 bow tubes); 1 x 2cm (0.8in) gun

22ND FLOTILLA (47 BOATS)

Type	Boats assigned
Type IIB	U-8, U-11, U-14, U-17, U-18, U-19
Type IIC	U-56, U-57, U-58, U-59
Type IID	U-137, U-138, U-139, U-140, U-142, U-143, U-144, U-145, U-146, U-147, U-149, U-150
Type VIIA	U-28, U-30
Type VIIC	U-71, U-78, U-96, U-235, U-239, U-316, U-339, U-349, U-350, U-351, U-369, U-552, U-554, U-555, U-560, U-717, U-721, U-924, U-1197, U-1198
Type VIIC/41	U-1103, U-1167
Type IX	U-37

22ND FLOTILLA BASE LOCATIONS

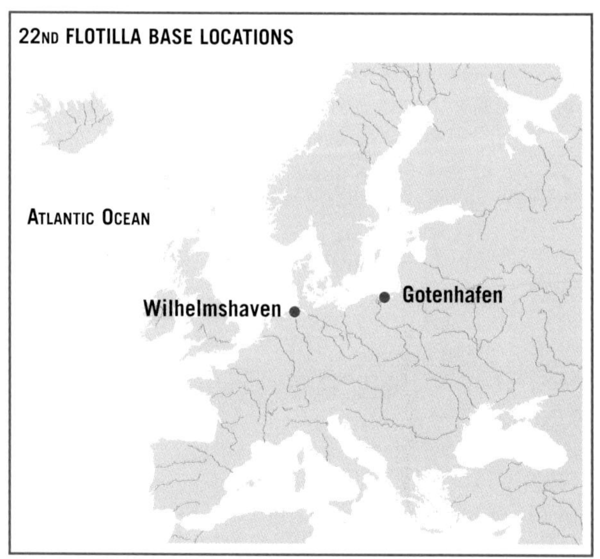

22ND FLOTILLA BOATS LOST WHILE TRAINING/BOATS THAT MADE OPERATIONAL PATROLS WHILE TRAINING					
U-Boat	**Type**	**Commissioned**	**Flotilla(s)**	**Patrols**	**Fate**
U-28	VIIA	12-Sep-36	1 Dec 1943 – 17 Mar 1944	School boat	Sunk by accident in port at Neustadt 17 Mar 1944. Raised in Mar 1944 and stricken 4 Aug 1944
U-30	VIIA	8-Oct-36	1 Dec 1943 – 12 Jan 1945 from 24. Flottille	School boat	Used in the last months of the war as a range boat. Scuttled 4 May 1945 in Kupfermühlen Bay
U-56	IIC	26-Nov-38	19 Dec 1940 – 30 Jun 1944 (operational Jun/Aug 1941) from 24. Flottille	School boat. 12 patrols. 3 ships sunk: total 8860 GRT; 1 auxiliary warship sunk: total 16,923 GRT; 1 ship damaged: total 3829 GRT	to 19. Flottille
U-96	VIIC	14-Sep-40	1 Jul 1944 – 15 Feb 1945 from 24. Flottille	School boat	Sunk 30 Mar 1945 by US bombs at Wilhelmshaven
U-139	IID	24-Jul-40	1 May 1941 – 2 May 1945 (operational 22 Jun 1941 – 31 Jul 1941)	School boat. 2 patrols	Scuttled 2 May 1945 at Wilhelmshaven
U-140	IID	7-Aug-40	1 Jan 1941 – 31 Mar 1945 (operational 22 Jun 1941 – 31 Aug 1941) from 1. Flottille	School boat. 3 patrols. 3 ships sunk: total 12,410 GRT; 1 warship sunk: total 209t/206 tons	to 31. Flottille
U-142	IID	4-Sep-40	19 Dec 1940 – 1 May 1945 (operational 22 Jun 1941 – 31 Aug 1941) from 24. Flottille	School boat. 4 patrols	Scuttled 2 May 1945 at Wilhelmshaven
U-144	IID	2-Oct-40	20 Dec 1940 – 10 Aug 1941 (operational from 22 Jun 1941)	School boat. 3 patrols. 1 warship sunk: total 209t/206 tons	Sunk with all hands 10 Aug 1941 in Gulf of Finland, torpedoed by the Russian submarine SC-307. 28 dead
U-149	IID	13-Nov-40	1 Jan 1941 – 8 May 1945 (operational 22 Jun 1941 – 31 Aug 1941) from 1. Flottille	School boat. 1 patrol. 1 warship sunk: total 209t/206 tons	Transferred from Wilhelmshaven to Scotland 30 Jun 1945 for Operation *Deadlight*. Sunk 21 Dec 1945 in position 55.40N, 08.00W

23 Unterseebootsflottille

The original 23rd Flotilla was a combat unit operating in the eastern Mediterranean in 1941 and 1942. Based at Salamis in Greece, it was disbanded and its surviving boats absorbed into the 29th Flotilla. However, the flotilla was revived a year later in the Baltic.

THE 23RD FLOTILLA WAS re-established in September 1943 as a training flotilla, under the command of *Korvettenkapitän* Otto von Bülow. Like the 19th and 24th Flotillas, its main purpose was to train future U-boat commanders.

Bülow was an experienced U-boat ace, and his task, along with the other experienced officers who served as instructors, was to present the trainee commanders with the kind of problems they could expect to face in combat.

Based at Danzig, the 23rd Flotilla was disbanded and evacuated in March 1945 as advancing Soviet forces approached the city.

23RD FLOTILLA (11 BOATS)	
Type	**Boats assigned**
Type VIIA	U-29
Type VIIB	U-52
Type VIIC	U-80, U-97, U-133, U-704, U-903, U-904, U-922, U-923, U-975

Commanders

Korvkpt. Otto von Bülow *(Aug 1943 – Mar 1945)*

23RD FLOTILLA BASE LOCATION

24 Unterseebootsflottille

The 24th Flotilla was founded in November 1939. Until March 1940 it was known as the *Unterseebootsausbildungsflottille* (U-boat training school flotilla), and then until June 1940 it was redesignated as the 1. *Unterseebootsausbildungsflottille*.

Like the 23rd Flotilla, which though earlier numerically was actually founded later, the 24th Flotilla trained future U-boat commanders in a course known as the *Kommandantenschiesslehrgang*, or KSL. Each KSL course lasted four weeks, during which up to 12 U-boat officers received their final training in operations and tactics before being assigned to a boat in a front flotilla.

Before arriving at the 24th Flotilla, the prospective submarine commander would have served for at least six months aboard a surface warship, during which time he would have completed a naval armament course that would have introduced the basics of gunnery, torpedo operations and anti-aircraft defence.

Originally, the flotilla had been set up to provide officers with underwater attack training, which included the firing of training torpedoes at real targets, but in the middle of war the emphasis was changed to include training in underwater detection techniques, and in using the information so gained to escape an enemy attack.

24TH FLOTILLA (53 BOATS)	
Type	**Boats assigned**
Type IIB	U-8, U-9, U-14, U-18, U-19, U-121
Type IID	U-56, U-142, U-143, U-148, U-151, U-152
Type VIIA	U-28, U-29, U-30, U-34
Type VIIB	U-46, U-52, U-101
Type VIIC	U-71, U-72, U-80, U-96, U-236, U-251, U-287, U-351, U-393, U-554, U-555, U-560, U-579, U-612, U-704, U-747, U-748, U-749, U-750, U-763, U-821, U-982, U-1161, U-1162, U-1192, U-1193, U-1195, U-1207
Type VIIC/41	U-999, U-1007, U-1008
Type IXA	U-38
Type IXB	U-103
UA	UA (ex-Turkish)
0 21 class	UD-4 (ex-Dutch)

24TH FLOTILLA BASE LOCATIONS

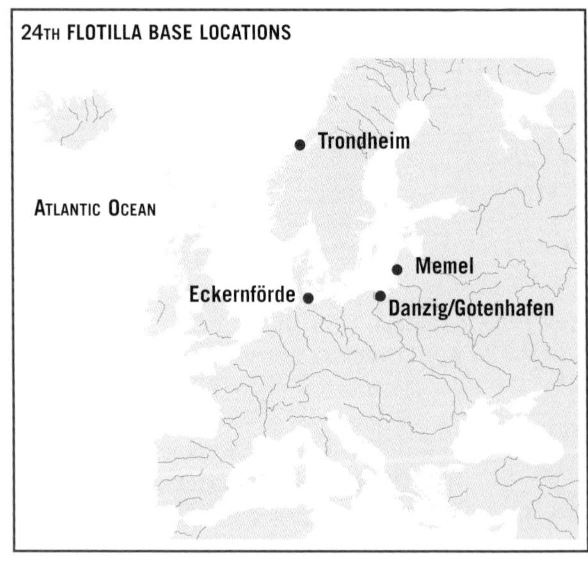

Baltic base

Initially based in the eastern Baltic, the flotilla was briefly moved to Norway during the early months of Operation *Barbarossa* to avoid conflicting with operational units, but was back at Memel by September 1941. The flotilla was disbanded in March 1945, as Allied troops advanced into Germany from east and west.

Commanders

Korvkpt. Hannes Weingärtner *(Nov 1939 – Jun 1940)*
Kpt. z. S. R. Peters *(Jul 1942 – Jan 1943)*
Fregkpt. Karl-Friedrich Merten *(Mar 1943 – May 1944)*
Korvkpt. Karl Jasper *(May 1944 – Jul 1944)*
Fregkpt. Karl-Friedrich Merten *(Jul 1944 – Mar 1945)*

24TH FLOTILLA INSIGNIA

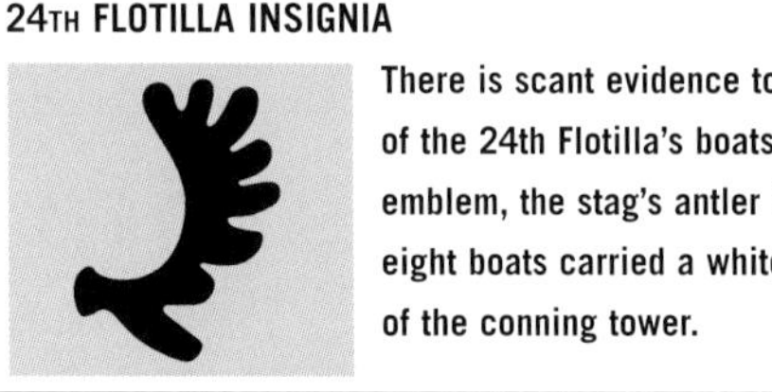

There is scant evidence to suggest that any of the 24th Flotilla's boats used the official emblem, the stag's antler insignia. At least eight boats carried a white 'V' on the side of the conning tower.

25 Unterseebootsflottille

The 25th Flotilla was founded in April 1940. Its main purpose was to put newly commissioned boats still going through their working-up training through a course of live torpedo firing.

THE BOATS TOOK four weeks to complete their training before going on to a final tactical exercise with the 27th Flotilla. The 25th Flotilla operated until the end of the war, being disbanded on 13 May 1945.

Commanders

Korvkpt. Ernst Hashagen *(Apr 1940 – Dec 1941)*
Korvkpt. Karl Jasper *(Dec 1941 – Aug 1943)*
Fregkpt. Karl Neitzel *(Aug 1943 – Jan 1944)*
Korvkpt. Robert Gysae *(Jan 1944 – Apr 1945)*
Korvkpt. Wilhelm Schulz *(Apr 1945 – May 1945)*

25TH FLOTILLA INSIGNIA

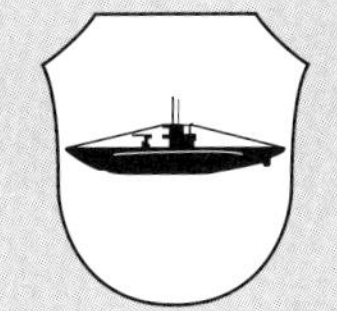

Although the 25th Flotilla had its own insignia of a U-boat silhouette on a white shield, none of the new boats that passed through wore it, since none of them were assigned permanently to the formation.

25TH FLOTILLA BASE LOCATIONS

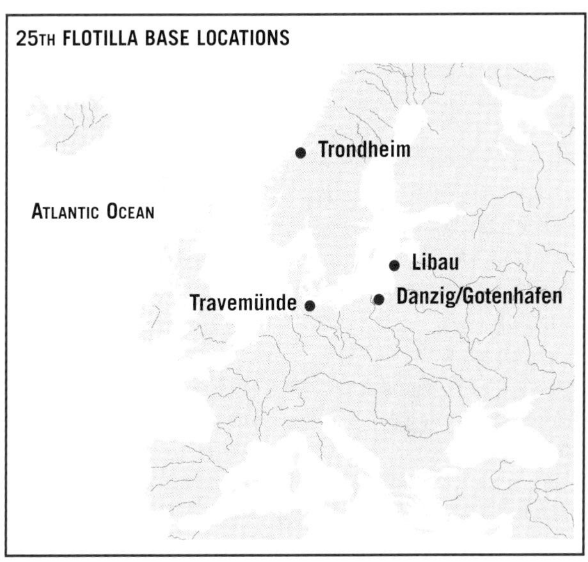

26 Unterseebootsflottille

Like the 25th Flotilla, the 26th Flotilla was set up to put newly commissioned boats still going through their working-up training through a course of *Torpedoschiessausbildung*, or training in live torpedo firing.

THE 26TH FLOTILLA was founded in April 1941. The boats usually took three to four weeks to complete their training before going on to a final tactical exercise with the 27th Flotilla. The training torpedoes used were standard G7e weapons without warheads, and could be recognized by double white bands around the nose. Some weapons were fitted with lights to allow night shooting practice to be assessed.

The 26th Flotilla was disbanded in May 1945, when Germany surrendered.

Commanders

Korvkpt. Hans-Gerrit von Stockhausen *(Apr 1941 – Jan 1943)*
Korvkpt. Karl-Friedrich Merten *(Jan 1943 – Apr 1943)*
Fregkpt. Helmut Brümmer-Patzig *(Apr 1943 – Mar 1945)*
Korvkpt. Ernst Bauer *(Apr 1945 – May 1945)*

26TH FLOTILLA BASE LOCATIONS

26TH FLOTILLA INSIGNIA

Unlike the 25th Flotilla, the 26th Flotilla did have boats permanently assigned, and there is no record that any of them carried the unit's official insignia. Most were former combat boats with their own symbols.

26TH FLOTILLA (7 BOATS)

Type	Boats assigned
Type VIIB	U-46, U-48, U-52, U-101
Type VIIC	U-80, U-351
Type IXA	U-37

27 Unterseebootsflottille

The 27th Flotilla was founded in January 1940 as a *TaktischeAusbildungUnterseeboote*, or tactical training flotilla. This was the final stage of training for new U-boat crews. After a boat was commissioned, it was sent to the U-boat Acceptance Command, where it was checked for mechanical or structural faults.

From the Acceptance Command the new boat was attached to a training flotilla, where instructors would put the new crews through a course designed to familiarize them with the kind of problems that occurred on operations. The crews would then would pass through one of the shooting flotillas, where they received practical instruction in firing torpedoes.

The graduation course was run by the *Technische Ausbildungsgruppe für Frontunterseeboote*, usually known as the *Agru Front.* The key element of the *Agru Front* course was the final war game, which came under the operational control of the 27th Flotilla. This was a simulated convoy battle in the Baltic. Boats usually arrived on the course in groups of 10 to 12, and a boat and its crew had to pass the course before being declared fit for operations.

By the later stages of the war, German training facilities were being put under severe strain, and the competent crews that had passed out early in the war were not matched by their successors. Before the war and in the early years of the conflict, all officers were seaman above all, and the relatively small numbers of boats meant that the U-boat arm could pick and choose from officers who displayed real leadership ability. Unfortunately, by the later years of the war the massive increase in size of the U-boat arm meant that suitably capable officers were much harder to find.

Training strain

Recognizing the fall in quality, in 1943 the instructors added a ten-day pre-tactical course before the convoy exercise. However, this was not enough to make up for the deficiencies. A really bad performance meant that a boat could be held back for further training, taking part in the final war game twice or more. On some courses the instructors

Commanders

Korvkpt. Ernst Sobe *(Jan 1940 – Dec 1941)*
Fregkpt. Werner Hartmann *(Dec 1941 – Oct 1942)*
Korvkpt. Erich Topp *(Oct 1942 – Aug 1944)*
Kptlt. Ernst Bauer *(Oct 1944 – Mar 1945)*

27TH FLOTILLA (1 BOAT)

Type	Boats ordered
O 21 class	UD-4 (ex-Dutch)

27TH FLOTILLA BASE LOCATION

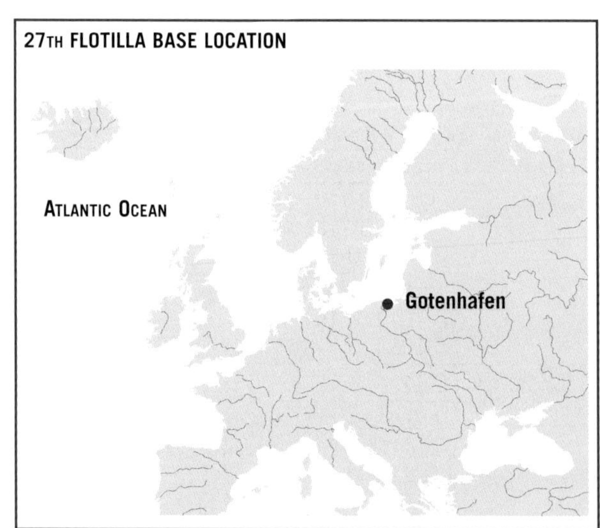

would have liked to fail every boat passing through. However, such was the pressure on the U-boat arm in the Atlantic that the staff at the *Agru Front* were forbidden to fail more than two boats per course.

Many years later, *Kapitänleutnant* Klaus Korth remembered how depressing it was to hear that crews he knew needed more training had been lost on their first or second operational patrols. However, there was little he or any other instructor could do. Any complaints went as far as Admiral Friedenburg, who agreed with the instructors, but were ignored by Admiral Dönitz and the naval high command, who needed boats at sea.

The 27th Flotilla was the last training station for new U-boats before they were overhauled, armed and filled with supplies for the long and dangerous voyage to their operational bases in France and Norway.

The flotilla was finally disbanded in March 1945.

31 Unterseebootsflottille

The 31st Flotilla was founded in September 1943 as an initial training unit, tasked with taking inexperienced crews and giving them the basics of U-boat operations.

THE FLOTILLA BECAME the initial Type XXI training unit. Crews had to learn new techniques to handle the sheer speed of the revolutionary 'Electro Boat'. Some of the boats went on to the 4th and 11th Flotillas for operational training, but most were still undergoing basic training at the end of the war.

The flotilla was disbanded in May 1945 when Germany surrendered, but one boat did not come in quietly. The Type VIIC boat U-977 left Kristiansand, Norway, on 2 May 1945 for a combat patrol in the English Channel. When Germany surrendered a few days later, the boat was outbound in Norwegian waters. The commander, *Kapitänleutnant* Schäffer, did not wish to surrender and decided to head for

Commanders

Kpt. z. S. Bruno Mahn *(Sep 1943 – Apr 1945)*	Korvkpt. Carl Emmermann *(Apr 1945 – May 1945)*

31ST FLOTILLA BASE LOCATIONS

BOATS THAT TRAINED WITH THE 31ST FLOTILLA

Type	Boats ordered
Type VIIC	U-708, U-712, U-720, U-721, U-722, U-733, U-746, U-747, U-748, U-768, U-771, U-772, U-773, U-774, U-775, U-776, U-777, U-778, U-779, U-903, U-905, U-907, U-922, U-924, U-975, U-977, U-982, U-1101, U-1132, U-1192, U-1193, U-1194, U-1196, U-1197, U-1198, U-1201, U-1204
Type VIIC/41	U-999, U-1000, U-1001, U-1002, U-1003, U-1004, U-1005, U-1006, U-1007, U-1008, U-1009, U-1010, U-1013, U-1014, U-1015, U-1016, U-1017, U-1018, U-1019, U-1020, U-1021, U-1022, U-1023, U-1024, U-1103, U-1167
Type IXC/40	U-1224, U-1225, U-1226, U-1227, U-1228, U-1229, U-1230, U-1231, U-1232, U-1233, U-1234, U-1235
Type XXI	U-2501, U-2502, U-2503, U-2504, U-2505, U-2506, U-2507, U-2508, U-2509, U-2510, U-2511, U-2512, U-2513, U-2514, U-2515, U-2516, U-2517, U-2519, U-2520, U-2521, U-2522, U-2523, U-2524, U-2525, U-2526, U-2527, U-2528, U-2529, U-2530, U-2531, U-2533, U-2534, U-2535, U-2536, U-2537, U-2538, U-2539, U-2540, U-2541, U-2542, U-2543, U-2544, U-2545, U-2546, U-2548, U-2551, U-2552

Argentina. Many of the crew were of the same mind, but those with families did not want to go. Schäffer gave the married men the chance to go to ashore, and 16 men, about a third of the crew, were landed on the Norwegian coast near Bergen on 10 May, where they were taken prisoner and transferred to England. On the same day, U-977 with its diminished crew submerged on a *Schnorchel* run to the Cape Verde Islands which was to last for 66 days – the second longest continuously submerged voyage of the war.

Crossing the equator on 23 July, U-977 arrived in Mar del Plata, Argentina, on 17 August after a voyage of 108 days. The boat and crew were interned and were later handed over to the Americans.

31ST FLOTILLA BOATS LOST WHILE TRAINING/BOATS THAT MADE OPERATIONAL PATROLS WHILE TRAINING

U-Boat	Type	Commissioned	Flotilla(s)	Patrols	Fate
U-708	VIIC	24-Jul-42	16 Mar 1945 – 3 May 1945 from 21. Flottille	Initial training	Scuttled 3 May 1945 at Wilhelmshaven. Broken up in 1947
U-733	VIIC	14-Nov-42	1 Mar 1945 – 5 May 1945 from 21. Flottille	Initial training	Sank 9 Apr 1943 at Gotenhafen after a collision. Raised and repaired. Scuttled 5 May 1945 in Flensburg Fjord after being crippled by bombs and aircraft guns. Broken up in 1948
U-746	VIIC	4-Jul-43	1 Mar 1945 – 5 May 1945	Initial training	Scuttled 5 May 1945 in Gelting Bay, after being bombed. Broken up in 1948
U-747	VIIC	17-Jul-43	1 Apr 1945 – 1 Apr 1945 from 24. Flottille	Initial training	Destroyed 1 Apr 1945 in Hamburg, by US bombs
U-768	VIIC	14-Oct-43	14 Oct 1943 – 20 Nov 1943	Training	Sank after a collision with U-745 in the Gulf of Danzig 20 Nov 1943. No casualties – 44 survivors
U-776	VIIC	13-Apr-44	13 Apr 1944 – 8 May 1945	Training plus 1 patrol	Surrendered at Weymouth, England, 20 May 1945. On display in the Thames at Westminster from 24 May. Operated by the Royal Navy as trials boat N 65 before being sunk 3 Dec 1945 in Operation *Deadlight*
U-777	VIIC	9-May-44	9 May 1944 – 15 Oct 1944	Training	Sunk 15 Oct 1944 at Wilhelmshaven in a British air raid
U-977	VIIC	6-May-43	1 Mar 1945 – 8 May 1945 from 21. Flottille	Initial training	Crew refused to surrender at end of war. Interned at Mar del Plata, Argentina, 17 Aug 1945 after a trip from Norway that included 66 days submerged. Transferred to United States 13 Nov 1945. Torpedoed as submarine target off Boston 13 Nov 1946
U-982	VIIC	10-Jun-43	1 Mar 1945 – 9 Apr 1945 from 24. Flottille	Initial training	Destroyed 9 Apr 1945 at Hamburg in an RAF bombing raid
U-1007	VIIC/41	18-Jan-44	1 Mar 1945 – 2 May 1945 from 24. Flottille	Initial training	Scuttled 2 May 1945 at Lübeck after a rocket attack by 4 Typhoons of No. 245 Sqn RAF. 2 crewmen killed
U-1013	VIIC/41	2-Mar-44	2 Mar 1944 – 17 Mar 1944	Training	Collided with U-286 17 Mar 1944 in the Baltic east of Rügen and sank. 25 dead and 26 survivors
U-1015	VIIC/41	23-Mar-44	23 Mar 1944 – 19 May 1944	Training	Collided with U-1014 in the Baltic west of Pillau and sank. 36 dead and 14 survivors
U-1103	VIIC/41	8-Jan-44	1 Mar 1945 – 8 May 1945 from 22. Flottille	Initial Training	Transferred from Kiel to Scotland 23 Jun 1945 for Operation *Deadlight*. Sunk by naval gunfire 30 Dec 1945
U-1132	VIIC	24-Jun-44	1 Feb 1945 – 4 May 1945 from 5. Flottille	Training	Scuttled 4 May 1945 near Flensburg in Küpfermühlen Bay
U-1167	VIIC/41	29-Dec-43	1 Mar 1945 – 30 Mar 1945 from 22. Flottille	Initial Training	Sunk 30 Mar 1945 at Hamburg-Finkenwärder, after being damaged by British bombs. 1 crewman killed
U-1196	VIIC	18-Nov-43	1 Mar 1945 – 3 May 1945 from 21. Flottille	Initial Training	Stricken in Aug 1944 after a torpedo accident. Scuttled 3 May 1945 at Travemünde
U-1197	VIIC	2-Dec-43	1 Mar 1945 – 25 Apr 1945 from 21. Flottille	Initial Training	Damaged by bombs at Bremen and stricken at Wesermünde 25 Apr 1945. Sunk as a target by US Navy in the North Sea in Feb 1946
U-1201	VIIC	13-Jan-44	1 Mar 1945 – 8 May 1945	Training	Severely damaged by US bombs at Hamburg 11 Mar 1945. Scuttled 3 May 1945
U-1224	IXC/40	20-Oct-43	20 Oct 1943 – 15 Feb 1944	Training	Transferred to Japan as RO-501 15 Feb 1944. Sunk with all hands northwest of Cape Verde Islands 13 May 1944, en route to the Far East, by Hedgehog and depth charges from the destroyer escort USS *Francis M. Robinson*. 48 Japanese seamen killed
U-1234	IXC/40	19-Apr-44	19 Apr 1944 – 31 Jan 1945	Training	Collided with a steam tug in fog and sank at Gotenhafen 14 May 1944. 13 dead and 43 survivors. Raised, repaired and recommissioned 17 Oct 1944
U-2505	XXI	7-Nov-44	7 Nov 1944 – 3 May 1945	Training	One of 3 Type XXI boats buried in the wreckage of the Elbe II bunker in Hamburg
U-2509	XXI	21-Sep-44	21 Sep 1944 – 8 Apr 1945	Training	Sunk 8 Apr 1945 at Blohm und Voss, Hamburg, in a British bombing raid
U-2514	XXI	17-Oct-44	17 Oct 1944 – 8 Apr 1945	Training	Sunk 8 Apr 1945 at Hamburg by bombs
U-2515	XXI	19-Oct-44	19 Oct 1944 – 11 Mar 1945	Training	Damaged in Dec 1944 in the Baltic Sea by a mine. Sunk 17 Jan 1945 in dock at Hamburg, by bombs while damaged sections were being replaced
U-2516	XXI	24-Oct-44	24 Oct 1944 – 9 Apr 1945	Training	Sunk 9 Apr 1945 at Kiel, by bombs
U-2521	XXI	21-Nov-44	21 Nov 1944 – 3 May 1945	Training	Sunk 3 May 1945 in the Flensburg Fjord by rockets from Typhoons of No. 184 Sqn RAF. 44 dead. Previously credited to a British Liberator which actually sank U-579
U-2523	XXI	26-Dec-44	26 Dec 1944 – 17 Jan 1945	Training	Sunk 17 Jan 1945 in dock at Hamburg, by bombs
U-2524	XXI	16-Jan-45	16 Jan 1945 – 3 May 1945	Training	Scuttled 3 May 1945 southeast of the island of Fehmarn in the Kattegat after a rocket attack by Beaufighters of Nos. 236 and 254 Sqns RAF. 1 crewman killed
U-2530	XXI	30-Dec-44	30 Dec 1944 – 20 Feb 1945	Training	Sunk 31 Dec 1944 in a bombing raid on Hamburg. Raised in Jan 1945. Further damaged in raids 17 Jan 1945 and 20 Feb 1945
U-2537	XXI	21-Mar-45	21 Mar 1945 – 8 Apr 1945	Training	Sunk by US bombs 31 Dec 1944 while fitting out. Raised, damaged again 15 Jan 1945. Destroyed by British bombs 8 Apr 1945
U-2542	XXI	5-Mar-45	5 Mar 1945 – 3 Apr 1945	Training	Sunk 3 Apr 1945 on the Hindenburg Bank at Kiel, by bombs

32 Unterseebootsflottille

The 32nd Flotilla was founded in April 1944, primarily to train crews of the new high-performance Type XXI and XXIII 'electro boats'. However, only two of the larger boats were assigned, and after less than a month they were transferred to the 4th Flotilla.

THE TYPE XXIIIS WERE SMALL coastal boats, armed with only two torpedoes. Designed to mount short-duration patrols, they were equipped with *Schnorchels* and it was expected that they would spend most of their time submerged. As a result, they had no exterior decking, which caused considerable underwater drag on more conventional boats.

Type XXIIIs were equipped with a very large battery capacity, which meant that they were faster when submerged than on the surface. Very manoeuvrable, they could crash-dive in only nine seconds, which made them popular with crews, for whom Allied air attacks had become the major threat.

However, the sheer speed at which the boat could dive meant that crews had to be absolutely certain all hatches were secure: any water flowing into the boat could cause disaster, and U-2331 was lost in such a diving accident while training with 32nd Flotilla.

A further problem was the fact that the boat's safe operating depth had been vastly overestimated at some 250m (820ft), which was the kind of depth later Type VIIs could achieve safely. In fact, the true safe operating depth for the Type XXIII was only 80m (260ft), and crews had to be careful when crash-diving not to descend too rapidly.

The flotilla was originally located at Königsberg in East Prussia, but was transferred to Hamburg in January 1945 after Kurland was isolated by the advancing Red Army. The flotilla was disbanded in May 1945, when Germany surrendered.

Commanders

Fregkpt. Hermann Rigele *(Apr 1944 – Mar 1945)*	Korvkpt. Ulrich Heyse *(Mar 1945 – May 1945)*

32ND FLOTILLA (43 BOATS)

Type	Boats ordered
Type XXI	U-3001, U-3002
Type XXIII	U-2321, U-2322, U-2324, U-2325, U-2326, U-2327, U-2328, U-2329, U-2330, U-2331, U-2334, U-2335, U-2336, U-2337, U-2338, U-2339, U-2340, U-2341, U-2342, U-2343, U-2344, U-2345, U-2346, U-2347, U-2348, U-2349, U-2350, U-2351, U-2352, U-2353, U-2354, U-2355, U-2356, U-2357, U-2358, U-2359, U-2360, U-2361, U-2362, U-2363, U-2364

32ND FLOTILLA BASE LOCATIONS

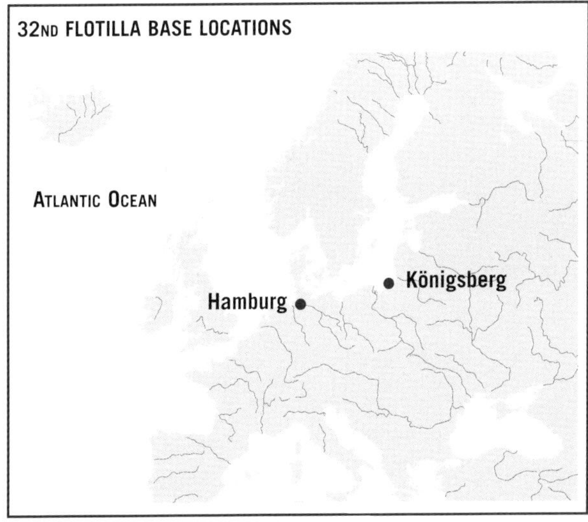

31ST FLOTILLA BOATS LOST WHILE TRAINING

U-Boat	Type	Commissioned	Flotilla(s)	Patrols	Fate
U-2331	XXIII	12-Sep-44	12 Sep 1944 – 10 Oct 1944	Training	Sank 10 Oct 1944 near Hela in an accident. 15 dead and 4 survivors
U-2338	XXIII	9-Oct-44	9 Oct 1944 – 4 May 1945	Training	Sunk 4 May 1945 east-northeast of Fredericia by Beaufighters of Nos. 236 and 254 Sqns RAF. 12 dead and 1 survivor
U-2340	XXIII	16-Oct-44	16 Oct 1944 – 30 Mar 1945	Training	Sunk 30 Mar 1945 at Hamburg by British bombs. Wreck broken up
U-2342	XXIII	1-Nov-44	1 Nov 1944 – 26 Dec 1944	Training	Sunk 26 Dec 1944 in the Baltic north of Swinemünde by a mine. 7 dead
U-2344	XXIII	10-Nov-44	10 Nov 1944 – 18 Feb 1945	Training	Collided with U-2336 and sank 18 Feb 1945 north of Heiligendamm. 11 dead and 3 survivors

U-boat operations – Atlantic Theatre

The Battle of the Atlantic was one of the key campaigns of World War II. Lasting from the first day of the conflict to the last, it was a war of weapons and tactics, with the early German advantage giving way to an Allied victory as new technology proved decisive.

The successful prosecution of Britain's war in Europe depended upon a steady flow of shipping reaching the United Kingdom from across the Atlantic and from the Empire beyond. The primary weapon employed by Germany in its attempts to strangle this flow was the U-boat, though at the outbreak of war elements within the *Kriegsmarine's* high command expected great things from surface raiders. However, although these achieved some successes, many were hunted down by the much larger Royal Navy. U-boats, on the other hand, were much harder to find, and presented a serious threat to Britain's Atlantic lifeline.

The capture of France and Norway in 1940 meant that Germany's U-boats no longer had to make the long and dangerous transit up the North Sea and around the northern coasts of the British Isles to reach the main shipping lanes. Based in French Atlantic ports, the few boats available to the *Kriegsmarine* were able to wreak havoc in Britain's western approaches as well as in convoy attacks in mid-Atlantic and on British shipping off West Africa.

America's entry into the war in December 1941 saw the *Kriegsmarine* extend its U-boat operations to the North American coast. The US Navy was slow to institute convoys, and the U-boats had an easy time finding targets at night, silhouetted as they were by the bright lights of American cities. A general blackout would have cut losses, but was delayed by six months primarily due to opposition from the tourist trade! In the meantime, the U-boats were wreaking havoc on America's coastal trade; so much so in fact that the German crews called this their second 'Happy Time'.

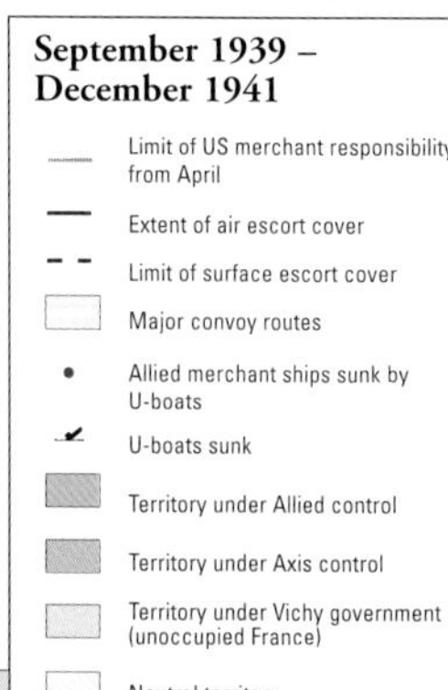

▶ September 1939 – May 1940

In 1939 Admiral Karl Dönitz had only 56 U-boats in service, of which only 22 were ocean-going types. Initially, pickings for the U-boat commanders were rich, as their boats sank merchantmen returning individually to Britain.

Even when convoys were established, they could only be escorted through 15 degrees of longitude at either end of the transatlantic route due to a lack of suitable escorts. Even so, the U-boats were little more than a nuisance – until the fall of France.

▶ June 1940 – March 1941

The lessons of 1917, when unrestricted U-boat warfare had almost brought Britain to its knees, had been largely forgotten by the Royal Navy between the wars, though the British were quick to re-establish convoys in the face of the U-boat threat. Even so, losses were heavy once the U-boats began operating from French ports, reaching 1.6 million tonnes (1.57 million tons) between June and November 1940. The British were particularly unprepared for the German tactic of night-time surface attacks. So successful were the U-boats that their commanders and crews were to remember this period as the 'Happy Time'.

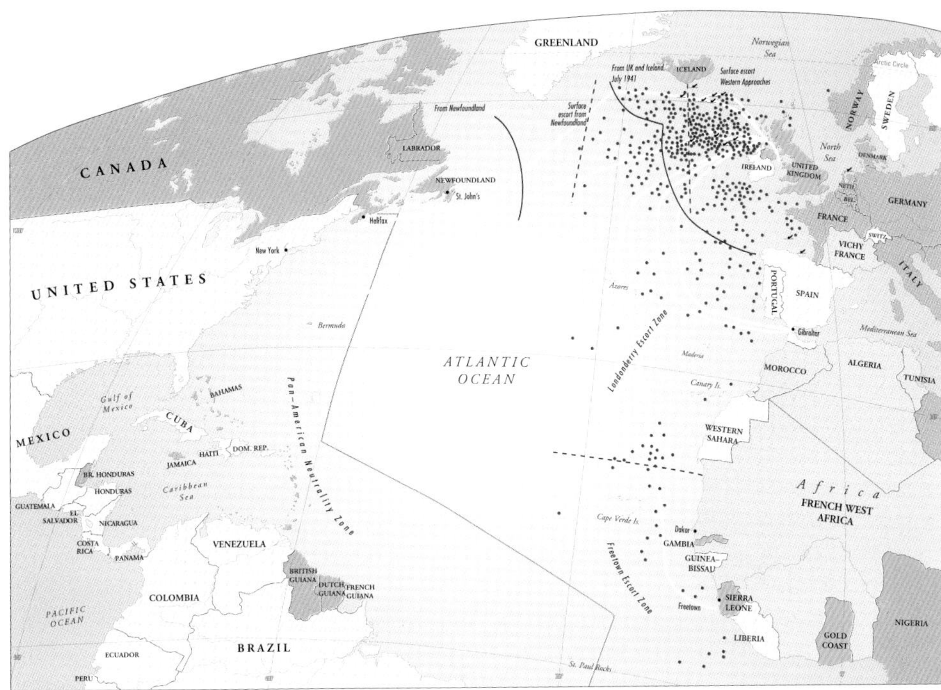

▶ April – December 1941

In 1941, the *Kriegsmarine* still had too few U-boats to control the convoy routes. Improvements in British convoy tactics and the advent of a new type of escort, the corvette, made the U-boat mission harder. Increasing Canadian strength and the decision by the United States to escort convoys out of their ports further strengthened the British position. The American decision involved the US Navy in a 'secret' shooting war, in which US escorts attacked if first attacked by U-boats. However, the introduction of Wolfpack tactics – the use of multiple boats making coordinated attacks on a single convoy – negated the effects of improved British convoy tactics.

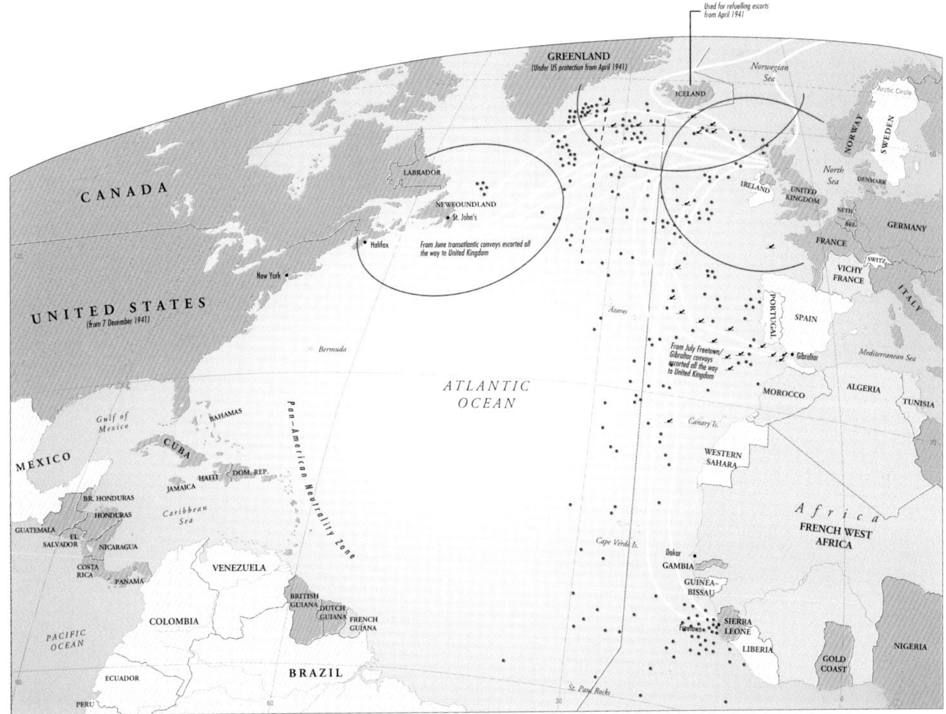

▸ January 1942 – February 1943

In July 1942 the Americans finally instituted a convoy system, so the U-boats moved south to the Caribbean where they could strike at the vital oil supplies coming out of Maracaibo. As the US convoy system expanded to include these areas, the U-boats prepared to move back to the shipping lanes of the North Atlantic. By now, the *Kriegsmarine* had more than 300 U-boats in service, and by November 1942 Allied shipping was being sunk at a rate of more than 700,000 tonnes (689,000 tons) every month.

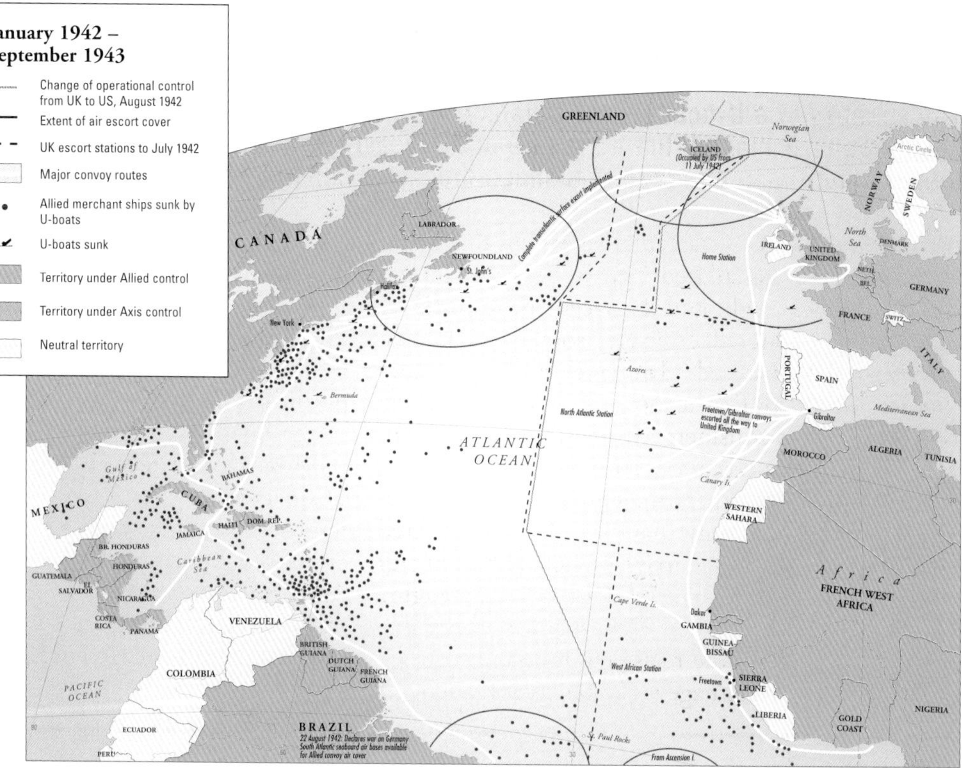

▸ March – September 1943

Between May and August 1943, 98 new U-boats were commissioned – but 123 were lost in action. Each of those losses represented a trained crew perished or taken prisoner. By the end of 1943, the *Kriegsmarine* knew that the average U-boat was unlikely to survive for more than three or four patrols, many being sunk by Allied aircraft as they transited the Bay of Biscay. In 1943 the U-boats sank 463 ships of 2.6 million tonnes (2.55 million tons): in 1944, though more than 400 boats were in commission, they sank only 132 ships totalling 770,000 tonnes (758,000 tons).

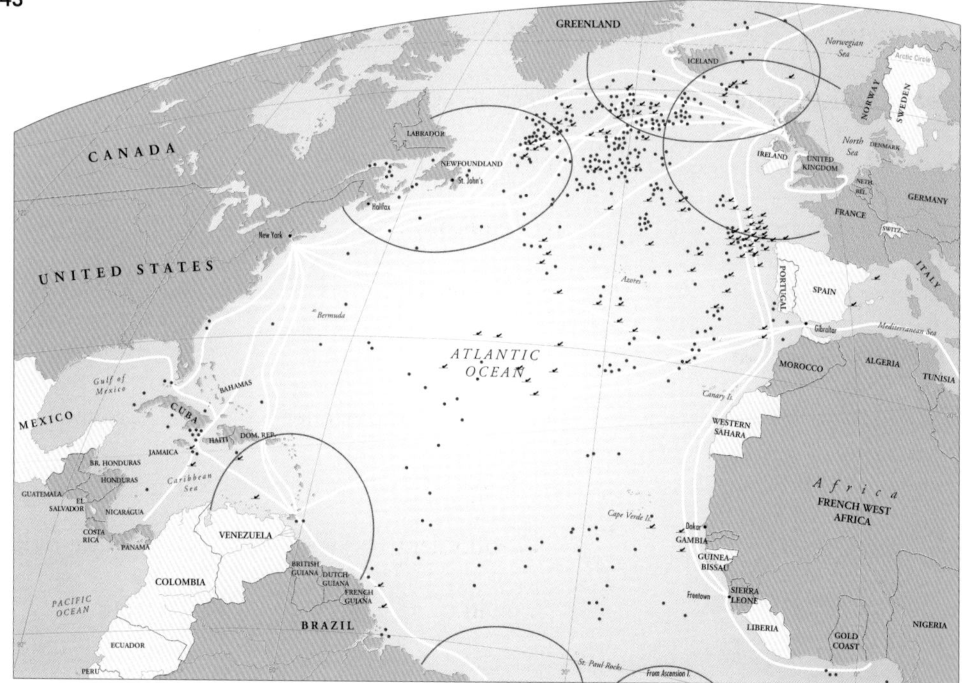

Tonnage definitions

The success of a U-boat or a commander was sometimes calculated by the number of ships destroyed or damaged, but was more often measured in the tonnage of shipping sunk. However, there is more than one type of tonnage measure, depending on the type of vessel.

THERE ARE FOUR CATEGORIES by which tonnage of a vessel is calculated: gross registered, net registered, deadweight and displacement tonnage.

- Gross Registered Tonnage, sometimes known simply as Registered Tonnage and generally abbreviated as GRT, is a measure of volume where 100 cubic feet is considered the equivalent of a ton. This is the total internal capacity of a vessel.
- Net Registered Tonnage is a commercial measure, describing only that part of the Registered Tonnage that is used to carry commercial freight. All spaces that are not revenue producing – the engine compartment, ship's stores, crew spaces and the like – are deducted from the registered tonnage.
- Deadweight Tonnage is the carrying capacity of a vessel in terms of weight rather than volume, and is measured in tons or tonnes.
- Displacement Tonnage is the actual weight of the ship and is equal to the weight of water displaced by the vessel. It is measured in imperial tons (2240 pounds per ton) or in metric tonnes (1000 kilograms).

Most U-boat records were measured in GRT or Displacement Tonnage. GRT was applied to merchant vessels as well as to auxiliary warships such as Armed Merchant Cruisers or AMCs, Merchant Aircraft Carriers (MAC ships), and small vessels like trawlers pressed into patrol or anti-submarine duties. Displacement Tonnage refers solely to vessels built as warships.

Kriegsmarine officer ranks

There were minor differences between the *Kriegsmarine* and the Allies, the latter having no equivalent for *Fregattenkapitän,* which could be described as a junior Captain's rank.

KREIGSMARINE RANK	BRITISH EQUIVALENT	US EQUIVALENT
Fähnrich zur See	Midshipman, cadet	Midshipman, cadet
Oberfähnrich zur See	No equivalent	Ensign
Leutnant zur See	Sub-Lieutenant	Lieutenant – Junior Grade
Oberleutnant zur See	Lieutenant	Lieutenant
Kapitänleutnant	Lieutenant-Commander	Lieutenant-Commander
Korvettenkapitän	Commander	Commander
Fregattenkapitän	No equivalent	No equivalent
Kapitän zur See	Captain	Captain

Key Sources

Books

Högel, Georg. *U-Boat Emblems of WWII.* Atglen, PA: Schiffer Military History, 1999.

Macintyre, Donald. *The Battle of the Atlantic.* Barnsley, UK: Leo Cooper Ltd, 2006.

Mallmann-Showell, Jak P. *U-Boats Under the Swastika.* Shepperton, UK: Ian Allan Publishing, 1987.

Rohwer, Jürgen. *Axis Submarine Successes of World War II.* Annapolis, Md.: Naval Institute Press, 1999.

Rössler, Eberhard. *The U-Boat.* London: Arms and Armour Press, 1981.

Williamson, Gordon. *Wolfpack: The Story of the U-boat in World War II.* Oxford: Osprey Publishing, 2005.

Wynn, Kenneth. *U-Boat Operations of the Second World War (Vols 1 and 2).* London: Caxton Editions, 1997.

Websites

www.uboat.net

www.ubootwaffe.net

www.uboatwar.net

www.u-boot-greywolf.de

U-Boat Index

Page numbers in *italics* refer to illustrations and photographs.

General Index

Page numbers in *italics* refer to illustrations and photographs.

INDEX